A GUIDE TO
TREKKING IN NEPAL

STEPHEN BEZRUCHKA
THE MOUNTAINEERS
SEATTLE

THE MOUNTAINEERS: Organized 1906 " . . . to explore, study, preserve, and enjoy the natural beauty of the Northwest."

First edition, 1972; second edition 1974; third edition 1976; all by Sahayogi Press, Kathmandu, Nepal
Fourth edition published January 1981 in the United States by
The Mountaineers, 715 Pike Street, Seattle, Washington 98101.
This edition made possible through the courtesy of Sahayogi Press, Kathmandu, Nepal.
First printing, February 1981; second printing, February 1982; third printing March, 1983

Published simultaneously:
> In Nepal by Sahayogi Press, Tripureshwar, Kathmandu
> In the United Kingdom and Europe by Cordee, 249 Knighton Church Road, Leicester, England LE2 3JQ
> In Canada by Douglas & McIntyre Ltd., 1615 Venables Street, Vancouver, British Columbia V5L 2H1

Manufactured in the United States of America
Book design by Marge Mueller
Cover photo: *Trekking below Annapurna South on the lush southern side of the range.* Photo by Gordon Wiltsie.
Title photo: *Dhaulagiri towers above the Kali Gandaki Valley seen in route to the Annapurna Base Camp.* Photo by Peter Banys.

Library of Congress Cataloging in Publication Data
Bezruchka, Stephen.
    A guide to trekking in Nepal.

    Bibliography: p.
    Includes index.
    1. Nepal—Description and travel—Guide-books.
2. Hiking—Nepal.   I. Title.
DS493.3.B49   1980   915.49′604   80-27091
ISBN 0-89886-003-2

Nepal is there to change you, not for you to change it. Lose yourself in its essence. Make your footprints with care and awareness of the precarious balance around you. Take souvenirs in your mind and spirit, not in your pockets. Nepal is not only a place on the map, but an experience, a way of life from which we all can learn.

CONTENTS

MAPS

Mount Everest. It was first climbed in 1953 by Sir Edmund Hillary and Tenzing Norgay. (Stephen Bezruchka)

FOREWORD

I first visited the Khumbu area of Nepal in 1951 and took part in the initial reconnaissance of the great icefall and the southern approaches to Everest.

I can clearly remember my first walk up the Everest valleys—the unbelievable summits, the dense forest around Tengboche, alive with colorful birds and nervous musk deer, the upper valleys clothed in dark green juniper and azalea. It was a unique experience and everything was so incredibly beautiful.

What a change there is today! The summits are still there of course—floating high above man's mess and destruction—but the Khumbu valley is now an ecological slum. Erosion is everywhere; tins and trash clutter up the paths and campsites. You are lucky if you see a single juniper; the forests are being destroyed, and the traditional culture is being crushed by the insidious economic machine.

As you trek through Nepal, you have to be blind if you cannot see the changes taking place. Population pressure pushes agricultural terraces higher and higher on steep hillsides; there is widespread and growing erosion; and "tourist" routes are clearly defined by cigarette packages and used toilet paper.

Nepal is still very beautiful—surely one of the world's great trekking paradises. But those of us who take advantage of these charms have great responsibility. We can play an active part in Nepal's future by making positive efforts to leave the mountains and walkways cleaner than we found them, taking care not to abuse local customs and traditions, and limiting our use of energy to a minimum so there may be something left for future generations.

Nepal must be saved—and we can help do it.

Sir Edmund Hillary

PREFACE

This book initially arose from my experience in Nepal during 1969 and 1970. Before leaving on my first trek, I tried to amass as much information as possible about the country and the activity. But there was comparatively little to be found, especially about trekking.

But lack of information did not seem to deter the growing number of people who set out on treks in Nepal. People would often decide to go after talking to others in a Kathmandu restaurant. Almost the next day, they would strike out for the hills with a vague idea of where they were going and what they could expect. This kind of adventure is almost unknown in most parts of the West.

This guide attempts to help trekkers without greatly diminishing their sense of adventure. Perhaps travelers who have some idea of the route, what is involved in a trek, and a description of the people and countryside can better appreciate the people, their culture, the mountains and valleys, and the striking, haunting beauty of Nepal.

I have tried to include a vast amount of information in this book. Most trekkers' queries are answered somewhere. It is, I hope, comprehensive, but an attempt to consume all of it at once will result in indigestion.

In Section I, the first four chapters, and to some extent the fifth, are helpful in planning your trek. I feel that Chapter 4, "Interacting With Nepal," is the most important part of the book. If you follow the advice in it, both you and your Nepali hosts will have a better experience. Chapter 5, "Health Care," should not only be read before you go; it is useful for reference as health problems arise on the trail. It is particularly important to keep referring back to the section on altitude illness if you are going to high elevations. Chapter 6, "Nepali for Trekkers," can help you start learning enough of the language to increase your enjoyment of your trip and ease the difficulties of finding your way. The chapter's pages are edged in gray so you can find them quickly while trekking.

Section II contains the various route descriptions. It is very important to read the introduction to the section, "Following the Route Descriptions," in order to understand the system in which the route information is given. If the times given between towns seem too short, reread the introduction to the section. The route descriptions answer the frequently asked question, "How much farther," and they include tidbits of information about some of the sights.

Section III contains chapters with some information about Nepal's natural history and people. But as you travel, you may find that the information in these two chapters and in the rest of the book is not enough to satisfy your growing curiosity about Nepal. If so, you can find sources of more comprehensive information on the subjects that interest you in the "Recommended Reading" section at the back of the book. There is also a list of addresses of sources that may be helpful in arranging your trek or supplying information.

This edition is the third revision of a work that was first published in 1972. It was the first trekking guidebook to Nepal. Response to the previous editions has been quite gratifying, and it appears that the book fulfills a definite need. Several Nepalis have even made use of it! While other trekking books have now appeared, this remains the only comprehensive guide.

Ritual bathing under the 108 water spouts at Muktinath. (Brot Coburn)

Information for this book has been gathered from many sources, including Nepalis of the hills and towns, seasoned trekkers, anthropologists, naturalists, photographers, and concerned readers of previous editions. Most of it is based on my personal experiences in Nepal over many years. Although this is the third revision, I'm sure that inaccuracies and omissions continue. These are my responsibility alone. I hope that users of this guide will continue to note errors and incomplete or outdated information on availability of food and shelter and other matters. I would be grateful for any suggestions sent to me in care of the publisher.

In preparing past editions I have been helped by many people. Special thanks are due to: Michael Abramson, Ross Anthony, Charles Bailey, Deepak Bajracharya, Terrence Bech, John Dickinson, Luke Golobitsh, Ane Haaland, Gerald Hankins, Mary Lynn Hanley, Herbert Hultgren, Cathy Johnson, John Lehmkuhl, David Lichter, Sue Malick, Donald Messerschmidt, Dorothy Mierow, Ted Moore, Mary Murphy, Jonathan Nicholas, Michael Payne, Robert Rieffel, Janice Sacherer, Karna Sakya, Warren Smith, Adam Stainton, Gay Troth, and Per Wegge.

Ramesh Kumar Sharma of Sahayogi Prakashan Publishing Company has supported the book from its conception. My debt of gratitude to him will never be paid.

My porters, Sherpas, and friends in Nepal have made the book possible by assisting on my treks and enabling me to become addicted to their country. I am especially grateful to Ang Dawa Sherpa, Dorje Tsering, Jaku Man Tamang, Karsang Jigme, Nima Tundu Sherpa, and Ram Bahadur Tamang.

In preparation of this edition, special thanks are due to: Kristin Adams, Peter Banys, Gordon Benner, Diane and Edwin Bernbaum, Peter Byrne, Karin Carrington, Malinda Chouinard, Joan Firey, Ane Haaland, Peter Hackett, Mary Lynn Hanley, Cathy Johnson, Nick Langton, Jay Longacre, Donald Messerschmidt, Ted Moore, Dawa Norbu, David and Kathy Peterson, Jennifer Read, Robert Rieffel, and Daniel Taylor-Ide. John Pollock supported this fourth edition in many important ways. Ann Cleeland was instrumental in shaping this edition through her critical comments and painstaking help. The design of the book was creatively done by Marge Mueller. Donna DeShazo did a fine job in production. Critical comments by Broughton Coburn, Dayl Donaldson and John Ricker helped shape the final form of the book. Bruce McKinney translated the manuscript into proper English and improved the book both structurally and stylistically. To all who helped I am most grateful.

SECTION I
ABOUT TREKKING

Along the pilgrimage route to Muktinath. On the left is the Thorung La, the pass leading to Manang. (Brot Coburn)

Namaste, *the traditional greeting, done with hands pressed together, will welcome every traveler to Nepal. (Ane Haaland)*

WHAT TO EXPECT

A hundred divine epochs would not suffice to describe all the marvels of the Himalaya.

Sanskrit proverb

What kind of experiences will you have in Nepal? Think of waking up early one morning and directing your gaze to the north. It is quite cloudy, but for some reason, you lift up your eyes. There it is—the triangular rock and snow face of Machhapuchhre. But it is not even 23,000 ft (7000 m) high! How could it look so big? Or you are walking along the trail when you suddenly hear, "Good morning, Sir," spoken in perfect English. You turn around, astonished, to see an ordinary-looking Nepali. Yes, the speaker is a Gurkha soldier, retired from the British Army. The two of you pass many miles talking together. Or it is the day's end and you are resting after the walk, looking at a Western book or magazine that you carry. Soon you are surrounded by children who gaze intently at the pictures. You want to tell them that the world those pictures represent is not better than theirs. Or after you have walked for eleven days, you reach the top of a hill and suddenly see Mount Everest and Ama Dablang. Everest is over 6000 ft (1800 m) higher, but you hardly notice it; Ama Dablang excites you all the time you are near it. Or it is spring and you have toiled to get far above the valley. The rhododendrons make the mountains look like a paradise. They are red in many places; yet the colors can be light, and even beautifully white. Every day there will be many times like these when you will forget the miles you have yet to go, the vertical feet yet to climb, the load on your back. And you will vow to return.

Nepal is a land of unparalleled variety. Imagine a rectangle, 500 miles by 150 miles, divided lengthwise into three strips. The northernmost strip is mountainous; it includes eight of the ten highest mountains in the world. This Himalayan region is sparsely settled by people who speak languages of the Tibeto-Burman family and practice Tibetan Buddhism. The southernmost region, which is the narrowest of the three strips, is called the Tarai. It is an extension of the Gangetic plain of northern India. This area is populated by people who speak Indo-European languages and practice Hinduism. The animals of the south belong to a different realm than the animals of the north. In between the two outer strips lies an interface region of hills and valleys. The inhabitants speak languages of both the Tibeto-Burman and Indo-European families and generally practice Hinduism with many Buddhist and shamanistic influences.

Climatically, the country has subtropical, temperate, and alpine regions, determined by elevation. It contains examples of most of the vegetation zones of the world.

The economy is basically subsistence agriculture. Nepal has most of the statistical characteristics of the world's poorest countries in terms of per capita income, literacy, and infant mortality. The high rate of population growth—doubling time is about thirty years—threatens to outstrip food production. Another serious problem is deforestation due to the search for wood for fuel and construction. The result is erosion and loss of topsoil.

What to Expect

Nepal is the world's only Hindu monarchy. The King, Birendra Bir Bikram Shah Dev, is a direct descendant of Prithvinarayan Shah who unified the country in the 1760s. For over a hundred years, until 1951, Nepal was ruled by a sequence of hereditary prime ministers, the Ranas. During this period Nepal was essentially cut off from outside influences. Because of its forbidding mountains to the north and deadly malaria endemic in the Tarai to the south, Nepal was never successfully invaded by a major power.

After the Chinese occupied Tibet in 1959, many Tibetans fled to India and Nepal where they settled in refugee camps. The northern border of Nepal was closed for some time, but restrictions now have been relaxed somewhat so that trade goes on, though it is not the extensive commerce it once was. Most Tibetans in Nepal have successfully adapted to their new environment.

After an attempt at democracy in 1959, the country was ruled by a system of participatory councils, but with real power vested in the King. In the spring of 1980 a popular referendum was held to determine if the country should allow multiple political parties. The proposal was defeated. It remains unclear how Nepal's government will change as a result of the popular pressures that are becoming more commonplace in Third World countries.

Nepal was closed to foreigners and foreign influence until 1951 and did not officially open its doors to tourists until a few years later. But by 1978, over 125,000 tourists were visiting the country each year, and massive amounts of foreign aid had started Nepal on the road to modernization and development. Major contributors of aid are India, China, the Soviet Union, and the United States. It remains to be seen whether this economic assistance will improve the lot of Nepali farmers. In the past, most aid has been given primarily for political reasons, although Nepal is a non-aligned country and has declared itself a zone of peace. So far most of Nepal remains largely untouched by the ways and ideas of the West.

It is this land of contrasts that beckons those who are willing to travel, as the Nepalis do, on foot. Indeed, walking is the only means of reaching most destinations, since Nepal still has the fewest miles of roads in proportion to area or population of any country in the world. The trails that trekkers use are the public transportation and communication routes for the local people.

Trekking, as described here, means travel by foot for many days. During this time, travelers can spend nights in the homes of local people, or camp by themselves. They can eat either local food or food they have brought with them. In fact, on many journeys through populated areas to lonely heights, it is customary to try all of the above variations.

Trekking is a very healthy activity, although not without its hazards. It is strenuous and burns calories, so that many overweight people shed their excess load along the trail. Smokers may cut back on their consumption of cigarettes. And everyone feels his or her muscles strengthen and firm up. To be sure, there are hazards and lower standards of hygiene. Furthermore, modern health care is not available in the hill and mountain areas. But when sensible precautions are taken, few get sick in Nepal. To the contrary, most people find it physically and spiritually enlightening.

1 TREKKING STYLES AND RELATED ACTIVITIES

There are three basic approaches to trekking, but within each there are many variations as well as some related activites that can be enjoyed during or between treks. The style you choose depends on your budget, time available, and personal preferences. In addition, the areas you wish to visit dictate certain choices. Finally, your choice depends on what you want from your trek.

TREKKING WITHOUT A GUIDE

This mode, also known as the "live off the land" approach, is very popular among budget-conscious travelers as well as those who wish to live among the people of Nepal during their treks. This is a good way to learn Nepali. You can sleep and eat with the local people or, in areas where there are no inhabitants, carry your own food and shelter. Along the popular routes, your main human contacts may be with other similar-minded trekkers. Food can often be purchased at the last inhabited place on your route, but be sure to check availability beforehand. Local porters can be hired at this stage.

In some areas, for example from Pokhara to Thak Khola, or in Khumbu, more luxurious accommodations and eating places cater to trekkers. These establishments provide Western style food and comforts. They are, of course, more expensive than the facilities found along the trails less popular with tourists. But they do allow trekkers to travel without a great deal of hassle.

With few people in the party, large distances can be covered quickly if necessary or desired. Such travel, especially on the standard treks described in this book, can be very rewarding and expenses can be quite low. Daily costs, not including any porters, are usually less than $3 per person.

Disadvantages of this mode of travel include wasting considerable time in Kathmandu organizing affairs, getting lost occasionally—especially when traveling off the standard routes, and often being limited in the areas you can travel to.

Trekkers who choose to travel without a guide are more likely to be disappointed in some of their expectations than those who have their treks catered through a professional agency, although many people seem to manage quite well. But the advantage of trekking without a guide is that learning to deal without the cultural props you grew up with can be a very educational and enlightening experience. Attempting to view the world through Nepali eyes may be the best lesson trekking in Nepal has to offer.

TREKKING WITH A GUIDE

This mode of travel can mean arranging and outfitting a large trek just as a professional agency would do. Or it might mean simply hiring a guide to accompany a small group. A guide can keep the party on the correct trails and may sometimes cook, carry a load, or attend to other chores. Porters, that is people hired strictly for load-carrying, can be taken on along the trail when necessary, or hired in Kathmandu before starting a trek. The guide can take care of this. Parties may camp all the way; or they may eat and sleep in local homes or hotels, and camp only where necessary. Those camping all the way must carry considerable food and equipment. A guide can be hired either privately, or through a trekking agency. The agency can also make other arrangements, such as providing equipment and porters.

Parties wishing more of a spirit of adventure—and a savings on wages—can hire an inexperienced guide. Such a person may be an older Sherpa who has been a porter for treks and mountaineering expeditions, or a youngster eager to break into the business. Such people can be excellent and will often do much more than guide—they can cook, carry things, and help in other ways. On my first trek in Nepal in 1969, I hired a young inexperienced Sherpa. We both learned a great deal and enjoyed ourselves immensely. He has since gone on to become an excellent guide, and now with his brother runs a company that supplies dehydrated foods to trekkers.

The advantage of trekking with a guide is that it allows considerable flexibility in the choice of route, diversions, and scheduling. There is also a greater opportunity for interacting with the local people encountered in route, especially if the party and the number of assistants (guides and porters) are small. However, arranging all this after arriving in Nepal can be time-consuming and somewhat difficult.

Trekking in a modest style is a good means of getting money into the hands of people in the hills of Nepal, since the villagers who provide food, run the inns, and work as porters benefit directly. This may be a more effective means of economic assistance than international aid. Costs for this style are less than for professionally arranged treks, and depend on the number of assistants hired.

TREKKING WITH A PROFESSIONAL AGENCY

While initially only Mountain Travel, founded by the indomitable Himalayan veteran, Lieutenant Colonel James Roberts, was able to offer comprehensive trekking arrangements for the traveler, many similar businesses operate today (see Addresses in Appendix).

Many travel agencies and organizations based in other countries organize groups for treks to various regions of Nepal. The actual arrangements for the treks are customarily handled by one of the approved trekking agencies in Nepal. No listing of such agencies is given here, but information about them can be obtained from travel agents in your own country. Even though a particular trekking agency in Nepal works with an affiliated agency in your country, you can usually deal directly with the Nepali agency if you prefer.

This mode of travel is expensive but it offers a degree of luxury that is not available in the others. Treks are organized for both large and small groups and are usually conducted by Sherpa guides called Sirdars, who are often famous for their mountaineering exploits on Himalayan expeditions. The guides speak sufficient English to ally fears of language difficulties. A large retinue of porters insures that nothing essential to the comfort and well-being of trekkers is left behind. The parties usually camp in tents near villages and skilled cooks prepare fine meals. Most of the necessary equipment is provided. These parties often have someone with medical expertise along, and emergencies can usually be handled more quickly than in less experienced groups. There is also no need to spend time planning for all these arrangements in Kathmandu.

Such parties usually have to stick to a pre-determined route and schedule, so there is less leeway for interesting diversions or layovers. Members of large parties must generally keep together. Trekkers in professionally organized parties are usually rather insulated from the local people encountered in route. Indeed, the participants tend to relate exclusively to one another, to the guides, and to other employees of the trek.

This kind of travel is especially suited for those who have neither the time nor the desire to make their own arrangements, but wish to enjoy the scenery of the country. The costs, exclusive of air fares and charters, run from about $20 to $100 per person per day and vary according to the length of the trek and the number of people in the party. Arrangements must usually be made before leaving your own country, either directly or through agents. In contrast to people who prefer other styles of trekking, those who embark on this type of trek are paying for comfort and security.

TREKKING ALONE

Trekking groups can literally be any size. People travel alone, with two or three friends, or in groups of twenty or more. The larger parties are more unwieldy, though some prefer the companionship of numbers. The fewer the "sahibs," the greater the likelihood of interaction with local people. I strongly recommend that trekkers traveling alone hire a guide or porter. Women should try to find a woman porter or guide. Nepalis find it difficult to understand why foreigners, especially women, would travel alone—indeed most Nepali women wouldn't. Not that there is any particular hazard; it is just safer with a companion. Local people seem to consider a woman traveling alone a witch or a person of low morals. The same caution applies to men, but it is more common to see a man traveling alone in Nepal.

There have been rare instances of attacks on trekkers, usually those traveling alone in remote areas. These are probably due to misunderstandings. If you follow the principles outlined in Chapter 4 and are sensitive to your hosts, you should have no problem. Travel in Nepal is certainly safer than in most other countries, including your homeland!

TREKKING WITH SMALL CHILDREN

Small children need not be left at home in order for the adults of a family to enjoy a trek in Nepal. Certainly a trek with children will be different from one without children, but it need not be any less enjoyable or memorable. In fact, children can be real icebreakers in an alien land; they provide a common link with which the local people can identify.

The Nepali village people are open and friendly for the most part, and the sight of a trekking family will interest them. Although a small child may initially be overwhelmed by the interest of outsiders, an exciting cultural exchange can be encouraged if the child becomes accustomed to the local people. Flexibility in the itinerary is particularly important if the family hopes to achieve this communication. Many of the difficulties encountered in trekking with children in Nepal can be overcome if the family tries some overnight trips near home. In this section, problems specific to Nepal will be discussed, and in Chapter 5 there is an important section on health care for children. It should be read concurrently.

Don't assume that treks must be modest in scope. One family with children, aged four and six, trekked with another family with a child of six. They covered almost 500 miles in fifty-five days from Pokhara to Baitadi in the extreme western part of Nepal. This trek was more ambitious than most people would choose to undertake with children of that age, but for them it was a wonderful experience that none of them will forget. The two families, by carrying moderate packs themselves (30 to 50 lb, 13 to 23 kg) and living off the land insofar as possible, were able to get by with only two porters. They never carried any of the children except across streams or rickety bridges. Thus the pace was slower than that of normal adults, but they compensated for this by increased attention to peripheral activities such as photography and birdwatching. The children appeared to thrive on the physical exercise. They received lots of personalized attention from their parents and were constantly stimulated by new sights and activities. At the end of the day, they had little energy left and usually fell asleep soon after dinner.

It may not be inappropriate to consider taking older children out of school for a trek. Understanding school officials will probably agree that what the children learn on the trip far outweighs any loss in book learning. Parents can help children keep journals of their activities and adventures, which will aid them with their writing and provide a resource for later use.

Younger children need not be left at home. Infants older than six months can trek, though I would recommend that only breast-fed infants be taken. One trekking family with a two-year-old found it most convenient that the child was still breast feeding. In Nepal children nurse at their mother's breasts until they are quite old. Certainly this is the most sanitary method of feeding, and it has many other health benefits.

Families with younger children have carried them in a back- or front-style pack carrier. A back carrier with an elevator seat is probably best. Other families hire a porter, the best being a woman—a Sherpani or hill Nepali. Most such women have children themselves and enjoy singing and playing with the child. They usually prefer carrying the child in a *Doko*, a conical wicker basket, using a tumpline. A foam pad for the inside and an umbrella attached to the basket rim for shade keep the child comfortable. It is not unreasonable to carry a child up to 44 lb (20 kg) in this manner. Some children, especially active ones, may not tolerate being carried in a basket by a stranger. The method you choose depends on your personal preferences. Certainly carrying your own child can contribute to an important relationship with him or her.

Children in diapers need not be a problem. Some parents prefer disposable diapers. Never dispose of them in a hearth fire in a Nepali home. Burn them out of sight of others and bury the ashes. Infants might need six a day, while two a day should be enough for semi-toilet-trained toddlers. A few disposable diapers may come in handy in case of diarrhea, even for a toilet-trained child. Disposable diapers are not available in Nepal. Actually, I feel it is preferable to use cloth diapers, which either you or the porters wash. It is not a chore that a porter can be expected to do, but an arrangement can be worked out beforehand. Try to avoid pollution of streams when washing diapers. Nepali children never use diapers as we know them. A "potty" or chamber pot for toilet-trained children may be helpful. Otherwise, unfamiliar surroundings may make defecation difficult for them.

Food for children can vary a great deal. The children of one trekking family soon became willing consumers of *daal bhaat*, the local rice and lentil dish. Those on treks organized by professional agencies have few problems if the cook

A potter carrying his wares in a Doko *by means of a tumpline. The basket could carry your child. (Ane Haaland)*

prepares familiar foods. A great deal depends on the parents' attitude and their children's food fussiness. It may be wise to keep some favorite snacks handy.

Parents who have hiked with their children under various conditions should have no difficulties choosing clothing for them. The new synthetic-pile garments worn over a zippered pajama suit, may be the best choice for cold days. Such clothes are warm, light in weight, and quick drying.

Most children, like many adults, find it difficult to be continually stared at. This is the case when staying in a Nepali home that is not set up as a hotel with

Children are great "ice breakers" in Nepal. (Ted Moore)

separate rooms for trekkers. A tent gives your children a familiar place to go, away from the prying eyes of the crowds that always assemble to stare at the funny little white children. Children may find it reassuring to sleep between their parents when staying in unfamiliar surroundings.

Your children may be surprised to see that Nepali children have few toys. It is wise to bring a few items to keep your children amused since they won't be as inspired by the beauty of the countryside as you. Playing with toys with the Nepali children could be fascinating for your children, but avoid setting an unfortunate precedent by indiscriminately giving out toys to local children. Nepali children are quite happy with the toys they have, and they could become quite depressed if they knew about the toys they don't and can't have.

Be aware of the physical hazards in Nepal. There are plenty of places inside homes, along the trails, and in the fields where a slip or fall could be disastrous for a child. Dogs (particularly rabid ones) represent an occupational hazard for trekkers in Nepal, and even more so for children. Exercise extreme caution around all dogs and villages as options after being bitten are few and unpleasant. Although they are not known to be carriers of rabies, water buffalo frequently have surly dispositions and delight in charging small children.

Like most aspects of trekking in Nepal, the experience of going as a family can be rewarding and enlightening if you prepare yourself adequately.

TREKKING IN THE MONSOON

In Nepal all paths and bridges are liable to disappear or change at no notice due to monsoons, acts of Gods, etc.

Note on trekking map, 1972

Although many consider it out of the question, trekking during the rainy season has been discovered by a select few "Nepalophiles." There are several reasons to consider joining these eccentrics. Many people can come to Nepal only during the Western summer holidays, which correspond to the monsoon. Some want to trek when popular trails are not packed with foreigners. Others are interested in the plant and animal life that is most spectacular at this time. It is undeniably a most beautiful time of the year. Everything is lush and green. The clouds perform dramatically, and periodically part to reveal the splendor of spectacular vistas. Mountain views during the monsoon may be unforgettable. The high country is alive with activity as people pasture their animals on the upper slopes.

There are problems, however. Everything tends to get soaked. Trails are often very muddy, always wet, and sometimes treacherous. Distant views are clouded most of the time. Bridges sometimes wash out, necessitating time-consuming and difficult detours. What may have been a trickle in the dry season becomes a deep, fast torrent in the monsoon. Travel thus often involves fording rivers. At times you may have to wait a day or two for the water level to drop enough for a safe ford. To make matters worse, leeches populate the forests at higher altitudes (see Chapter 5), while mosquitoes abound at lower elevations.

Yet, just as you adjust to trekking in Nepal during the dry season, so you can adapt your life-style to the monsoon. Certain items of equipment are essential: a waterproof cover for your pack, sheets of plastic for the porter loads, an umbrella, and footwear with good traction, preferably Vibram soles. Skirts for women, preferably with a hem about calf length, and shorts for men are the most practical clothing. Although women should wear skirts in towns for cultural reasons (see Chapter 4), many prefer to wear pants on monsoon soaked trails and only change into skirts when they stop for the evening in a village. Most waterproof rain parkas and cagoules are not very useful—if you do not get wet from the outside, you will soak in sweat from the inside. The new gear made from Gore-Tex, a fabric that breathes, yet is waterproof if kept clean, may be suitable for the monsoon. Gore-Tex jackets with underarm zips allow considerable ventilation, as do pants with side zips. Pile clothing or garments of synthetic, down-like material are useful in the wet high altitudes.

In planning a monsoon trek, do not plan on covering too much distance in a short time. It is hard to equal dry season trekking times. Many of the trails will be different during the monsoon. Drier ridges are usually taken instead of the flooded valley bottoms. Take time to enjoy village life, to sample the fruits and vegetables in season, and to enjoy the prodigious plant life. And do not tell too many people how much you enjoyed it!

MOUNTAINEERING

Among the first outsiders to come to Nepal were mountaineers looking for ways onto the highest summits. Much of the early descriptions of the countryside comes from them. The history of climbing on the highest peaks is itself fascinating, and has recently been well-chronicled by Louis Baume in *Sivalaya* (see Recommended Reading).

Besides the many expeditionary peaks, there are eighteen minor peaks, called trekking summits, which can be climbed by trekkers if they get the proper permits. The fact that they are called trekking summits in no way implies they are trivial. Some are difficult and dangerous, and a few have only recently had first ascents. Further information on these climbs can be obtained from mountaineering journals, trekking agencies, and the climbing community.

To attempt one of these peaks, application must be made to the Nepal Mountaineering Association (NMA), G.P.O. Box 1435 Ram Shah Path, Kathmandu. The current General Secretary is T. C. Pokharel. Permission is granted for two weeks and may be extended for another two weeks. This period applies only to the time spent at or above base camp. Applications are on a first come–first served basis and are not transferable. The current fee is Rs. 315 for each member of the party. There is a minimum fee of Rs. 1,260 for peaks higher than 20,014 ft (6100 m) and of Rs. 630 for lower peaks. The charge for the time extension is twenty-five percent of the original fee. Fees are payable at the time of application and are non-refundable. Climbers can apply after they arrive in Nepal.

A Sirdar, or guide, registered with the NMA must accompany each party. He must be paid Rs. 30 plus food and tent accommodations. If he is required to go above base camp, he must be furnished with climbing equipment and clothing, and insured to Rs. 75,000. All climbing must be clean: hardware must be removed and camps left clean. Finally, a report must be submitted to the NMA upon return. Applications should include the climbing fee and the following information: the name of the peak; the period of time for which the permit is requested; the route (peaks can be climbed by any route); the name and nationality of each member of the party; the name, nationality, passport number, and home address of the leader; the appointed representative in Kathmandu (usually a trekking agency); and the name and organization or address of the guide or Sirdar.

The trekking peaks, grouped according to area and using the term *Himal* which means range, are:

Khumbu Himal
Island Peak (6189 m)
Kwangde (6187 m)
Kusum Kangru (6369 m)
Lobache East (6119 m)
Mehra Peak (5820 m)
Mera Peak (6437 m)
Pokalde (5806 m)
Rolwaling Himal
Pharchamo (6318 m)
Ramdung (6060 m)
Langtang Himal
Ganja La Chuli (5846 m)

Ganesh Himal
Paldor Peak (5928 m)
Manang Himal
Chulu East (6059 m)
Chulu West (6583 m)
Pisang (6091 m)
Annapurna Himal
Fluted Peak (6390 m)
Hiunchuli (6441 m)
Mardi Himal (5586 m)
Tent Peak (5500 m)

As for expeditionary peaks, the general rules and regulations are too lengthy to document here. These rules can be obtained from the Ministry of Tourism in Kathmandu and have been listed in the journal, *Off Belay*, April, 1978. Essentially, a license must be obtained by application to the Ministry of Tourism "with the recommendation of a reputed and recognized mountaineering institution in the appropriate country, or the embassy of that country in Nepal." Usually this is the national alpine club, if one exists. A royalty of Rs. 10,000 to Rs. 15,000 must be paid, and the party must take a liaison officer chosen by the government. There are rules governing what he must be provided and paid; these rules also describe his duties and functions. There are similar rules regarding the Sirdar and high altitude porters. Penalties for disregarding the rules include banishment from Nepal for three to five years or disqualification from climbing in Nepal for five to ten years. An institution that disregards the rules can be disqualified from sponsoring climbs for three years.

Certain peaks are open to all climbers, others to Nepali climbers only, and still others to joint expeditions. The peaks for all climbers are:

Everest (8848 m)	Langtang Lirung (7220 m)
Kanchenjunga (8598 m)	Baruntse (7220 m)
Lhotse (8501 m)	Annapurna South Peak (7219 m)
Makalu (8475 m)	Manaslu II (7154 m)
Yalung-Kang (8420 m)	Ganesh Himal II (7150 m)
Dhaulagiri (8167 m)	Gaurishankar (7150 m)
Manaslu (8156 m)	Pumori (7145 m)
Annapurna (8091 m)	Mount Api (7132 m)
Annapurna II (7937 m)	Ganesh Himal III (7132 m)
Kangbachen (7937 m)	Tilicho (7132 m)
Nuptse (7879 m)	Ganesh Himal IV (7102 m)
Himalchuli (7864 m)	Glacier Dome (7069 m)
Peak 29, also called Dakura (7835 m)	Nilgiri North (7061 m)
Dhaulagiri II (7751 m)	Kanguru (7010 m)
Dhaulagiri III (7715 m)	Langtang Himal (6986 m)
Jannu (7710 m)	Numbur (6954 m)
Dhaulagiri IV (7661 m)	Nilgiri Central (6940 m)
Fang (7647 m)	Kanjiroba (6882 m)
Makalu II (7640 m)	Patrasi (6860 m)
Dhaulagiri V (7617 m)	Ama Dablang (6856 m)
Annapurna III (7548 m)	Nilgiri South (6839 m)
Annapurna IV (7525 m)	Kangtega (6809 m)
Gangapurna (7455 m)	Nampa (6754 m)
Ganesh Himal I (7405 m)	Baudha (6672 m)
Churen Himal (7371 m)	Thamserku (6623 m)
Chamlang (7319 m)	Dhampus (6012 m)
Dhaulagiri VI (7268 m)	Kagmara I (5960 m)
Putha Hiunchuli (7246 m)	Jagdula (5791 m)

The summits for Nepali expeditions only (and those foreigners allowed to accompany those expeditions) are:

Gyachung Kang (7922 m)	Dorje Lakpa (6990 m)
Omi Kangri (7922 m)	Bhrikuti (6720 m)
Jongsang (7473 m)	Changla (6715 m)
Gurja Himal (7193 m)	Kerolung (6681 m)
Chamar (7177 m)	Nala Kankar (6635 m)

RIVER RUNNING

Over the last ten years, many of the great rivers of Nepal have been run by rubber rafts, canoes, kayaks, and other craft. There is nothing unique about rivers in Nepal as far as such activities are concerned. There are the usual difficulties in transporting the boats to the starting point and arranging to have them picked up at the destination. Rivers commonly rafted include the Trisuli and the Gandaki. You can arrange motor transportation to and from these rivers. Another popular choice is the Sun Kosi. You can go by vehicle to the starting point, but you must fly back from Biratnagar after the journey. Rivers like the Bheri, the Marsyangdi, and the Arun offer more challenges because of logistic problems. Others like the Karnali are perhaps beyond the limits possible today.

While some professional river runners have done expeditionary trips independently, most people deal with agencies in Nepal that specialize in rafting (see Appendix for Addresses).

RUNNING

Running, which has become very popular in the West, has in some measure come to Nepal. While few Nepalis run regularly along the trails, stories abound of incredibly short times taken by Nepalis, usually as mail runners for mountaineering expeditions. Recently Jay Longacre became known in much of Nepal as "The American Runner" for his 4¼ day run from Kathmandu to Kala Pattar near the base of Mount Everest, a journey that takes more than 15 days to trek. Few people will want to challenge that record, but some may wish to combine running with trekking. The following information is taken from Jay's experiences in Nepal.

Most of the information for trekkers applies also to runners and won't be repeated here. The problems of altitude illness are very important and the cautions in Chapter 5 must be heeded. Physical conditioning does not prevent these problems. Runners, if they are alert to the symptoms, should at least be able to descend quickly to safety. If they persist in ascending despite serious symptoms, their risk is certainly greater. However, most runners won't be able to continue running, even with mild symptoms.

One danger of steep mountain running is the possibility of falling off the trail. If a runner stumbles, he should try to fall on his hands and knees onto the dirt. If he tries to remain upright, he may lurch off the trail and down the mountainside. To prevent injury, runners must master the techniques of running downhill. To avoid falling and injuring joints, a runner must shorten his stride, strike heel first with the knee slightly bent, and lean backward as little as possible. Practice it on hills near home first.

Proper shoes and clothing are basics for a pleasant run. Ripple-soled running shoes are preferable to waffle-soled shoes. The latter tend to wear quickly and to grip the trails too well, permitting feet to slide within the shoes. This causes blisters. Running without socks may help prevent blisters and it enables the runner to walk through water and across rivers easily.

Basically there are two ways of running outside the major cities and towns in Nepal: long solo runs covering two or more days and 50 mi (80 km) or more; and daily runs of more than an hour, alone or with a group, along or close to one of the main trekking trails. On long solo runs, you should retain a Sherpa guide (not a porter) to meet you at the end of your run with extra clothes and other needed supplies. On the run itself you need to carry sunscreen, Vaseline, soap, face mask, wool mittens, one suit of long wool underwear, cap with a long bill, nylon all-weather suit, Nepali money, cup, sleeping bag, water bottle, iodine, map, pen, notebook, flashlight, sunglasses, extra clothes, and this book. All of this will fit into a small pack, and needn't weigh more than a few pounds. Wear shorts, tee shirt, and running shoes.

For daily runs along a main trekking route, hire a Sherpa guide to carry your sleeping bag and supplies. He can help by explaining the trails and by leaving earlier to wait for you at difficult or confusing areas. On these daily runs, you need only carry a cup, soap, Vaseline, sunscreen, camera, iodine, and water bottle.

It is important to force yourself to drink frequently to prevent dehydration, even if you don't feel thirsty. It is unlikely you could drink too much.

Runners have greater difficulty with anal irritation than trekkers. After each bowel movement, wash to help prevent irritation. Use the water in your bottle if necessary.

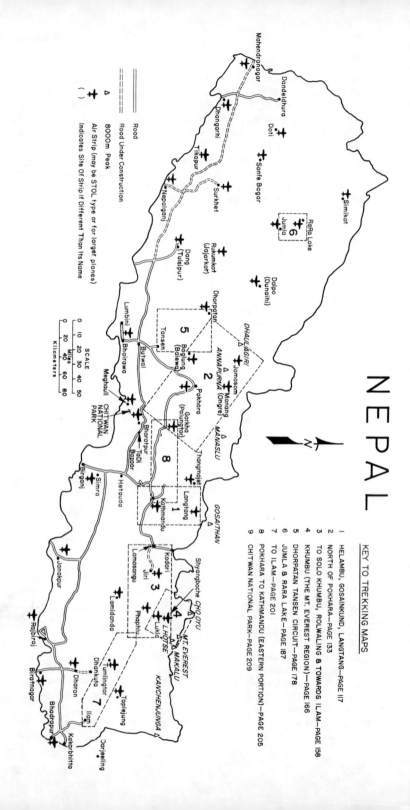

2 CHOOSING A TREK

*Just go on and on . . . Do you see the mountain ranges there, far
away? One behind another. They rise up. They tower. That is
my deep, unending, inexhaustible kingdom.*

Henrik Ibsen, *The Master Builder*

In choosing a trek, many factors must be considered. Important among them
are the time available, the strength and ability of the members of the party, and the
desires of the trekkers. Certain treks offer majestic mountain scenery; others a
glimpse of hill life in Nepal; still others spectacular floral displays. Routes can be
linked to provide many different experiences. Some entail entering potentially
dangerous mountain terrain. Finally the time of year is very important, as certain
treks are difficult, if not impossible, during heavy snowfalls. Others are very
uncomfortable in the pre-monsoon heat.

WEATHER

The usual trekking season lasts from October to May. During the remainder of
the year, the monsoon makes traveling wet and offers little in the way of mountain
views. In addition, leeches abound.

During October and November the skies are clear and good views can be expected. Occasional short storms may occur and the temperature often goes below
freezing at night above 10,000 ft (3050 m). This is the most popular time for trekking.

December and January are the coldest months, but there is little snowfall.
Again, excellent clear views are common. Temperatures constantly plunge below
freezing at night above 10,000 ft (3050 m), and below 0°F (– 18°C) at altitudes
above 14,000 ft (4300 m). Some inhabitants of the northern Himalayan region head
south for the winter at this time. It can be a hauntingly beautiful time of the year to
trek.

February and March bring warmer weather, but frequent storms and considerable snowfall at higher altitudes. Birds and flowers, especially the rhododendrons, are seen at the lower altitudes. Toward the end of March, haze—caused by
dust from the plains of India—and smoke from local fires often obscure distant
views. In addition, it becomes much warmer in the regions below 3000 ft (1000 m).

April and May are less suitable for trekking because of the heat—sometimes
100°F (38°C)—at altitudes below 3000 ft (1000 m). Also the haze mars distant
views of the peaks. During these months, however, you encounter many species of
plant and animal life not seen at other times. As the season progresses, the
magnificent rhododendrons bloom at higher and higher altitudes until the flowers
reach the tree line. Occasional pre-monsoon storms clear the haze and cool the atmosphere for a few days. While temperatures below freezing can be encountered
above 12,000 ft (3600 m), it becomes quite warm below 8000 ft (2500 m) and almost
oppressive below 3000 ft (1000 m).

Depending on the year, travel in the high country can be difficult because of
heavy snowfalls, especially during January, February, and March. Passes, such as

the Trashi Labtsa, the one near Gosainkund, and the Ganja La heading north into Langtang, are best attempted in autumn through December, or in later spring.

Trekking in the monsoon (June to the end of September) can be undertaken by the keen or experienced. Rain, mist, and fog can be expected almost daily, but occasionally clouds part to give spectacular views of the mountains. The flora are usually at their most colorful.

It is important to keep in mind that mountain weather is highly unpredictable. Classical signs of a storm approaching, such as a cirrus-clouded sky or a fall in barometric pressure, can be misleading. To estimate temperatures, note that for a rise of 100 m, the temperature falls about 0.65°C; or for a rise of 1000 ft, it falls about 3.5°F.

HELAMBU, GOSAINKUND, AND LANGTANG

The trekking most accessible to Kathmandu is in Helambu, Gosainkund, and Langtang, all north of the capital city. There are trails linking the three regions, and as many can be visited as time and conditions permit. The minimum time for a brief visit is a week. Two weeks would allow you to combine two of the regions, and in three weeks you could enjoy the entire area.

Helambu is the region closest to Kathmandu. It is best approached from the northeast rim of the Kathmandu Valley. The name refers to a region at the north end of the Malemchi Khola (river). It is inhabited by Sherpas, though they are not closely related to the famed Sherpas of the Everest area. This region south of the main Himalayan chain provides an example of typical hill life in Nepal. A circuit can be made through the area with minimal backtracking if snow does not prevent travel on one high-level stretch. The trails are fairly good and only a few sections are difficult to follow. Cooked food and lodging are easily available, except on the high-level stretch. The route begins in areas of Hindu influence and goes through Buddhist villages. Side trips are possible and linkups can be made with Gosainkund and Langtang, weather conditions permitting. There are distant views of the Himalaya on the high-level stretch in good weather, except during the late spring when they may be obscured by the haze. Rather than backtrack to Kathmandu, you could vary your exit to reach the Kathmandu-Kodari Road, either at Panchkhal if you head south from Tarang Marang, or at Baliphi if you take the Panch Pokhari side trip.

Gosainkund is the site of seven lakes that lie south of a major ridge between Helambu and the Trisuli river to the west. The area is uninhabited for the most part, but every August as many as 50,000 pilgrims crowd into the area for a festival near a lake that figures prominently in Hindu mythology. Trekkers may wish to visit this area from Trisuli Bazaar and, if conditions permit, cross a moderate pass to link up with Helambu. In the spring when rhododendrons are in bloom, it is a spectacular area. Below the lakes to the west, but above the Trisuli, is a cheese factory and a little-used Buddhist temple. Trekkers heading into this area must be self-sufficient.

Langtang is a Himalayan valley that lies north of both Helambu and Gosainkund. It is inhabited by Tibetan people and provides a glimpse of mountain life. Trails are straightforward, yet you can head east in the Langtang Valley beyond the last habitation to spectacular remote mountain areas, taking various side trips. Food and lodging are available for the most part. Linkups with Gosainkund are reasonably simple, but those with Helambu require crossing a substantial pass.

Either way, you must be self-sufficient. There is an airstrip in the Langtang Valley at Kyangjin where planes can be chartered. They can be used to leave the area, but should not be taken in because the altitude gain is too abrupt. Most of Langtang and Gosainkund has been included in Langtang National Park in an attempt to preserve their beauty.

NORTH OF POKHARA

The area north of Pokhara is popular both with trekkers new to Nepal and with veterans. The mountain scenery is as spectacular as any in Nepal, especially on the high routes. The many different ethnic groups are as interesting, if not as famous, as the Sherpas of Khumbu. Some of the areas provide perhaps the finest native cuisine in rural Nepal. One ethnic group, the *Thakali*, run numerous inns and hotels in the area. They have adapted their menu in many cases to the palates of foreign trekkers and can provide food and accommodations for those who wish to avoid local diets and the lodgings used by hill Nepalis. Finally, and perhaps most significantly, most of the treks in this region traverse through many different ecological zones. They begin with the customary terraces of the hills, encounter rain, deciduous, and pine forests, pass through arid, desert-like country similar to the Tibetan Plateau, and even reach alpine areas. Remarkable transitions through different areas, each with its customary animal life, can be made in a week or less.

Perhaps the most famous trek is from Pokhara to the Kali Gandaki river and up it to the Thak Khola region and to Jomosom, the administrative center of Mustang District. This route does not go higher than 10,000 ft (3048 m) and is not too strenuous. Along the way there are plenty of inns and hotels that cater to single trekkers or small parties. The trek is quite suitable for those traveling without guides or porters. The trail goes through an incredible variety of vegetation and follows one of the deepest gorges in the world between Annapurna and Dhaulagiri. On this route you are likely to encounter colorful mule caravans made musical by the tinkling of neck bells. Several side trips out of the Kali Gandaki Valley are possible. They are strenuous, but they reward tired hikers with spectacular views. This is a justifiably popular trek, and the only way to avoid meeting other trekkers all along the trail is to take the side trips. Ten days is the minimum time for a round trip to Jomosom. Most parties prefer to take two weeks and travel up to Muktinath (12,475 ft, 3802 m), an ancient pilgrimage site a day beyond Jomosom.

The Annapurna Sanctuary, the basin southwest of Annapurna that is the source of the Modi Khola, is a fine objective for those who wish to trek only a short time, yet include a trip into alpine country. There is not quite the same variety in vegetation as on the trek up the Thak Khola since you never get north of the main Himalayan chain. The *Gurung* villages in route are particularly colorful. Ten days is the minimum time. Snowfall and avalanche hazards may make it difficult, if not impossible, to reach the sanctuary in winter.

Manang, the region north and east of the Annapurna massif, is a third worthwhile objective north of Pokhara. This area was finally opened to foreign travel in 1977. The people of the villages of Manang are traders and many of them, world travelers. The scenery north of the main Himalayan chain is spectacular. It takes over a week to reach the town of Manang. Beyond, a high pass, the Thorung La, leads over to Muktinath. This pass can be difficult or impossible in the winter and early spring because of snow. But for those able to cope with the high altitudes,

A Gurung *tending goats during the monsoon at a high pasture north of Pokhara.* *(Donald Messerschmidt)*

the pass allows a complete circuit of the Annapurna massif without backtracking. While you can usually travel to Manang carrying only minimal food and shelter, it is necessary to be self-sufficient to cross the Thorung La.

The classic trek in this region, combining Manang and Thak Khola in a circuit, covers more than 150 mi (240 km) and requires at least three weeks. The Thorung La Pass is best crossed from Manang to Thak Khola in order to take advantage of better campsites and allow enough time for acclimatization. It is feasible to include the Annapurna Sanctuary on the circuit. There is an airstrip at Jomosom, and scheduled or charter flights from Kathmandu can shorten treks. You should not fly to Jomosom and then attempt the crossing to Manang unless you spend enough time acclimatizing. The altitude gain is too abrupt for safety.

Many trekkers with less time make a circuit from Pokhara to Ghorapani, down the Kali Gandaki to Baglung, and then to Pokhara. Others take short one- to three-day trips directly north of Pokhara to Ghachok, Siklis, and other *Gurung* villages.

Pokhara can be reached from Kathmandu by foot, road, or air, or from India by road or air. Flight delays to or from Pokhara are common during the peak tourist season, so it is best to make reservations as far in advance as possible. A week or more may be necessary.

SOLU-KHUMBU

Solu-Khumbu is the district south and west of Mount Everest. It is populated by Sherpas, an ethnic group that has achieved fame because of the exploits of its men on mountaineering expeditions. Khumbu is the name of the northern half of this region, which includes the highest mountain in the world and many of the 8000 m (26,247 ft) summits. Most of Khumbu is part of Sagarmatha National Park. Solu, the southern portion, is less rugged, but it has many interesting monasteries and villages.

The attractions are the majestic mountains, the villages in the high mountain valleys, the associated monasteries, and the interesting inhabitants. The area is popular, and outside of the monsoon, many trekkers are encountered. Some potential visitors might be put off by this, but where else can you find so many of the world's highest mountains together with communities of people living among them? By contrast, the inhabited areas of the Karakorum in Pakistan are few and the villages are far from the great mountains there. Actually, less than 10,000 people a year visit Khumbu, while many more crowd into small areas of well-known European and North American mountain parks in a weekend! While you can count on meeting many trekkers on the standard route to the base of Mount Everest, it is quite possible to spend time in Khumbu and its environs without meeting other trekkers. For almost two weeks in the autumn recently I did not see a single trekker on part of my wanderings in Khumbu and on the trek out. And I didn't concoct a devious route to avoid people. This should not be taken as a plea to get more trekkers into Khumbu, merely a statement that while it is popular, you needn't always feel crowded.

Travel to and from Khumbu can pose logistic problems. Royal Nepal Airlines (RNAC) now has scheduled flights from Kathmandu to Lukla, an airstrip located one to two days south of Namche Bazaar, the entrance to Khumbu. While getting flights to Lukla can be a problem, finding a seat back to Kathmandu can be even more trying since weather sometimes delays landing for weeks! Several hundred trekkers can be stranded there, with their patience wearing thin as they find themselves belatedly close to the pressures of modern civilization. There are other airstrips in the region, but the one at Shyangboche, close to Namche Bazaar, is even higher and best avoided for flights in. For most trekkers, it is not useful for flights out, as the planes landing there do so only to service the Everest View Hotel. Trekkers who land at high altitudes such as at Lukla and venture into the rarefied altitudes are at greater risk of altitude illness. Thus it is preferable to walk to Khumbu, and to fly out if you can tolerate delays. Part of the pleasure of walking to Khumbu is in enjoying the beautiful countryside of hill Nepal and in anticipating your arrival in Khumbu as you follow the footsteps of many mountaineering expeditions.

Two weeks is the minimum time I would recommend spending in Khumbu if your goal is the foot of Everest. If you walk from Lamosangu on the Kathmandu-Kodari Road and fly back, the entire trip takes three to four weeks. Walking to and from Khumbu makes the trip at least a month and probably more. Other approaches to Khumbu on foot include walking to Rolwaling from Barabise on the Kathmandu-Kodari Road or crossing the Trashi Labtsa Pass. Another attractive exit is to walk southeast to Ilam. Also you can enter and leave from the Tarai. Finally, airstrips at Phaphlu in Solu, at Rumjatar and Lamidanda in the south, and at Jiri in the west can shorten approaches or exits.

For those planning to trek on their own, there should be few problems obtaining cooked food and shelter on the standard route to Khumbu, and, except for the last day, on the trek to the base of Mount Everest. However, shortages do occur at times, and it is best to carry some food in reserve. While a Sherpa guide or porter may not be absolutely necessary, there is a great advantage in having one whose home is in Khumbu. He can often give you a hospitable base of operations, and hospitality in the area.

WESTERN NEPAL

Generally, the part of Nepal west of the Kali Gandaki river is not often visited by trekkers. The facilities for trekkers are few and distances are great. There are very few roads suitable for launching treks and, unless you charter a plane, air transportation is difficult. Food is sometimes impossible to obtain. Except for the treks near the Dhaulagiri Range, there are few trails that provide views of spectacular mountains. In fact, Dhaulagiri is the only 8000 m peak in Nepal west of the Kali Gandaki. The feeling of being right in the mountains that is common in, say, Khumbu, is rare here.

In spite of the difficulties, the rewards are many. The hills of western Nepal are characterized by majestic forests and interesting vegetation. Population pressures have yet to contribute to extensive deforestation. The country is very rugged, and in the northern reaches, has a feeling of openness. The people are very interesting. The farther west you go, the less contact they have had with Westerners. This can create difficulties in getting their cooperation.

One trek is a circuit from Pokhara to Dhorpatan, returning via Tansen, the capital of an old kingdom. It can be walked in less than two weeks. From Tansen you can either return to Kathmandu by road via Pokhara, or motor to Bhairawa in the Tarai and fly from there. The trek can be shortened using regular RNAC flights to Balewa near Baglung, and charters to Dhorpatan. Food and lodging are available along most of the route. There are excellent views of the Dhaulagiri Range and you can take side trips into more mountainous country.

Another trek is a circuit from Jumla to RaRa Lake, the site of a national park. Jumla is reached by scheduled planes, but getting a seat on a return flight can be difficult due to weather problems. Food and shelter must be carried on the week-long circuit. Finding the way can be a challenge, so those on their first trek in Nepal should hire a guide if they are not on a professionally organized trek.

In general, if this is your first visit to Nepal, choose one of the other treks unless you have some specific reason for wanting to trek in western Nepal. On the other hand, if you are a veteran trekker, and are looking for new, exciting, interesting experiences, go west and enjoy them.

OTHER TREKS

The treks described in Chapter 11 include an exit from Khumbu across the Trashi Labsta, a high pass to the west (18,885 ft, 5755 m), and through Rolwaling to the Kathmandu-Kodari Road. The pass is strenuous and hazardous, and unsuitable for neophyte trekkers. Some mountaineering experience is required, and food and shelter must be carried. The trek takes a minimum of ten days. It is best attempted in the early autumn or late spring. The route can be followed in reverse to visit the Rolwaling Valley, an incredibly steep-walled valley inhabited by Sherpas. It is a fine

Irrigated rice terraces. (Ane Haaland)

objective in its own right, although it is not advisable to cross from Rolwaling to Khumbu because of the abrupt altitude gain. Careful parties can do it successfully if they take time to acclimatize.

Another exit from Solu-Khumbu, this one suitable for all trekkers, is the walk from Namche Bazaar to Ilam. It takes about ten days and is best done during the winter when there is little haze from the plains of India to obscure the view. Also, the weather in the lowlands is coolest at this time.

The trek between Pokhara and Kathmandu, like that to Khumbu, goes against the grain of the land, but the difference in elevation between the ridges and the valleys is much less. It is an easy and convenient trip for those who wish to eat local food and sleep in Nepali homes. The scenery is typical of the hills of Nepal, and there are spectacular views of distant high mountains. The trek is also interesting from a historical point of view, especially the town of Gorkha from where the founder of modern Nepal, King Prithvinarayan Shah, made conquests in the eighteenth century. Indeed many of the places along this route figure strongly in the story of the unification of the country. It is quite a short journey, a matter of five or six days if you take a jeep or bus between Trisuli and Kathmandu. People who do not want to take the road or wait for a plane to or from Pokhara can follow this route. It is a good introduction to trekking in Nepal. The Pokhara-Kathmandu road runs about a day's walk south of the trail and is much less scenic.

In contrast to treks to hill and mountain regions, a trip to Chitwan National Park provides an example of the country, people, animals, and vegetation of the Tarai. Like other treks described in this book, it can be done economically. About five days is an appropriate time to spend on the round trip from Kathmandu.

There are, of course, many fine trekking areas that are currently restricted. Nevertheless, many unrestricted areas not described in this book provide excellent trekking. Areas you might consider include the Arun Valley in the east, the Bara Pokhari Lekh north of Chiti, the upper Chepe and Darondi Kholas, and the area south of Ganesh Himal, all in central Nepal. But before trying one of these, get some experience on the more popular treks.

In the future, areas of Nepal previously closed to trekkers may be opened up. Many of the restrictions were imposed due to the disdain for the prevailing rules and limits shown by earlier travelers. If all trekkers abide by the regulations, there may be fewer restrictions imposed on travel due to the transgressions of a few.

After gaining some basic experience in Nepal on some of the treks described in this book, the person yearning for adventure can easily strike out to visit places where few outsiders have been. The opportunities are endless.

SUMMARY OF TREKS

Easiest
> Pokhara to Kathmandu

Moderate
> Dhorpatan circuit
> Gosainkund
> Helambu
> Jumla to RaRa Lake circuit
> Langtang
> North of Pokhara
> Rolwaling Valley

More difficult
> High altitude wanderings north of Pokhara, in Khumbu and beyond
> > Rolwaling
> High passes such as the Ganja La, Trashi Labsta and Thorung La

Shortest (a few days)
> Initial part of most any trek
> Flying to Shyangboche, Langtang, Lukla, Dhorpatan, or Jomosom; walking
> > a day or two without altitude gain; and flying back

Around a week
> Gosainkund
> Helambu
> Khumbu—flying in and out, but not going to Everest Base Camp or Kala
> > Pattar
> Langtang
> Pokhara–Kathmandu
> RaRa Lake circuit

Two weeks or more
> Dhorpatan circuit
> Combining two areas north of Kathmandu
> Khumbu—flying in and out, and visiting the Everest Base Camp and Kala
> > Pattar
> To Manang and back from Pokhara
> Rolwaling
> To Thak Khola heading north from Pokhara

Three weeks or more
> Dhorpatan circuit with side trips
> Helambu, Gosainkund, and Langtang
> Khumbu with plenty of side trips or walking from Kathmandu and back
> North of Pokhara with lots of side trips or the Annapurna circuit

Most Spectacular Mountain Scenery
> Annapurna circuit
> Khumbu
> Upper Langtang Valley
> Manang
> Side trips north of Pokhara such as Annapurna Sanctuary, Annapurna
> > Base Camp, Dhaulagiri Icefall, Tilicho Tal, or Dhampus Pass
> Upper Rolwaling Valley

Good springtime introduction to flora, especially rhododendrons
> Dhorpatan circuit
> Gosainkund, Helambu, and Langtang
> RaRa Lake circuit
> Rolwaling
> Solu-Khumbu

Winding down the trail near Syang in Thak Khola. (Ane Haaland)

3 PREPARATIONS

If anything can go wrong, it will.

Murphy's Law

Trekking in Nepal, like any other activity, is usually more successful if the participants are prepared, and if they have some idea of what to expect. Those who know before they leave home that they want to trek in Nepal should attempt to equip themselves adequately before they leave. The many people who decide to trek only after they arrive in Nepal must acquire equipment there. Since this is not always easy, it is better not to come totally unprepared.

VISAS AND PERMITS

Most travelers to Nepal need a visa. This can be obtained from one of the Nepali Embassies and Consular Services in eighteen countries throughout the world. The visas are valid for up to one month. Two passport-size photographs are necessary for the application, and travelers should bring a dozen or so for use in formalities.

Visas valid for one week only are issued at entry points to Nepal. The main entry points are: (1) Kathmandu, for those arriving by air; (2) Kodari along the Nepal-Tibet border (currently not used by tourists, but may be opened if travel to the Tibetan Region of China becomes established); (3) Birgunj across from Raxaul, India, on the main road from India to Kathmandu; and (4) Sunauli across from Nautanwa, India, near the town of Bhairawa on the road from India to Pokhara. Other border points with India, less used by tourists, are: DhangaDi, Jaleswor, Kakarbhitta, Kakarhawa, Koilabas, Mahendranagar, Nepalganj, and Rani Sikijahi. Travelers coming by road need a *carnet de passage* for their vehicles. There is also bus service on the main roads.

Nepali Embassies and Consular Services are located in Edgecliffe, Australia; Vienna, Austria; Dacca, Bangladesh; Brussels and Antwerp, Belgium; Rangoon, Burma; Peking and Lhasa, Peoples Republic of China; Cairo, Egypt; London, England; Bonn, Dusseldorf, Frankfurt, and Munich, West Germany; Paris, France; Hong Kong; New Delhi and Calcutta, India; Tokyo, Japan; Beirut, Lebanon; Islamabad, Pakistan; Bangkok, Thailand; Washington, New York, and San Francisco, United States; and Moscow, Soviet Union.

Trekking regulations change from time to time, so it is wise to check by writing to one of the trekking agencies. At present, permits are required for all areas except the Kathmandu and Pokhara valleys and Chitwan National Park. Several areas of Nepal, mostly those on the northern border, are restricted, and permission to trek there is not granted. It is important to respect these restrictions, as many have been imposed after indiscretions by trekkers.

Under current regulations, trekking permits are issued at the Central Immigration Office of the Home and Panchayat Ministry, His Majesty's Government (HMG), on Ram Shah Path in Kathmandu. A visa extension is issued first, then a trekking permit for one trek at a time. The places that you are permitted to go are stated on the permit. A general prescribed route must be taken. In applying, state the northernmost town in each major valley as well as names of towns with police check posts. Two passport-size photographs are required. The trekking permit must be presented at all police check posts along the route and annotated by the post nearest to the destination. It is a good idea to have the permit annotated at all check posts, since this verifies that you have in fact traveled with the permit. This may be helpful in getting visa extensions. The permit must be surrendered on return to Kathmandu. A trekking agency can handle many of the formalities.

The limit for tourist visas is three months. Extensions for one month at a time can be obtained through the Central Immigration Office on Ram Sha Path in Kathmandu. An initial visa of one month can be obtained from Nepali Embassies abroad, or a one-week visa can be obtained at an entry point to Nepal. Thereafter, you are required to show bank receipts to verify having exchanged $5 in U.S. currency for each day of the proposed extension. Extensions can usually be granted only in Kathmandu, though occasionally it may be possible to obtain one-week extensions in Pokhara or at a police post.

Visa and trekking permit formalities tend to take some time. Count on at least two days. All government offices are closed on Saturday, the weekly holiday. Other holidays are frequent.

It cannot be too heavily stressed that you should attempt to put forward a pleasant image in dealing with the immigration officials. They do not understand the ways, habits, dress, or customs of many Westerners. They are wary of people who attempt to get visa extensions indefinitely under the pretext of trekking, but who, in fact, wish to become residents of Kathmandu Valley. Be considerate, dress neatly, and try to minimize the element of distrust that Nepali officials may have of foreigners. You will have fewer problems if you do so.

Four areas of Nepal have been designated national parks. They are the Langtang, RaRa, Royal Chitwan, and Sagarmatha (Everest) national parks. Foreigners must pay a fee and obtain a park permit at the entrance. Buying wood from locals or taking it from the forests is illegal in the parks. All travelers are required to carry non-wood stoves and fuel. Violators can be arrested and fined.

MAPS

Modern topographical maps suitable for trekking are difficult to find for most areas of Nepal. The country was surveyed between 1924 and 1927 by clandestine workers for the Survey of India. They ventured through the country with concealed survey instruments and did a creditable job. While the altitudes on their maps are usually not correct, the relative features of the topography south of the Himalaya are portrayed well. But the trails are not always marked accurately. The 1:250,000 series (one inch = 3.9 miles) of this survey is not generally available. Like most Indian cartographic materials, its distribution is restricted to official agencies. In the United States, the U.S. Army Map Service, Corps of Engineers, has printed these maps under the title Series U502. The sheets most useful to trekkers are:

NG 45— 3   *Kanchenjunga* (toward Darjeeling)
NG 45— 2   *Mount Everest* (Kathmandu to Khumbu and Rolwaling)
NG 45—14   *Tingri Dzong* (north of above sheet)
NG 45— 1   *Kathmandu* (Gorkha to Kathmandu and north)
NG 45—13   *Jongkha Dzong* (north of Kathmandu)

NG 44—16   *Pokhara* (north and west of Pokhara)
NG 44— 4   *Tansing* (south of above sheet)
NG 44—11   *Jumla* (Jumla to RaRa Lake)

These maps can be seen at the Library of Congress in Washington, D.C., or at the Lamont Library of Harvard University in Cambridge, Massachusetts, as well as at other places. Some government offices in Kathmandu have maps from this series on display.

A scaled-down version of the Survey of India maps on the scale of 1:506,880 (one inch = 8.0 miles) is available to the public. These maps, Series U462, are published by the British Ministry of Defense. They can be seen at His Majesty's Government (HMG) Tourist Office in Kathmandu. A blue non-topographical version with recently built roads and airstrips is also sometimes available. A further scaled-down updated version on the scale of 1:780,000 (one inch = 12.3 miles) is available from the American-Nepal Map Project, c/o M. S. Holloway, P.O. Box 12130, San Diego, Calif. 91212. Either of these versions gives general impressions of the topography, but few towns are marked and the delineation of the trails is not quite accurate. Nevertheless, they are the best general maps of Nepal available.

Maps produced for aircraft navigation are available from: Distribution Division (C-44), Office of Aeronautical Charts and Cartography, National Oceanic Survey, Riverdale, Maryland, 20840. They portray the topography well, but do not show most villages or trails. In the 1:500,000 (one inch = 7.9 miles) series, four sheets cover Nepal—PC-H-9A, 9B, 9C, and 9D. In the 1:1,000,000 (one inch = 15.8 miles) series, ONC-H-9 covers all of Nepal.

The Survey of India completed an aerial survey of Nepal in the early 1960s to produce maps on a scale of 1:63,360 (one inch = 1.0 mile). They are excellent, but almost impossible to find because of restrictions on distribution.

Several series of maps produced in Nepal have appeared recently. The first, entitled Annapurna and Dhaulagiri Himal, was done by Dr. Harka Gurung on the scale of 1:253,440 (one inch = 4 miles) and indicates ridges, trails, and drainage features in an easy to use fashion. It is out of print, but occasionally available. This series was followed by several others: first the Mandala Maps, and then other series from several sources, including the recent Survey of India maps. Contours, trails, and towns are shown on most of them, but the altitudes, trails, and towns are not always accurate. They are dyeline copies of artwork and the copies are poor. Nevertheless, they are sufficient for most trekking purposes. Maps to cover most of the commonly trekked areas are available sporadically. Titles include: *Kathmandu, Helambu, Langtang, Gosainkund; Pokhara to Jomosom, Manang; Lamosangu to Mount Everest; Kathmandu to Pokhara; Jomosom to Jumla and Surkhet; Jugal Himal; Khumbu Himal; Kanchenjunga, Makalu, Mount Everest; and Jumla to RaRa.*

Other productions are expected. A recent series, published by M.L. Maharjan, has a map covering the Annapurna region. Another covers the Everest trek and beyond to the Arun. Inquire at Graphics Rachana, Dharma Path, Kathmandu, for maps produced in Nepal. Another useful map is *Royal Chitwan National Park Map,* published by Tiger Tops.

Because of extensive mountaineering interest in the Khumbu region, there are excellent maps of it and of some nearby areas. Currently the best available are six published by Kartographische Anstalt Freytag-Berndt und Artaria, Vienna, Austria. The *Tamba Kosi-Likhu Khola Nepal* sheet covers about five days of the hill portion of the trek to Khumbu. The *Shorong/Hinku* sheet covers the next portion to just below Namche Bazaar. The *Khumbu Himal Nepal* sheet covers the region from Namche Bazaar north. The *Lapchi Kang Nepal* and *Rolwaling Himal (Gaurisankar) Nepal* sheets cover the trek from the Kathmandu-Kodari Road to Rolwaling and beyond. The *Dudh Kosi* sheet covers the southern part of Solu. These modern topographic maps on the scale of 1:50,000 (1 inch = 0.8 mile) are produced by the Research Scheme Nepal Himalaya and are accurate in almost all respects. An earlier version of the *Khumbu Himal* sheet was published in 1957 as *Mahalangur Himal.* It covers only an area close to Mount Everest and has a scale of 1:25,000 (one inch = 0.4 mile).

Currently in production in the same series are sheets covering Langtang/ Jugal Himal and Khumbakarna Himal. The latter will cover the area east of the *Khumbu Himal* sheet. Another sheet in the series covers the Kathmandu Valley. These maps are occasionally available from the Thyssen House offices located on the road to Swayambhunath in Kathmandu. They can also be purchased from Geographische Buchhandlung, Rosenthal 6, D-8000 München 2, West Germany. They are expensive, but map-lovers will find them hard to resist. In this text, they are often referred to as the Schneider maps, after the mapmaker.

There is a series of ecological maps published by the Centre National de la Recherche Scientifique, 15, quai Anatole-France, 75700, Paris, France. They are useful because they show vegetation zones and contain some ethnographical information. Presently available are:

Carte Ecologique du Nepal Region Annapurna-Dhaulagiri 1:250,000 (one inch = 3.9 miles)
Carte Ecologique du Nepal Region Jiri-Thodung 1:50,000 (one inch = 0.8 mile)
Carte Ecologique du Nepal Region Kathmandu-Everest 1:250,000 (one inch = 3.9 miles)
Carte Ecologique du Nepal Region Tarai Central 1:250,000 (one inch = 3.9 miles)
Carte Ecologique du Nepal Region Ankhu-Khola-Trisuli 1:100,000 (one inch = 1.6 miles)
Carte Ecologique du Nepal Region Biratnagar Kanchenjunga 1:250,000 (one inch = 3.9 miles)

Many accounts of mountaineering expeditions include maps that are useful to trekkers. Map sellers handling many of the maps not published in Nepal include: Edward Stanford Limited, 12-14 Long Acre, London WC2, England; Reise und Verkehrsverlag, Gutenbergstrasse 21, Stuttgart, West Germany; and Zumsteins Landkartenhaus, Liebkerrstrasse 5, 8 München 22, West Germany.

The maps in this book are intended to help the reader visualize the route descriptions. They are drawn to scale and have the towns and trails described in the text. Except for major ridge features and drainage systems, little else is depicted. Town placements are often somewhat arbitrary, since some towns have houses spread out rather than clustered together. Trekkers not especially interested in maps should find them adequate, but those who appreciate good maps should try to obtain the Schneider maps.

EQUIPMENT

Although much of the equipment is the same, trekking in Nepal is different from backpacking as the term has come to be known in North America and

Western countries. My equipment preferences are based on considerable and varied experience in Nepal. Much of the equipment described is current "state-of-the-art" gear. This is not really necessary for trekking, but it is important to have equipment adequate for the conditions. I have used many different types of gear while trekking in Nepal, sometimes going quite simply, though never as simply as the local Nepalis.

To minimize customs hassles and delays, trekkers should carry equipment with them into Nepal if possible, rather than shipping it separately. If you must ship equipment and supplies into Nepal, arrange for at least the last part of the journey to be by airfreight. Delays are fewer that way and customs duties are generally less. Shipping by sea is fraught with risk. Be prepared for delays no matter how you ship. The only sure way to have the gear you want when you want it is to bring it all with you. I have waited over a month to receive an airfreight shipment! In such circumstances, check daily at the airport or employ someone to check for you. But even then expect delays.

After your trek you can ship your goods out of Nepal in various ways. Airfreight is reliable, but expensive, except for large shipments. Surface parcel post is slightly less reliable. The best shipping agencies in Kathmandu do a good job of packing and mailing goods, and the bureaucratic hassles and time involved in doing it yourself can be eliminated.

Camping and mountaineering equipment used by Sherpas on mountaineering expeditions is often available for sale or rent in Kathmandu, Pokhara, and Namche Bazaar. Prices vary from cheap to outrageous, and the quality is not uniform. Many trekkers sell their equipment after their treks by means of notices in restaurants and hotels. The variety of equipment available, like everything else in Kathmandu, is never constant. Some people are able to pick up everything they need in the city, but it is safer to come at least minimally prepared.

Footwear

Comfortable footwear is a must, but opinions vary widely on what types are best. I prefer a Vibram-soled mountaineering boot for the high country where snow, ice, or rock is anticipated. But at other times I wear a pair of rubber-soled leather scampers or light, flexible Vibram-soled boots with uppers above the ankles. I wear wool socks over a light, thin pair of synthetic socks. It is difficult to find footwear to fit large feet (size 11 American or 44 European) in Nepal. Make sure that your boots or shoes are well broken in before the trip. On long treks, there may be considerable wear, especially to the uppers. Bring stitching material and epoxy glue for the soles. In snow or wet weather, appropriate waterproofing material is needed.

Some trekkers wear high top hunting boots all the time. I find them unnecessarily restrictive and uncomfortable as well as hot and sweaty. Others swear by sneakers, running shoes, or tennis shoes. Rubber-soled shoes with fabric uppers are very cheap and easily obtainable in Nepal. The Chinese-made variety is quite durable. These shoes are rarely found in the bazaars outside the Kathmandu Valley, and even then, only in small sizes. They work quite well, but I would be cautious wearing them in hot weather because the feet may sweat a great deal and develop blisters quickly. I also find that they provide little support under the sole of the foot. Some find training flats for runners and joggers quite suitable below the snow line. A type of footwear known variously as a thong or a chapal, consisting of a sole with a strap passing between the toes and over the front of the foot, is widely available in Nepal. It is unsuitable for constant walking, but can be comfortable off the trail. It is good to have some sort of light footwear to change into at the end of the day.

Experiment with various ways of lacing boots or shoes. Try lacing tightly to the instep, then tying a knot and lacing loosely the rest of the way. On some boots, avoiding some of the first lacing holes and lacing diagonally may prevent painful infolding of the leather. Always tighten the laces for a steep descent.

The secret of foot care is in the socks. The outer pair, which should be soft and woolen to absorb moisture, should be changed frequently. Thick outer socks made of synthetic material (acrylic or nylon) should be avoided since they do not absorb sweat well and often lead to blisters. But synthetic socks as thin inners are excellent. Thin slippery socks worn within heavier ones allow the feet and the inner socks to slip around inside the outer socks. This decreases stress and helps prevent blisters. A plastic bag over the inner sock may prevent the inside of the boot from getting wet and help keep feet warm in cold, snowy conditions. Some people advocate changing socks twice a day or more, keeping a pair drying outside the pack. Try this if you are having trouble with your feet. Be sure to take enough pairs, say four to six, for the journey. Also take some wool for darning. Again, large size socks are unavailable. For prevention and care of blisters, see Chapter 5. In the high, snowy regions, gaiters or spats of various types can be useful in keeping snow out of boot tops.

Clothing

Loose trousers for men, long skirts for women, and shirts with pockets are good basic garments. Wool clothing is traditionally chosen because it feels warm when wet. Knickers, also called plus-fours, are versatile for men since they can be ventilated easily. Long thermal underwear is good at high altitudes, especially during the winter months. Wool has traditionally been considered best for these garments, but new synthetic fabrics such as polypropylene keep moisture away from the skin and are more comfortable when the wearer sweats. Sweaters, worn with an outer nylon shell, provide wind protection and variable degrees of warmth depending on the number of layers. A down jacket is a light, efficient alternative to a sweater, but down is useless when wet. Synthetic, fiber-insulated clothing is good for wet weather. A recent improvement in clothing are the warm, efficient, synthetic pile garments. Like wool, they are warm when wet, but also dry out quickly. Some advocate down pants for sitting around in the cool high campsites; synthetic pile pants are also good. Garments that can be easily put on over existing clothing are the most versatile. A hat is important on cold days since considerable heat can be lost from the scalp because of its particularly good blood supply. A hat with a wide brim is best at high altitudes in order to shade the eyes from the sun. Dark glasses or goggles are also essential at high altitudes, especially on snow where the sunlight is exceptionally intense. Such eye protection should have eye shields to prevent light from coming in from the sides. They should absorb all ultra-violet light and at least ninety percent of visible light. Mittens are better than gloves for cold weather. Fingerless gloves or ones made of thin silk or synthetic material are good for operating cameras or attending to other intricate details in the snow.

It is difficult to stay dry in rainy weather while walking. Those wearing waterproof garments tend to sweat inside them. The new Gore-Tex fabrics are a definite improvement over the old coated nylon gear because they are waterproof if kept clean, yet breathe better than other waterproof fabrics. Jackets and pants with zippered areas under the arms and down the legs are preferable, since they have better ventilation. In the hundred-percent humidity of an intense rainfall, no clothing can breathe, so you will probably get wet from the inside no matter what. In those circumstances, light clothes and an umbrella or loose fitting poncho may be the best compromise.

Men should bring shorts for the hot low altitudes. Skirts for women should be light synthetic or cotton fabrics for the lowlands, but wool for the high country. (For the rationale behind skirts for women, see the next chapter.) A bathing suit can be useful.

Since individuals vary, it is difficult to give specific details regarding how many garments of a particular type will give the required warmth at a particular temperature range. Many of the temperature ranges encountered are familiar. Most people can expect to be reasonably comfortable at high altitudes with thick wool pants, two sweaters, a wind jacket, mittens, a hat, wool socks, and heavy boots. You may feel chilly in the morning when it could be well below freezing, yet sweat later in the day as you exercise in the sun.

Sleeping Gear

A good sleeping bag is essential for those who contemplate going to the cold high elevations. A down or synthetic fiber mummy bag is usually necessary for comfort at temperatures below freezing. A bag with a full zipper is more versatile since it is comfortable at cool high altitudes and in warm low country. A washable sleeping bag liner solves some hygiene problems. An air mattress provides a comfortable night's sleep, and to me, at least, is worth the extra effort needed to carry it. The short, rubberized nylon models, extending from the knees to the shoulders and weighing less than a pound, are sufficient. Bring a repair kit for it. Some prefer a foam pad or nothing at all. A sheet of plastic under the sleeping bag helps keep equipment clean and dry. This is a good item even in hotels and on the floors of people's houses.

Those who plan to sleep outside or in a tent at low temperatures (below freezing, or on snow or ice) should be aware that a sufficient thickness of insulation is necessary under you as well as over. Most sleeping bags do not provide enough since the filler compresses under the weight of the body. Anything that can trap air and provide a quarter to a half inch of insulation is sufficient. An ideal item is a closed cell foam pad. Of course, jackets, clothing, rope, rugs, packs, or other items can serve as well.

For those going only to low altitudes, or planning a trek in the monsoon below 7000 ft (2150 m), a lightweight blanket may be sufficient.

Shelter

Your route and preferred style dictate whether you need a tent. If you prefer to camp, or desire privacy even occasionally, a tent is necessary, except along certain routes where hotels with private rooms are common. A tent is a must at high altitudes if there is no shelter. A lightweight nylon tent good enough to withstand high winds and snow is necessary for the high passes, but a lean-to made from a sheet of plastic and some cord can weather some of the heaviest of storms if properly pitched. Bivouac sacs used by mountaineers are light, efficient shelters good for occasional use. In some areas you can stay in herding huts called *goTh.*

Preparations

Shelter can sometimes be found in caves or beneath overhanging rocks. Be sure you have enough adequate shelter for all the members of your party if you are going to high altitudes. It is not unheard of for porters to die of exposure and hypothermia in the parties of thoughtless trekkers. My relationship with porters has always been better when I showed them the tent they will use in the high passes before we left our point of departure.

Packs

Perhaps the most suitable and comfortable carrying device for trekking is the contoured pack frame made of aluminum or a light alloy. The load is placed in a bag that attaches to the frame. Frames with padded waist bands allow you to transfer the weight from your shoulders to your hips. Waterproof nylon bags with outside pockets are best since they allow easy access to selected items during the day. The sleeping bag is usually stuffed in another bag and attached to the frame below the pack bag. Recent models of internal frame packs and soft packs are probably equally suitable. With soft packs, the load must be arranged carefully in order to be comfortable. Equipment and supplies that the porters carry can be packed in sturdy duffel bags, preferably ones that can be locked.

While I understand the "carry it all yourself" philosophy, it makes little sense to laden yourself down like a pack animal and then wear yourself out carrying the load. There may be little for you to enjoy except the feeling that you did it. Porters are quite inexpensive, and by hiring them, you contribute directly to those who need it. I, for one, feel I must always carry something. I usually limit myself to forty or fifty pounds (I weigh 190 lb), but I reduced this when going above 12,000 ft, (3657 m). I did make the mistake of starting off on my first trek with fifty or sixty pounds on my back and, after some days, I developed back strain that didn't disappear for quite a while. So start off light and get used to carrying a load gradually. Members of mountaineering expeditions do this.

Cooking Gear

Light nesting pots are available in Kathmandu. Two or three should suffice for a small group cooking together. Spoons are the ideal general purpose utensil, and pocket knives are a good accessory. Quality Swiss pocket knives are hard to come by in Kathmandu. A combination salt and pepper shaker is useful if you season your food. Plastic scouring pads are handy for cleaning pots, but steel pads are easier to find.

Because travelers have placed great pressures on the scant forests remaining in the high altitude areas, regulations require that all trekkers and their porters, cooks, and guides be self-sufficient in the national parks. And I strongly recommend that trekkers use kerosene stoves at all times when they cook for themselves, especially in the high altitude areas. Kerosene is the only fuel available in the hills. Even then its availability is sporadic outside of popular places like Namche Bazaar. Furthermore, its quality is low and at times unsuitable for burning in some stoves. So fuel must sometimes be carried from Kathmandu. The quantity needed depends on whether snow must be melted for water, the efficiency of the stove, and the number in the party. About three liters will last a party of three for a week if snow must be melted. Plastic jerry cans for fuel are available in Kathmandu. Kerosene stoves of Indian manufacture are readily available in Kathmandu, but they are generally bulky and heavy. The light Swedish stoves are sometimes found in stores selling trekking and climbing gear. In my experience, the Swedish stoves seem to operate well at high altitudes on the impure kerosene found in the hills. Be sure to carry appropriate spare parts and a funnel containing a wool filter. Try the stove out before you leave.

Miscellaneous

A medical kit is essential (see Chapter 5).

Food is best packed in plastic bags and then put into labeled cloth bags tied with string. Plastic bags can be purchased in Kathmandu. Be sure to take extras. (Sheet plastic is also available. It is a good item for protecting porters and loads in the rain.) Cotton bags can be sewn by a local tailor, but nylon stuff sacks are, perhaps, a better choice.

It is important to consider what might break down and carry appropriate spare parts. A sewing kit is indispensable and a sewing awl for heavier items may be very useful. Epoxy glue can repair most things if used discriminately. In Kathmandu, ask for the brand, Aryldite, in stores carrying Indian products. A pair of pliers can be useful; the combination wrench, pliers, and screwdriver originally made for ski troops, is ideal. A pocket knife with a few gadgets on it will also come in handy.

A water bottle of at least one quart (liter) capacity should be carried for each person in the party. Water is often scarce and must be treated before use. Buy plastic jerry cans and bottles with good stoppers and screw tops in the Kathmandu bazaar. Take biodegradable soap in a container. A washcloth or towel and a toothbrush are good to have. A small flashlight or torch is very useful—the plastic kind is warmer to handle in cold weather. Indian D cell batteries are about the only kind obtainable outside of Kathmandu. Take candles to read by at night, matches in a waterproof container, and toilet paper. It is wise to have at least one compass in the party. Magnetic declination in Nepal is less than two or three degrees west in most places and can be overlooked for most map work. A pair of binoculars, an altimeter, and a thermometer can be helpful.

Insects are not usually a problem in the high country, but those traveling extensively in the lowlands during the warmer months or during the monsoon should use mosquito netting while sleeping and insect repellents (the ones with N, N-diethyl-meta-toluamide are the best) while traveling.

Consider taking a portable tape recorder to capture the local music and other sounds of Nepal. Cassette tapes of various manufacture and D, C, and AA batteries are available in Kathmandu.

"Photography is a magical process that has given Sahibs all over the world the chance to rest under the guise of business" states naturalist Ed Cronin in *The Arun* (see Recommended Reading). So photographic equipment is a must! Take lots of film from home; a polarizing filter to cut out haze and dramatize the sky; an ultra-violet filter for each lens; lens-cleaning equipment such as a brush, paper, and fluid; an electronic flash run by battery rather than by a rechargeable unit; and various lenses. Don't use wide-angle lenses on distant mountain scenes as the main features will come out too small. Many photographers use only a moderate wide-angle lens and a telephoto lens, omitting the standard lens. A zoom lens could also be valuable. A tripod may be too heavy if you have to carry it, but a small light camera clamp can be made into a tripod when mounted on the cross-piece of a pack frame propped up with a stick or an ice axe. A self-developing picture camera is great, except that you may be besieged by Nepalis who want their pictures taken.

Most trekkers carry reading matter and writing materials. Rereading a journal kept on a trek taken years ago can be a most rewarding experience.

The equipment game can be, and often is, carried to extremes. Cronin describes how, relying on the Boy Scout spirit of preparedness, he emerged from the plane at a remote airstrip on his first trip to Nepal. He was dressed in his custom-designed field jacket, complete with dashing epaulets and eleven pockets offering precise space for various necessities from compass to moleskin to a waterproof container of matches. Around his neck he carried two camera bodies and a host of lenses and light meters as well as a pair of binoculars and a tripod. Descending laboriously from the plane, he noticed that all eyes were on him. "I thought at the time this was because I was new and lacked a sunburn, but later realized it was because I carried more wealth on my person than the average porter . . . could accumulate in a lifetime," he said. He later described all the difficulties he had walking with this paraphernalia.

For many reasons, including some important ones to be discussed later, be reasonable in what you bring, and keep most of it packed until needed.

FOOD

The type of food available in the hills varies depending on the place and the season. It is also somewhat dependent on who has gone before you. Many locally grown items are available during the autumn harvest time, but in late spring vegetables and other commodities may be scarce. Fruits, a real treat, are available in season. On the more popular routes, such as in Khumbu, Helambu, Langtang, Thak Khola, and some parts of Manang, many items normally only available in large cities can be purchased.

Below, the starred (*) items are sold in most hill bazaars, and can sometimes be purchased in people's homes. The remainder, except as noted above, can only be bought in Kathmandu, Pokhara, or cities in the Tarai. Although the metric system is being introduced, the traditional system of measure is used here where appropriate. Volume is measured in *maanaa*. One *maanaa* equals twenty ounces or 2½ cups (0.7 l). Eight *maanaa* equal a *paathi*. The basic unit of weight is the *paau*, about half a pound (0.2 kg). Four *paau* equal a *ser*, and three *ser* equal a *dhaarni* or six pounds (2.7 kg).

Rice* is the staple food of richer Nepalis, but it is not easily obtainable in the northern regions. It is measured by volume. Most Nepalis eat large quantities of it daily. Try to buy the kind with unbroken grains.

Lentils,* or chick peas, are made into a soup called *daal*. It is poured over rice to make the staple meal. A *maanaa* of lentils should last two or three people for about three meals.

Assorted vegetables* are obtainable locally. A list of them is given in Chapter 6. They are eaten in comparatively small amounts by the Nepalis, except in Solu-Khumbu and Langtang where entire meals usually consist of potatoes.

Noodles are rarely found outside of Kathmandu, Namche Bazaar, Langtang, and other areas of Tibetan influence.

Tea* is the staple drink, usually taken sweet with milk. Five hundred grams should last two or three people most of a month. In Khumbu and other areas of Tibetan influence, Tibetan tea is served with butter and salt. It is delicious, but it is an acquired taste.

Coffee is sold only in the instant variety from India.

Grinding corn. (Brot Coburn)

Sugar* is sold either by weight or volume. It is a comparative luxury and is sometimes hard to find in the hills. About twenty *paau* should last a small party for almost a month.

Milk is best carried in powdered form. If mixed dry with sugar before adding hot tea or coffee, it should dissolve well. Several kilograms should last a month. Cans of condensed sweetened milk are often sold in the hills. This product, which is made in China, is excellent. Fresh milk should be heated to the boiling point before being consumed.

Salt* of the finely granulated iodized variety is available in Kathmandu. Only coarse rock salt is available in the hills. Both are measured by volume.

Pepper* and other spices should be bought in Kathmandu. Many unfamiliar, exotic spices are used in the hills.

Oats are another item that lend variety to a diet. They are available in Kathmandu.

Cheese is usually available at the dairy on New Road or Lainchaur in Kathmandu. It is made from yak's milk in Langtang. Canned cheese made in India is also available. Cheese can be purchased at certain times at plants in Langtang, at Thodung, and at Sing Gomba near Gosainkund.

Butter can also be purchased at the dairies in Kathmandu. It does not keep

Churning butter. (Brot Coburn)

long if unrefrigerated. Indian butter is available in cans. In the hills clarified butter called *ghiu** is available.

Peanut butter and various **jams** are a treat, but the ones that come in glass jars must be repackaged as it is not practical to carry glass.

Biscuits* made by the Nebico Biscuit Company in Kathmandu are excellent, as are the more expensive Indian cookies manufactured under license from British affiliates.

Candy* is a good source of quick energy during the day. Try the milk bonbons made by Nebico. Buy them in the kilogram package. Chocolate bars of Indian manufacture are available.

Roasted flour* is a common food in the hills. It may be of wheat, barley (*tsampa*), corn, or millet. Mixed with water and spices, it is sometimes the only food you can get.

Soup mixes, cooked and poured over rice, make a good substitute when *daal* is not available. The Indian brands are not as good as those made in the West. However, most American groceries can be obtained only from the U.S. Commissary by Embassy and Aid for International Development employees. Got any friends?

Eggs* are available wherever there are laying chickens. This includes most places except the high mountain areas.

Dehydrated foods suitable for trekking and mountaineering expeditions are produced in Kathmandu by Trekkers Foods, G.P.O. Box 304, Kathmandu. (At the time this book went to press, this was the only producer of dehydrated foods in Kathmandu.) These foods are of good quality, are quite reasonably priced, and require less fuel to cook than many other foods. They are available in many supply stores in Kathmandu and some in Pokhara. Products currently available follow, but those marked with the symbol (**) are not available in the autumn or winter: powdered soup (tomato, onion, and cream of tomato, spinach, and potato); dried vegetables (carrots, onions, spinach, cauliflower**, cabbage**); dried fruits (pineapple, apple, naspati—like pear, persimmon**, mango**, papaya**); granola; muesli (a breakfast cereal); wheatmeal porridge and tomato drink powder. New products may be available in the future.

Many luxury items such as Indian-canned fruits, vegetables, and meat are sold in Kathmandu, but they are quite heavy. Foods taken on mountaineering expeditions find their way into shops in the appropriate areas—for instance, around Namche Bazaar, north of Pokhara, and near Langtang. The variety and quality vary greatly.

You may want to bring other items from home that aren't available in Nepal—drink mixes, soup mixes, freeze-dried meats, vegetables, and desserts. Of course, none of them are necessary, but it may be enjoyable to celebrate at certain times during the trek. I personally like to take powdered grapefruit drink.

Note that few meat items are mentioned. Most Westerners are used to meals centered around meat, but this is not so in Nepal. Occasional bits of meat may turn up among the vegetables and you can ask to have a small dish served to you with your *daal bhaat.* You can buy a chicken in the hills and have it cooked. Where meat is available, it must be requested separately—at a small extra cost. If you are in good health, you can survive and remain quite healthy without any meat. For more on nutrition, see Chapter 5.

GUIDES AND PORTERS

Sherpas are an ethnic group who have become famous for their exploits on mountaineering expeditions. As commonly used, the term Sherpa does not stand for a specific job description, but for a group of people who originally migrated from eastern Tibet and settled in the Solu-Khumbu region of Nepal. They have often been employed by trekkers as guides, cooks, and porters. But the term Sherpa at times refers to anyone of any ethnic group who does those tasks. People of ethnic groups other than Sherpas—*Tamang* and Tibetans, for instance—are increasingly being used as guides. Many of them are quite capable.

People trekking in Nepal for the first time will generally have fewer problems if they have a guide or Sirdar. It may be difficult to hire one during the busy autumn season. The current rate for guides is about Rs. 30 per day with food provided by the trekker. Guides often demand considerable equipment, and since this custom is becoming established, you may find it difficult to avoid. These experienced people do not carry loads, and usually do not cook either; they confine their activities to guiding, hiring porters, and attending to various logistical matters. Most guides speak some English, and some speak varying degrees of French, German, Japanese, and other languages due to their close contacts with foreigners on treks and mountaineering expeditions.

Sometimes younger people with little experience or knowledge of English, who are nevertheless enthusiastic and quite capable, can be hired for less. Such people are, in a way, more desirable, especially for the trekker who wants as few assistants as possible and wants to learn some Nepali. Sometimes these workers may carry a porter's load and do some cooking in addition to guiding.

For a large party not eating locally, a cook, and perhaps a helper, are needed. The guide can usually suggest a Sherpa cook. Porters are also hired by the guide, or by you if you do not have a guide. The wage for porters has recently been set by the government at Rs. 21 per day up to an altitude of 12,000 ft (3700 m) and Rs. 30 per day over 12,000 ft (3700 m).The porter provides his or her own food. But it is often possible to make a contract with a porter to carry the load a certain distance, and this may work out to be cheaper. Porters usually carry their own food. They can be hired through the trekking agencies in Kathmandu, or in other areas at airstrips, restaurants, and hotels frequented by foreigners. Some trekkers prefer to bring reliable people with them from Kathmandu to the beginning of a trek. Porters hired locally may be Sherpas or Tibetans in Khumbu, Tibetans in Pokhara, *Gurung* north of Pokhara, *Tamang* in Kathmandu, or people of other ethnic groups depending on the area. Women as well as men can be good porters, but so far they have not become involved in guiding.

Porters carry their loads—usually around 65 lb (30 kg)—by means of a tumpline or *naamlo,* a band going around the load and around the forehead. You need only put the load in a sack or duffel bag. Or porters use a *Doko,* a conical basket available for a few rupees throughout much of Nepal. Anything can be carried in it, and an outer wrapping of plastic can keep the load dry when it rains. Even if you give your porters a modern pack frame to carry, most of them will disregard the straps and waist belt in favor of a tumpline which supports the weight from their foreheads. Items carried by porters receive rough treatment, and it is best to carry fragile items yourself.

All transportation costs such as bus or plane fares to the actual beginning of the trek are the responsibility of the trekker. In addition, if the trek does not leave an employee at his home or point of hiring, you are obligated to pay for his return, at half the daily rate. Travel is faster on the return trip, so the number of days this journey will take should be agreed on in advance.

When you hire porters and Sherpas, you are taking responsibility for them. If they get sick or injured, see to it that they get suitable medical attention. Many lowland porters have never been on snow or in below-freezing temperatures. They may not be aware of conditions in the places you want to take them. Provide them with footwear, clothes, bedding, and shelter if necessary.

The following scene is all too common. The sahib is in his tent, comfortable and warm in his down sleeping bag sitting on a thick foam pad. His down jacket and pants are stuffed in the corner. Outside, huddled together by some rocks used as a windbreak, his wet, shivering porters do not sleep a wink all night. The sahib wonders why they are so slow the next day.

If you have a Sherpa guide, it is his responsibility to see to the needs of the porters, but this does not relieve you of responsibility. Recently several porters died needlessly on high passes in storms when they were abandoned by guides. In a storm, it may be prudent to sit low and wait it out rather than try to cross a pass to keep on schedule. Equipment for porters can be rented in Kathmandu. Make sure the porters understand that the equipment is a loan, not a gift.

Some people advise trekkers to give guides and porters cigarettes occasionally, or even regularly. Smoking is well established in Nepal, but I feel that it is unethical to further this unhealthy habit, especially for those who don't smoke. If you do smoke, it may be unreasonable not to share your cigarettes. But don't make a habit of buying cigarettes for the employees. There are many other ways to share your satisfaction with them on the trip and to show your appreciation for their efforts at its end. Give them a smile, a look through your camera or binoculars, or a gift. Good gifts include used clothing, pocket knives, pencils, paper, discarded containers, sewing needles, and strong thread.

Do not overlook the possibility of using animals to carry loads. This is especially feasible in Khumbu and other northern regions. On one occasion we used a yak and on another, a *zopkio*—the sterile male offspring of a cow mated with a yak. The animals are remarkably sure-footed, but the *zopkio* has a much better disposition than the yak, which requires pulling and pushing at times. However, the yak can withstand more cold than the *zopkio*. Either can carry a hundred pounds or more. In some areas horses can be used. Sometimes a person whom you may want to hire as a porter will carry nothing, but use a pack animal. In this case, the person is paid as a porter, or two, depending on the load carried by the animal. Be sure that the arrangement is clear beforehand.

AIRCRAFT

Small Short Takeoff and Landing (STOL) aircraft can be chartered to small airstrips in many parts of Nepal. Helicopters can also be chartered for travel to trekking sites, although this is rare for most tourists. Helicopters are used more commonly for sightseeing and rescue. The planes are usually single engine Pilatus Porters carrying 900 to 1100 lb (400 to 500 kg). Twin Otter planes carrying more than twice that load can also be chartered. Charters are arranged in Kathmandu through the offices of Royal Nepal Airlines (RNAC), which also has regularly scheduled flights to many small airstrips. These are usually cheaper than charters, but you can only be sure of the reservations from Kathmandu to the place in question. Reservations for the return trip can be made in Kathmandu, but this is usually not very helpful, and everything has to be rearranged at the remote airstrip. For example, it is notoriously difficult to get a reservation back to Kathmandu from the STOL strip in Jumla.

By making arrangements to fly, it is possible to complete treks in a shorter time and occasionally to prevent backtracking. In addition, the views are often incredible, and the thrill of a spectacular landing is not quickly forgotten. However, this mode of travel is expensive.

Charters are usually arranged to bring a party into a high altitude area. The quick gain in elevation can be very fatiguing and the time lost recuperating from the sudden rise can sometimes equal the time necessary to trek to the area. Even more important for quite a few trekkers, such rapid elevation gain has resulted in death from altitude illness, especially high altitude pulmonary edema. Hence, given the choice, it is better to arrange a charter to return from the area and to acclimatize by walking in.

CARS, BUSES, AND TRUCKS

> *A fast approach by plane robs the journey of anticipation; a slow approach by road always begins with the hope of a pleasant trip, and continues with the hope of simply reaching the destination.*
> George Schaller, *Stones of Silence*

Private bus companies provide service over Nepal's main roads. The routes most often used by trekkers are Kathmandu to Barabise and Lamosangu for treks east; Kathmandu to Trisuli for treks north; Kathmandu to Pokhara for treks north of Pokhara; and Bhairawa to Pokhara for western treks. Further information is given in the route descriptions. Riding on these buses is usually an unforgettable experience. They often tax the trekker as much as two weeks' walk with a pack. Most trekkers are willing to put up with the slow, pitching buses in order to save time. Trekkers may sometimes be able to purchase rides on trucks transporting goods; this may even be preferable to the crowded buses. It may make sense for a large party wishing to transport all its gear, porters, and trekkers to the start of a trek to hire taxis or other private vehicles. Trekking agencies, of course, usually make these arrangements and provide pickup services.

MONEY

Nepali currency is the medium of exchange in Nepal. In the not too distant past, bartering was the common means of trade and commerce in the hills, although Indian coins were occasionally accepted. Ten years ago trekkers were advised to take mostly coins of low denomination. Now I recommend taking one-, five-, and ten-rupee (*rupiyAA*) notes as well as five or ten rupees in five-, twenty-five-, and fifty-*paisaa* coins. There are 100 *paisaa* in a rupee. A rupee is equal to about 8½ cents (U.S.) at the 1980 exchange rate. In Solu-Khumbu, Thak Khola, and other areas of wealth, 100-rupee notes can often be broken. I have even been asked by locals to change 1000-rupee notes. Some trekkers manage to do business with foreign currency such as U.S. dollars in wealthy areas. But this is illegal except at certain locations, such as the Everest View Hotel in Solu-Khumbu. It is easiest to exchange currency at banks in Kathmandu and Pokhara. While banks do have branches in most of the district centers, exchanging foreign currency at them can be time consuming and difficult, if not impossible. But like most encounters with Nepali bureaucracy, it is fascinating.

Many trekkers barter clothes and equipment for Nepali crafts, meals, and lodging. Western goods can also be exchanged for cash at times. The local people like to obtain useful foreign goods in this way. I usually travel with minimal gear that is difficult to replace in Nepal and do most of my commerce with cash. Some who are in Nepal for short periods of time, exchange, sell, or give away much of their clothing and equipment toward the end of their trek.

It is best to take new currency on your trek. Exchange worn tattered notes for crisp new ones in Kathmandu. People in the hills will often refuse a ragged, torn note. Similarly coins that are worn thin may be refused. As for the amount of money to take, it depends on your style of trekking. If everything has been arranged by a prepaid trekking company, little money is needed. If you are traveling without porters or guides and eating food locally, $2 to $3 (U.S.) per person per day takes care of the necessities. Carry enough funds for contingencies. Generally you get a great deal of value for the money spent in Nepal. Don't lose that perspective.

The prices throughout this book are based on 1980 rates. Although you may well find the prices higher when you reach Nepal, you'll at least have some idea of what to expect.

---

4 INTERACTING WITH NEPAL

Madam, this is Nepal. In America you can be a bird in a gilded cage. Here the bird is free. And for that there is a price.
A Nepali to an inconvenienced and angry trekker

For many years, few indulged in trekking in Nepal, and their impact on the country was rather small. But the large numbers of people who have begun trekking in recent years are causing many changes, good and bad, in the landscape and the people of Nepal. Generally, trekkers are unaware of these changes until, reflecting later, they wonder what is happening.

This chapter, then, attempts to provide not only basic information on day-to-day trekking, but also food for thought on how to help preserve the character of trekking in Nepal.

TREKKING LIFE

Variables such as the type of trek, the size of the party, and the area visited all affect the way you organize your daily trekking activities. Trekkers employing Nepali assistants are advised to adhere to a schedule compatible with them. Trekkers traveling in areas where there are few foreigners and who wish to eat local food, must also adhere to the local schedules.

Though local schedules vary depending on the area and the village, the following general outline gives you some idea of what to expect. In the hills, people get up around sunrise, sometimes have a brief snack, then work until the mid-morning meal about 10 A.M. Work then continues until the late afternoon, and is followed by the second meal of the day. A snack immediately preceding this meal is not uncommon. Since activities coincide with the period of daylight, people tend to go to sleep soon after sunset. In the mountains a more Western schedule is common. People wait until it warms up a little before engaging in much activity. They generally eat three meals a day.

Thus, a reasonable schedule for trekkers not too insulated from the local lifestyle is to begin around sunrise, or just before. After a snack or hot drink, begin walking in the cool morning until 9 or 10 A.M. Then stop at a *bhaTTi* (local inn) for food, or cook your own along the trail. If traveling away from the trails frequented by foreigners and eating in the local inns, the food is *daal bhaat*, a large quantity of rice, with a lentil soup poured over it. There are usually some cooked vegetables available, and occasionally you may be able to get an egg or some meat. Unlimited quantities of *bhaat* (rice) are included in the meal, but the *daal* (lentils) and vegetables are rationed. The food requested in a *bhaTTi* is usually not cooked until after you order, so the entire food stop takes approximately two hours. In some inns catering to trekkers, ready-cooked food is available.

If eating in a *bhaTTi* frequented by Nepalis, spoons are seldom available. You must either provide your own, or eat with your right hand as Nepalis do. It is not

During a relaxed moment at her roadside tea shop, a Thakali *woman puffs on her* chilim *(clay pipe). (Mary Lynn Hanley)*

considered impolite to make slurping noises while eating, and a burp is often taken as an appreciation of the meal. Sometimes, while waiting for a meal to be cooked, you can obtain a snack (*khaajaa*) such as roasted corn (it does not pop like the Western variety). Often tea is available too, but the farther north you go along trails frequented mostly by Nepalis, the more scarce it becomes. In many areas of Buddhist influence in the northern regions, only Tibetan tea served with butter and salt is available. Large quantities of this broth are consumed by the *BhoTiya* of this region, and you may acquire a taste for it, too. Along certain northern routes frequented by trekkers, tea with milk and sugar is often available.

Just as tea shops can be found only in certain areas, local inns are often limited to regions settled by *Thakali*, the traditional innkeepers, though people of other ethnic groups also run them. *BhaTTi* are especially scarce in the west. When you cannot find one, villagers are often willing to provide food and shelter in their own houses. This generally is not possible, however, in Brahman and *Chetri* dwellings. To ask, you must first attract the attention of someone inside the house (never go in without being invited). Call out a suitable term of address (see "Nepali for Trekkers") and wait for someone to appear. Then make your request.

It may be difficult to find people prepared to cater to trekkers on the less frequented trails, but on the popular trails it is much easier. In route to Khumbu and in Khumbu, Langtang, Helambu, Gosainkund, and north of Pokhara, many establishments cater specifically to trekkers. They often sell foods carried in from big towns and bazaars, and hoteliers will generally cook meals for you at other than the usual times. Most of these places have signs; others can be found by asking around. A variety of non-Nepali meals are available, depending on local supplies. This is not gourmet cooking, and the local people do not eat it. Those who sample local foods may be surprised and become converts to the tasty varieties of this simple cuisine.

With the first meal of the day in your stomach, the rest of the day's trail awaits your feet. Along the way you may pass tea shops and stop for refreshment. Trekkers may pass pastures and shepherds in the high country, and may be able to obtain some fresh milk or yogurt.

During the day's walk, you may pass through several villages and farming areas, cross major rivers, climb to the crest of one or more ridges, and descend down into the valleys again. When trekking without a guide, it is necessary to constantly ask the name of the current village and the way to the next village. There are few trail signs in Nepal, and finding the route is a matter of asking the way as Nepalis do. Often you may be confused by the answers Nepalis give to your questions. If so, repeat the question or phrase it differently until you are satisfied with the response. The problem may be your pronunciation. Ask the next person on the trail, too. It's all part of the fun of trekking and finding your way in Nepal. Along the more popular routes local people make a commotion when they think you are on the wrong trail. This can create problems when you deliberately wish to take a side trip. When asking the way, keep in mind both the next town's name as well as a larger, well-known town farther along. Often the names of small settlements may not be known, but everyone knows the names of big centers. Because of a lack of standardized spelling, names on many maps may lead to improper pronunciation.

Nepalis are eager to please Westerners and in their enthusiasm to do so, often give incorrect answers to questions. For example, a Nepali might say that a particular destination you ask about is close when it is actually a long way off. Or he might say that the trail you are on goes to the place you are asking for, rather than upset you by telling you the truth. And people who don't understand your questions sometimes answer nevertheless. Learning to get around these problems is all part of the experience. It isn't insurmountable or fraught with hazard.

Trails in the high country where there are no settlements are a different matter. Travel along these is seasonal. Most Nepalis go there only during the monsoon when few trekkers are afoot. Animal trails may be confused with human trails. Forest, fog, or whiteout may make finding the route difficult or impossible. Trekkers have often become lost in such circumstances, and it is easy to remain lost for several days, especially if trying to bushwhack to a trail you don't know. If lost, backtrack to a point you know, rather than trying to force a way to some place you think you might know. It is prudent to travel with a guide in such country. Often one can be hired locally for a few days.

Trails vary considerably with the seasons. During and soon after the monsoon when the rivers are still swollen, travelers take ridge trails rather than those following the valley floors. But in the dry season, November through May, many trails on ridges are abandoned in favor of more direct river routes. Sometimes during the well-traveled dry season, tea shops spring up along the river routes. In addition, shortcuts across dry paddy fields are favored over the well-worn trails. These shortcuts can be numerous and at times misleading, but they are still preferable in most cases. By contrast, in warmer weather and during the monsoon, tea shops and *bhaTTi* reappear in the high country.

During the day you may pass many Nepalis who ask where you are coming from and where you are going. The accepted form of greeting or taking leave of a person is to place the palms of your hands together in front of your face as if to pray and say *namaste* or *namaskaar*. The latter is more respectful and formal. Both have the connotation of "I salute the god within you." Children will often badger you with endless greetings. Always use the less formal greeting with children.

In the late afternoon or sooner, look for a place to stay. Asking for a meal in the evening is equivalent to asking for a place to sleep. Along the popular routes, there is usually a hotel fee for sleeping in places that cater to foreigners. But in *bhaTTi* in the rest of the country, a place for the night is included in the charge for a meal. Hotels for foreigners often have extra sleeping space, and sometimes separate rooms with beds can be obtained. Some places have wood stoves or fireplaces for warmth. Charges are reasonable in view of the wood used. In the more typical *bhaTTi*, you sleep on the floor, often with many other travelers. Sometimes when the *bhaTTi* is particularly crowded, you may be shown a hayloft or other more simple accommodation. I sometimes prefer to sleep on porches outside the houses, as chimneyless and windowless interiors are often quite smoky. This is obviously impractical in most high, cool areas.

Trekkers traveling in the high country often stay at *goTh*, temporary shelters used by shepherds. Some are quite substantial structures, while others are only four walls or just the frames for the walls. When the shepherds bring their animals up to graze during the hot monsoon months, they bring mats to cover the frames. *Yersa* are groups of *goTh* used by those who pasture yak and sheep. If there is any doubt about whether these shelters will be available or if privacy is desired, it is safest to carry a tent.

If stopping to cook your own food along the trail during the day, expect to take two hours. Setting up camp in the evening takes half an hour, and breaking it the next morning takes almost an hour. To get a small group processed at a police check post takes half an hour. Do not produce your passport unless absolutely necessary or there may be further delays. Be patient and courteous in dealing with officials.

Trekkers on trips organized through an agency will tend to have customary meals at the usual times. Lunch is usually prepared by the cooking staff who then go on ahead. The staff sets up and breaks camp and makes sure that the trekker keeps to the correct trail. The Sirdar and other staff may be able to enrich the experience by explaining things seen, and also things not seen.

CROSS-CULTURAL CLUES

The fullest enjoyment of Nepal in its myriad aspects comes to those who attempt to transcend the cultural differences between themselves and their Nepali

Awaiting the evening meal in a Nepali home. (Ane Haaland)

hosts. These people are more easily accepted into the social framework of Nepal, and there are many rewards.

In the past, some trekkers have offended their Nepali hosts. They have misunderstood the actions and feelings of Nepalis, and their reactions have made a bad situation worse. Others have taken great advantage of traditional Nepali hospitality without considering the consequences. Still others, realizing how much further their money will go in this country, have made a big display of their wealth, both in handing out large (for Nepal) sums of money, and giving away many of their possessions. All of these actions create many misunderstandings, and affect the Nepalis' interactions with the next trekkers who come along. In an attempt to minimize these problems, here are some cultural **dos** and **don'ts**.

Many of the differences result from the Hindu concepts of purity and ritual pollution. As hill Nepal becomes increasingly Sanskritized, these differences become more important. Generally the *BhoTiya,* northern peoples of the mountainous regions, are less affected by these customs, but they have other customs that must be respected. For instance, the fire and hearth are considered sacred in Sherpa homes and in those of many other *BhoTiya.* Thus, do not throw any refuse into a hearth. The important thing is to observe what Nepalis around you are doing, and to act accordingly.

Hindus are concerned about ritual pollution of food when it is touched by anyone outside their caste or religion. As a foreigner, you are outside the caste system. Often you are considered an outcaste or untouchable. Thus, do not touch any cooked foods on display, though it is usually all right to handle uncooked foods such as fruit and raw vegetables. When drinking from a container used by others, avoid touching your lips to it; pour the liquid into your mouth. Similarly, when drinking from a water bottle, do not touch your lips to it—at least not in sight of your hosts. Wait for food to be served to you rather than helping yourself. Do not give leftovers to your hosts, even though they may be rare delicacies brought from home. Do not offer a person anything from which you have taken a bite or sip. This is the *juTho* concept of food—if any food is touched by someone's mouth, the entire plate is contaminated and the utensils must be washed before anyone uses them. By the same token, all leftover food or drink must either be thrown away or fed to animals. The only exception is that a wife may eat from her husband's plate. Hence, do not accept more food than you can eat, and in a tea shop, make sure you put your empty glass where the Nepalis put theirs. Furthermore, since Westerners are considered outside the Hindu caste system, trekkers who visit Brahman houses or villages can expect to be served food apart from others, usually outside their host's house. They will not be allowed to sleep in a Brahman house.

Don't touch food with your left hand. Nepalis use the left hand for cleaning after defecating, and it is offensive for them to see food in it. Eat with your right hand and use your left for picking up a glass or holding something nonedible. Before and after meals, you will be offered water and a place to wash your hands and rinse your mouth. Wash your hands separately, or your left one not at all. Your right hand may be used to wipe your mouth, never your left. Give and receive items with your right hand. Similarly, don't touch anyone with your left hand. In eating *daal bhaat* and vegetables, the meal is served in separate containers, so keep them that way, except for small portions that you mix on your plate prior to eating. It is, of course, possible to eat with a spoon or chopsticks, which may be available along the more popular trekking trails. But try eating with your right hand. It's fun!

Shoes are considered the most degrading part of your apparel, so keep them on the floor or ground. Remove them before putting your feet up on anything. Shoes, especially leather ones, should always be removed before entering any kind of temple, *gomba,* or monastery. Do not touch anyone with your shoes. The greatest insult you can give a Nepali is to kick him or her with your shoe. Follow the example of your host in deciding whether to remove shoes before entering a Nepali home. If in doubt, remove them. When sleeping in a temple or *gomba,* don't point your feet at the images.

Before sitting down on the ground, you will almost always be offered a mat to sit on. When sitting, do not point the soles of your feet at anyone. Nepalis will not step over your legs and feet. Be sure to draw them up to make a path for anyone coming or going. As you go farther north, these concepts of purity and pollution become more relaxed. Watch your hosts and adjust your habits accordingly.

Nepali women bathing at the hot springs at Tatopani north of Pokhara. (Brot Coburn)

This mantra, Om Mani Padme Hum, *is carved on* mani *stones throughout the northern regions. Its mystical syllables can be heard in the murmur of pious Buddhists saying their prayers along the trail. (Mary Lynn Hanley)*

Many Western habits are offensive to Nepalis. Some, such as shaking hands, using dry toilet paper, carrying around a used handkerchief, and eating without washing, seem unsanitary to many. Women wearing short skirts, shorts, or pants are considered lewd by many Nepalis.

A *lungi* or tube of material can be purchased in any cloth shop and custom-sewed in ten minutes into a suitable garment for women. Perhaps easier to wear is the *AAgl* or *chubaa,* a long, sleeveless *BhoTiya* dress that ties in back. It can expand after dinner, yet be svelte and fashionable. It can sometimes be purchased ready-made from cotton, or it can be made from wool or polyester. Long skirts brought from home are also excellent, but more expensive. The experience of choosing material and having a garment tailor-made for you in Kathmandu is alone worth the nominal cost.

Trekkers often like to relax in hot springs or to swim in rivers or lakes. Nepalis are usually very shocked if this is done with genitals exposed. Women should not bare their breasts, especially those who have not borne children. Men may go bare-chested while swimming, but not at other times. If you wish to bathe in the nude, do it out of sight of Nepalis. This may sound prudish to some, but remember that you are a guest in their country and should respect their values. Recall how you have reacted upon observing foreigners with strange customs and habits in your own country.

While traveling, you may pass Buddhist *mani* walls containing tablets with prayers carved on them in handsome Tibetan script. Walk by them, keeping them on your right, as Buddhists would do as a sign of respect. Similar treatment is given to the *chorten* and stupas, commemorative mounds sometimes modeled after those at Swayambhu or Baudha. If in doubt as to whether a structure is one of these, walk by it on the right. When visiting a monastery or *gomba,* a few rupees for the upkeep is expected as a gift. In paying respects to the abbot of a monastery, offer him a ceremonial scarf, or *kata,* obtained from another monk.

It is very easy to forget these suggestions. Indeed, Nepalis along the well-traveled routes don't expect trekkers to respect local customs. It is partly for this reason that traditional Nepali hospitality is less obvious along these routes. If you do something that offends Nepalis, they usually do not let you know because they don't want to displease you. But among themselves, they have less respect for you. Conversely, if you take the effort to respect Nepali customs, you will find yourself more respected.

PRESERVING THE TREKKING EXPERIENCE

> *Tourism is thus not only the goose that lays golden eggs, but it also fouls its own nest.*
> Dr. Kamal Kumar Shrestha, Nepali chemist

When the first trekkers came to Nepal, the reaction among the hill people was uniform. The visitors were given hospitality and respect, and their actions were watched carefully. With the passage of time and many travelers, patterns of interaction developed. As the kinds of people who came to trek changed, so did the Nepalis' reactions.

The first travelers were interested in mountaineering or research. Some people, generally well-to-do, came just to see the country. All traveled similarly, with large numbers of porters, much equipment, and imported food. They tended to be quite generous, both with their money and their equipment. Lavish tips and presents were offered. More often than not, local feelings were not respected, and customs were violated. Travelers began to be viewed as a source of income and goods. Since they were usually able to pay outrageous prices for Nepali goods and services, this came to be expected. Traditional hospitality remained and has to this day, but it is much less spontaneous and more dependent on money, especially along the more frequented routes.

At the other extreme, in the late 1960s and early 1970s, very budget-conscious travelers and "hippies" came onto the scene. Their actions and customs were different from those of the earlier travelers. Often they lived and kept themselves in a dirtier state than many of the Nepalis. Their drug habits were also viewed with suspicion. While Nepalis have used marijuana and hashish for years, it is used in moderation and only among some older people in society. The new travelers would sometimes run off without paying for food or services. Occasionally, they would even steal precious items. Indeed, once Nepalis realized that art objects had value other than religious, they too began to steal them to sell on the black market.

The result of all this is that trekking in many areas has become essentially a commercial venture in which attempts are made to relieve travelers of their goods and money. Nepal used to be famous as a place where travelers had absolutely no worries about theft and violence. Now some trekkers complain of theft. Petty vandalism and thievery of packs and luggage left on top of buses is no longer rare. And misunderstandings have been created that have resulted in attacks and robberies, but these are rare.

Another aspect of travel in Nepal that contributed to its popularity was the availability of cheap labor. Porters could be hired for very low rates. Trekkers who could not afford it at home could have servants to do many of the distasteful and laborious chores of camping and backpacking. Porters and assistants were sometimes thought of as less than human. This was evident in the lack of responsibility that many took toward their employees. Porters often carried their loads through the cold and snow with no shoes, clothing, or bedding. A considerable number died in the service of trekkers, usually in high areas during bad weather. At times porters who were sick or injured were abandoned by the sahibs.

What can be done to improve the situation? First, it is important to understand the custom of bargaining, which is almost universal in Asia. The locals regard it as a game and not as an impediment to friendship. But once a price is agreed upon, it is "fixed." Westerners, by contrast, often harbor bad feelings after the bargaining process. Language trouble can also create misunderstandings. I can well remember bargaining once with a taxi driver to take me to the start of a trek out of the Kathmandu Valley. He named a price, and I began to bargain with him, but named a higher price, as my command of numbers in Nepali was poor. He quickly agreed, and it was only as the ride began that I realized my mistake. Nevertheless, I paid the price I had agreed to.

Try to find out the going price for something before you begin bargaining. Failure to do so hurts everyone. As an example, if a Nepali will sell an egg to his neighbor for Rs. 1, but finds he can get Rs. 2 from a trekker, he will be less likely to sell that egg to his neighbor. Thus the price of eggs goes up. The Nepali gets hurt, but not the trekker, to whom the difference in price is negligible. Such inflation has become quite common.

Thus, in dealings with people, pay the going rate. Never walk off without paying. In tipping people for their services, be reasonable. Some people tip much more than the salary they are paying. This only reinforces the belief that the sahib does not know the value of his money, and thus should be relieved of as much of it as possible. Bringing small gifts for people who have helped you along the way is a good idea. But beware of the long-term repercussions of anything you do. When a friend of mine who was working in family planning in Kathmandu in 1969 suggested that I distribute condoms during my treks, it seemed a great idea. Reluctant to demonstrate their proper use to adults, I blew them up as balloons for children. This was a highly successful public relations gesture, but I learned later that people following my path were besieged with requests for condoms and balloons. Currently such litter abounds. Bring small useful items like strong sewing thread, needles, cloth, and rope.

It is interesting to watch patterns of begging develop along the trekking trails over the years. When I first came to Nepal in 1969 there was little begging in the hills, and the few who did were almost all children who wanted candy. Yet children and others along the trekking trails are now constantly begging for candy, money, pens, and cigarettes. A few hours walk off these trails, people do not beg at all. In areas such as Thak Khola where many types of trekkers are seen, people who beg tend to approach those who appear to be well-to-do. When I visited Manang after only a few rather lavishly organized treks had been through that area I was constantly besieged. Indeed, it was expected that I should give freely to everyone, presumably because earlier parties had done so. Intransigent trekkers like me have had children throw stones at them for not giving in to begging. Yet over the pass in Thak Khola the pressure to give was much less, presumably because the children

Sometimes a group of men from a village will travel to a trading post days to weeks away to bring back supplies for the coming year. (Donald Messerschmidt)

and others realize their requests will be better rewarded by trekkers in large groups.

Nepalis have had good dental hygiene in the past, due mostly to their low consumption of sugar. Don't work against this by giving candy. Heavy cigarette smoking is a major factor contributing to the high rate of lung disease in Nepal. Don't encourage this by handing out cigarettes, especially to children. Handing out money to everyone who asks for it further propagates the image of the fat, rich tourist who does not have anything better to do with it. Giving money for posing for pictures is similarly not a good idea. Parents of Nepali children are usually quite ashamed to learn that their children have been begging, and they try to stop it.

Trekkers may sometimes encounter beggars to whom it is appropriate to give. There are few traditional beggars in the hills, but occasionally *saddhus,* or holy men, travel through begging as part of their life-styles. Food such as rice is an appropriate gift for them. Sometimes destitute people are encountered and gifts of clothing, food, and occasionally money are appropriate. Note the actions of Nepalis around you when deciding whether to give.

In general, pay for your food and lodging at the going rates and reward those who have done favors for you in some special way. In buying food, realize that you may be consuming important nutrients that the people of the area need, but are willing to forgo because of the relatively high price they can get from trekkers. Off the main trails used by trekkers, villagers may be very generous and offer more food than they can easily afford to give. Decline excessive hospitality. Whatever you do, be careful not to set a bad precedent. It is all too easy for the foreign

Nepali life: carrying water, spinning wool, making gravel. (Ane Haaland)

traveler to instill inappropriate hopes and desires in Nepalis by thoughtless acts and gestures.

Many trekkers purchase art and craft objects in the hills. Sometimes they buy valuable old art objects, usually at modest prices. This is expressly illegal; it is prohibited to remove any valuable old items from their origins. Even transporting idols and artifacts can result in imprisonment, and this has happened to several trekkers. Steadfastly deny any interest in old art, for if you don't, you encourage Nepalis to steal objects from sanctuaries, monasteries, or temples in order to sell them to foreigners. Theft of such items by trekkers themselves is totally reprehensible.

Some Nepalis have taken to fraudulently "antiquing" art. The old-appearing *thangka,* scroll painting, brought out of a chest in Helambu and sold as an antique is common. So-called old jewelry peddled by *BhoTiya* is another example. It may even be difficult to obtain government permission to export fraudulently antiqued works of art or objects of religious value. Permission must be obtained from the Archaeological Department in Thapathali in Kathmandu.

Beware of other amazing items for sale. Recently in Manang I was shown what appeared to be a huge (ten-carat or more) diamond that its owner said he found lying on the ground near a mountain glacier. He went to great lengths to "prove" to me that it was not glass and said he wanted only Rs. 300 for it. I was entertained, but not convinced. There are many good locally made craft items in certain areas. Purchasing these at the going prices is certainly beneficial to the local economy.

Try to prevent petty thievery by keeping a watchful eye on your possessions. In the past, sahibs tended to leave expensive cameras and other gear lying around. It became clear to the Nepalis that if the sahib did not value his possessions, then he would not miss them. Carry around only the equipment that you expect to use a great deal. Try to have all your gear stowed inside your pack and duffel, and keep the pockets done up. Lock items whenever possible. When traveling by bus with your belongings in the luggage rack on top, either have someone in the party ride on top with them, or be watchful of people climbing on top when the bus stops. It helps to keep all easily removed items buried deep inside the luggage.

Respect people's desires not to be photographed. Many, especially elderly villagers, believe that being photographed can shorten their lifespans. Sometimes if you talk with them a while, they will consent. Otherwise there are many who enjoy being photographed, and their smiles will grace your pictures for years. Don't promise to send copies of photographs to people unless there is a reasonable chance that you can do so. Sending photographs through the mail in Nepal is completely unreliable unless the letters are registered, and even then I wouldn't advise it. Better to send them with another traveler, or through your trekking agency in Kathmandu.

In the past, medical facilities were very scarce in Nepal, and foreigners were almost the only source of Western medicines. It became traditional to consider each passing traveler a doctor, and indeed, many people, both medical and nonmedical, used to devote a considerable part of their energies to treating the local ills. I feel that this effort is probably not warranted, and may even do more harm than good. To begin with, it helps destroy confidence in health care services developing in rural areas. Besides the facilities staffed by doctors along the trails, there are many health posts manned by auxilary health workers. It is very doubtful that ephemeral medical care such as a trekker could dispense would result in a cure or significant benefit to the sufferer. Furthermore, the idea that a little medicine might help a sick person and enable him or her to get to proper medical aid just does not hold up. Based on my personal experience as a doctor working in a remote area of Nepal and on discussions with other medical personnel, giving medicine to someone whom you wish to refer to another facility is almost certain to deter that person from acting on the referral. Finally, the idea that a little aspirin won't hurt anyone is untenable because, since it will not effect a cure, it may help destroy confidence in Western medicine. In a country with many different medical practices, it is best to introduce those aspects of Western medicine that definitely work. This may seem like a very inhumane and hard-nosed attitude, especially for a physician, but it is in Nepal's best interests.

CONSERVATION

Take nothing but pictures, leave nothing but footprints.
Sierra Club motto

In addition to the effect trekkers have on the people of Nepal, they may leave a profound impact on the countryside. Nepal's limited supply of firewood is being rapidly consumed and there are few reforestation projects. As a result, Nepal's biggest export is probably the extremely valuable topsoil being eroded away into rivers to be washed into India. Trekkers increase the demand for wood, especially in alpine areas where forests are being cut down near tree line to provide it. In addition, *goTh*, temporary herding huts, are sometimes dismantled by trekkers or their porters who need firewood for warmth and cooking. Use of wood for trekking, especially in the high altitude areas, must stop if trekking is to be a resource-conserving activity. Some may argue that wood is a renewable resource, while kerosene is a non-renewable fossil fuel. True, but in Nepal the deforestation problem is far too severe to be further worsened by trekkers. The local people need the wood for themselves, and even for them, it won't last forever.

When camping, especially in the frail alpine meadows, be careful not to add to erosion problems. It takes many decades to produce the vegetation that can be carelessly torn away by a boot or killed by a tent. Similarly, when following trails, stay on the path and do not cut switchbacks. If the vegetation surrounding the trails erodes, it is much more likely that the trail will wash out during the torrential monsoon.

For some popular trails, the route description might as well read, "Follow the line of sahib's garbage—film boxes, food wrappers, foreign cigarette boxes, tin cans—for a week to reach the superb alpine pastures and majestic viewpoints." Many parties have littered areas of Nepal so that they are reminiscent of the overused campsites, trails, and countryside of North America. It is really not necessary to provide labels from many foreign lands for the bored trekker to read. Carry your wrappers and other items throughout the day, and burn them in the evening. Flatten tin cans after burning, and bury them. Remember, however, not to throw any items into your host's hearth fire. Metal and glass containers can be given as gifts to villagers. Nepalis discard little that does not quickly decompose. It is the foreigner who brings non-biodegradable items into the hills and leaves them there. Remember that your actions will be a model for Nepalis and that you owe it to trekkers following you to provide them an experience uncluttered by your litter.

Cutting fodder for buffaloes takes much time and puts pressure on Nepal's forests. (Brot Coburn)

Children playing on a ping or Nepali-style ferris wheel. (Ane Haaland)

Disposing of body wastes is another problem facing trekkers. Those on large organized treks often erect enclosed latrines at campsites. The feces and other material are then buried. This commendable practice avoids the unsightliness and potential for disease of piles of feces, each with a topping of toilet paper. Travelers who are not on organized treks that provide portable toilets should ask if there are communal latrines (*chaarpi*) in the villages, or if a family has one. One of the many positive changes over the past decade has been the establishment of latrines in certain heavily trekked areas. There are latrines in many of the villages in Thak Khola and other areas. Although not always maintained, they are often excellent facilities. Most homes in Khumbu have a convenient latrine arrangement on top of the hay pile situated in an alcove off the second floor. However, in most of Nepal, you will have to do as the Nepalis do. Usually they perform their eliminations before dawn or after sunset in various places near the village. They carry a *loTaa*, or container of water, to wash themselves. I recommend that you find a corner of a field or other sheltered spot away from running water and bury your feces, or at least cover them with stones. Burn the toilet paper. Often you will find pariah dogs that eat feces—indeed these are often summoned by villagers to clean up after young children. Disgusting as it may seem to non-Nepalis, it is certainly preferable to some alternatives. Whatever you do, be sure to exercise appropriate modesty and get out of sight of others. You never see a Nepali in an act of defecation. I wish I could say the same for trekkers. Nepali women and men often urinate discreetly by hunkering in their skirts. Some women trekkers find this quite appropriate if wearing long skirts with no underpants. But urination generally poses few problems. Women should be careful to dispose of tampons and applicators properly since they have been turning up as children's toys!

Finally, in whatever you do, realize that you are not alone. If you carry off one *mani* stone from a prayer wall, saying that one less will make no difference, realize what would happen if everyone did so. If we who travel in this exotic country respect its culture and customs, perhaps its spectacular countryside and the experience which we have found so worthwhile can be preserved for the benefit of Nepalis and the enjoyment of future trekkers.

This traditional medical practitioner in western Nepal will chant and beat his drum for many hours to drive out the evil spirit causing disease in a sick child. These shamans co-exist with the modern medical practices slowly being introduced. (Stephen Bezruchka)

5 HEALTH CARE

*I suffered increasingly from mountaineer's foot—reluctance to
put one in front of the other.*

H. W. Tilman, *Nepal Himalaya*

Trekking in Nepal need not be a great risk to your health in spite of what many
Westerners may think. If the preventive measures described here are strictly
followed before and during your stay in Nepal, you should enjoy reasonably good
health. Field treatments and procedures are given for the medical problems you
may encounter in the hills. These are based on my own experiences as a physician
who has worked and trekked in the hills of Nepal, and on discussions with other
experienced trekkers.

What follows may seem frightening to would-be trekkers who are used to the
professional medical care available in modern society. In Nepal you may be a
week's walk or more from a doctor. Tens of thousands of trekkers have followed
precautions similar to those outlined here and have had a most enjoyable and
healthy journey. Awareness and prevention are the keys. A lot of information is
provided, some of which may cause anxiety. But it is better to have advice
available should it be needed, rather than to disclaim any potential for illness. For
most people, trekking is not dangerous; it is the beginning of a new vitality.

PREPARATIONS AND POST-TREK PRECAUTIONS

Many people come to Nepal with no hiking experience and, though in poor
condition, take on their first trek, walk a hundred miles or more, and thoroughly enjoy themselves. Still, I strongly recommend that those planning to trek undertake a
conditioning program. Running several miles a day is about the best single condi-
tioner. Taking hikes uphill with a heavy pack is a good activity to put variety into
the regimen. Bicycling, cross-country skiing, swimming, and other aerobic activities are also excellent. But all of them must be started months ahead of time
and carried on regularly with increases in the amount of exercise each week.
Toughen your feet and break in your footwear through progressively longer hikes.
Applying tincture of benzoin to your feet over pressure points may toughen the
skin.

Before you leave for Nepal, visit your physician and get a cholera innoculation
if required for international travel at that time. The following immunizations are
recommended: Sabin trivalent polio, typhoid, tetanus-diphtheria, and perhaps
smallpox. These vaccinations should be recorded on a World Health Organization-
approved International Certificate of Vaccination that can be obtained from the
health department in your country's national government offices.

Obtain a tuberculin test, and consider the BCG immunization against tuber-
culosis. The cholera vaccine requires a booster every six months. In Nepal you can
get one at Shanta Bhawan or Bir hospitals in the Kathmandu Valley, but the stamp
for the International Certificate of Vaccination is obtainable only at Bir Hospital.
Have a thorough physical examination and let your physician know the nature of

the activities you will be engaged in and the altitudes you hope to reach. Visit a dentist to have potentially disabling dental problems cared for. There is no easily accessible good dental service in Nepal.

Those with active chest and heart diseases that limit physical activity should avoid going to high altitudes. Individuals with the following conditions **definitely** should not go to high altitudes: primary pulmonary hypertension, cyanotic congenital heart disease, absence of the right pulmonary artery, chronic pulmonary disease with arterial unsaturation, coronary artery disease with severe angina or cardiac failure, congestive failure with arterial unsaturation, and disablingly symptomatic cardiac arrhythmias. In the interest of specificity these are listed in medical terms to be interpreted by doctors.

Recently some people who had serious pre-existing diseases have died while trekking. Those with sickle cell disease or sickle cell trait greatly increase their risk at high altitudes. People with recurrent deep vein thromboses and pulmonary emboli should also avoid high altitudes, but those with essential hypertension tolerate high altitudes well. Our knowledge of the effect of high altitudes on people with mild or moderate chronic disease, as well as on the elderly, is woefully inadequate. Information on drug effects at high altitudes is similarly lacking. Certainly many people in their 60s and 70s have trekked at high altitudes in Nepal with no problems. If you are in that age range and enjoy good health and physical conditioning, by all means consider trekking in Nepal, at least at moderate altitudes. You could later consider trying the high passes. Anyone with chronic diseases not discussed here should seek the advice of a knowledgeable physician and, if given the go-ahead, should first make supervised visits to high altitudes near home. Similarly, those who wonder if they have the physical stamina for trekking should first take hilly hikes lasting several days near their homes.

Consult your physician about taking malaria suppressants. Malaria used to be endemic in the Tarai, but today it has been somewhat controlled in most areas. Nevertheless, incidents of malaria continue to occur. The usual form of protection is to take a suppressant, for instance, 500 mg of chloroquin weekly. The chances of contracting malaria while trekking in the hills and mountains are slight outside of the monsoon, especially above 4000 ft (1200 m). But you may wish to take the drug as an additional protection. If so, start taking the pills two weeks before you reach the first area where there is a chance of getting malaria. Do not discontinue them until two months after you have left all infected areas, and until you are in an area where good medical care is available in case an attack occurs after you stop the drug. There is no chloroquin-resistant falciparum malaria in Nepal.

Discuss the medical supplies mentioned here with your physician. Drugs and most supplies can be bought cheaply in Kathmandu. Moleskin, iodine water purification tablets, and modern sunscreens may only be available in the United States and Europe. Moreover, a few items available in Kathmandu, such as elastic or adhesive bandages, are inferior to those made in the West.

Finally, arrange to get a gamma globulin injection just before you leave home. This provides partial protection against infectious hepatitis, long feared by travelers to Asia. Presently the U. S. Public Health Association advises 5 ml every four months regardless of body weight. If traveling for more than four months, you can get a gamma globulin injection at 1 P.M. any Wednesday at the Kalimati Clinic in Kathmandu. Gamma globulin does not offer complete protection. It lessens the risk so that if you follow other safeguards while in Nepal, you will probably not end up in the hepatitis ward of Shanta Bhawan Hospital.

After you return home from trekking, you should have your stool examined for ova and parasites. In particular, rotten-egg burps suffered during diarrhea may be an indication of giardiasis, a common treatable parasitic disease. It is a good idea for anyone returning from Asia to have a stool examination, even if the person never had diarrhea there. Several people have written to me, pleased that they followed this recommendation and discovered parasitic infestations that were easily treated. You should also repeat your tuberculin skin test if it was previously negative.

HEALTH CARE OF CHILDREN

For those trekking with children, it is essential that a knowledgeable physician or other health professional be consulted before you leave home in order to get specific information appropriate to your children and their needs. See this person well in advance—several months may be necessary—to ensure that the required immunizations can be obtained in time. If it is decided that your children should take chloroquin as a malaria prophylactic, pills of appropriate size can be obtained at stops in route, for instance, in Hong Kong, or sometimes in Nepal. Small dose tablets are not easily available in the United States or Canada.

The greatest health risk for children trekking in Nepal is the hazard of fecal-oral contamination. Children at oral stages tend to put everything in their mouths. Human and animal feces are everywhere, and tend to get into the hands and mouths of children. The problem is compounded because children with diarrhea and vomiting can get dehydrated quickly. Since there are essentially no medical care facilities in the hills, each family is on its own. Take solace in knowing that most trekking families have no problems.

Prevention is the key. Watch what your child puts in his mouth. Iodize or boil all water for drinking and feed your child only cooked food. Keep materials for making oral rehydration solution on hand in case diarrhea or vomiting develops. If the liquid losses in stool or vomitus are replaced gradually, no serious problems should result. In Kathmandu an oral rehydration powder called RD-Sol can be purchased in the drug shops. Mix one packet with two cups (half-liter) of boiled or iodized water, and feed it to the child by spoon or cup a little at a time. Try to get the child to drink as much liquid as he has lost. Check for signs of adequate hydration such as normal frequency and amount of urination, moisture on the lips and mouth, and fairly normal behavior of the child. If in doubt, get the child to take more fluids. Do not use opiates or other similar drugs to "plug up" diarrhea in children. Do not use tetracycline drugs in children under age eight. If you lack a commercial oral rehydration powder such as RD-Sol, a substitute can be made up almost anywhere. Add one three-finger pinch of salt, and a three-finger scoop of sugar to one *maanaa* (2½ cups or 570 ml) of boiled or iodized water. Add some orange or lime juice if available.

Colds and other upper respiratory infections are very common in Nepal, and your children may get their share. One family found a bulb syringe handy for clearing their two-year-old's snotty nose.

Children's doses for drugs are not given here. They vary, of course, with the age and weight of the child. Be sure to discuss which drugs to take, and their doses with your health consultant. Liquid doses are best for young children.

The hazards of high altitudes are no different for children than for adults, except that it may be more difficult to determine whether a particular child's health problem is due to altitude or to some other cause. One family recently took their twenty-one-month-old child to 16,500 ft (5000 m) without difficulty, after appropriate acclimatization. I have seen Sherpa mothers carry their one- or two-month-old babies over 19,000 ft (5800 m) passes. And a woman who was six months pregnant ascended to 24,000 ft (7300 m). Such extremes are not recommended. Families should limit their treks to 13,000 ft (4000 m). All people with children who venture to high altitudes should descend immediately if there is any difficulty in acclimatizing. The safety margin in waiting out the minor symptoms of altitude illness is significantly less in children than in adults.

THE MEDICAL KIT

A very basic medical kit is proposed here so that trekkers will be reasonably prepared for problems. Most of the items can be purchased quite cheaply in Kathmandu. Since the greater part of its contents will remain unused, it can be considered a kind of insurance. In most developed countries, prescriptions are required for some of the drugs. An understanding physician should give you these if you carefully explain why you need them. Do not use these medications when medical assistance is available nearby. The procedures outlined here are only field approximations in most cases, and proper diagnosis is very important.

Names of drugs are always a dilemma. While the official or generic names are generally the same throughout the world, the advertising or brand names vary greatly from place to place. The generic names are used here whenever possible.

My recommended medical kit—enough for a party of two—includes:

Moleskin—Felt padding about one millimeter thick with adhesive backing, used for the prevention of blisters. About half a square foot per person should be enough. It is not available in Kathmandu, but adhesive tape or zinc oxide strapping can be used as a substitute.

Bandages—One roll of two-inch cotton gauze, one roll of two-inch adhesive tape, and five to ten adhesive bandages per person for small wounds.

Elastic Bandage—One three-inch roll for relief of strains and sprains.

Thermometer—One that reads below normal temperatures (for diagnosis of hypothermia) as well as above (for fever).

Miscellaneous—Scissors, needle or safety pin, and forceps or tweezers.

Plastic Dropper Bottles—One-ounce size for iodine and tincture of opium.

Water Purification Chemicals—Tetraglycine hydroperiodide or iodine in various forms (see next section).

Leech Repellent (Optional)—For those trekking during the monsoon. Dibutyl Phthalate—not available in Kathmandu—is reputed to be effective for four hours if applied to the skin. Many insect repellents are also effective. Clothes sprayed with 30 ml of Dibutyl Phthalate at strategic areas where the pests might enter are safe for up to two weeks. Clothes can also be treated by soaking them in a concentrated salt solution.

Iron Pills (Optional)—Ferrous Sulfate tablets (200 mg) for women only. Take one per day, and discontinue after your trek.

Nose Spray or Drops—Phenylephrine HCL (one-half percent) for stuffed noses and sinuses. In Kathmandu a product called Fenox (one-fourth percent active substance) is available in convenient 15 ml dropper bottles. Put two drops of the more concentrated solution in each nostril two or three times a day when symptomatic and when changing altitude.

Nasal Decongestant (Optional)—For those used to taking these tablets for colds.

Antihistamine—For treating symptoms of colds and hay fever. If you do not have a favorite, try chlorpheniramine maleate tablets (4 mg).

Aspirin or Similar Drug—Twenty-five tablets (five-grain, 325 mg) of aspirin for relief of minor pain, for lowering temperatures, and for symptomatic relief of colds and respiratory infections. Acetaminophen is an appropriate substitute for those who can't tolerate aspirin.

Codeine—Fifteen tablets (30 mg) for relief of pain and cough.

Drugs for Diarrhea and Dysentery—Tincture of Opium (the most concentrated), 1 oz (30 ml), or Camphorated Tincture of Opium (less concentrated, but the only form available in Kathmandu) 8 oz (250 ml). More expensive alternatives (see next section) include Lomotil and loperamide tablets.

Antibiotic—In increasing price order, tetracycline capsules (250 mg), penicillin G tablets (400,000 units), penicillin V tablets (250 mg), ampicillin capsules (250 mg), or amoxicillin capsules (250 mg). Bring forty capsules or tablets of any one. People who are allergic to penicillin should not take ampicillin or amoxicillin either. Instead they should take tetracycline or erythromycin tablets (250 mg). Of the drugs available in Kathmandu, ampicillin and tetracycline are good choices. A cephalosporin such as cephalexin capsules (250 mg) offers the broadest spectrum of protection of any oral antibiotic, but it is quite expensive.

Sunscreening Preparation—One with a Sun Protection Factor (SPF) of ten to fifteen in order to get adequate protection from the sun on snow slopes at high altitudes. Zinc Oxide, an opaque ointment, is the only effective sunscreen available in Nepal. Sunscreens are best applied one or two hours before exposure, and reapplied after heavy sweating. Be sure to apply them over all areas that can receive direct or reflected sunlight, especially under the nose, chin, and eyebrows. Lip balms containing effective sunscreens should also be used.

Topical Ophthalmic Antibiotics—For instance, Ten Percent Sodium Sulfacetamide (15 ml) made by Royal Drug in Kathmandu. Many antibiotic products are made for treatment of conjunctivitis or eye irritations, but in choosing one, avoid all penicillin products since the chance of becoming sensitized to them is great if they are used on the skin. The same goes for any antibiotic if you may want to take the active ingredient internally. Good choices of ophthalmic antibiotics are those that contain bacitracin, chloramphenicol, neomycin, or polymixin. Avoid any that contain steroids such as betamethasone, cortisone, dexamethasone, hydrocortisone, prednisone, or others.

Malaria Suppressant (Optional)—Chloroquin, for instance, if one is taken.

These items are considered a bare minimum by some, too much by others; they are clearly adequate for most situations. Other items are mentioned in the next section, and can be added if desired. I would never go into the hills without tincture of opium, aspirin, iodine, a sunscreen, and an antibiotic. Physicians accompanying a group to high altitudes might find a stethoscope and an ophthalmoscope useful.

HEALTH AND MEDICAL PROBLEMS

The vast majority of diseases that plague the trekker in Nepal are transmitted by food or water contaminated by infected human or animal feces. You should assume that all water and uncooked foods in Nepal are contaminated. Prepare food and water properly to render them harmless.

Water

The safest procedure is to boil drinking water vigorously for ten minutes. This kills all bacteria, viruses, and parasites. The next best is to treat the water with iodine, which kills most organisms, but may not kill all the viruses, one of which is reputed to cause infectious hepatitis. There are two methods of adding the required amount of iodine to water. One is to add two drops of two percent Tincture of Iodine solution to 8 oz (one cup, 250 ml) of water, stir, and wait ten minutes before using. If the water is cloudy, add twice the amount of iodine. The iodine can be carried in a small plastic dropper bottle. The other method involves using tetraglycine hydroperiodide tablets, also called water purification tablets iodine (Globaline, Potable Aqua). Add one tablet to a quart (liter) of water. After it has dissolved, stir the water and leave it for ten minutes before using. The Tincture of Iodine method is best suited for small quantities, while the tablets are useful for water in canteens.

Another technique for iodination of water is to place 4 to 8 g of crystal iodine (USP grade resublimed iodine) in a 1 oz (30 ml) clear glass bottle with a plastic top. Fill the bottle with water and shake it vigorously. Allow the crystals to settle to the bottom. Add half the bottle of solution to each quart (liter) of water, and wait for fifteen minutes before consuming the water. Refill the bottle, and reuse it. This technique can be used about 1000 times before the iodine is depleted. If the water is unusually contaminated, allow it to stand for forty minutes before using it. People with no access to a chemical supply store may find iodine crystals difficult to obtain. Sometimes a drug store can supply them. Try any method using iodine at home first to make sure you are not allergic to it. This is rare, but not unknown.

Several new products, such as the Walbro Water Purifier, that treat water by passing it through a device are available. I have no personal experience with any of these devices and can see no advantage to the trekker in using them. The standard water filters used in homes and restaurants in Asia are not effective by themselves in filtering out bacteria, viruses, and parasites.

On organized treks, trekkers are sometimes told the water they are given has been boiled, when in fact it hasn't. I always assume that "boiled water" has not been boiled, unless I have supervised it.

You must be cautious with all water ingested, even that used for brushing teeth. Water used for cleaning open wounds is best boiled first and left to cool. Get used to the idea that if it does not taste like iodine, it is not water (unless it has been boiled).

Chlorine (Halazone) is widely used as a water purification agent, but it is not as effective as iodine because the spectrum of organisms it kills is smaller. Chlorine is useless against amebic cysts, while iodine has been shown to kill these hardy creatures. Most trekkers will probably decide to add iodine to their water rather than boil it.

Food

Thoroughly cooked foods can be considered safe, but only if they are eaten soon after cooking. Fruits and vegetables that are eaten uncooked must first be washed and peeled under sanitary conditions. Leafy vegetables must be cooked, since it is not clear how effective it is to wash them in an iodine solution. Thus peel it, cook it, or forget it.

Food prepared by Nepalis can be assumed to be safe if it has just been

Water buffalo milk is delicious, however it should be heated to the boiling point before drinking. (Brot Coburn)

cooked and not allowed to be contaminated by flies. Contamination is possible from the plates the food is served on, but this is very difficult to control.

Milk should always be heated just to the boiling point and allowed to cool before drinking, unless it is known to be already pasteurized. Curds are made from boiled milk and can be assumed to be safe unless recontaminated. This can easily occur, especially if flies have been allowed to sit on the surface. Scraping off the top layer should then be sufficient. If milk has been diluted with water, it is necessary to boil the mixture for ten minutes. Buttermilk and cottage cheese, especially when prepared by herdsmen in their alpine huts, can be considered fairly safe. The dairy in Kathmandu pasteurizes its milk. Most of the ice cream in Kathmandu is risky.

It is difficult to follow rigorous advice concerning alcoholic drinks. To be safe, avoid them all. *Rakshi,* distilled from a fermented mash, is perhaps the safest since it has been boiled. The *Thakali* frequently serve *daru,* a *rakshi* that is very much like sake. The common fermented drink is called *chang* by Sherpas and Tibetans, and *jAAR* by other Nepalis. Unless the water from which it is made is known to be pure, it is possible to get sick from it (a hangover notwithstanding). However, many trekkers will find it very difficult to abstain.

Honey is often obtained in the hills from beehives located on cliffs. The bees are smoked out by Nepalis dangling on primitive ladders made of reeds. If this honey is from rhododendron flowers, it may contain a potent neurotoxin (poison). Locals are often aware of this. Cooking the honey is reputed to destroy the toxin. On one of my treks in a remote region we obtained some cliff honey and later consumed part of it. An hour later, my companion began to feel ill and then became comatose. He required rescue, but recovered fully. We subsequently cooked the honey, but days later his Nepali companion ate some and developed similar, though less severe, symptoms. Be careful of unknown local honey.

Nutrition

The University of Hawaii *Nepal Health Survey* concluded that the dietary intake of Nepalis is adequate, except that it is deficient in Vitamins A and C and riboflavin. However, clinical signs of deficiency are occasionally observed only with regard to Vitamin A. Iodine deficiency is also found in the hills and people with goiters are sometimes seen.

A recent survey of trekkers' diets in Nepal showed that many are inadequate in protein and caloric intakes. Rice and lentils (*daal bhaat*) in large quantities is a reasonable source of calories and protein. Trekkers should make sure that they periodically eat green vegetables and pigmented fruits and vegetables to get sufficient Vitamins A and C. Those worried about their protein intake because of the relatively meatless diet should ask at Nepali homes for some roasted soybeans (*bhaTmaas*). These are pleasant to munch on along the trail and they contain more protein per unit weight than any other food including meat.

For insurance, some trekkers might want to take a vitamin pill daily. Women might also want to take an iron pill daily, as the local diets do not contain much iron. Women do lose a significant amount of iron monthly through menstruation. However, neither of these supplements should be necessary for healthy trekkers who spend a few months walking around in the hills.

Diarrhea and Dysentery

Diarrhea and dysentery are the most common problems among trekkers. The term diarrhea as used here means frequent passage of loose stool. Dysentery means forms of diarrhea in which the stool often contains blood and mucus. Sufferers may also have stomach cramps and fever. Diarrhea is much more common among trekkers than dysentery.

General principles in either situation are to note the number and nature of the stools and to begin taking clear fluids such as water, weak tea with sugar, juice, clear soup, or soda pop that has been left to stand until the carbonation is gone. Drinking lots of fluids is necessary to avoid dehydration. Perhaps the best liquid to take is an oral rehydration solution. RD-Sol, a powder manufactured in Nepal by

Royal Drug Company, contains the needed salts. Mix one small bag with a pint (half liter) of water and drink it in small sips. Take ten drops of tincture of opium in a small amount of water after each loose stool, up to five times a day. A teaspoon of the deodorized tincture (paregoric), two or three Lomotil tablets, or loperamide tablets can be substituted. Treatment with opiates and synthetic anti-motility agents may actually prolong illness in those afflicted with certain forms of dysentery, so don't take them indiscriminately.

If this relieves the symptoms, return to solid food gradually. If it does not and you have two or three loose stools a day with no blood or mucus but feel well enough to continue, omit taking the tincture of opium and go on. Often the diarrhea will subside of its own accord. On the other hand, if you have dysentery, especially with nausea, vomiting, and fever, rest and begin the antibiotic with an initial dose of two pills followed by one pill every six hours, preferably before eating. People with such symptoms will rarely be able to continue at the time, but with rest and constant intake of fluids, the symptoms should disappear in a few days. It is important to continue taking fluids, even if only small portions can be taken at any one time.

A remedy that I personally use and find effective, yet whose effectiveness I am unable to document rigorously, is the following: With the first episode of diarrhea I take one tetracycline capsule (250 mg). The symptoms usually subside rapidly and no further treatment is necessary. Stubborn cases may require a day or two of medicine, taking one capsule four times a day. This is not a recognized treatment protocol and, as a physician, I can see how taking only one capsule could mask more serious illness. Trekkers may wish to experiment with this method. I would be eager to hear their comments on it.

Another effective remedy for diarrhea is a bismuth subsalicylate suspension such as Pepto-Bismol. It has also been shown to work as a prophylactic agent. No side effects have been reported. The dosage of 60 ml (4 tbsp) taken four times a day is effective for either purpose, but this necessitates carrying enough for a cup a day. But a half pound (225 g) a day (not counting the weight of the container) works out to some 15 lb (7 kg) for a month's trek.

There are many other treatment regimens for diarrhea and dysentery. In fact, almost every traveler knows of several. One drug, a combination of diphenoxylate and atropine, has been marketed and heavily promoted under the trademarked name Lomotil. It is used much the same as tincture of opium, but it has not been shown to be superior, in spite of its much higher cost. A newer similar drug, also no better, is loperamide. An old favorite is the widely touted iodochlorhydroxyquin, marketed under the name Entero-Vioform. People take it either prophylactically or for diarrhea. However, a study of people using this drug for prophylaxis in Mexico showed it was no better than a placebo (sugar pill). And a recent study has implicated this drug in causing eye and nerve damage. I would not recommend it. I similarly would not recommend the use of the drug Mexaform.

Other drugs have been used for prophylaxis of traveler's diarrhea. Sulfa drugs and neomycin as well as bismuth subsalicylate have been shown to be of some benefit in controlled studies. Other recent studies have confirmed the prophylactic benefit of the tetracycline drugs. Doxycycline, available under various brand names, was the particular drug studied. A dose of 100 mg (one capsule) taken once a day with meals to avoid side effects, is effective according to two studies. Use of the drug for longer than three weeks is not recommended. It should not be used by pregnant women, children under eight, or people allergic to tetracyclines. It is quite expensive, often costing a dollar a day. Individuals taking such drugs may theoretically risk other infections with bacteria such as salmonella and shigella. Another theoretical risk is the development of resistant strains of enteropathogenic *E. coli* bacteria (the causative agent of most forms of traveler's diarrhea). Cases of photosensitivity have occurred among people using doxycycline for prevention of diarrhea in Nepal. They become sensitive to the sun, and are sunburned much more easily than others on the trek. If you suspect this is happening to you, discontinue the drug immediately. As with any drug, the potential hazards should be weighed against the potential advantages. I do not recommend this drug as a prophylactic except to those who have previously had incapacitating traveler's diarrhea, or who are very worried about getting it. Since the usual forms of diarrhea that trekkers get are self-limiting, most people can get by quite well by treating episodes as they occur.

Altitude Illness*

Problems with altitude can strike anyone, even at relatively low altitudes such as 8000 ft (2450 m). Indeed some have died from altitudes at this level. But in general, trekkers going to higher altitudes quickly are more severely affected. People who fly to a high altitude and then proceed to an even higher area or cross a pass should be especially wary. Examples include flying to Lukla and Shyangboche and going on to Everest Base Camp; flying to Jomosom and crossing the Thorung La; or flying to Langtang and crossing to Ganja La. Statistically, some symptoms will be felt by two-thirds to three-fourths of those going to high altitudes, especially to 14,000 ft (4200 m) or above. Those hiking up will have fewer problems than those flying up. Serious illness occurs in perhaps two to three percent of people who go to high altitudes.

Altitude illness can be prevented by acclimatization, that is by a gradual rate of ascent, allowing sufficient rest at various intermediate altitudes. It is a totally preventable problem. The proper amount of rest and rate of ascent vary greatly from individual to individual, and even over time in the same individual. For example, one person who previously had climbed Mount Everest later had difficulties at lower altitudes from ascending too rapidly. Dr. Charles Houston, who has done extensive research at high altitudes, says a cautious rate of ascent that would ensure comfort and safety for almost anyone is to take five days to reach 11,000 ft (3350 m) and six more days to reach 15,000 ft (4500 m). Above 15,000 ft (4500 m), climb 500 ft (150 m) a day. However, most parties could safely go at a slightly faster rate, allowing one day of acclimatization for every 3000 ft (900 m) gained between sleeping sites above 10,000 ft (3000 m). This is feasible only if everyone is on the lookout for the signs and symptoms of maladaption to high altitudes. If the party acts appropriately should anyone develop altitude illness, serious problems can usually be avoided.

For example, in ascending to Everest Base Camp, Kala Pattar, or anywhere above 15,000 ft (4500 m) allow at least two rest and acclimatization days. One stop could be at 11,000 ft (3350 m), and the other at 14,000 ft (4250 m). On these days, people who feel good could take an excursion to a higher point, but return to sleep at the same altitude as the night before. In Khumbu a rest day at Namche Bazaar

---

*Much of the information here on altitude illness is taken from *Mountain Sickness* by Dr. Peter Hackett (see Recommended Reading). He has perhaps more experience in dealing with altitude illness in Nepal than any other physician.

or Tengboche, followed by another at Pheriche, would be the minimum requirement. Then spend a night at Lobuje, and ascend to Kala Pattar the next day, returning to Lobuje for the night. Climb high and sleep low.

There are other factors besides a slow rate of ascent that help in acclimatization. A large fluid intake to ensure good hydration is a key. Four quarts (liters) or more a day of liquid are usually necessary. Urine volume should always exceed one pint (one-half liter) daily, preferably one quart (one liter). The urine color should be almost clear. A strong yellow color indicates that more fluids should be drunk. Some trekkers and Himalayan climbers find that measuring urine output daily with a small plastic bottle helps ensure adequate hydration. A simpler way to measure urine output is to wait until you are absolutely bursting before urinating. The volume is then close to half a liter. Empty a full bladder at least twice a day. One sign of adaptation to altitude is a good natural diuresis (passage of lots of urine). If this is not found, be cautious. An easy way to judge the presence of dehydration is to compare heart rates standing and lying down, with a thirty-second interval between. If the rate is twenty percent greater in the standing position, the individual is significantly dehydrated and should consume more fluids. This can be water, tea, soup, or broth. Alcoholic drinks should be avoided by dehydrated individuals, and at high altitudes by everyone. Besides being detrimental to acclimatization, the effects of alcohol at high altitude may be impossible to distinguish from symptoms of altitude illness.

Proper nutrition is another factor in acclimatization. Caloric intake should be maintained and the diet should be high in carbohydrates. The tasty potatoes found at high altitudes in Nepal are an excellent source of carbohydrates. A good appetite is a sign of acclimatization. Avoid an excessive salt intake at high altitudes; indeed cut back somewhat if you habitually consume a great deal of salt. Don't take salt tablets.

Rest is also important. Over-exertion does not help acclimatization. Give up part of your load to Sherpas and other high altitude dwellers who are already well acclimatized and can carry loads with ease. Avoid going so fast that you are always stopping short of breath with your heart pounding. A rest step and techniques for pacing yourself by checking your heart rate are described in the introduction to Section II. Plan modest objectives for each day so that you will enjoy your stay in the heights.

Many people who frequent the mountains and often make rapid changes in altitude find that forced deep breathing helps reduce the mild symptoms of altitude illness. However, if done to excess, it can produce the hyperventilation syndrome in which shortness of breath, dizziness, and numbness are present. Breathing in and out of a large paper or plastic bag for a few minutes will relieve these symptoms.

Finally there is a drug that may help in coping with high altitude in certain situations. Acetazolamide (Diamox) has been shown to be beneficial in those who fly to high altitudes. The dose is 250 mg by mouth twice a day begun two days before the flight and continued for three days after ascent. It can also help when begun upon arrival at high altitude by plane, and may have some benefit to those who walk to high altitudes. Side effects often noted are an increased urine output, and some numbness and tingling. Trekkers flying into a high altitude area such as Lukla, Shyangboche, Langtang, Dhorpatan, Jomosom, and Manang might consider taking it. But even they should not use it routinely because of the side effects and, perhaps more importantly, because of the false sense of security it may provide. Users may not heed the early warnings of grave problems and continue ascending to their deaths. The drug only prevents certain symptoms and probably not the serious life-threatening ones.

Other drugs used for prevention are at best controversial and studies on their effectiveness are conflicting. Furosemide, also called frusemide (Lasix), has been studied by the Indian Army and found to be helpful, but all the other studies attempting to confirm it have in fact found it to be harmful as a prophylactic. Antacids to alkalinize the urine have been proposed as part of a comprehensive program to acclimatize but at present there is no controlled evidence to support their use.

Most people trekking to high altitudes experience one or more **mild symptoms of altitude illness.** The symptoms include:

Nausea
Loss of appetite
Mild shortness of breath with exertion
Sleep disturbance
Breathing irregularity, usually during sleep
Dizziness or light-headedness
Mild weakness
Slight swelling of hands and face

As long as the symptoms remain mild, and are only a nuisance, ascent at a modest rate can continue. Symptomatic treatment with medicines may be helpful. If several of the mild symptoms are present and the climber is quite uncomfortable, ascent should be halted and the victim observed closely. If there is no improvement after a few hours, or after a night's rest, descent on foot should continue until the symptoms are relieved. Then ascent at a more gradual rate can be considered.

Serious symptoms of altitude illness are a grave matter. They include:

Marked shortness of breath with only slight exertion
Rapid breathing after resting—twenty-five or more breaths per minute
Wet, bubbly breathing
Severe coughing spasms that limit activity
Coughing up pinkish or rust-colored sputum
Rapid heart rate after resting—110 or more beats per minute
Blueness of face and lips
Low urine output—less than a pint (500 ml) daily
Persistent vomiting
Severe, persistent headache
Gross fatigue or extreme lassitude
Delirium, confusion, and coma
Loss of coordination, staggering

If anyone in your party develops any of these symptoms, he or she should descend IMMEDIATELY, on the back of a porter or animal to avoid undue exertion. Dr. Peter Hackett, states, "There are three rules for treatment: descent, descent, descent!" The victim should be kept warm and given oxygen if it is available. After a descent of several thousand feet, relief may be dramatic. At the point where relief occurs, or lower, rest a few days. Then consider ascending cautiously again.

It cannot be stressed too strongly that you must descend at the onset of serious symptoms. If in Khumbu, go to the hospital at Kunde, or to the Trekkers'

Aid Post at Pheriche, if that is on your descent route. A pressure chamber to simulate the effects of descent is being tested in Pheriche, so this could hold some hope for the future. Don't stop descending in Pheriche unless the victim is considerably better. Trekkers have died in Pheriche from not heeding this guideline. Don't wait for a helicopter to rescue you; it may only take out a body. Many trekkers, including Olympic athletes, physicians, and experienced climbers, have died in Nepal from altitude illness because they failed to heed symptoms when they occurred. Don't be another statistic in this totally preventable problem.

The essential material on altitude illness has already been covered, and what follows is for trekkers who are particularly interested, or who are suffering from altitude illness.

Altitude illnesses observed in Nepal include: acute mountain sickness (AMS), high altitude pulmonary edema (HAPE), peripheral edema (PE), cerebral edema (CE), and high altitude retinal hemorrhage (HARH).

AMS commonly comes on after being at high altitudes for one to two days. A variety of symptoms are experienced, most often a persistent headache, usually present on awakening, The mild symptoms listed here also occur. Irregular or periodic breathing during sleep, called Cheyne-Stokes respiration, is common. The rate and depth of respiration increase to a peak, then diminish, stopping altogether for fractions of a minute, then increasing again. If none of the serious symptoms are present, there is no cause for concern. Young people seem to be more susceptible to AMS. Physical fitness *per se* is of no benefit. This is true for most altitude illness. The treatment is to deal with each symptom with whatever means you have, and to ascend slowly or rest, depending on the severity of the problem. Acetazolamide, if available, may be effective in treating the symptoms of AMS. Try a 250 mg tablet before bed and upon arising to see if it helps the headache and malaise. It may also help ensure a good night's sleep. (Do not take sleeping pills at high altitude; they may worsen symptoms and be dangerous.) The effectiveness of acetazolamide for **treating** symptoms of AMS has not yet been documented. It is important to make sure that mild weakness does not progress to the serious symptom of gross fatigue or extensive lassitude in which the person becomes unable to care for himself. Don't leave such a person alone, for the mild condition may progress and the victim can become helpless.

Tests for coordination should be taken. An easy one is called tandem walking. After resting, see if the person can walk a straight line by putting the heel of the advancing foot directly in front of the toe of the back foot. Slight difficulty is tolerable if 12 ft (4 m) can be covered in a straight line. If in doubt, compare the individual with someone who is having no difficulty. In exhaustion, hypothermia, or intoxication, mild degrees of loss of coordination (ataxia) can be seen, but there should be no staggering or falling. Another test is to have the person stand, feet together, arms at the side (or in front), and eyes closed. If the person sways considerably, significant loss of coordination (ataxia) is present. Again, use a non-affected member of the party as a measure. Ataxia is a sign of serious illness, possibly CE, and the person should descend while he is still able to do so under his own power, but always with someone else.

HAPE, the presence of fluid in the lungs, is a grave illness and is probably present if the respiratory problems on the above serious symptoms list are noted. The heart and breathing rates are useful clues. Do not delay in descending with individuals with these symptoms as death can be only a few hours away. Usually there are also some signs of AMS. Trained people using stethoscopes may hear sounds called rales in the lungs of trekkers with no symptoms. This is common and no cause for alarm. It may be difficult to differentiate HAPE from lung infection. In fact, both may be present. If there is any doubt, especially if the person is getting worse, descend. Individuals with chest disease are more susceptible to HAPE as are people who have previously suffered from it. People under age twenty-five are also more susceptible. Those with upper respiratory infections or common colds are probably not at any increased risk. Oxygen and morphine may be beneficial, but it appears doubtful that other drugs used to treat pulmonary edema at sea level are effective. If descent is impossible, oxygen and morphine could be tried as a last resort. One altitude illness expert, Dr. Herbert Hultgren, has recently published a study suggesting that mild to moderate HAPE at a relatively low altitude (12,300 ft, 3750 m) can be treated by bed rest alone. This was done by trained clinicians in a modern hospital in Peru, however, and cannot be recommended as the therapy of choice in Nepal. Descend!

PE—swelling around the eyes, face, hands, feet, or ankles—is present in some degree in many visitors to high altitudes. Women seem to be affected more than men, but this doesn't appear to be related to the menstrual cycle or to taking birth control pills. The hands are the part of the body most often affected. Rings on the fingers and constricting clothing or pack straps should be removed or loosened. Swelling of the feet and ankles should be treated by rest and elevation of the legs. Facial swelling, especially if severe enough to shut the eyes, requires descent. In general, check for other symptoms, and if any of the serious ones are present, descend. Otherwise, if the swelling is not especially uncomfortable or disabling, cautious ascent can continue. But such swelling can be an early indication of failure of the body to adapt to high altitudes. A diuretic to increase urination can be administered if swelling is a problem, but again, watch for other serious symptoms.

CE or swelling of the brain is a serious disorder that fortunately is not common at the altitudes trekkers visit. Nevertheless, it has killed quite a few. It usually occurs after a week or more at high altitudes and begins with mild symptoms that progress to the serious ones. Usually the heart and lung symptoms are not prominent. Characteristic features are severe lassitude, lack of coordination, and total apathy, leading to coma and death. Do not leave such a person alone assuming that he is tired. Check for ataxia (loss of coordination) and descend. Oxygen and steroids may be useful adjuncts in treatment. For those trained in the use of an ophthalmoscope, swelling of the optic nerve in the eye can be an indication of problems. Difficulty with the tandem walking test is probably better as an early sign.

HARH or bleeding in the retinas of the eye is more common at extreme altitudes than at those the trekker is likely to reach. But it does happen to trekkers occasionally and usually is symptomless unless the vision clouds somewhat, or the bleeding is near the macula or center of visual acuity in the eye. Double vision or noticeable blind spots are sufficient cause for descent. Vision clears and bleeding resolves at lower altitudes.

All this may seem frightening to the trekker bound for the heights, but the information has to be put in perspective. If you have previous high altitude experience, you have some idea of what to expect (though altitude illness continues to strike groups led by Himalayan "experts"). If you have not been to high altitudes, don't be scared away from enjoying the mountains of Nepal. Be prudent. Ascend at a rate appropriate for the entire party—that is at the rate appropriate for the individual having the greatest difficulty. Know the symptoms of altitude illness and what to do about them. If descent becomes necessary for some members of the party, make sure they are not sent down alone, but are cared for by responsible, informed people. Don't always assume that your hired employees understand altitude illness. There have been incidents in the past when people with obvious serious altitude illness were put into tents to rest unobserved and were discovered dead in the morning. With people better informed today, this shouldn't happen. Above all, use common sense. You are not in Nepal to race up to base camp even if it kills you, but to enjoy the country and its people in all their varied beauty.

Foot Care

It is easier to prevent foot problems than to treat them. Well-fitting boots or shoes and proper socks are a must (see Chapter 3). Blisters tend to form on the same spots time and again, so prophylactic application of moleskin or adhesive tape is beneficial. Tincture of benzoin can be applied to the skin to toughen it. The tape or moleskin tends to spread the friction over a larger area and reduce local stress between layers of the skin. When you feel a tender or hot spot on the skin while walking, stop and investigate. Put a generous piece of moleskin or adhesive tape over the area. Don't remove it for several days; otherwise you may pull some skin off with it. Rather than wait for hot spots to develop, begin your trek with moleskin applied to potential areas.

It is important to keep the feet dry. Change socks frequently in hot weather, and do not wash or soak your feet too often. By keeping feet dry, you develop callouses over pressure points, and this protects your feet against blisters. Sometimes callouses can get too thick and cause painful problems. Soaking them in warm water will soften them, and they can sometimes be peeled back with a knife.

Once a blister has formed, there are two schools of thought on what to do. Some advocate leaving the blister alone, in fact protecting it by cutting a hole of the same diameter as the blister in a piece of moleskin and applying that around the blister. Several thicknesses of moleskin may be necessary in order to have the moleskin level with the top of the blister. Eventually the blister will go away of its own accord. The alternative is to drain the blister with a needle. Sterilize the needle in a flame until it turns red hot and allow it to cool. The needle should be inserted at the edge of the blister right next to the good skin. Then apply a sterile dressing or some moleskin. I prefer the latter routine.

Do not go barefoot in Nepal. The risk of picking up infections is great. Hookworm is spread this way.

Aches, Strains, and Sahib's Knee

Various muscle aches and strains often result from hiking and carrying a pack. if you get these, lighten the load or reduce the activity. If pain is particularly severe, take two aspirin tablets every six hours. Soaking the painful area in hot water usually helps, as does an elastic bandage on knees and ankles when you must continue walking.

Absorb the shock of the descent by bending the knees when the lower foot contacts the ground. Take short, choppy strides. Once the quadricep muscles involved get into shape, this method is much less tiring than keeping the knees stiff. Turning feet sideways on steep descents is also helpful. Be sure to keep your shoes or boots laced tightly during descents to avoid toe blisters. If you take long strides with your legs fully outstretched, the pads of cartilage in the kneejoint and the supporting ligaments will absorb the shock. Injury or strain of these parts is called "Sahib's Knee" and it demands that you stay off your feet until the knees heal. If any walking must be done, wrap an elastic bandage around the knee and three to four inches above and below it. Moist heat may also help, as will aspirin. A good preventive measure is to strengthen the quadricep muscles by raising the legs with knees unbent and weights on the ankles.

Hypothermia

This condition, often termed exposure, occurs when loss of body heat exceeds gain, and body core temperature drops. The body gains heat by digesting food, from an external source, and through muscular activity, including shivering. Loss occurs through respiration, evaporation, conduction, radiation, and convection. The combination of physical exhaustion and wet or insufficient clothing, increased by failure to eat, dehydration, and high altitude, can result in death in a very short time, even at temperatures above freezing. People venturing into cold, high regions must take adequate steps to prevent hypothermia, and should be able to recognize its signs and symptoms. Be especially alert to its development in lowland porters who may be inadequately clothed for cold.

Initial symptoms of hypothermia are marked shivering and pale skin, followed by poor coordination, apathy, confusion, and fatigue. As temperature drops further, speech becomes slurred, and the victim has difficulty walking. Even at this stage, an external source of heat is needed to warm the victim. Further lowering of core temperature results in cessation of shivering, irrationality, memory lapses, and hallucinations. This is followed by increased muscular rigidity, stupor, and decreased pulse and respiration. Unconsciousness and death soon follow. Symptoms can appear in a few hours after the onset of bad weather, and the situation can quickly progress to the point where the victim cannot perform the functions necessary for survival. Hypothermia is easily diagnosed with a low-reading thermometer. Mild degrees of hypothermia are present when body temperature is below 94°F (34.4°C).

Treatment consists of applying heat rapidly to the person's body core. Remove wet clothing and put the person in a sleeping bag together with a source of heat—a warm naked person. If possible feed the victim warm drinks and sweets. Set up a tent, dig a snow cave, or seek shelter. On one of my treks, a companion developed hypothermia on a high rainy pass. Taking turns, we carried him down to a pasturing shelter where I put him in my sleeping bag with me to warm him up. He recovered the next day.

Frostbite

Frostbite is a condition of frozen body tissues. Fingers, toes, ears, noses, and chins are most commonly affected. Fortunately it is rare in trekkers because the temperature extremes necessary are not usually encountered for long periods of time. But it has happened. Prevention is a matter of having adequate clothing and equipment, eating adequate food, and avoiding dehydration and exhaustion. Extreme altitudes increase the potential of the problem, as does a previous history of frostbite. Frostbite can occur at relatively low temperatures if there is significant wind and if the victims are inadequately equipped and suffer from dehydration and exhaustion. Affected tissues initially become cold, painful, and pale. As the condition progresses, they become numb. The trekker may then forget about the problem with serious consequences.

An earlier reversible stage is frostnip. At this stage the affected area becomes numb and white. Treatment consists of rapid rewarming by placing the part against a warm area of the body—an armpit, a hand, the stomach of the victim or another trekker. Once normal color, feeling, and consistency is restored, the part can be used, providing it is not allowed to freeze again. A part of the body that has suffered frostnip before is more likely to get frostbite again.

Once an extremity has become frozen and seriously frostbitten, it is best to keep it that way until help and safety can be reached. A frozen foot can be walked on to leave the cold area. Do not rub snow on the frozen area. Once feasible, the treatment is rapid rewarming in a water bath between 100° F (37.7° C) and 108° F (42.2° C). Thereafter the victim requires expert care in a hospital and is not able to walk. Like most medical problems associated with trekking, prevention is far better than treatment.

Heat Injury

Not only does travel in Nepal pose problems in coping with extreme cold, but also in dealing with extreme heat. Both can happen during the same trek if it is from the hot lowlands to the cold, windy, snowy heights. Heat produced by the body is eliminated mostly by the skin through evaporation of perspiration. Acclimatization to heat takes about a week. When the body becomes able to sweat more without losing more salt, the ability to exercise in a hot environment improves. Maladaptation to heat can be prevented by an adequate intake of fluids and salt. Thirst mechanisms and salt hunger may not work adequately, so extra salt and water should be consumed. In humid regions where evaporation is limited, it is a good idea to rest in the shade during the hottest part of the day. Cover the head and wear light colored clothing to reflect sunlight.

Signs and symptoms of heat exhaustion are a rapid heart rate, faintness and perhaps nausea, vomiting, and headaches. Blood supply to the brain and other organs is inadequate because of shunting of blood to the skin. The patient's temperature is normal. If the victim is treated with shaded rest, fluids, and salt, recovery is usually rapid.

Heat stroke is a failure of the sweating and heat regulation process, usually because of fatigue of the sweat glands themselves. The victim rapidly becomes aware of extreme heat, then becomes confused, uncoordinated (ataxic), delirious, or unconscious. Characteristically, the body temperature is very high, 105° F (40.6° C), or higher. The skin feels hot and dry and does not sweat. Treat immediately by undressing the victim and cooling him by any means available. Immersion in cool water, soaking with wet cloths, and fanning are all appropriate. Massage the limbs vigorously to promote circulation. Continue cooling the body until the temperature is below 102° F (38.9° C). Start cooling again if the temperature rises. The victim should be watched closely for the next few days. Strenuous exercise should be avoided.

Animal Bites

Loud, threatening dogs are sometimes met along the trail. They threaten mostly, but just to be sure, carry a long stick and pass them assertively. I particularly remember the angry dogs in Jubing. Often you meet large Tibetan mastiffs, but they are usually chained, except possibly at night and near herders' camps.

In case of an animal bite, try to capture the beast and keep it alive for seven to ten days. If the animal is healthy after that, you do not have to worry about rabies. A dead animal's brain can be examined for rabies by medical personnel, but this is not as reliable as direct observation of a live animal.

Often a dog's bite can be explained considering the circumstances surrounding it. In such cases, it is wise to inquire seven to ten days after the incident to see if the animal has undergone any unusual changes. But in case of an unprovoked, unexplained attack, get yourself and the animal, if possible, to Kathmandu as soon as possible. Two incidents of dog bite occurred during our treks in 1969 and 1970. Once a person entered a courtyard quickly, and without looking, thrust a leg near a bitch that was nursing her pups. Circumstances explained the bite and observation of the animal several days later alleviated any worries. Another time, I heard squeaking noises coming from a covered basket and went over to investigate. As I crouched down to look, the mother of the litter in the basket sunk her teeth into my posterior! Again explainable.

Treat a bite by washing the site immediately with soap and water as well as salt and water. Wash and irrigate the wound for half an hour or more. In animal experiments, washing alone has been shown to be effective in preventing rabies after inoculation of a wound with rabies virus. Irrigation with a quaternary ammonium solution (cetrimide or benzalkonium chloride, also found in the antiseptic Savlon) within twelve hours has also been found effective in animal tests.

If rabies is suspected, speed of evacuation is essential so that the vaccine can be administered as soon as possible. Once symptoms occur in the person bitten, it is too late to begin treatment. The decision to seek help may be difficult if the animal bite is unprovoked and the animal appears healthy. If other animals in the area have been acting strangely recently, there may be an epidemic. In order to contract rabies, it is necessary that the animal's saliva penetrate the skin, either through the bite itself or through a previous wound.

Leeches

Leeches, abundant in the forests above 4000 ft (1220 m) during the monsoon, usually gain entrance to the skin at the ankles or around the neck. You may feel a sharp sting at the moment you are bitten, but often the pests are discovered only later. It is best to stop periodically and remove them from your socks, shoes, and anywhere they may have gained access. Remove them by holding a lighted match or cigarette to them, or by putting salt or iodine on them. Pulling them off also works and probably does not result in the head remaining imbedded more often than the other methods. The resulting wound tends to bleed considerably afterward. Control it with a clean pressure dressing, and if it gets secondarily infected afterwards, treat it as you would any infection. Try one of the leech repellents mentioned in The Medical Kit section of this chapter.

Small Wounds and Infections

It is important to clean with soap and water any wound that breaks the skin. Avoid using the common antiseptics, as they may damage healthy tissue. A large wound should be covered with a sterile dressing that should be changed periodically until a good clot has formed and healing is well underway. It is then best left uncovered.

A wound infection is often the result of contamination and is evidenced by signs of inflammation and pain a day or more after it occurs. In this case, soak the wound in hot water for at least fifteen minutes. Afterwards, cover it with a sterile dressing. With severe spreading infections, one antibiotic pill should be taken every six hours, preferably on an empty stomach. For abscesses such as boils or carbuncles, the treatment is similar to that for wound infections, except that antibiotics probably do little to help unless the boils are a recurring problem. Drain the abscesses by soaking them in hot water for fifteen minutes five or six times a day.

Constipation

This is not nearly the problem diarrhea can be. A bulky diet usually prevents difficulties with bowel movements. If constipation does occur, drink plenty of fluids. Try a cup or two of hot water, tea, or coffee upon waking in the morning. In rare cases, mild laxatives may be needed. Better to just wait until the bowels do the job on their own.

Burns and Sunburns

Burns are common among Nepali infants who walk or crawl too close to a fire and fall in. The severity of a burn depends on its area, its depth, and its location on the body. First degree burns are superficial—they do not kill any of the tissue, but produce only redness of the skin. Second degree burns kill the upper portion of the skin and cause blisters. In third degree burns damage extends through the skin into the underlying tissues. First degree burns require no treatment, but for the others, wash the area gently with iced or cold water, if possible, and cover with a sterile dressing. Ointments are of no use and may increase the danger of infection. Burns that cover more than twenty percent of the body surface are usually accompanied by shock, which is a serious threat to life. Attempt to get the injured person to drink plenty of fluids mixed with salt. Aspirin or codeine, two tablets every six hours, may help relieve pain. There is little you can do for extensive burns except evacuate the person to medical help.

Sunburn is common among trekkers visiting high altitudes where there is less atmosphere to filter solar radiation, and where snow and ice can reflect additional radiation. Effective sunscreening agents are listed as contents of the medical kit. Be sure to protect the lips and under the chin and nose when on snow. When sunburn occurs, it should be treated in the same way as any other burn.

Eye protection in the form of dark glasses is needed on snow, and generally at high altitudes. In an emergency, lenses made of cardboard with a thin slit to see through can be used. Hair combed over the face, a method favored by Sherpas and Tibetans, is effective. Otherwise, snow blindness, a painful temporary condition, can result. The condition gets better in a few days. Darkness and cold compresses over the eyes may help relieve pain. For severe pain, take aspirin or codeine, two tablets every six hours.

Common Cold

Upper respiratory infections including the common cold are very prevalent in Nepal. Medical science does not seem to offer any widely agreed upon remedies. Linus Pauling, a Nobel Prize winning chemist, has popularized taking large doses of Vitamin C to prevent a cold, and to cure it in its early stages. But there is certainly less than universal confidence in this method. There are plenty of other ways to deal with a common cold. Rest if possible, drink plenty of fluids, and take two aspirin tablets every four to six hours. Do not smoke. Gargle with warm water and salt for a sore throat. Decongestants have been used for years by many people. Recently some evidence from experiments has suggested that the antihistamine chlorpheniramine maleate may be helpful in reducing the annoying symptoms of nasal stuffiness associated with a cold. You may want to try taking a tablet (4 mg) four times a day. I would avoid decongestants containing many different drugs. People with high temperatures should not continue trekking. Normal temperature is 98.6°F (37°C), but there is no reason to be concerned if temperatures measured orally remain below 100°F (38.9°C).

Coughing

Coughing normally brings up sputum and is beneficial in ridding the body of it. Sometimes, however, an annoying cough occurs that even after a few days, does not produce sputum. If this happens, take one or two tablets of codeine (30 mg), every six hours for a day. Do not attempt to suppress those coughs that produce some sputum. Read the section on altitude illness to make sure you are not dealing with a form of it. General measures in treating an annoying cough include drinking plenty of fluids and breathing moist air. The latter is difficult in dry mountain areas. Hard candy or throat lozenges may provide some relief at night.

In addition to altitude illness, serious coughing could be due to a pneumonia. An affected individual would have high fevers, sputum thick with pus and streaked with blood (but not frothy) and often localized chest pain that is most severe at the end of a deep breath. The sick person is usually too ill to travel. Treatment consists of two antibiotic tablets every six hours, aspirin for fever and pain, and plenty of fluids.

Conjunctivitis

This is an inflammation of the delicate membrane that covers the surface of the eye and the undersurface of the eyelid. The eye appears red and the blood vessels on its surface are engorged. The flow of tears is increased and exudate may be crusted in the margins of the eyelids and eyelashes. Irritation from the ubiquitous smoke in Nepali homes is a common cause, especially among the Nepalis. Apply ophthalmic antibiotic ointment or solution beneath the lower eyelid next to the eye every four hours until the symptoms disappear.

Appendicitis

Sometimes trekkers, out in the remote hills, are worried about appendicitis. The chances of it occurring are very slight, so this is offered only for your peace of mind. The pain usually starts in the mid-abdomen, soon shifts to the right lower quadrant, and becomes accompanied by nausea. Persistent diarrhea is rare with appendicitis. In a case where appendicitis is suspected, give two tablets of an antibiotic every six hours and evacuate the patient. Cases of acute appendicitis may respond to antibiotics and even improve by themselves without treatment.

Dental Problems

Dental problems are unlikely among trekkers if they see a dentist before coming to Nepal. For simple toothache, a small wad of cotton soaked in oil of cloves and inserted in the appropriate cavity often relieves pain. Codeine and aspirin, two tablets every four to six hours, help relieve severe pain. Abscesses characterized by swelling of the gums and jaw near the site of the toothache, and often accompanied by fever and chills, call for extraction. In the interim, take an antibiotic tablet every six hours.

Sinusitis

Sinusitis is an inflammation of the sinuses, often following a cold. It is characterized by headaches of a dull nature, pain in the sinuses, fever, chills, weakness, and swelling of the facial area. Some or all of these symptoms may be present. For severe symptoms, record the fever and chill temperatures, rest, drink plenty of fluids, and take two aspirin every four hours for the fever and phenylephrine nose drops three times a day. Start an antibiotic if the temperature is less than 97°F (36.0°C) during a chill or more than 101°F (38.3°C) when feverish. In this case, take two tablets of the antibiotic immediately, followed by one tablet every six hours, preferably on an empty stomach. This course should be continued for seven days no matter when the symptoms subside.

Psychological and Emotional Problems

Trekkers and travelers to exotic countries can, and sometimes do, have emotional problems adjusting. Reasons are many: being separated from friends and familiar places; adjusting to a very different environment; being seemingly surrounded by poverty, filth, and disease; realizing that you are essentially alone a week or two from "civilization" and 15,000 mi (24,000 km) from "home" by plane; being sick and not eating well; being dirty and unkempt; and realizing that trekking is not all it was cracked up to be. (I can well remember squatting in the bush with diarrhea on the first few days of my first trek in Nepal on my first journey away from North America, and pondering whether this was my reaction to being separated from my familiar environment.)

As with most health matters, prevention is the key to not getting "burned out." Steps for prevention depend on the individual. For some, it may be ensuring that you are with friends with whom you can share the experience. For those who are fastidious in their personal habits, it may mean a daily bath, shaving every day or every other day, keeping hair combed, and putting on a clean change of clothes every few days. For some it may mean acceptance of the reality that the schedule they have set for themselves is too ambitious, or that difficulties in adjusting to altitude will prevent them from getting to that famous viewpoint or crossing that pass. For all, it should include being aware of what is in store during the trek and being prepared for it psychologically as well as physically.

What if you are getting quite depressed or close to a "nervous breakdown?" First, do some familiar, relaxing, comforting routines, such as bathing, shaving, washing your clothes, or putting on clean ones. If alone, find other trekkers to join. If carrying a heavy load, hire a porter. If sick and weak, rest and eat better foods frequently during the day. If consuming marijuana and other mood altering drugs, stop them. If appalled by the conditions in Nepal and among the Nepalis, take comfort in the fact that you can leave if you choose. If your mood does not improve, head back to Kathmandu or Pokhara by plane if possible. But be careful not to end up waiting a week for a plane when you could have walked in three days. If you have trouble adjusting to conditions in Nepal, don't go to India.

Few people end up having to curtail their trek in Nepal for these reasons. Rather, many will undergo a "culture shock" upon returning home as, based on their experience in Nepal, they question the values of the environment they have grown up in. But trekking in Nepal is not for everyone. If it isn't for you, don't despair. There are many other superb activities elsewhere waiting for you.

EMERGENCY CARE AND RESCUE FACILITIES

Nepal's health plan involves setting up hospitals staffed by physicians in each of the seventy-five districts. They are intended to provide secondary health care. Primary health care is provided by health posts scattered throughout each district. These are staffed by paramedical personnel and provide basic facilities. Tertiary care is provided by a few major hospitals throughout the country, with the best in Kathmandu. However, to date, district hospitals are set up in only about forty-five places.

If faced with an emergency in the hills, you must choose between trying to reach one of the hospitals or clinics listed here and trying to get word to Kathmandu to effect an air rescue. If an air rescue is necessary, head for a STOL landing strip if one is near, or send to Kathmandu for a helicopter. Most STOL airstrips do not have frequent or even regular service, so a fixed wing aircraft should be sent for. Air rescue is usually impossible during the monsoon.

Hospitals, Aid Posts, Airstrips, and Radio Stations

HELAMBU, GOSAINKUND, LANGTANG

The only facilities available are at the government hospital in Trisuli where there is also a radio and telephone to Kathmandu. A STOL strip is located near Kyangjin in the Langtang Valley. The nearest radio station is on the Bhote Kosi at Rasuwa Garhi on the Tibetan border. In winter, the STOL strip in Thangmojet across the Bhote Kosi may be the only recourse. There is also a little-used strip at Likhu near Trisuli.

NORTH OF POKHARA

There is a regional government hospital, radio service to Kathmandu, and an airport in Pokhara. Radio stations are located in Kusma, Baglung, Beni, and

Jomosom. STOL strips are found in Jomosom and in Balewa south of Baglung across the river from Kusma. There are district hospitals in Baglung and Jomosom.

SOLU-KHUMBU AND ROLWALING

There are radio stations at Jiri, Namche Bazaar, Kunde, Tengboche, Pheriche, Salleri, Charikot (south of Rolwaling), and Lamobagar (north of the Rolwaling River). STOL strips are found at Jiri, Phaphlu, Lukla, and Shyangboche. There are government health facilities in Jiri, Namche Bazaar, and Charikot. Hospitals built by Sir Edmund Hillary and staffed by New Zealand physicians are found in Kunde and Phaphlu. There is a Trekkers' Aid Post operated by the Himalayan Rescue Association at Pheriche. It is staffed by a doctor during most of the trekking season.

FROM NAMCHE BAZAAR TOWARD DARJEELING

There are radio stations at Chainpur, Khanbari, Taplejung, Phidim, Bhojpur, Terhathum, Dhankuta, Dharan, Ilam, and Chandragari, and STOL strips at Tumlingtar and Taplejung. There are government hospitals in Chainpur, Taplejung, Bhojpur, and Dhankuta. The British Military Hospital is at Dharan.

POKHARA TO KATHMANDU

In addition to the facilities in Pokhara and Trisuli already mentioned, there are radio stations in Ghorkha and Kuncha; a STOL strip at Palungtar near Tadi Pokhari; and a government hospital at Ghorkha. The United Mission runs a hospital at Ampipal.

WESTERN NEPAL

In addition to the facilities in Baglung and Beni already mentioned, there are radio stations in Jumla and Tansen. STOL strips are found at Dhorpatan, Jumla, and RaRa Lake. There is a government hospital in Jumla.

The radio stations listed here are civilian operated, part of the telecommunication system. The messages are delivered through the Telecommunication Central Office in Kathmandu. In addition, there are other wireless systems in operation, but their use is normally restricted. In an emergency, it may be possible to use them. Ask at police check posts or army installations.

Emergency Messages and Rescues

In writing a message and organizing a rescue, it is important to provide the proper information and make sure it reaches the proper place. It is wise to send several messages to different organizations to ensure that at least one is delivered. Addresses should include enough redundancy to speed delivery. Rescue messages should be sent to one or more of these:

—The trekking agency that organized the trek, if applicable.

—Royal Nepal Airlines Corporation, Charter Division, RNAC Building, New Road, Kathmandu (Phone 14511, extension 147 or 137).

—The embassy or consulate of the victim.

—Himalayan Rescue Association, G.P.O. Box 435, Ghantaghar, Kathmandu Phone: 16514.

The message should contain the following information:

—Degree of urgency. **Most Immediate** means death is likely within twenty-four hours. **As Soon As Possible** is used for all other cases in which helicopter rescue is justified.

Health Care

—The location, including whether the victim will remain in one place or be moved down along a particular route. If the pickup place is above 10,000 ft (3000 m), give the altitude. Generally, 17,000 ft (5000 m) is the limit for helicopter pickups.

—Medical information, including the type of sickness or injury, and whether oxygen or a stretcher (as for back injuries) is needed.

—The name, nationality, age, and sex of all people to be evacuated.

—The sender's name and organization, along with information on the method and source of payment for the rescue. Generally, RNAC will not fly rescues without written assurance of payment. This can sometimes be provided by the embassy of the victim.

A rescue can take several days, especially if a runner has to be sent with the message, or if there is airplane trouble. It is wise to move the person along the route, waiting each day until 10 A.M. to start. In each sleeping place, a large smoky fire should be built each morning, and a landing site cleared and marked with a large X, preferably using international orange garments.

The cost of a helicopter rescue is high—an hour of helicopter time costs over $500. This has to be borne by the party involved, unless rescue insurance has been taken out previously. Some trekkers might wish to obtain a comprehensive travel, accident, and rescue insurance policy before they leave home. Some of the general insurance companies in Kathmandu may be able to provide this, but I have had no personal experience with them. If you have not dealt with a trekking agency, it may be prudent to make yourself known at your country's embassy in Kathmandu, in case they receive a rescue telegram. Westerners working in remote areas in Nepal have posted bonds in Kathmandu to pay for a rescue should it be needed. It all depends on your inclination and life-style.

6 NEPALI FOR TREKKERS

To speak a foreign language well . . . we must imitate and mimic the whole time. We must never imagine that our efforts will be laughed at. There are so many dialects . . . that speaking incorrectly does not sound so odd as it might in another country.

G.G. Rogers, *Colloquial Nepali*

Nepali is an Indo-European language that is really not very difficult to learn. Here an attempt is made to introduce the trekker to enough Nepali words and phrases to get by in the hills. It is especially advisable for those trekking without an English-speaking guide to make some effort to learn minimal Nepali. Nevertheless, people have trekked without guides and without any knowledge of the language.

The problem of learning the language is complicated by the lack of suitable books for the student. The best aids available at present are the Summer Institute of Linguistics' *Conversational Nepali* course, the book *Basic Course in Spoken Nepali,* and the *Basic Gurkhali Dictionary* (see Recommended Reading). Without some principles of grammar, the dictionary is of little use. Brief phrase books, which occasionally become available in bookstores in Kathmandu, are of some value.

PRONUNCIATION AND GRAMMAR

Nepali is written in Devanagari script. In order to avoid learning it, a system of transliteration to the Roman script is used here. Many of the letters denote their usual sounds. Only the special sounds are described.

STRESS

The stress usually falls on the first syllable (**chhaá mal**) unless the first syllable has a short vowel and is followed in the second syllable by a long one. Then the stress falls on the second syllable (**pa kaaú nos**).

VOWELS

a	like the *a* in *balloon.*
aa	long like the *a* in *father* or *car.*
i	like *ee* in *beer,* the short and long forms are pronounced similarly.
u	like *oo* in *mood* or *root,* again with long and short forms similar.
e	like *a* in *skate* or like the French *e* as in *cafe.*
ai	a diphthong with first element like the *a* in *arise* and the second like the *y* in *city.* Together, somewhat like the *ay* in *laying,* but not like the sound of the word *eye.*
au	a dipthong in which the first element is like the *a* in arise and the second like the *u* in *put.*
o	like *o* in *bowl* or *go.*
aau, aai, and eu	not diphthongs, but vowels pronounced separately one after the other.

CAPITALIZED LETTERS

Except for T, R, and D, a capital denotes nasalization of that letter.

DENTAL AND RETROFLEX CONSONANTS

t   pronounced unaspirated with the tip of the tongue on the teeth as in the French *petite*.

T   like the *t* in *little,* with the tongue slightly recurved when it meets the roof of the mouth.

d   dental like the French *d* in which the blade of the tongue is pressed behind the upper teeth.

D   pronounced with retroflexion of the tongue. Turn the tongue back in the mouth, press the underside of it against the palate and pronounce the *d* in *dog*.

R   also pronounced with retroflexion of the tongue.

ASPIRATED CONSONANTS

Nepalis differentiate between aspirated and unaspirated consonants. This is quite difficult for native English speakers. Aspiration is indicated by an *h* following the consonant. Consciously avoid breathing hard or aspirating on the consonants when not followed by an *h*.

The exception to the above rule in the transliteration scheme employed in this book applies to *ch* and *chh*. Only the latter is aspirated.

chh   press the blade of the tongue behind the upper teeth and try to say *ts*. At the same time exert strong breath pressure so that when the tongue is released from the teeth, there is a loud emission of breath. Listen to a native Nepali speaker.

ch   the unaspirated form as in *chalk, Chinese.*

MISCELLANEOUS

k   like *c* in *cat.*

y   like *y* in *yeast.*

s   like *s* in *song.*

j   press the blade of the tongue against the upper teeth with the tip of the tongue pointed down and say *j* as in *January*. It is somewhat like *dz* and is especially found in words coming from Tibetan dialects.

Other consonants should present little difficulty. When two consonants come together, be sure to pronounce them individually.

GRAMMAR NOTES

• All verbs come at the end of the sentence.

• Questions are formed simply by raising the voice pitch at the end of the sentence.

• The *ne* ending at the end of a verb, such as **janne** or **basne**, is a present tense neutral form, which can be used with any of the personal pronouns.

• When translated into Nepali, the prepositions *in, to, for,* and others are suffixed to the words they refer to. Throughout this chapter, these "postpositions" have been enclosed in parentheses for easy identification. For example, **malaai,** meaning *to me,* has been written **ma(laai)** *me (to).*

PRACTICE BEFORE YOU GO

> *To aquire a language is to learn the spoken utterance. The natural receptive medium is, therefore, the ear, not the eye. It is an art very much akin to music.*
>
> G. G. Rogers, *Colloquial Nepali*

The following may seem formidable if you are just going on a short trek. Do not be daunted. It is here in case you need it. You will find, however, that a minimal knowledge of the language is indispensable on the trail where people normally cannot speak or understand a word of English.

If you have a few days in Kathmandu before you set off, you can practice a little in a familiar and exceedingly helpful environment.

First ask your hotel receptionist or some friendly waiter in a restaurant you frequent to read the word list to you. Repeat it after him until you get a feel for the pronunciation. This should take about 15 minutes and will probably make you instant friends with your Nepali helper. Then try it out. For example, practice your Nepali in a restaurant.

Say:

chiyaa   dinos
tea   please give me

or:

bill dinos
bill   please give me

or:

menu   dinos
menu   please give me

Later when it is time to pay, say:

khaanaa   (ko)   kati?
food   for   how much

raising your voice pitch at the end of the sentence to indicate a question. Have the person answer in Nepali rather then English. People are usually more than happy to repeat the Nepali number for you and translate it into English. If you feel clumsy or shy about any of this, always smile. It works like magic to ease every situation. Smiling is the Nepali way of getting over tense or slightly embarrassing situations.

When you go to a bazaar and wish to buy an item, point to it and say:

yasko   kati?
for this   how much

The person may answer in Nepali or English, but try to come away from the transaction able to understand the Nepali number.

If you do this each time, you should soon be able to understand spoken Nepali numbers, or at least the main ones. This is a tremendous asset on the trail where people often do not know the English numbers.

If you do not understand, or want something repeated, say:

hajur
excuse me

By the time you reach this stage, you will already be experiencing the hospitality that even the tiniest knowledge of Nepali inspires.

Now try asking for directions:

paaTan jaane baaTo ho?
Patan going to road is it

meaning: Is this the road to Patan? On the trail where there are no road signs, this direction finding question is essential.

Now add some vocabulary to the skeleton. If you do not want much food, say:

ali ali dinos
very little please give me

Ask for **dhai** instead of yogurt, **paani** instead of water. Ask for the time, bargain, use the terms of address.

By asking questions in Kathmandu, you can get used to hearing some of the many types of responses. Basic communication in Nepali will lose some of its terrors, and you will be far more competent in dealing with situations in the non-English-speaking world on the trail.

It's easy. Now go straight to your hotel receptionist and begin reading the word list with him.

WORD LISTS

FOOD

bananas	**keraa**	meat	**maasu**
beans	**simi**	milk	**dudh**
beer	**chang** (Tibetan),	millet	**kodo**
	jAAR (Nepali)	onions	**pyaaj**
biscuits	**biskooT**	oranges	
bread		(tangerines)	**suntalla**
(unleavened)	**roti, chapaati**	peanuts	**badaam**
cabbage	**bandaa kopi**	potatoes	**aalu**
carrots	**gaajar**	pumpkin	**parsi**
cauliflour	**kauli**	rice (uncooked)	**chaamal**
chicken	**kukhura**	cooked rice	**bhaat**
chillies	**khursaani**	rice and lentils	**daal bhaat**
corn	**makai**	roasted flour	**saatu** (Nepali),
eggs	**phul**		**tsampa** (Tibetan)
boiled eggs	**umaleko phul**	salt	**nun**
fish	**maachhaa**	snacks	**khaajaa**
flour	**piTho, aaTa**	soy beans	**bhaTmaas**
white flour	**maidaa**	spirits	**rakshi**
whole wheat		sugar	**chini**
flour	**gahUko piTho**	sweets	**miThai**
food	**khaanaa**	tea	**chiyaa**
greens (spinach)	**saag**	tomatoes	**golbhEDa**
lemons	**nibuwaa**	vegetables	**tarkaari**
lentils	**daal**	water	**paani**
limes	**kaagati**	drinking water	**khaane paani**
mangoes	**Amp**	boiled water	**umaleko paani**

hot water	**taato paani**
washing water	**dhune paani**
yogurt	**dhai, mAI**

OTHER USEFUL NOUNS

airport	**giraund**
good bridge	**pul**
makeshift bridge	**saanghu**
cave	**wodaar**
distance unit (two to three miles)	**kosh**
dog	**kukur**
downhill	**worallo**
friend	**saathi**
my frlend	**mero saathi**
hill	**lekh, dandaa, pahaaD**
inn, lodging	**bhaTTi**
kerosene	**maTTitel**
large knife	**khukuri**
lake	**pokhri, tal**
light (lamp)	**batti**
load	**bhaari**
pass	**bhanjyang**
porter	**kulli**
river	**khola, kosi, nadi**
road	**baaTo**
snow	**hiU**
snow peak	**himal**
spoon	**chamchaa**
stone rest spot	**chautaara**
store	**pasal**
temporary shelter	**goTh**
toilet	**chharpi**
uphill	**ukaalo**
volume unit (2½ cups)	**maanaa**

OFTEN-USED VERBS

please ask	**sodhnos**
to buy	**kinnu**
please cook	**pakaaunos**
enough	**pugyo**
can get	**paainchha**
please give	**dinos**
go	**jaane**
impossible (It cannot be done)	**sakdaaina**
possible (It can be done)	**sakchha**

I need	**chaahinchha, chaaiyo**
please sit down, stay	**basnos**
stay, stop, rest, sit	**basne**
it will take (two hours)	**(dui ghanTaa) laagchha**
I don't understand	**bujdaina**

ADJECTIVES AND ADVERBS

after	**pachhi**
good	**ramro**
not good	**ramro chhaina, naramro**
here	**yahAA**
very little	**ali ali**
slowly	**bistaari**
spicy (hot)	**piro**
sweet	**guliyo**
tasty	**miTho**
for this	**yasko**
where	**kahAA**
quickly	**chhito**

TIME

now	**ahile**
today	**aaja**
tomorrow	**bholi**
day after tomorrow	**parshi**
yesterday	**hijo**
hour	**ghanTaa**
day	**din**
week	**haptaa**
morning	**bihaana**
early morning	**saberai**
afternoon (12 A.M. to 4 P.M.)	**diuso**
evening (4 P.M. to 8 P.M.)	**beluki**
night	**raati**
What time is it?	**kati bajyo**

MONEY

small change	**paisaa**
how much	**kati**

paisaa is the smallest unit
sukaa = 25 **paisaa**
mohar = 50 **paisaa**
rupiyAA = 100 **paisaa**

DAYS OF THE WEEK

Sunday	**aitabaar**
Monday	**sombaar**
Tuesday	**mangalbaar**
Wednesday	**budhabaar**
Thursday	**bihibaar**
Friday	**sukrabaar**
Saturday	**sanibaar**

NUMBERS

1	**ek**	13	**tera**
2	**dui**	14	**chaudha**
3	**tin**	15	**pandhra**
4	**chaar**	16	**sora**
5	**pAAnch**	17	**satra**
6	**chha**	18	**aThara**
7	**saat**	19	**unnaais**
8	**aaTH**	20	**bis**
9	**nau**	25	**paachis**
10	**das**	30	**tis**
11	**eghaara**	40	**chaalis**
12	**baara**	50	**pachas**
		60	**saaThi**
		70	**sattari**
		75	**pachhattar**
		80	**ashi**
		90	**nabbe**
		100	**say**
		200	**dui say**
		1,000	**ek hajaar**
		½	**aadha**
		1½	**DeDh**
		2½	**aDhaai**

ANSWERS

Nepalis either repeat the verb you have used in your sentence to indicate agreement with you (more frequent), or they use one of the following terms:

it is	**ho**
there is	**chha**
please sit down, stay	**basnos**
okay (polite)	**hunchha**
okay (very polite)	**haas**
okay	**hajur**
yes	**ju**
yes	**A**

On the negative side they might repeat the verb in its negative form:

cannot get	**paaindaaina**
cannot stay	**basnu sakdaaina**
not permitted	**hundaaina**

or they might use the negative form of the verb "to be":

it is not	**hoina**
there is not	**chaaina**
no	**ahA**

Shaking of the head in a diagonal fashion can mean yes. You may initially think it means no.

THANK YOU

Westerners are always eager to thank people as part of common courtesy. While Nepali does have a word connoting gratitude (**dhanyabaad**), native speakers do not use it in the sense that we would. You may hear this word used by some trekkers along the popular trails, and the locals are becoming accustomed to hearing it, but it is still outside of their custom. It is best for trekkers to get used to the Nepali social custom of not thanking, except by using the English words where they are understood. Buddhist highlanders in Nepal (*BhoTiya*) do have a word (**thuDichhe**) that is used more like our "thank you."

PHRASES

Talking to Porters

Here are some useful words and sentences to aid in making arrangements with porters and in giving them instructions on the trail. To avoid misunderstanding later, arrange these details before setting off: the destination; approximately how many days the porters will be needed; the rate per day and whether it includes food; pay for porters returning without a load; and whether the porters have the necessary equipment, especially if you will be traveling through snow or during the monsoon.

I am going to Namche Bazaar.	**namche bazaar jaane.** Namche Bazaar go
I will need porters for one week.	**ek haptaa (ko) kulli chaahinchha.** one week (for) porters need.
I will need five porters for two days.	**dui din (samma) pAAnch kulli** two days (up to) five porters **chaahinchha** need
How much per day?	**din (ko) kati?** day (for) how much
with food?	**khaanaa khaaiera?** food with
without food?	**khaanaa nakhaaiera?** food without
Fifteen rupees without food is enough.	**pandhra rupiyAA khaanaa** fifteen rupees food **nakhaaiera pugchna.** without is enough

For returning, ten rupees per day is enough.

pharkaaunda din (ko) das
returning   day (for) ten
rupiyAA pugchha.
rupees   enough

Without load.

bhaari chhaaina.
load   there is not

With load.

bhaari chha.
load   there is

After one week.

ek haptaa pachhi.
one week after

Do you have warm clothes?

nyaano lugaa chha ?
warm   clothes do you have

Do you have a carrying basket?

doko chha ?
carrying basket do you have

Please show me your warm clothes tomorrow.

nyaano lugaa bholi dekhaaunos.
warm   clothes tomorrow please show

Go quickly.

chhito jaane.
quickly go

Go slowly.

bistaari jaane.
slowly go

Walk near me.

masanga jaane.
with me go

We will stop (stay or rest) now.

ahile basne.
now stay

We will stay here.

yahAA basne.
here stay

We will stop after one hour.

ek ghanTaa pachhi basne.
one hour after stop

Please ask where to stay.

kahAA basne sodhnos.
where stay please ask

Please ask about food.

khaanaa (ko laagi) sodhnos.
food (about) please ask

We need firewood.

daauraa chaahinchha.
firewood need

Please cook food.

khaanaa pakaaunos.
food   please cook

tea.

chiyaa
tea

bread.

roti
bread

Are you hungry?	**bhok laagchha?** hunger strikes
Do you want to rest?	**bisaaune ki?** rest or

Ask and You Will Not Get Lost

Is this the road to Namche Bazaar?	**yo namche bazaar jaane baaTo ho?** this Namche Bazaar going road is this
How many hours to Namche?	**namche (samma) kati ghanTaa** Namche (up to) how many hours **laagchha?** does it take?
It will take one hour.	**ek ghanTaa laagchha.** one hour it will take
Is there an inn in Namche?	**namche (maa) bhaTTi chha?** Namche (in) inn is there
Can we get food in Namche?	**namche (maa) khaanaa paaincha?** Namche (in) food get
Is the trail good enough to take or not?	**baaTo (maa) chhiRnu sakchha** road (on) get through possible **ki sakdaaina?** or impossible
Impossible. Cannot be done.	**sakdaaina.** It cannot be done
Where are you going?	**kahAA jaane?** where go
Can I come with you?	**sangaai jaane?** with you go
What is the name of this town?	**yo gaaU (ko) naam ke ho?** this town (of) name what is
What is the name of the next town on the trail?	**yo baaTo (maa) kun gaaU** this road (on) which town **parchha.?** must it be
Where is there a weekly market?	**haaT bajaar kahAA chha?** market where is there
What is your caste? (ethnic group)	**tapAAlko jaat ke ho?** your caste what is

Finding a Place to Eat or to Stay

Porters can be very helpful in finding a lodging for you in town, especially if they have been over the trail before. If you are on your own, try these sentences:

Where can I get food?	**khaanaa kahAA paainchha?** food where get
There.	**utaa** or **tyahAA.** there
Here.	**yahAA.** here
Please sit down.	**basnos.** please sit down
Can I get food in Namche?	**namche (maa) khaanaa paainchha?** Namche (in) food get
potatoes?	**aalu** potatoes
Where can I stay?	**kahAA basne?** where stay
Is there a place to stay in Namche?	**namche (maa) baas paainchha?** Namche (in) stay get
You cannot stay.	**baas paaindaaina.** stay cannot

Food

ASKING AT THE HOUSE

Can I get food here?	**khaanaa yahAA paainchha?** food here get
biscuits?	**biscooT** biscuit
tea?	**chiyaa** tea
Please cook rice and lentils for me.	**daal bhaat pakaaunos.** lentils rice please cook
Please do not make it too spicy.	**piro nabanaaunos.** hot please do not make

DURING THE MEAL

There is a fairly strict Hindu etiquette to be observed while eating. Breach of these rules is grossly insulting. It is wise, therefore, to read about Nepali customs in Chapter 4 before you venture to eat in a Nepali home.

Please give me more rice.	**bhaat dinos.** rice please give
vegetables.	**tarkaari** vegetables

Give me only a little.	**ali ali dinos.** a little please give
It is tasty.	**miTho chha.** tasty it is
That is enough.	**pugyo** enough

BUYING FOOD TO CARRY WITH YOU

Can I buy flour?	**piTho kinnu paainchha?** flour buy can I
bread?	**roti** bread
uncooked rice?	**chaamal** uncooked rice
Please give me five **maanaas** of flour.	**pAAnch maanaa piTho dinos.** five maanna flour please give

PAYING

How much for this?	**yasko kati?** for this how much
How much for food?	**khaanaa (ko) kati?** food (for) how much
tea?	**chiyaa (ko)** tea (for)
one day?	**ek din (ko)** one day (for)
one **maanaa**?	**ek maanaa (ko)** one maanaa (for)
I will pay only three rupees.	**tin rupiAA maatrai dinchhu.** three rupees only I give
Please give me my change.	**paisaa dinos.** change please give

Getting Someone's Attention

In Nepal, people address each other using kinship terms whether they are related or not. Rather than grunting or shouting "hey you," here are some more pleasant ways of attracting people's attention. Listen and you will hear Nepalis using these terms all the time.

To get a man's attention	**hajur.** (this also means *yes, sir* and *I did not hear you*)

A man a little older than you	**o** **daai** or **daaju.** hey older brother
A woman who is a little older than you	**o** **didi.** hey older sister
A man old enough to be your father	**o** **baabu.** hey father
A woman old enough to be your mother	**o** **amai.** hey mother
A girl younger than you	**o** **bahini.** hey younger sister
A boy younger than you	**o** **bhaai.** hey younger brother
Once you have their attention:	**namaste**, or more politely, **namaskaar.** Translated literally, this greeting means: "I salute the God in you."

Time

People like to ask you for the time on the trail, and if you know the first twelve numbers, you can easily answer.

What time is it?	**kati** **bajyo?** how many bells
It is two o'clock.	**dui** **bajyo** two bells.
I will go today.	**aaja** **jaane.** today go
tomorrow.	**bholi** tomorrow
now.	**ahile** now
I will stay for one day.	**ek** **din** **basne.** one day stay
one week.	**ek** **haptaa** one week
Can we get bread early in the morning?	**roti** **saberai** **paanichha?** bread early morning get

Emergencies

I am sick.	**biraami chhU.** sick I am.
My friend is sick.	**mero saathi biraami chha.** my friend sick is.

Where is a hospital?	**aaspital kahAA chha?**	
	hospital where is	
police post?	**thaanaa**	
	police post	
army post?	**aarmi berik**	
	army barrack	
district headquarters?	**sadar mukaam**	
	headquarters halting place	
radio?	**aabaa**	
	from the sky	
airstrip?	**hawai jahaaj giraund**	
	air vehicle ground	

I have a message to be radioed to Kathmandu.

kaThmaanDu (maa) pathaaune
Kathmandu (to) to send
samaachaar chha.
message there is

Please take it to Namche.

namche (maa) puraaidinos.
Namche (to) please take

I need a person to carry me.

ma (laai) bokne manche chaahiyo.
me (for) carrying man need

Please carry me to Shyangboche.

shyangboche (maa) malaai
Shyangboche (to) me
boknos.
please carry

The author and a native Nepali have prepared a 48-minute cassette of the contents of this chapter. Each word and phrase is spoken once in English, then twice in Nepali. The cassette provides a useful introduction to the language for trekkers. It may be obtained by sending $6.00 in U.S. funds to:

Nepali Language Tape
Post Office Box 122
Seattle, Washington 98111

Please add $1.00 (U.S.) if overseas airmail is desired. Allow six weeks for delivery in U.S. or via airmail overseas, ten weeks otherwise.

SECTION II
THE ROUTES

The fortress town of Jharkot in Mustang. (Ane Haaland)

FOLLOWING THE
ROUTE DESCRIPTIONS

No one goes so far or so fast as the man who does not know where he is going.

H. W. Tilman, *Nepal Himalaya*

In the trail descriptions that follow, treks are not set out on a day-to-day basis. Instead of adhering to a schedule, each party can adjust for long rests or interesting diversions. Those committed to straight traveling can count on covering about six to eight hours of the given route times in a day, allowing a two-hour food stop during mid-morning. In the winter there is less daylight than at other times, and smaller distances can be covered.

In the route descriptions that follow, the times listed between points are generally those I took myself. They *do not* include any rests. This has been strictly adhered to, initially by subtracting all rest times, and more recently by using a chronograph. Over most of the trails I carried a moderately heavy pack.

The times are fairly uniform in that, if a person takes ninety minutes to cover a stretch listed as taking an hour, then it will take him one and a half times as long as the time listed to cover any other stretch—providing the same pace is maintained. Some people have commented that they find the times too long, while most find them too short. The latter is usually because they do not subtract rest times from the total. The times are in boldface to make them easier to total. They help trekkers know what to expect, and thus find the way more easily, and they make it easier to plan where to eat and spend nights.

Experienced trekkers find that often the first day on the trail seems fast. The next two or three days can be slow and painful. As the body strengthens and adjusts to the pace, the miles and hills seem to go by more effortlessly.

Everyone should learn the rest step for ascents. As you advance your uphill foot, plant it and then, before transferring your weight to it, consciously rest briefly with your weight on your downhill foot. Do this continuously and the hills come easier. On descents, tighten your shoe or boot laces so that your toes are not crammed into the front of the boot with each step. Take short steps, bending your knees to absorb the energy of the descent. Be limber.

Monitoring your pulse by placing your fingertips on a wrist or neck artery is an effective way to gauge your pace. Maximal heart rate can be determined by a sustained strenuous activity for a short time (for instance running at full speed for 1½ mi or 3 km, bicycling up a steep hill, or running on a treadmill). About sixty or seventy percent of the heart rate after such exercise is an appropriate target pulse for sustained activity. Try maintaining your pace to produce this heart rate, or less, and see if you fatigue easily. Most people following this method find a speed that produces an optimal heart rate (related to oxygen consumption) which they can maintain without getting short of breath or fatigued. This may help you maintain a pace without tiring, especially climbing uphill. Some people, myself included, find this too technical and just walk at a comfortable pace.

Along the trail to Muktinath. (Brot Coburn)

Following the Route Descriptions

The altitudes listed in the descriptions are taken from two sources: recent maps whose accuracy can be trusted, and my altimeter, a Thommen instrument, which is affected by temperature fluctuations. The readings have not been corrected for temperature changes, but they are adequate to indicate the order of climbing or descending. Ascent rates of 2000 ft (600 m) per hour are difficult to maintain for any length of time. Most hikers find 1000 ft (300 m) per hour a reasonable rate if the trail is good and they climb steadily. Similarly, a descent rate of 1500 ft (450 m) per hour is reasonable. Altitudes are usually converted from feet into meters and are not rounded off, although they are only approximations at best and can be in error by a few hundred feet. Altitudes of most towns in the hills are difficult to interpret accurately since several hundred feet of elevation may separate the highest and lowest parts of a town.

Routes are described in one direction only. They can easily be followed in the opposite direction. The time for a trip in the reverse direction can be figured approximately if altitude to be gained or lost and the rate of ascent or descent are taken into consideration.

Directions in the trail descriptions are given with reference to the compass. In addition, right- and left-hand sides of rivers are indicated to avoid confusion. Right (R) and left (L) refer to the right and left banks when *facing downstream*. Compass directions, for the most part, are general and may be a little off in some places. However, they are adequate for finding your way.

A *chautaara,* referred to in the trail descriptions, is a rectangular rock platform with a ledge for resting your load. Sometimes a pipul and a banyan tree are planted side by side in the center. You can look forward to these welcome structures found on many of the well-traveled routes. A *chorten* is a Buddhist religious structure, often cubical with carved tablets. The term, entrance *chorten,* refers to a covered gateway or arch decorated with Buddhist motifs. A stupa is a very large *chorten. Mani* walls are rectangular and made of stone tablets carved with mantras and prayers.

Names of towns and villages are taken from two sources: maps and other documents, and my own attempts at transliterating the names I heard. Errors crop up in both sources. One reason is the lack of a completely standardized spelling. Many names from the early Survey of India maps are quite inaccurate, especially in the northern regions. In some places when I asked four or five people the name, I heard four or five variations. Place names in Nepal are not unique. There are many Bhote Kosi's (rivers from Tibet), Beni's (junctions of two rivers), and Deorali's (passes). In addition, some villages may be called by two different names, but this should not cause much confusion in actual practice.

The pronunciation and transliteration guide in Chapter 6 indicates the correct way to pronounce the place names. It is important to place the stress on the first syllable of most words, for instance, Kathmandu, Pokhara, and Tengboche. The transliteration system is the same for words of both Nepali and Tibetan origin. The meaning of capital letters occurring within words is explained in Chapter 6. Place names are capitalized in spite of the transliteration system. The only place names that would be capitalized if the transliteration scheme were followed strictly are *RaRa* and *RiRi.* The correct spelling of Kathmandu in this transliteration system is kaaThmaanDu, but for the sake of convenience, the common spelling is used.

In the route descriptions, the names of some towns are in boldface. They are usually large, well-known places whose names the trekker should use when asking the way.

7 HELAMBU, GOSAINKUND AND LANGTANG

(Map No. 1, Page 117)

These regions offer the trekking that is most convenient to Kathmandu. Beginning from Kathmandu, the basic trek through Helambu, making a circuit from Pati Bhanjyang, is described. Included is an alternative exit from Talamarang to the Kathmandu-Kodari Road as well as an alternative journey out of Helambu to Panch Pokhari, and then down to the Kathmandu-Kodari Road. Visits to Gosainkund and Langtang beginning at Trisuli to the northwest of Kathmandu with routes linking them with Helambu are described. An alternative route goes to Langtang with the return via Gosainkund and Helambu. Langtang, Gosainkund, and the northern part of Helambu have been designated a national park with headquarters at Langtang village.

HELAMBU

Helambu or Helmu is the name of a region at the northern end of the Malemchi Khola Valley. The Helambu trek starts from **Sundarijal**, a small dam and hydroelectric station in the northeast corner of the Kathmandu Valley. More precisely, it begins west of Sundarijal at the end of the auto road where the large water pipe comes out of the hill.

There is no bus service to this point. A taxi could be hired. The cheapest way to go there is by bus to Baudha, boarded at the northern end of Ratna Park opposite the Park Restaurant. Stay on the bus until it reaches the turnaround point several hundred yards east of the stupa. At this point the road forks—the right branch going to Sankhu, and the left to Sundarijal. Begin on this left fork and walk **two to three hours** along the level road until it forks again near the edge of the valley. The left fork goes a short distance to a gate and the water treatment plant. Follow the right fork until it ends near a large water pipe. Cross under the pipe and proceed along its west side. Much of the way is up stairs. The trail reaches a clearing with an open building in **half an hour**. Continue until you come to a school on your left. Then just beyond, turn left to cross over the dam of a water reservoir (5200 ft, 1585 m).

Climb through wet, subtropical forest to an oak forest, and on to **Mulkharka** (5800 ft, 1768 m), a scattered *Tamang* village. The trail continues up, first in open country, then in oak forest, and reaches the few houses of **Chaubas** (7525 ft, 2233 m) in 1½ **hours**. The trail then ascends for another **half hour** to a pass, **Burlang Bhanjyang** (8000 ft, 2438 m), with a few houses below it on the north side. This pass marks Kathmandu Valley's rim, here known as the Shivapuri ridge. The trail descends through a pleasant oak forest, past one house on the left, **Chisapani** (7200 ft, 2194 m), to a flat portion where another trail joins from the right. In clear weather there are good views of the Himalaya to the north. In the spring rhododendrons bloom here. The trail continues to descend through open farmland to reach

Helambu, Gosainkund, and Langtang

Pati Bhanjyang (5800 ft, 1768 m), sitting in a saddle 1¾ **hours** from the pass. There is a police check post here.

From here, there is a choice of two routes. One continues along the general ridge system heading north, and eventually descends east to the Sherpa village of Malemchigaon. The other heads east, descends to the Malemchi Khola, and proceeds up its east (L) bank toward Tarke Ghyang, situated opposite Malemchigaon on the east side of the river. The ridge route goes much higher (almost to 12,000 ft, 3658 m) than the other route, and there may be snow on its upper portions in the late winter or early spring. There are no permanent villages between Kutumsang and Malemchigaon on this route, but if you leave Kutumsang in the morning, you should reach Malemchigaon that evening. This part of the route offers excellent views of the mountains. If it clouds over, as often happens late in the day, consider spending a night up high in a *goTh* or shelter used for pasturing animals. Then hopefully, you'll have good views the next morning.

The circuit to the north along the ridge and the return via the east side of the Malemchi Khola Valley is described. But if the weather is bad, it is wise to head up the east (L) side of the Malemchi Khola and then, if conditions have improved, to return via the high route. In this case, follow the directions in reverse.

To head north from Pati Bhanjyang, climb up the north side of the hill forming the saddle to the left of a long house. Shortly (100 ft, 30 m), the trail forks. The right fork heads to Thakani, a *Tamang* village, and beyond to the Talamarang Khola and Malemchi Khola. This is where it meets the return path.

Take the left fork instead, climb a little, and contour for **half an hour** to reach another saddle (5800 ft, 1768 m). Continue climbing north for 1¼ **hours** to the town of **Chipling** (7100 ft, 2165 m), scattered along the hillside. Climb on, taking the uppermost fork at major junctions, up to 8050 ft (2453 m), then begin descending through the oak forest to **Gul Bhanjyang** (7025 ft, 2142 m), a *Tamang* village 1¾ **hours** from Chipling. The trail is not very direct over this portion. A **few minutes** north of the town, reach a clearing and a trail junction where the left fork contours while the right climbs near the ridge. Take the right fork. Almost an **hour** beyond Gul Bhanjyang at 7975 ft (2430 m), there is another fork. Take the left fork up to 8350 ft (2545 m) just west of the summit of the hill and descend to the few houses of **Kutumsang** (8100 ft, 2468 m) situated in a pass. Reach it in 1¾ **hours**. At the pass, you can take the right fork and contour for **ten minutes** to **Bolumje**, more houses, and perhaps a better place to stay. There are no permanent villages between this town and Malemchigaon, a day away.

In bad weather you could continue along the right fork to the Malemchi Khola Valley and proceed high up on its west (R) bank to Malemchigaon. In route, you would pass the villages of Nalemgorkha and Kwagaon. This route takes about **ten hours**. After the last tributary, climb up a small ridge for 1500 ft (458 m) to Malemchigaon (8400 ft, 2560 m), situated in a clearing. But this route has little to recommend itself. It is steep and narrow in places, and slippery when wet.

From Kutumsang or Bolumje the trail ascends the hill to the north. From Bolumje, pass two *chorten,* then reach a *mani* wall (8250 ft, 2515 m) in **ten minutes**. Climb through a prickly-leaved oak forest that becomes a rhododendron and fir forest in its upper reaches. Reach a notch containing three *chorten* (10,600 ft, 3230 m) after climbing for 2½ **hours**, mostly on the east side of the main ridge. If starting from Kutumsang, the trail initially keeps close to the ridge crest. Just beyond the notch is a clearing. Continue, keeping more level, on the west side of the ridge. Another clearing containing some *goTh* (10,450 ft, 3185 m) is reached in **half an hour**. At the north end of the clearing, a little to the west, there is a fresh water

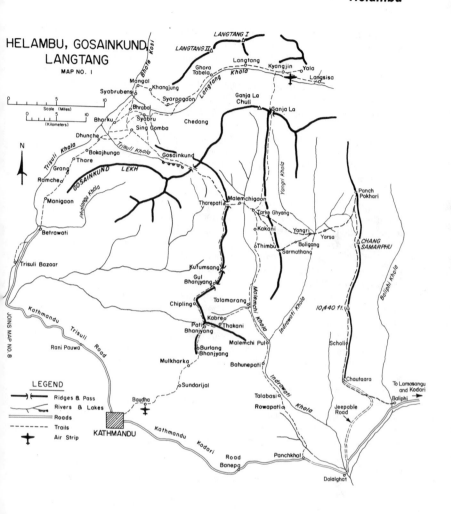

HELAMBU, GOSAINKUND
LANGTANG

MAP NO. 1

spring. Water can be difficult to find along this ridge during dry weather. From here on, there are two route choices. One keeps close to the ridge crest, the Turin Danda, while the other contours over portions on the west side.

From the clearing, contour on the west side to reach **MangegoTh** (10,775 ft, 3285 m) in **half an hour**. This is the largest group of *goTh* before Tharepati. Continue north on the east side through pleasant rhododendron forests. Cross over to the west side in **fifteen minutes**, then contour to reach some *goTh* (11,125 ft, 3390 m) in **less than half an hour**. Continue on the west side to the ridge crest in another **forty-five minutes**. A **few minutes** beyond in a notch on the ridge (11,800 ft, 3597 m), you can look across the valley to the east and see a tight cluster of houses some 3000 ft (913 m) below you. If this town of Tarke Ghyang is east-southeast of you (slightly south of east or about 117°), you are in the correct notch. The notch is north of a *chorten*. If the village of Tarke Ghyang cannot be

117

seen because of bad weather or haze, continue north along the trail. If in **fifteen minutes** you cross the crest of the ridge to the west side and see two clusters of *goTh,* Tharepati, 100 ft (30 m) below you, then you have the correct notch. There are many trails on this portion from Bolumje to Tharepati, so the specific one you take may be different from those described. Keep to the ridge crest for the most part. There may still be some signs in English to help locate the trails.

You can reach the notch in some **five hours** from Kutumsang, and in clear weather you should have fine views of the mountains. As mentioned before, consider spending a night in one of the *goTh* in route to enjoy views in the morning. If, instead of descending from the notch, you continue to the two clusters of *goTh* called Tharepati (11,800 ft, 3597 m) and then beyond to the north, the trail leads to the Gosainkund Tal in a day.

To continue to Malemchigaon and the villages of upper Helambu, descend east from the notch mentioned above along a poorly defined trail that heads north and down. Good trail sense is an asset here. There are blazes on the oaks to mark it. Eventually you enter a rocky streambed (9600 ft, 2926 m). Follow it down about 200 ft (61 m). About 1½ **hours** from the notch, at 9400 ft (2865 m), you reach a clearing with a few *goTh* and, beyond, a fork in which the right branch descends to cross a tributary (8265 ft, 2520 m) after **forty minutes**. A short climb brings you to **Malemchigaon** (8400 ft, 2560 m).

The people here call themselves Sherpas, but their relationship with the Sherpas of Solu-Khumbu, at least as evidenced by the infrequency of intermarriage, is distant. The dialects spoken are also different. Here you will find a *gomba* on the east end of the town, and an interesting rock home of a hermit on the west end.

There are no more towns farther up this valley, so to go to Tarke Ghyang, proceed down to the south of the *gomba* through an entrance *chorten* and descend a small ridge. About 1000 ft (304 m) below, there are some large rocks, and farther below, a large bridge over the river. Reach it (6200 ft, 1890 m) in **one hour** from Malemchigaon. Cross to the east (L) bank and head up southward to a *chorten*. Here, turn east and climb a little until a trail branches to the right across some terraces. Continue, contouring mostly, up a little and across two tributaries. After the second crossing, the trail rises more directly, and **an hour** from the bridge, reaches a small treeless *chautaara* (7200 ft, 2194 m). Another 1000 ft (304 m) of vertical climbing brings you to a *chorten* and shortly beyond, to a tight cluster of houses called **Tarke Ghyang,** another Sherpa village (8400 ft, 2560 m), 1¼ **hours** from the *chautaara.*

From Tarke Ghyang you can head east up past the schoolhouse and then north to reach the Ganja La, a high pass (16,805 ft, 5123 m) leading to the Langtang Valley, in three days. Food, shelter, and fuel have to be carried, and the party should be equipped for snow climbing. This route is described in the reverse direction later in this chapter. Or, from Tarke Ghyang, you can head up to the ridge crest to the southeast and east to Panch Pokhari, a series of small lakes (about 13,000 ft, 3968 m) that are pilgrimage sites. There is a fine view from the ridge nearby. You can then head to the Kathmandu-Kodari Road. This is not a well-traveled route and there are few houses along the way. However, it is an alternate exit from the Helambu area. This route description follows that for the stretch from Talamarang to the Kathmandu-Kodari Road. The third route from Tarke Ghyang follows the river southward.

To take this third route, head south at the low end of the village past the large new *gomba* and rows of *mani* walls to cross a stream. Take the lower fork just beyond, and after an **hour**, cross a tributary (7000 ft, 2134 m) to **Karkani,** a small scattered Sherpa village (6750 ft, 2058 m) **half an hour** after the tributary. Upon rounding the next ridge crest, you reach a clearing in the oak forest with *chorten, mani* walls, and an entrance *chorten*. Descend from here into the valley of the next tributary. Rather than head east to cross the tributary upstream from the main river, the trail descends near the ridge past a large *chorten*. In 1½ **hours** from Kakani, you reach **Thimbu**, another scattered Sherpa and *Tamang* village (5000 ft, 1524 m). Below it, the trail descends for **fifteen minutes** to cross the next tributary (4550 ft, 1486 m).

The trail now follows the east (L) bank of the Malemchi Khola, close to the water for the most part, but rising occasionally to clear difficult stretches. The forest is again subtropical. In **less than an hour**, descend to a suspension bridge across the river (4050 ft, 1234 m). Do not cross it, but continue on the east (L) bank, crossing several tributaries along the way. About 1½ **hours** beyond the first suspension bridge, you come to the third bridge (3500 ft, 1067 m). Cross this to the west (R) bank and continue south on a wide trail that was once a road but is now in disrepair. There is an interesting looking Brahman village (Sarha) on the right, and 1¼ **hours** beyond the suspension bridge, you pass high above another. Then **shortly**, you descend to **Talamarang** (3150 ft, 960 m), a town with shops and teahouses.

There are two route choices from here. One ascends the tributary lying south of the village to rejoin the outward bound route at Pati Bhanjyang. The other continues south along the west (R) bank of the Malemchi Khola, crosses to the Chak Khola after five hours, and reaches the Kathmandu-Kodari Road at Panchkhal where you can board a bus for the remainder of the journey. This route takes only seven hours to the road, remains quite level, and follows a wide path almost suitable for a jeep; but it covers over twenty miles. The other route follows an ill-defined trail up a riverbed for several hours and involves a vertical ascent of 4700 ft (1433 m), followed by a descent of 2700 ft (823 m) to the Kathmandu Valley. This route takes eight to nine hours to Sundarijal and should be taken if bad weather prevents you from having good views of the peaks on the way to Pati Bhanjyang, or if you are traveling in the spring when the lower route is much hotter.

Return via Pati Bhanjyang

To return from Talamarang via Pati Bhanjyang, cross the suspension bridge over the tributary, the Talamarang Khola, and head west up its south (R) bank. Stay close to the river most of the time. Try to follow a small trail which meanders about the river and crisscrosses it irregularly. The forest is chir pine and chilaune again. Almost **three hours** later (4700 ft, 1433 m), cross a large landslide through which a prominent tributary from the south trickles. **Half an hour** beyond on the south (R) bank of the Talamarang Khola near the hill to the south, you come to a small water-operated mill (4750 ft, 1448 m). A trail rises near the mill and essentially climbs the ridge north of the tributary valley mentioned before. Follow the trail to the *Tamang* village of **Kabre** (5500 ft, 1676 m) which is **forty-five minutes** from the riverbed.

Continue along the ridge through oak forest past another *Tamang* village. Take the right fork beyond to head west and rise to a *chautaara* (6050 ft, 1844 m) **thirty minutes** from Kabre. The trail continues to ascend and reaches a ridge crest (6200 ft, 1890 m) in **twenty minutes** near the *Tamang* village of **Thakani**. There are good distant views from here in clear weather. The trail now crosses to the south side of the ridge and contours, heading west, for 1¼ **hours** to the trail you took on the way out, just north of Pati Bhanjyang. Descend to **Pati Bhanjyang** in a **few minutes** and retrace the route described earlier to Sundarijal.

Return via Panchkhal

To proceed to the Kathmandu-Kodari Road from Talamarang, cross the bridge over the tributary and continue south on a wide trail. Vehicles have succeeded in motoring most of the way on the road, but presently it is not in good repair. There are large boulders and washouts obstructing the way. You are in sal forest and non-cultivated areas for the most part.

Follow the west (R) bank of the Malemchi Khola for 1½ **hours** until you see a large suspension bridge over the river and a cluster of houses on the west (R) bank. This is **Malemchi Pul Bazaar** (2775 ft, 846 m). Another 1¼ **hours** brings you to **Bahunepati** (2660 ft, 811 m), the largest bazaar in route. A further 1¼ **hours** along the much wider valley brings you near another suspension bridge spanning almost the entire valley floor. There is a town, Talabasi (2575 ft, 785 m), at the west end of the bridge. The road passes west of the town, heads over to the hillside on the west, and ascends it to a saddle to the west. The town of **Rowapati** (3075 ft, 937 m) is on the saddle **an hour** beyond the bridge. The trail now enters the next valley west of the Malemchi Khola containing the Chak Khola. Continue south above its east (L) bank for 1¼ **hours** until you cross to the west (R) bank (2600 ft, 793 m). The trail then ascends and winds for **twenty minutes** to reach asphalt (2920 ft, 890 m). Turn right and pass mileage marker No. 47 to reach a cluster of houses by the road in **fifteen minutes.** This is a part of the town **Panchkhal** (3100 ft, 945 m). Buses going to Kathmandu stop here every few hours.

Panch Pokhari

For people who approach Helambu from the west or south, this is an alternative means of return to the highway through an area south and east of Helambu. While slightly longer, it does offer some fine scenery and a ridge route which is cooler during the hot months. From Panch Pokhari (five lakes) itself, there is no view of the snow-covered mountains because the cirque the lakes are set in faces southeast. But a **half-hour** climb to the crest of the cirque yields a spectacular vantage point. Five or six days should be allowed for the trip.

From Tarke Ghyang, follow the main trail along the ridge crest to Sarmathang. It is a pleasant **three- to five-hour** walk via a level trail contouring around two subsidiary ridges. Panch Pokhari is on the next ridge to the east, so it is necessary to cross the Indrawati Khola in between. Descend, while going diagonally north, to **Boligang** in 1½ **hours,** passing **Samil** about half way. The trail is rather obscure and the town, inhabited by Sherpas and *Tamangs*, is notably poorer than the Sherpa villages of Helambu. Continue heading north along a better trail which reaches the town of **Yangri** near the intersection of the Ripar Khola and the Indrawati Khola in **one hour.** This town may be reached more directly from Tarke Ghyang by climbing up (2000 ft, 609 m), crossing the ridge directly, and descending via the Ripar Khola to Yangri.

Cross the river at each of the branches over somewhat treacherous bridges and take a short steep climb along a cliff between them. Instead of taking the path diverging right toward Bhotung, climb straight up through millet fields to **Yarsa** in **one hour.** From Yarsa, take the main path on the left, going gently up, but avoiding steeper alternative paths, past *chorten* and clusters of houses until you come to a rushing stream in **one hour**. Cross the stream on a bridge and then go steeply up on your left along a well-built trail. Half way up, take the steeper path (the other trail flattens) and reach the crest in **one hour**.

The trail continues gently up for **fifteen minutes** to **Dukang**, a settlement with two permanent houses and many *goTh*. This is the last human habitation for the next several days. Panch Pokhari can be reached from here in one rather long day.

Go rather steeply up to reach another ridge crest in **1¼ hours**, then contour left for **one hour** to a stream. Here the trail is easy to lose due to floods, but proceed up the stony bed for a few hundred feet, cross a temporary bridge, and go diagonally left very steeply up the hillside. Soon the grade eases and in **forty-five minutes**, you enter pleasant terrain. Cross two streams (the last water before Panch Pokhari) and go left up across the hill. This section may be seen from the level section of the trail before the stream. In another **forty-five minutes**, gain the crest near some abandoned *goTh* and continue gently up to the left on fine rock slabs to reach the saddle (12,000 ft, 3658 m) in the Panch Pokhari ridge in **1½ hours**. There are numerous *chorten* and a trail shelter here, but water may be difficult to find.

The trail to Panch Pokhari runs along the left side of the ridge and is generally well-built, but it has numerous ups and downs that are tiresome at that altitude. Reach one slightly broken, but usable, shelter to the north of the ponds in **three hours** from the point of gaining the ridge. There is room for only three or four people to sleep on the boards, but many more could be accommodated on the dirt, and there are plenty of fine camping places. Since the area is just above the tree line, firewood is scarce. But there may be a large pile of sticks about **fifteen minutes** down the trail. There is a Hindu shrine and numerous Buddhist prayer flags nearby, making it a very peaceful place. From the cirque crest (about 13,000 ft, 3962 m), there is a splendid view of the Himalaya all the way east from Langtang to beyond Everest.

The return to the Kathmandu-Kodari Road is almost entirely along a ridge route with only a couple of short climbs to break the 11,000 ft (3354 m) descent. Follow the ascent route back for **two hours** to the shelter (12,966 ft, 3958 m) in the saddle north of Chang Samarphu. The old trail went up almost to the summit, but the new route skirts the west side of the peak on a nearly level trail consisting of easy slabs. Rejoin the former trail in **1½ hours** at the col on the south side where there are remains of some *goTh*. The next hill is also skirted on its west side in **half an hour**. Midway on this section are a couple of caves suitable for housing four or five people, but the nearby watercourses are sometimes dry outside of the monsoon. About **ten minutes** short of the next col there are some meadows which provide excellent camping and some shelter in abandoned *goTh*. Water is available at a good stream at the col, but there is no camping site any closer.

From the col, take the main trail which branches east (left). At first it is fairly level, then goes upward, crosses several streams, and reaches the crest in **1¼ hours**. From the open, flower-filled meadows, there are fine views of the mountains. Now descend rather steeply for 500 ft (152 m), then go down more gradually over a series of bumps to reach the lowest col (10,440 ft, 3182 m) before the peak in **1½ hours**. The remains of many fires indicate where water is found some 200 ft (61 m) east in small semi-clear pools. Camping sites as well as some small grass and leaf lean-tos are available. This is the last water for about five hours.

Proceed diagonally, going gently up, around, and down the west side of the peak (10,440 ft, 3187 m) until in **1½ hours**, four chimney-like cairns are reached just beyond a shallow, sandy depression in the ridge. There is a good view from here of the ridge below as it goes south before doglegging southwest. The fine trail continues **one hour** down to the dogleg, then stays fairly level for another 1½ **hours**. An obvious level trail cuts off to the left (southeast) here and goes out to the end of a subsidiary ridge. Then it heads down steeply to a series of plateaus where the first houses are found and where water is probably available, though not along the trail. As you descend, the town of Scholi can be seen. Farther away, Chautaara, which has a particularly large, white building, is nestled in a saddle in the ridge.

Continuing, skirt gently down across the southwest face of a large hill where two small streams join. Cross the saddle to the east side of the next hill and drop steeply down to **Scholi**. It has a small bazaar with a rest house about **forty-five minutes** from the stream crossing and perhaps 2½ **hours** from the beginning of the steep descent. From Scholi, proceed for 1½ **hours** along a very wide, flat trail which meanders along the ridge top and around hillocks, then goes more steeply down to **Chautaara**. This fairly large bazaar is the district headquarters. There is a jeep road which is sometimes open to the Kathmandu-Kodari Road. The foot trail follows the motor road east for 1½ **hours** until you come to two tea shops. From here, descend steeply to **Baliphi** on the main road where a bus to Kathmandu is available.

GOSAINKUND

Here is the description of a trek from Trisuli, up the Trisuli Valley to the sacred lakes of Gosainkund and beyond to Helambu. Such a circuit may be about the best possible short trek from Kathmandu. It takes a minimum of a week, and food for two or three days must be carried.

Trisuli can be reached from Kathmandu on foot in 1½ days, or by bus in four to five hours from Pakanajol in the northwest corner of Kathmandu. Consider a side trip to the old fort of Nuwakot as described in Chapter 11. From Trisuli you can proceed north up the east (L) or west (R) bank of the river.

The route up the east (L) bank has more rises and dips, but it can be motored by rugged vehicles. The route on the west paralleling the water reservoir and canal is quite flat. To take the west bank trail, climb up behind the bazaar (1775 ft, 541 m) to reach the canal flowing to the penstocks of a hydroelectric power project. Follow the road to the east of the canal. Beyond the reservoir, the water pipe crosses the river. You cross on a catwalk beside the pipe (1900 ft, 579 m) **one hour** from Trisuli. On the east (L) bank the trail joins the road and continues north through sal forest. The pipe crosses to the west (R) bank again, but you stay on the east (L) side until the road ends **half an hour** beyond the crossing near a partial dam across the Trisuli Khola. There are a few houses here, but the main town of **Betrawati** (2100 ft, 641 m) is **twenty minutes** beyond at the junction of the Phalangu Khola and the Trisuli. Cross the suspension bridge over the tributary and climb a bit to the town of **Bogata** (2350 ft, 761 m). Now climb through an oak forest to a chir pine forest, then through open country on a wide trail to **Manigaon** (3925 ft, 1196 m) 2½ **hours** from Betrawati. The trail continues north, in and out of tributary valleys, to reach **Ramche** (5875 ft, 1791 m) in 2½ **hours**. Here national park entry permits must be purchased. Another **hour** brings you to the next *Tamang* village, **Grang** (6200 ft, 1890 m).

Continue contouring another 1½ **hours** to **Thare** (6525 ft, 1899 m). There are good views of Langtang I and II along the way. To the north up the main valley, Tibetan peaks are visible. Another **hour** brings you to **Bokajhunga** (6200 ft, 1890 m).

The trail through oak forest here is exceptionally pleasant. Another 1½ **hours** brings you to **Dhunche** (6450 ft, 1966 m), a main village at the junction of the Trisuli Khola and the Bhote Kosi. There are shops and a police check post here.

From Dhunche, there are two routes to Gosainkund. The newer trail is initially the same as that heading to Langtang. Head east, taking neither of the first two left forks **twelve and eighteen minutes** from town. Contour for **half an hour**, then take a left fork (6000 ft, 1829 m) beyond His Majesty's Government (HMG) Agricultural Project below you. Descend to a cantilever bridge (5775 ft, 1700 m) some **ten minutes** beyond. Cross the Trisuli Khola, which drains the Gosainkund Lekh, to the north (R) bank, and climb up a steep, but pleasant, oak-forested gully to reach a crest with a trail junction (6450 ft, 1966 m) after **fifteen minutes.** The trail that climbs to the east heads to Gosainkund, while the one going northwest, heads toward Langtang. Take the trail climbing to the east and follow it for approximately **five hours** to **Sing Gomba** (10,675 ft, 3254 m). Pass through oak forests to reach an impressive fir and rhododendron forest.

The old trail to Gosainkund heads east and contours from the water spout at the lower end of Dhunche. Do not take the right fork that ascends **forty-five minutes** beyond this. Continue past the turnoff for the new trail. In **half an hour** you reach the Trisuli Khola near some mills. The bridge here has collapsed, so you must ford the river (6375 ft, 1943 m). The trail heads east on the north (R) side. It is a climb of 8700 ft (2652 m) to the pass. The first 4300 ft (1311 m) are rather steep and there is little water. You reach **Sing Gomba** (10,675 ft, 3254 m) in **4½ hours.** At junctions, take the upper fork. The pleasant easy-to-follow trail passes through hillsides ablaze with rhododendrons in season. There are no permanent settlements beyond Dhunche for about three days. Sing Gomba is inhabited during the less severe part of the year when people there can provide food and shelter for trekkers. An HMG cheese factory, Chauchan Bari, is located there.

From the *gomba,* head east along the south side of the ridge, following a wide trail. At first, where there was once a big burn, the slope is covered with *Piptanthus nepalensis* shrubs with yellow flowers. Then the trail enters a rhododendron and fir forest, and crosses to the north side of the ridge. In 1¼ **hours**, reach a *goTh* (11,550 ft, 3520 m) where the trail is joined by the one coming up from Syabru. (If coming from Syabru, take the trail up the ridge from the village, past a water-driven prayer wheel, and follow a faint trail to gain the ridge here.) Continue for **forty-five minutes** on the north side to the few *goTh* called **Laurebina** (12,800 ft, 3901 m). Water is scarce here. In good weather there are views of Himalchuli, Peak 29, Manaslu, and Ganesh Himal to the west, Tibet to the north, and Langtang Himal to the northeast. Climb on, reaching a *chautaara* with poles sticking out of it (13,000 ft, 3962 m), then in a **little over half an hour**, cross the ridge to the south side (13,600 ft, 4145 m). Beyond, you begin to see the lakes. The first is Bhutkunda, followed by Nagkunda, and then **Gosainkunda.** This third lake (14,100 ft, 4298 m) is reached in **forty-five minutes.** There are two stone huts on the north shore.

Every year during the full moon between mid-July and mid-August, thousands of pilgrims and devotees come to bathe in this lake and to pay homage to Shiva. There are several legends, all similar, concerning the formation of this lake and its significance. One story is that the gods were churning the ocean, hoping to obtain from it the water of immortality. Some poison arose from the seas, and Shiva, realizing that the poison might harm the gods, drank it. The poison caused him a great deal of pain and thirst, as well as a blue discoloration of his neck. To relieve the fever and suffering, Shiva traveled to the snows of Gosainkund. He thrust his trident, or *trisul,* into the mountainside and three streams of water sprang forth

The clouds part near Langtang. (D. L. Golobitsh)

which collected in the hollow beneath, producing the Gosainkund Lake. Shiva stretched along the lake's edge and drank its waters, quenching his thirst. There is said to be an oval-shaped rock beneath the surface near the center of the lake. Worshippers say they can see Shiva reclining on a bed of serpents there.

In good weather, consider climbing the hill to the north for a view. To continue to Helambu, contour the lake and ascend past four more lakes (Bhairunkunda, Saraswatikunda, Dudkunda, and Surjekunda—often they may be covered with ice) to the pass (15,100 ft, 4602 m) in an **hour**.

From the pass, descend to the southeast, keeping generally to the northeast (L) side of the valley, and head for the prominent notch in the distance. In an **hour** reach some stone *goTh* frames (13,000 ft, 3962 m). Shortly beyond, descend a ridge with a waterfall on your left. There is a campsite (11,900 ft, 3627 m) **forty-five minutes** farther. Soon the trail crosses a stream and passes by another picturesque waterfall. About **forty-five minutes** from the first campsite, there is another under the overhanging rocks of **Gopte** (11,700 ft, 3566 m). The notch (11,675 ft, 3559 m) you saw earlier is reached in **forty-five minutes**. Some **forty-five minutes** later, there are more overhanging rocks. The trail continues through beautiful rhododendron forests and in **half an hour**, crosses a tributary from the north (10,550 ft, 3216

m) to ascend through juniper woods. It reaches a series of *goTh* called Tharepati (11,500 ft, 3505 m) just below the ridge west of the Malemchi Khola in another 1¼ **hours**. There are good views to the north from the crest of the ridge. A trail proceeds north near the crest, and leads over a high pass to the Langtang Valley.

From the ridge (11,875 ft, 3620 m) above the *goTh,* the trail follows the crest to the southeast and drops into a notch (11,800 ft, 3597 m) from which Tarke Ghyang is visible to the east-southeast as a tight cluster of houses on the east side of the Malemchi Khola Valley some 3000 ft (913 m) below you. To the south is a hill with a *chorten*. There are two choices now: descend from the notch to Malemchigaon, or head south along the main ridge to Kutumsang. Both of these trails have been described earlier.

LANGTANG

Langtang is a valley nestled in the Himalaya. It is best to carry some food in order to be able to explore the upper part of the valley. First the trip from Trisuli to Langtang, then several side trips up the valley are described. There is a high pass, the Ganja La, which links Langtang with Helambu. A brief description of this route is given. Return routes to avoid backtracking from Langtang, and linkups with Gosainkund, complete the description. An interesting and informative recent account of this area is given in Andrew R. Hall's "Preliminary Report on the Langtang Region" (see Recommended Reading).

To go to Langtang, follow the route already described to Dhunche in the Gosainkund section. From Dhunche (6450 ft, 1966 m) begin working east, not taking either of the two left forks **twelve and eighteen minutes** from town. Keep level and after a **half hour** from town, at 6000 ft (1829 m), take a left fork, beyond the HMG Agricultural Project and descend steeply to a cantilever bridge (5675 ft, 1930 m) some **10 minutes** beyond. Cross the Trisuli Khola, which drains the Gosainkund Lekh, to the north (R) bank and climb up a pleasant oak-forested gulley to reach a crest with a trail junction (6450 ft, 1966 m) after **forty-five minutes**. The right fork goes east to Gosainkund, while the left fork heading northwest is to Langtang. Take the left fork which forks again some **twenty minutes** later (6450 ft, 1966 m). The lower fork leads into the Bhote Kosi Valley, through a pleasant chir pine forest. After another **twenty minutes**, in sight of the next village, Bharku, there is another fork (6125 ft, 1867 m). The upper fork leads to the village and beyond to the new route into the Langtang Valley, while the left fork passes below the village to Syabrubensi and the older route to Langtang. This older route is described later as a variant for leaving the Langtang Valley. Continue to **Bharku** (6050 ft, 1844 m) **ten minutes** beyond.

To proceed on the new route, continue contouring and rising beyond Bharku through pleasant chir pine and rhododendron forests. Round a bend to a rest spot (7550 ft, 2301 m) with the first views up the Langtang Valley after 2¼ **hours**. Contour and descend another **forty-five minutes** to Syabru (6950 ft, 2118 m), a village strung out along a ridge. From Syabru there are trails ascending to Sing Gomba (three to four hours) and to Gosainkund (about seven hours). There are no settlements for at least a day's walk beyond Syabru. Shelter can be found under rocks, but food must be carried. To continue to Langtang, drop and contour across wheat fields to the east. Then descend and cross to the east (R) bank of a tributary (6375 ft, 1943 m) from the Gosainkund Lekh after **forty-five minutes**. Climb up a bit, then descend through a forest to reach the Langtang Khola (5450 ft, 1661 m) in **forty-five minutes**. A trail and several bridges cross the Langtang Khola and lead downstream to Syabrubensi. This difficult trail is passable only in the dry season, but can provide another route of return from the valley.

Continue upstream along the south (L) bank through a quite impressive gorge. In an **hour**, reach a rock shelter and cross a nearby tributary (6325 ft, 1928 m). Another **forty-five minutes** brings you to a new bridge (6700 ft, 2042 m) which is crossed to the north (R) bank. More rock shelters suitable for camping are found here. The trail continues climbing through rhododendron and prickly-leaved oak forests, to meet the old trail (7825 ft, 2385 m) from Syabrubensi in another **hour**. This old trail keeps high on the north side of the valley before descending to Syabrubensi. It is described later.

Notice how much drier it is on this side of the valley, which—because it faces south—receives more sunlight. Continue on up the valley, which widens out. **Half an hour** farther there is a *bhaTTi*, the Lama Hotel, and space for camping. Another **three-hour** climb brings you to the valley floor and the Nepali army post of **Ghora Tabela** (9450 ft, 2880 m). This was once a Tibetan resettlement project and may now have no permanent residents. A trekkers' lodge has been constructed here and may be in operation. Beyond, on the south side of the valley, are larch forests which turn golden yellow in the autumn.

Continue up the valley, passing several temporary settlements, then cross a tributary below a monastery after **1½ hours**. This active monastery is interesting and worth a visit. Note the glacier-worn *U* shape of the valley here, in contrast to the water-worn *V* shape of the valley below Ghora Tabela. Another **half an hour** brings you to beautiful **Langtang** village (10,850 ft, 3307 m), site of the Langtang National Park headquarters. Tourist facilities are being constructed here. Continue on up a moraine to cross a tributary (11,800 ft, 3597 m) after another **1½ hours**. The views become better with further progress, and looking back, you can see the impressive Langtang Himal. Another **twenty minutes** brings you to a trail fork (12,075 ft, 3680 m). The left fork goes to Kyangjin Gomba. Shortly beyond, on the right fork, is the HMG cheese factory and the summer pasturing settlements of **Kyangjin** (12,300 ft, 3749 m). Food and lodging can usually be arranged here.

Upper Langtang Valley

From Kyangjin there are several worthwhile excursions. You can head north to reach the glacier and icefall in less than three hours. Climb the lateral moraine to the left of the glacier. Or an hour's climb to the north up a small hill provides a good view. You can also proceed farther up the main valley. The STOL airstrip (12,100 ft, 3688 m) is half an hour beyond Kyangjin in the valley floor. There are many possibilities for short climbs, mostly to the north. There is another cheese factory at Yala, a 3½-hour climb from Kyangjin. A small summit with outstanding views can be reached from the factory.

To go to Yala, head east from Kyangjin, and after about **ten minutes**, contour the hillside to the north, reaching a few *goTh* in an hour. Another **hour's** contouring and climbing brings you to another series of *goTh* (13,650 ft, 4160 m). Round the ridge crest and contour another slope for **half an hour** to another ridge (14,400 ft, 4389 m). Climb north beside a small stream to reach the buildings at Yala (15,200 ft, 4633 m) in less than an **hour**. To reach Tsergo Ri (some call this Yala Peak), an excellent viewpoint, head west from Yala, or continue circling the hill, reaching the prayer flag-festooned summit (16,353, 4984 m) in **two hours**. To the south, you can see the Ganja La, a pass leading into Helambu. The surrounding peaks are quite spectacular. Many short climbs may suggest themselves to the experienced.

From Kyangjin, you can also head up the valley to Langsisa, the next to the last of the summer pasturing settlements. Cross an alluvial fan (12,250 ft, 3734 m) **twenty minutes** beyond and reach the airstrip, crossing its western end. In less than **half an hour**, reach the north (R) bank of the Langtang Khola and continue upstream. Another **forty-five minutes** brings you to a summer settlement (12,500 ft, 3810 m), and another **hour** brings you to a second. A big lateral and terminal moraine of the West Langtang Glacier looms ahead. Contour around its south terminus and reach the lone hut of Langsisa (13,400 ft, 4084 m) in another **hour**. Ahead lies the main Langtang Glacier, and the Tibetan border, a hard day's climb away (some trekking maps are grossly in error regarding the border). To the south lies beautiful Buddha Peak and the terminus of the East Langtang Glacier. Up this valley lies a difficult pass leading to the region east of Helambu. It was probably first crossed by H. W. Tilman in 1949. There are many places to explore.

There is a big reddish rock at Langsisa which, according to legend, is that color because a holy man living outside the valley lost his yak and trailed it to this place. The yak died here, however, and the Lama, wanting its hide, skinned it and spread the skin on a rock to dry. But the skin stuck and remains there on the rock to this day! This is the legend of the discovery of the Langtang Valley. "Lang" means yak, and "tang" means to follow. Hence the name. Also, a few miles up the valley to the southeast, two big rock gendarmes stand a hundred feet above the glacier. They are said to represent two Bhuddhist saints, Shakya Muni and Guru Rimpoche.

There are several possible linkup routes to avoid backtracking. From below Ghora Tabela, you can cross the Langtang Khola and ascend to the Chedang yak pastures and Laurebina on the main trail to Gosainkunda. This takes **two days** and requires a guide who is quite familiar with the route. You can also reach Malemchigaon from Chedang. From Syabru you can ask the way to Gosainkunda and to Sing Gomba. For experienced parties, the Ganja La leads to Helambu. This pass is normally possible from May to November, or sometimes longer in dry years. Food, fuel, and shelter must be carried for four to five days. It is necessary to have someone along who is familiar with the route, as it is quite easy to get lost in poor weather.

The Ganja La

To cross the Ganja La from Langtang Valley, go downstream from Kyangjin to a wooden bridge over the river. Downstream on the south (R) bank are a few huts. The trail enters the rhododendron forest and climbs to more huts, Ngegang (14,450 ft, 4404 m) in **two hours**. Another **four or more hours** brings you to the pass, which may be difficult to find. Keep to the west side of the valley coming down from the pass. The last 100 ft (30 m) to the pass (16,805 ft, 5122 m) is a scramble. Descend to the south into a basin, pick a route through the center among the moraines, and climb out of the basin. Then find the trail markers which head toward a stream. Follow the stream down to where it joins another stream to form the Yangri Khola, and follow it to some scattered summer pasturing huts (14,400 ft, 4389 m). This takes **three or four hours**. Climb out of the basin, and aim for a spur to the west of the main north-south ridge. Climb down to a series of huts in a meadow. This area is sometimes called Kelaung or Kelchung, and can be reached in **two hours** from the earlier huts. Continue south, crossing several shoulders and for the most part tending to the east side of the main ridge. Do not descend from the main high ridge. Reach another series of huts at Dukpu (13,200 ft, 4023 m) in 2½ **to three hours**. Ascend to a notch to the northeast of a prominent hill, and traverse fine rhododendron forests, crossing and recrossing the ridge crest. Pass through a clearing with a hut (10,900 ft, 3322 m) and head southwest, descending past Gekye Gomba to reach Tarke Ghyang in **three to four hours**. Routes linking Tarke Ghyang with Kathmandu have been described in the Helambu section of this chapter.

Langtang to Syabrubensi

If you came to Langtang without visiting Syabrubensi, consider varying your exit to Trisuli slightly by following the Langtang Valley downstream, high on the north side to Syabrubensi. Descend on the usual trail from Ghora Tabela, and after **one hour**, pass a bridge over the Langtang Khola (8625 ft, 2629 m). The bridge can be used to reach Gosainkunda via Chedang yak pastures as mentioned earlier. However, continue down to reach the trail junction (7850 ft, 2393 m) in another **forty-five minutes**. The left fork descends to the new bridge and Syabru. The right fork ascends through open, steep country where you might spot some interesting animals, such as a goral or serow. The trail passes a lodge and descends to the few houses of Syarpa or **Syarpagaon** (8225 ft, 2507 m) in another **hour**. Continue contouring and climbing on the steep valley wall for **two hours** until you round a ridge to an oak and blue pine forest and the valley of the main Bhote Kosi. A **thirty-to forty-five-minute** descent brings you to **Khangjung** (7250 ft, 2210 m), a scattered village with cultivated fields. At the lower end, the trail forks near a water source and *mani*. The right fork heads north to Rasuwa Garhi, while the left descends through terraces into chir pine forest to Mangal (4900 ft, 1494 m) near the bottom of the Bhote Kosi Valley in a **little over an hour**. Head downstream (south) from here, following the main trail on the east (L) bank of the Bhote Kosi for **half an hour** to **Syabrubensi** (4650 ft, 1417 m). This large town contains a settlement of Tibetan refugees as well as *BhoTiya* who call themselves *Tamangs*.

There are some hot springs near here which can be used for bathing. To reach them, cross the main suspension bridge over the Bhote Kosi and head downstream on the west (R) bank for about **ten minutes** to a small hot spring. There are other bigger ones below.

Syabrubensi to Sing Gomba

From Syabrubensi, cross the suspension bridge over the Langtang Khola to its south (L) bank. Heading upstream from here, you can take a trail to Syabru and on to Sing Gomba or Gosainkunda. Or you can walk for less than **ten minutes** downstream on the Bhote Kosi, take a left fork before some *mani* walls, and climb for about **six hours** to Sing Gomba and Chauchan Bari, the new HMG cheese factory (10,625 ft, 3239 m). This could provide a pleasant side trip for those basically retracing their steps to Trisuli, or it would be appropriate for trekkers who wish to visit the Gosainkund Lakes and cross over to Helambu. If taking this fork, climb steeply through chir pine forest to a *chorten* (6950 ft, 2118 m) in **two hours**. Another **fifteen minutes** brings you to a clearing with another *chorten* and good views north and west. Continue through wheat fields to **Bhrabal** (7450 ft, 2271 m) in a **few minutes**. About 125 ft (40 m) above this pleasant village, the trail intersects the trail from Bharku to Syabru at a *chautaara* and *mani* wall. However, continue climbing steeply up to the ridge, leaving terraces (8950 ft, 2728 m) after another **1½ hours** and climbing through oak forest. In an **hour** reach a clearing (10,250 ft, 3124 m) where the trail from Syabru joins. There are good views up the Langtang Valley and to the west. Climb for a **minute**, then take the right fork which contours through blue pine forest to reach a clearing (10,450 ft, 3185 m) in **half an hour**. Here the trail to Gosainkunda, beginning from across the Trisuli Khola at Dhunche, enters. Do not climb, but continue contouring through an impressive fir and rhododendron forest to reach **Sing Gomba** and the cheese factory, Chauchan Bari (10,625 ft, 3239 m) in **half an hour**. Accommodation can be arranged here. The trail beyond to Gosainkunda has already been described.

Syabrubensi to Trisuli

To head directly back to Trisuli from Syabrubensi, cross the Langtang Khola on the suspension bridge, and head downstream on the east (L) bank of the Bhote Kosi through chir pine forest. Follow the river, then climb to join the outgoing trail beyond **Bharku** (6125 ft, 1867 m) in **2½ hours**. The outward trail from this point has already been described.

8 NORTH OF POKHARA

(Map No. 2, Page 133)

Pokhara can be the starting point for at least five treks described in this book. The three described in this chapter are: the traditional trek to Thak Khola, Jomosom, and Muktinath; the trek to Manang starting at Dumre east of Pokhara; and the trip to the Annapurna Sanctuary. It is possible to combine all three in a circuit of the Annapurna massif with a visit to the so-called sanctuary. Such a trek combines spectacular mountain scenery with incredible ethnic and cultural diversity, and traverses through very different ecological life zones. This is justifiably a classic trek, among the world's best.

Two other treks starting from Pokhara are those to Dhorpatan and to Kathmandu. They are dealt with in Chapter 11.

TO THAK KHOLA AND MUKTINATH

The trek from Pokhara to Jomosom on the Kali Gandaki, or the Thak Khola as it is called in its northern portions, is perhaps one of the easiest, most comfortable, and most popular treks in Nepal. This is because there is relatively little climbing, cooked food and lodging are easily available along the entire route, and the terrain is more varied than on any other trek of comparable length. The trail to Muktinath, a Hindu and Buddhist pilgrimage site, a day's walk north of Jomosom, is described. While the route commonly follows passes among some of the highest mountains in the world, the scenery is not as exciting as in, say, Khumbu. However, there are several side trips that take the trekker up and out of the main valleys and closer to the main Himalaya. Several are briefly described.

Unless you plan a side trip to one of the areas where there are no inhabitants, there is no need to take any food or shelter. *BhaTTi,* local inns, can provide *daal bhaat* and rooms to sleep in. In some villages, hotels can provide more "Western" style food and accommodations. These places are run by *Newar* and *Thakali.*

Transportation from Kathmandu to Pokhara is available daily by RNAC plane and road, and from India by road. A walking route from Kathmandu is described in Chapter 11. You could take a plane to or from Jomosom and thus avoid backtracking, but this really is not worth it, since backtracking only increases your understanding and enjoyment of the area. Furthermore, it is difficult to count on getting a seat on a scheduled flight in Jomosom.

From the **Pokhara** airstrip (2686 ft, 819 m) you can board a bus or taxi to Mahendra Pul in the downtown area. The bus from Kathmandu also brings you here. From Mahendra Pul a bus or taxi can take you to the Shining Hospital, or you can walk. To do so, continue up to the upper end of the bazaar where the road descends a short hill. Near its bottom an **hour** from the airstrip, turn left and head toward the Multi-Purpose High School and the Shining Hospital. The hospital (the quonset huts in the field to your right), the first such non-government facility established in Nepal, has now merged with the Gandaki Anchal Hospital, which

Machhapuchhre from just north of Pokhara. (Stephen Bezruchka) 131

lies off the road to the south of Mahendra Pul. Continue north above the right bank of the Seti Khola, and after passing a river junction, cross the tributary Yamdi Khola to its left bank (3075 ft, 937 m). After passing through a small settlement, ascend to the Hyangja Tibetan Camp (3325 ft, 1013 m) **one hour** from the Shining Hospital. Food and lodging are available, and the handicraft center is well worth visiting. If you haven't seen a carpet factory in action, be sure to see the one here. The trail heads on to the town of **Hyangja** (3600 ft, 1097 m) in **forty minutes**, then enters the long, wide Yamdi Khola Valley whose floor is a series of irrigated rice paddies. Depending on the season, the route follows either through the paddies, or the small irrigation ditch on the northeast side of the valley. **Suikhet** is the name given to the small settlement near the area where the valley opens up (3650 ft, 1113 m) and to the few tea shops. Phedi (meaning foot of hill) is at the bottom of the hill to the south (3700 ft, 1128 m). Reached just after crossing the Yamdi Khola, this area is at the western end of the paddies about **one hour** from Hyangja. Climb the hill through sal forest to the south to reach **Naudanda** (4675 ft, 1425 m) on the ridge 1½ **hours** from Suikhet. The trail then goes west along the ridge. Phewa Tal, the lake at Pokhara, is visible to the southeast. There are stunning views of Machhapuchhre and the Annapurna range, so it is worthwhile to spend a night near here or near Chandrakot, either on the way out or on the return trip, in order to get clear views in the morning.

About **five to ten minutes** west of where you reach the ridge, and 125 ft (38 m) higher, the trail to Kusma forks left. But you keep close to the ridge and bear northwest. The trail continues in countryside reminiscent of Scottish highlands through **Paundu** (5650 ft, 1722 m) to the village of **KAAre** (5700 ft, 1737 m), which is in a pass. Continue through Jaljala (5275 ft, 1608 m) and **Lumle** (5300 ft, 1615 m) to **Chandrakot** (5250 ft, 1600 m) at the west end of the ridge. Reach KAAre in 1½ **hours** from Naudanda, Lumle in another **forty-five minutes**, and Chandrakot in a further **half hour**. Lumle is the site of a British agricultural development project where former Gurkha soldiers are trained in farming.

The views from Chandrakot, as from Naudanda, are unforgettable. The river, the Modi Khola, that flows south between the peaks Annapurna South and Machhapuchhre is crossed shortly. The Annapurna Sanctuary lies up this river beyond the gate formed by Machhapuchhre and Hiunchuli, the eastern outlier of Annapurna South. It is an interesting side trip.

The trail descends to the Modi Khola, follows its east (L) bank southward a short distance to a suspension bridge, and crosses to the prosperous town of **Birethanti** (3600 ft, 1097 m) 1¼ **hours** from Chandrakot. This is a good place to stock up on supplies, because prices go up the farther you get from Pokhara. From here, one trail heads up the Modi Khola on its west (R) bank toward the Annapurna Sanctuary. The trail to Thak Khola heads west. Just up from the town by a picturesque waterfall is a cool pool on the Bhurungdi Khola. If you swim here, be sure to wear clothing in order not to offend the Nepalis. Follow the Bhurungdi Khola westward through forests at first. Stay on its northeast (L) bank, passing a steel suspension bridge. Cross several tributaries, then pass through two settlements, Lamthali and Sudame. In times of low water the trail may even cross the main river to avoid steep areas. Do what the locals are doing, but stay on the northeast (L) bank except for these short diversions. **Hille** (5000 ft, 1524 m) is reached in **two hours**, and shortly beyond is **Tirkhedunga** (5175 ft, 1577 m). Farther on the branches of the Bhurungdi Khola are crossed on several bridges (5075 ft, 1547 m). The steepest climb so far, up to **Ulleri** (6800 ft, 2073 m), takes **two hours** from Hille. Note the handsome slate roofs on the houses here. In the upper part of the village,

Getting a haircut in Tatopani north of Pokhara. (Ane Haaland)

at a *chautaara* to the left as you ascend, you may find a rock tablet inscribed as a memorial to Ben, the son of anthropologist John Hitchcock. He died here suddenly while his father was doing field work.

From Ulleri, the trail climbs steadily, enters lush oak forests and crosses numerous small streams. It passes a rest house (*dharmsala*), but no habitation, until it emerges at **GhoRapani** (9350 ft, 2850 m), a cluster of hotels below the pass some **three hours** from Ulleri. GhoRapani, meaning "horse water," is a far cry now from the one building I saw there on my first trek in Nepal in 1969. Then it truly was a watering place for the horse caravans that traveled between Pokhara and Mustang. There are more hotels at the pass, GhoRapani Deorali, which is 250 ft (76 m) higher than the town. Trekkers should make certain they catch the views, either from below the pass to the north, from the pass itself, which is now considerably deforested, or from Poon Hill, which is 875 ft (267 m) higher than the pass on the ridge to the west. Reach the hill in less than an hour. There are trails and signs pointing the way to Poon Hill from GhoRapani and from the pass. Views of Dhaulagiri and the Kali Gandaki gorge are best in the early morning. From the pass, there is a trail following the ridge to the east to link with the trail from Ghandrung.

To continue to Thak Khola, descend through rhododendron forest, then prickly-leaved oak, to cultivated areas. Pass through the villages of **Chitre** (7600 ft, 2316 m) and **Phalate** (7400 ft, 2256 m) before reaching **Sikha** (6300 ft, 1920 m) **two hours** from the pass. The descent is unforgettable because of views of the immense (still unclimbed) south face of Dhaulagiri to the north. Descend, crossing a tributary and then some landslides, to **Ghara** (5550 ft, 1692 m) **less than an hour** from Sikha. Continue through a notch with a tea shop and descend to the south (L) bank of the Ghar Khola. Cross it on a wooden bridge (3850 ft, 1173 m) and reach the few houses called Ghar Khola above the junction of the Ghar Khola and the

Kali Gandaki. The trail to Beni crosses the Ghar Khola here to continue south on the east (L) bank of the Kali Gandaki. But you should head upstream, cross the Kali Gandaki on a suspension bridge, and go on to **Tatopani** (4000 ft, 1219 m) **1½ hours** from Ghara.

Tatopani is a prosperous *Thakali* town. It takes its name (literally "hot water") from the hot springs located along the banks of the river. One, near the middle of town, has been modified considerably from the simple pool I enjoyed on my first trip. Now the walls are cemented and the hot water piped in. Nevertheless, it still soothes aching muscles. Another more primitive hot spring is on the other side of the river north of town. Cross the river on a temporary bamboo bridge five minutes beyond the town and walk back to the spring.

Head north from Tatopani, pass the few houses of Jaltal, and note the junction of the Miristi Khola and the Kali Gandaki. If you venture from Lete to the north Annapurna Base Camp, you will reach this river in its upper portions. It could well be impossible to go upstream from here; there is no record of anyone having done so. Beyond, the trail actually tunnels through the hillside to a few more houses called Phuite. Stay on the west (R) bank of the Kali Gandaki and pass through Suki Bagar to reach **Dana** (4600 ft, 1402 m) after crossing a tributary, the Gatte Khola. This stretched-out town with a police check post is reached in about **1½ hours** from Tatopani. Farther north, don't cross the main river on the suspension bridge unless you are traveling during the monsoon. Instead, continue on the west (R) bank to Titre, then climb to the few houses of Rukse Khola, named after the tributary and its waterfall just beyond. Push on to **Kabre** (5600 ft, 1707 m) **1¾ hours** from Dana. Beyond, the valley narrows spectacularly and the cascading river torrent resounds across the canyon walls. The trail traverses this section and descends to the raging river (6300 ft, 1920 m). The trail used to be literally carved out of the canyon wall, but erosion and slides have made the old portion unusable. Continue upstream to a junction in the trail. During the monsoon, you must take the bridge above Dana, cross the Kali Gandaki on a suspension bridge, and rejoin the west (R) bank trail here. Nepal is full of such dry and wet weather trails—the dry weather trails are shorter, but only the wet weather trails are feasible during high water. Beyond, the trail reaches the strung out town of **Ghasa** (6700 ft, 2042 m) **three hours** from Kabre.

Note how remarkably the land has changed over this short stretch. You may have seen lizards below, but there are none beyond. The houses beyond here have flat roofs because there is less rainfall. Similarly, as you head north, you encounter more pine forests and fewer broad-leaved trees.

Continue north, cross a tributary, and pass through Kaiku and the few houses of Gumaaune (literally "walking around") to a new cement suspension bridge over the Lete Khola (8000 ft, 2438 m), a tributary from the west. Cross it to some bamboo teahouses. **Lete** (8100 ft, 2469 m), some **ten minutes** beyond, is **two hours** from Ghasa. There is a trail coming in from the southwest before you cross the Lete Khola. It offers a high route over the south shoulder of Dhaulagiri to Beni. Annapurna I, the first 8000 m peak ever climbed, can be seen to the east from Lete.

Heading north, pass through the spread-out village of Lete which blends into **Kalopani** (8300 ft, 2530 m). Reminiscent of tourist areas elsewhere, this town boasts a trekkers' campsite! West of here is one of the world's biggest open-book geological formations. Cross a tributary north of town to a good suspension bridge over the Kali Gandaki. Cross it in the dry season if there is a good temporary bridge to cross back over the Kali Gandaki farther upstream. Check what others are doing. If you cross to the east (L) bank here, the trail passes through Dhampu and Kokethanti before crossing back to the west (R) bank just below **Larjung** (8400 ft, 2560 m). It takes 1½ **hours** from Kalopani this way. In the monsoon, or if you wish to reach the area below the southeast Dhaulagiri icefall, stay on the west (R) bank and cross a river delta with its alluvial fan to reach the few houses of Chatang in **half an hour**. Just beyond is a *chautaara* with a plaque commemorating the 1969 Dhaulagiri tragedy in which seven members of an American expedition were killed in an ice avalanche. The trail to the icefall cuts off left just to the north. If continuing on to Larjung, cross another tributary, enter a pine and juniper forest, then cross the broad delta of the Ghatte Khola, wading where necessary, to rejoin the forest. Larjung is just beyond, perhaps 1¾ **hours** from Kalopani. To the west is the incredibly foreshortened summit of Dhaulagiri, almost 3.5 mi (5.5 km) higher than you.

From Larjung, head north, cross a tributary, and in a **few minutes** enter the fascinating town of **Khobang** (8400 ft, 2560 m). The trail passes through a tunnel, and doors to the houses open off it. The village is thus protected from the strong winds that blow up the valley almost every afternoon. There is a *gomba* to the east of the trail. Khobang is called Kanti in the northern portion. **Tukche** (8500 ft, 2591 m), a historically important town, is an **hour** beyond.

Tukche used to be an important center for the trade of Nepali grain for Tibetan salt through the valley of the Thak Khola. *Thakali Subbha,* or customs contractors, controlled it and exacted taxes at Tukche in the summer, and at Dana in the winter. When the Chinese occupied Tibet, the trade dwindled, and the enterprising *Thakali* turned their attention south and became more involved in business ventures around Pokhara and in the Tarai. Their spread throughout many of the trade routes in Nepal resulted in the establishment of many *bhaTTi,* even before trekking became popular. With the coming of foreigners, the *Thakali* developed hotel facilities for them. I urge you to try and find a traditional *bhaTTi* and sample a good Nepali meal of *daal bhaat taarkari* (lentils, rice, and vegetables). The *Thakali* prosper in whatever they turn to. In comparing my visits to this region almost ten years apart, I find the improvements impressive—water systems, latrines, more schools, indeed functioning schools, better trails, more varieties of crops, and cleaner homes. Of course, it is all relative. If this region strikes you as destitute and dirty, what would you think of the poor areas of Nepal? *Thakali* have always exhibited a strong ethnic group consciousness, and Thak Khola is their homeland.

A strong wind blows from the south up the valley, beginning in the late morning and lasting most of the day. This is probably caused when the air mass over the plateau to the north warms, rises, and creates a pressure difference. The wind is from the north in the early morning, so this is the best time to head south. As you go up the valley from Tukche, notice how there is relatively little vegetation on the valley floor itself, but there are trees and forests on the walls. This is because the valley floor is in a rain shadow due to the strong winds. When the wind is blowing, you may notice that there are no clouds over the center of the valley, but clouds do hang on the sides.

A trail to Dhampus Pass goes up the hill to the west of the *gomba* at Tukche. It is described later. The next town upstream is **Marpha** (8750 ft, 2667 m), some 1½ **hours** away. Marpha has a fine sewer system—a series of canals flowing down the streets. About **ten minutes** before Marpha, pass by the Government Agricultural Station, which has introduced new crops into the area. You may be able to purchase fresh fruit and vegetables in season. Marpha is another attractive town whose inhabitants call themselves *PaunchgaaUle,* people ethnically similar to the *Thakali.* Some of the hotels in Marpha, and also in Jomosom, advertise pony rides as far as Muktinath. The foot-weary trekker may welcome the opportunity to change his mode of travel. Dhampus Pass can also be reached from Marpha. To continue upstream, leave the town by the now familiar style of *chorten* and cross first a tributary, then another alluvial fan from the west, the Pongkyu Khola. The town of Syang is beyond, and its monastery is up the hill a bit farther.

On certain days during late October and early November, dance festivals staged by monks are performed in the *gomba* of Marpha, Syang, and possibly others. These are somewhat similar to the Mani-rimdu dance-drama festivals of Solu-Khumbu, and are definitely worth seeing. The Nepali name for such a festival is *dyokyapsi.*

Cross a tributary farther up the valley, and reach **Jomosom** (8900 ft, 2713 m), the center for Mustang District, 1½ **hours** from Marpha. There is a STOL airstrip here with scheduled service to Kathmandu. But because of the winds, service is rather unreliable. Other facilities include banks, a hospital, radio service, rather luxurious food and accommodations, and, of course, a police check post. This town has prospered immensely over the years and now has a large number of government employees who must be fed. Many of the pony caravans bring food to Jomosom.

The countryside to the north is very arid, not unlike the Tibetan Plateau farther north. To the south, Dhaulagiri impressively guards the Thak Khola Valley. It is much less foreshortened than at Larjung. To the east, across the river on a shelf of land, is the town of Thinigaon (9500 ft, 2897 m), reached in half an hour from Jomosom. Up the valley east of Thinigaon is Tilicho Pass and Tilicho Tal. The latter, at 16,140 ft (4919 m), is one of the highest, most spectacular lakes in the world. Once open to trekking, this area has recently been closed to access from Jomosom because of a Nepali army camp this side of the pass. The ban may someday be lifted. It takes at least two days to reach the lake from the valley floor, and caution must be exercised because of the rapid ascent.

To continue on to Kagbeni and Muktinath, head northeast on the west (R) side of the Kali Gandaki (you could also take the east (L) side, but this would probably require more river fording). Stay on the valley floor close to the river. In 1¼ **hours** reach a wooden cantilever bridge over the Kali Gandaki (9000 ft, 2743 m). You may need to wade some rivulets here. Once on the east (L) bank, head upstream for **ten minutes** to the trail junction of **Chyancha-Lhrenba** (9050 ft, 2758 m). The left fork continues up the river to **Kagbeni** (9200 ft, 2804 m) in **half an hour**, while the right ascends out of the valley and heads more directly to Muktinath. The right fork reaches the junction (10,350 ft, 3155 m) of the trail from Kagbeni to Muktinath in 1½ **hours**. The name Kagbeni aptly reflects the town's character—*kak* means blockade in the local dialect, and *beni* means junction of two rivers. And this citadel does effectively block the valley. River junctions are especially sacred to the local people. Since the town is at the confluence of trails from the north, south, east and west, the ancient king who sat here could control and tax the exchange of grain from the south and wool and salt from the north. The ruins of his palace, which can still be seen, are a reminder of the ancient kingdoms that predated the unification of Nepal. Some scholars believe the family that ruled here was related to the ancient kings of Jumla. The Sakyapa monastery here is rundown, but worth a visit. You may see two large terra-cotta images of the protector deities of the town—a male at the north end and a female at the south. This mingling of old animistic beliefs with those of the more developed religions is common in Nepal. People here call themselves *Gurung,* but are clearly not the same as the *Gurung* to the south. People from Tibet who have settled in Nepal often call themselves *Gurung* to facilitate assimilation. This practice has continued with the recent immigration of Tibetan refugees in the 1960s.

The impressive folding of the cliffs west of town illustrates the powerful forces of orogeny. You can just make out the crest of the Thorung La Pass up the valley to the east of town. Try and make out Kagbeni from the pass. The trail to Mustang and the Kingdom of Lo crosses the Kali Gandaki here and heads up the west (R) bank. In Kagbeni itself, there is a police check post. It is currently the northern limit for trekkers.

To go to Muktinath, cross the Dzong Khola, the tributary to the east, and head east through terraces to the trail's junction (10,350 ft, 3155 m) with the trail from Chyancha-Lhrenba in 1½ **hours**. Continue east, noting the caves on the north side of the valley. On a clear day, the walk along here can be ethereal, as the dry valley sparkles and the north wall seems suspended close to you. Contour above the town of Khyenghar (Khingar on some maps) to **Jharkot** (11,850 ft, 3612 m), an impressive fortress perched on a ridge 1½ **hours** from the trail junction above Kagbeni. Jharkot, called Dzar by Tibetans, is believed to have been the home of the ruling house of this valley. Note how some houses around the ruins of the fort are made of blocks of earth.

Continue climbing and contouring, often staying near an irrigation trough. Along the trail there are little piles of stones made by pilgrims returning from Muktinath in hopes of obtaining a better reincarnation. Go on to Ranipowa (12,225 ft, 3726 m), a large tin-roofed building in disrepair. Across the valley you can see extensive ruins of Dzong ("castle" in Tibetan) and the town built around it. **Muktinath** (12,475 ft, 3802 m) is less than **ten minutes** farther. Dhaulagiri looms impressively to the south.

Muktinath, located in a poplar grove, is a sacred shrine for Hindus and Buddhists alike. It is an ancient Hindu pilgrimage site mentioned in the *Mahabharata* (a book of Hindu mythology written about 300 B.C.) because of the presence of ammonite fossils. It is also a Buddhist pilgrimage site. Water is important in ritual purification for Hindus. The springs piped into the 108 waterspouts near the temple (which is dedicated to the Hindu deity Vishnu) are the focal point for the pilgrims. The Buddhists revere the fire from the natural gas jets that spout from earth, rock, and water. Certainly most of the pilgrims today are Hindus, predominantly the "twice-born" or high castes. For Nepali Hindus this place ranks with Gosainkunda and Pashupati as major pilgrimage sites. The "miraculous fires" can be seen in the Nyingmapa *gomba* south of the hotel and police check post. Here, curtained away under the altar, are the sacred flames. Your Sherpas and other Buddhist porters may ask you for a bottle to take some of the "water that burns" with them. Be sure to leave an offering for the upkeep of the temple. Devout Hindu pilgrims drink the water, but those who want to bathe in each of its 108 spouts do so quickly since the water is quite cold at this altitude. The area abounds with *chorten* and old Buddhist temples. There is a *dharmsala* and a hotel for pilgrims, but no village as such.

Many people from Mustang and other areas come to sell handicrafts to the pilgrims. Some sell a particular fossil called a *shaligram;* it is of a mollusc called an ammonite from a period roughly ten million years ago. These objects, treasured for worship by Hindus, are said to represent several deities, principally those associated with Vishnu, the Lord of Salvation.

To the east is the Thorung La Pass (17,650 ft, 5380 m) leading to Manang. Crossing it from Muktinath to Manang is more difficult than crossing in the other direction, for in the dry season there are few if any suitable campsites with water on this side of the pass. It is a very long day to ascend from Muktinath to the pass and then to descend to the first campsite on the other side. Altitude illness may jeopardize those who are unacclimatized. Crossing from Manang, on the other hand, is easier because of the comparatively long time spent at high altitudes before approaching the pass, and because of the higher campsites below the east side of the pass. The pass is often crossed from Muktinath, but it certainly is more difficult and hazardous. Under no condition should you ascend from either direction unless the entire party, including porters, is well equipped to camp in snow should a storm arise. The trail descriptions for the Manang to Muktinath crossing are given with the Manang section later in this chapter.

On the return journey, consider some variations such as: returning to Marpha via Thinigaon, approaching from Jomosom on the east (L) bank of the river; crossing to the east (L) bank near Larjung and Khobang and following this side to Dhamphu opposite Kalopani; following the east (L) bank through the narrow gorge between Ghasa and Dana; returning to Pokhara by following the Kali Gandaki south from Tatopani past Beni, Baglung, Kusma, and east to Pokhara. This last variation is described in greater detail later, but first some side trips out of the Thak Khola Valley are described. All are strenuous trips to substantial altitudes where food, fuel, and shelter must be carried. At certain times of the year, snow can make the trips almost impossible. Parties should be prepared for cold at any time of the year. It is always best to have someone along who is familiar with the route. You could climb out of the valley at other points and get good views of the mountains.

Dhampus Pass

Dhampus Pass (17,000 ft, 5184 m) connects the valley of the Thak Khola with Hidden Valley. It lies beyond the tree line and is often snowed in. Huts used for pasturing yaks are found in route to the pass, and can be used for shelter and cooking on the way up. There are no facilities at the pass. Carry food, fuel and shelter. Temperatures below freezing can always be expected and in the winter months the temperature drops below 0° F (−18° C). A trip to the pass is ideal for those who want a more intense experience with the mountains. Reach it from Tukche or Marpha by going to some yak huts (13,000 ft, 3962 m) the first day, and to the pass the next. This may be too rapid an ascent for many people. If you are unprepared to spend a night at the pass, you could go up and return to the yak huts in a day.

To trek from Tukche to Dhampus Pass, go to the large open field at the north end of the village. Just behind, to the east, is a steep earth cliff. Follow a plainly-defined switchback trail to the top and continue along the ridge behind the cliff. You pass through scattered apricot trees and horse pasturage for a mile to arrive at the base of a high rock cliff. Keeping well to the east, the trail ascends this steep, but not technically difficult, cliff, and comes out just above where the ridge plunges down to the Kali Gandaki far below. You are now on the end of the ridge defining the north side of the Dhampus Khola. There are fantastic views up the Kali Gandaki toward Mustang, and a panorama, from Tilicho Peak in the east round through the Nilgiris, the Annapurnas, and Dhaulagiri to Tukche Peak in the southwest.

Up to this point, the trail is fairly well-defined. But on the ridge it degenerates into myriad cow and yak trails, and you are pretty much on your own. Generally, from where the trail reaches the top of the ridge, continue up its north side for about two hours until you come to a low point (relatively speaking), then cross the south (Dhampus Khola) side of the ridge. Looking up the Dhampus Khola Valley, you can see a large rock ridge going off your ridge and dropping steeply into the Khola. It is perpendicular to your line of travel. Traverse upward slightly toward this ridge to a wide trail, which takes you around and behind the ridge. This is the main trail to the upper portion of the Dhampus Khola Valley, and is used by local herders taking their yaks up to graze during the summer. Yak yogurt is delicious and you should try to buy some at the herders' huts along the way.

After crossing the rock ridge, climb obliquely upward by obvious routes to Dhampus Pass, which is itself not visible at this point. If there is any question of cloudy weather, it is better to hire a local man from Tukche as a guide. Once clouds settle in, it is very easy to get lost. If fog becomes a problem, don't descend to the Dhampus Khola to escape, since the Khola is impassable due to rock cliffs in its lower portions. If you become confused in a fog, stay up high and traverse eastward back toward Marpha or Tukche. Again, be careful to descend if severe symptoms of altitude sickness come on.

Beyond the pass, you can descend into the upper (southern) end of Hidden Valley for excellent views of Dhaulagiri's north face and the glaciated pass called French Pass which lies between Dhaulagiri and her sister peak to the west, Dhaula Himal. You may see the remains of a plane near the pass. It is a Swiss Pilatus Porter that crashed in 1961. The plane was used to ferry people and loads from Pokhara for the Dhaulagiri Expedition. Semi-wild yak herds, snow leopards, and mountain sheep may be encountered in Hidden Valley.

Dhaulagiri Icefall

The area below the east Dhaulagiri icefall, where the American Base Camp of 1969 was located, abounds with yak pastures and is at a lower altitude than Dhampus Pass. It has correspondingly less severe conditions. The views of the mountains are excellent, possibly better than at Dhampus Pass.

To reach this area, proceed from the trail junction north of the few houses of Chatang between Kalopani and Larjung. The trail leaves the valley near a *chautaara* with a plaque commemorating the 1969 Dhaulagiri tragedy of the American Expedition to Dhaulagiri in which seven people were killed in an ice avalanche. Again, it is best to hire a local guide. The area below the icefall (12,400 ft, 3780 m) can be reached in a day from the Kali Gandaki. Beware of avalanches in the vicinity of the icefall.

Annapurna Base Camp

The route to the original Annapurna Base Camp was discovered by the French Expedition to Annapurna in 1950 led by Maurice Herzog. The French first tried to climb Dhaulagiri, but found it beyond their capabilities, and instead tried to find a way to the base of Annapurna. They had difficulty getting there from the Kali Gandaki, and the route still has a bad reputation. It is seldom used except by shepherds and mountaineering expeditions. However, in the relatively snow-free conditions of early fall and late spring, it is neither very difficult nor dangerous. The trail is often indistinct and traverses steep grassy slopes. Porters do not like this trail, but it is certainly no worse than little-used trails in many other areas of mountain wilderness.

On route to Annapurna Base Camp. (Stephen Bezruchka)

The views along the way are spectacular. The trail climbs steeply out of the Kali Gandaki Valley, the incredible gorge becomes more and more impressive. The views of Dhaulagiri and Annapurna from the crest of the ridge separating the Kali Gandaki from the Miristi Khola are breathtaking. Only from this perch (14,000 ft, 4267 m), some 7000 ft (2134 m) above the valley floor, can you appreciate just how high these mountains are. It is hard to believe that Dhaulagiri is the sixth highest mountain in the world from the foreshortened view from Kalopani. If you venture beyond the base camp toward Camp One on the north side of Annapurna, you can appreciate the impressive features of that side of the mountain.

There are neither villages nor shelter from Chhoya onward, so you must be self-sufficient for at least five days. It is best to hire someone from Chhoya to show the way. In times of high water, it may be impossible to cross the Miristi Khola and reach the base camp without building a bridge, an undertaking most trekkers prefer to avoid. But with the increasing number of expeditions to Annapurna, the chance of finding a usable bridge is good. Check beforehand to find out if there has been a recent expedition. In low water the river can be forded with some difficulty downstream. If there is no bridge, consider at least climbing to the height of land for the spectacular views.

If you are coming from the south, turn off the regular trail just after crossing the Lete Khola on a new suspension bridge. Keep close to the Kali Gandaki for some **ten minutes** before crossing the tumultuous river on a wooden bridge to reach Chhoya (8000 ft, 2484 m). If you are coming from the north, take a left fork a **few minutes** before reaching Lete and after passing through Upala Lete (8150 ft, 2484 m). This left fork takes you through a beautiful pine forest before you descend slightly in **ten minutes** to the same wooden bridge to Chhoya. You can get provisions in Chhoya or in Lete. From Chhoya, cross the delta of the Polje Khola and ascend to the few houses of Poljedanda (8175 ft, 2492 m). Then turn right and head southeast to the few more houses of Deorali (8275 ft, 2522 m) **half an hour** from Chhoya. This is the last village on the route. Here the trail forks left and you contour above fields to enter the valley of the Tangdung or Bhutra Khola, a little more than **half an hour** later. Contour below a small waterfall of a tributary to the main river (8075 ft, 2461 m) after a short, steep descent through forest. The river is 1¼ **hours** from Deorali. There should be a wooden bridge here unless it has been washed out during the monsoon. Fill up all your water containers as you may not get another chance during the next day.

The next section of the trail ascends 6000 ft (1829 m) and is unrelentingly steep. There are few suitable camping sites until near the end of the climb. After crossing to the southeast (L) bank, ascend a cliff and enter a mixed broad-leaved forest. The trail is easy to follow and the forest is pleasant. There are occasional vistas to inspire the weary. In the upper reaches you find areas of bamboo, then rhododendron, fir, and birch forests. In 2½ **hours**, reach a saddle called Kal Ghiu (11,000 ft, 3383 m). Some trekking groups call this place Jungle Camp. Camping is possible here if you can find water down the other side of the saddle. Keep close to the crest of the ridge as you pass several notches. Enjoy the rhododendrons in bloom in the spring. After keeping to the southeast side of the ridge and leaving the forest, the trail becomes fainter, reaches a minor ridge crest (12,600 ft, 3840 m), and crosses over to the northwest side. Keep climbing to a prominent notch with a *chorten* (13,350 ft, 4069 m) some **two hours** from Kal Ghiu. The views of Dhaulagiri are unforgettable.

The slope eases off now, and continues over more moderate grazing slopes to a place near a ridge crest called Sano Bugin (13,950 ft, 4252 m) where herders stay during the monsoon. There are rock walls here that the herders convert to shelters with the use of bamboo mats. If there is no snow to melt, water may be difficult to obtain. The gigantic west face of Annapurna, a challenge for rock climbers of the future, is before you. Head north along the ridge crest, or on the west side. The trail is marked with slabs of rock standing on end. In an **hour**, reach another ridge crest (14,375 ft, 4382 m) and cross to the southeast side of the ridge. This may be the "passage du avril 27" that Herzog's expedition discovered in order to get to the base of Annapurna. You are now in the drainage area of the Miristi Khola, the river that enters the Kali Gandaki above Tatopani.

Continue contouring for a **few minutes** to Thulo Bugin (14,300 ft, 4359 m) where herders stay. There is a small shrine here. Contour, crossing several tributaries of the Hum Khola, a tributary of the Miristi. The last stream (13,375 ft, 4077 m), reached in **half an hour**, is a little tricky to cross. Climb on, at first gradually, then more steeply, to reach a flat area sometimes called Bal Khola (14,650 ft, 4465 m) in 1¾ **hours**. Camp here, for there are few other suitable places until the river is reached. The west face of Annapurna looms before you. Local people do not venture much beyond here in their tending of sheep and goats.

Descend and round a ridge crest to the canyon of the Miristi Khola proper. The river is almost a mile below you, yet its roar can be heard. Continue on steep grassy slopes and pass an overhanging rock (14,075 ft, 4290 m) suitable for camping **forty-five minutes** from the high point. Descend more steeply on grass, cross a stream, and go down into shrubbery until it appears that a 1000 ft (300 m) cliff will block the way to the valley floor. The trail heads west to a break in the rock wall, and descends through the break to the river (11,550 ft, 3505 m) **1½ hours** from the overhanging rock. The gorge at the bottom is most impressive and gives a feeling of relative isolation. Head upstream on the northwest (R) bank. The dense shrubs may make travel difficult. There are campsites by some sand near a widening in the river (11,575 ft, 3528 m) where it may be possible to ford in low water. Otherwise, head upstream for **ten minutes** to a narrowing where there may be a bridge. Cross the river, if possible, and camp on the other side if it is late.

Once on the southeast (L) bank of the Miristi Khola, follow the trail upstream. The vegetation soon disappears as altitude and erosion increase. The trail becomes indistinct in the moraine. As the valley opens up, bear right to the east and leave the river bottom to climb the moraine to a vague shelf. Continue beyond to a small glacial lake in the terminal moraine of the North Annapurna Glacier. Cross its outflow to the right and climb the lateral moraine to the left. There are views of the Nilgiris to the west. The base camp for the various attempts to climb Annapurna from the north is on a flat shelf of land (14,300 ft, 4359 m) to the north of the glacier. There is a steep drop-off to the glacier valley to the south and east. The base camp is reached in **three to four hours** from the crossing of the Miristi Khola.

The view of Annapurna I from the base camp is minimal. Better views can be obtained by contouring and climbing to the east to a grassy knoll from which much of the north face can be seen. You could also proceed toward Camp I by dropping from the shelf and climbing along the lateral moraine of the glacier to 16,000 ft (4877 m). Exploratory and climbing journeys will suggest themselves to those with experience. The Great Barrier, an impressive wall of mountains to the north, separates you from Tilicho Tal. Be sure to take enough food to stay awhile and enjoy this unforgettable area.

Tilicho Tal

To reach Tilicho Tal, proceed up the trail from Thinigaon (9500 ft, 2895 m). It winds up the north side of the valley which leads to the pass to the east. There is little or no water along the lower part of the route. Pass through rhododendron, fir, and birch forests to reach alpine vegetation. Soon after crossing two tributaries, the trail leads to a *goTh* (14,000 ft, 2468 m) some **six hours** from Thinigaon. Another **day** takes you over the Tilicho Pass (16,730 ft, 5100 m) to the majestic ice walls beyond. The pass itself is not clearly seen from the *goTh*. It is glaciated, so those who are not equipped for ice climbing may prefer to head up one of the gullies north of the pass. This involves a greater climb, up to 17,500 ft (5334 m) or so, but it is preferable for most parties. A trip to the lake and climbs of nearby summits are rewarding. The lake is often frozen. Trekkers attempting to climb up to the lake from the valley in two days must be especially watchful for signs and symptoms of altitude sickness. They should descend at the first signs of severe symptoms.

Tatopani to Pokhara via Beni

The return to Pokhara from Tatopani via Beni mentioned earlier involves less climbing and does not necessarily take more time. It is not advisable to go this way in late spring as it is much hotter than on the higher route. To proceed from

Tilicho Tal, a lake situated at almost 17,000 ft (5000 m) with the immense wall of the Great Barrier to the south. (Brot Coburn)

Tatopani, cross the suspension bridge to the east (L) bank of the Kali Gandaki and cross the wooden bridge over the Ghar Khola to its south (L) bank to rejoin the Kali Gandaki. Proceed south on its east (L) bank.

After **several hours** on the trail, which in places is carved into the rock cliff and passes through subtropical valley forest, cross to the west (R) bank at **Tipling** (3400 ft, 1037 m) and climb high up the west (R) bank. Eventually descend to **Ranipauwa** (3900 ft, 1189 m) and cross the tributary Radughat Khola. Ranipauwa, some **six hours** from Tatopani, is the site of the annual *mela* (fair) that is usually in mid-November.

An **hour** after crossing the tributary, come to a suspension bridge over the Kali Gandaki just before **Beni** (2700 ft, 823 m), the administrative center for Mayagdi District. If you cross the bridge to the left bank, the important administrative and market town of Baglung (3200 ft, 975 m) is bypassed and the trail reaches Khaniyaghat below and on the side of the river opposite Baglung. This takes **three hours**. The view of the south face of Dhaulagiri from Baglung is quite incredible. Alternatively, by staying on the west (R) bank, and crossing the Mayagdi Khola at Beni, you can reach **Baglung** high above the river in **three hours**. Descending and crossing the Kali Gandaki to its east (L) bank, you can reach **Khaniyaghat** (2725 ft, 831 m) in **half an hour**. By proceeding to Balewa, **three hours** south of Baglung, you could reach an airstrip with regular RNAC service to Kathmandu.

From Khaniyaghat, continue south through sal forest to reach **Shastradara** (2550 ft, 777 m) in an **hour**. The trail follows close to the river to reach **Armadi** (2575 ft, 785 m) in **forty-five minutes**. Then climb a ridge to enter a wet subtropical forest leading to **Chamalgai** (3050 ft, 930 m) in another **forty-five minutes**. The cobbled path continues to **Kusma** (3000 ft, 914 m), the district center of Parbat District, in **half an hour**.

From Kusma there are two routes to Pokhara. One, which reaches the road south of Pokhara, is shorter and involves less climbing than the route described here. But it is much less scenic. This route is described going the other direction to Dhorpatan in Chapter 10.

For the other route, take the left fork at the east end of Kusma. Contour to the east and descend after **forty-five minutes** to a suspension bridge over the Modi Khola (2500 ft, 702 m). Three rivers meet here. Ascend up the valley of the middle one, the Rati Khola, to Dobila (3000 ft, 914 m). Don't confuse this town with the Dobila east of Baglung. Back in wet subtropical forest, the trail ascends to **Tilhar** (3600 ft, 1097 m) and **Sallyan**. It reaches the Bhaudari Deorali Pass (5500 ft, 1676 m) in about **four hours** from the Modi Khola. From the pass, the trail contours below the village of Paundur (5500 ft, 1676 m) to **Naudanda** (4782 ft, 1458 m) in another **four hours**. This town should not be confused with the Naudanda southwest of Pokhara.

There are two routes from Naudanda to Pokhara. One, the route of ascent from the Yamdi Khola via Suikhet, enters Pokhara from the north. The other goes along the ridge crest east of Naudanda to the town of Saranghat (5200 ft, 1585 m). About **half an hour** east of Naudanda, you reach a point on the ridge crest from which all the peaks from Dhaulagiri to Manaslu and Himalchuli can be seen. Soon after, descend to the west end of Phewa Tal (2500 ft, 762 m) and follow its north shore to the airstrip. It takes about **four hours** to reach the lake from Naudanda and another **hour** to reach the airstrip.

THE MODI KHOLA AND THE ANNAPURNA SANCTUARY

The valley of the Modi Khola west of Pokhara presents additional trekking possibilities. Those with insufficient time to trek to Jomosom and back (it requires two weeks), could consider a trek up the Modi Khola into the Annapurna Sanctuary. This term refers to the high basin southwest of Annapurna whose entrance is the narrow valley between Hiunchuli and Machhapuchhri. This vast amphitheatre surrounded by Himalayan giants was brought to the attention of the Western world by the British Expedition to Machhapuchhre in 1957. First the trek up the valley of the Modi Khola from Birethanti is described, then various possibilities linking this route with trails to Pokhara and Tatopani. The trail from Pokhara to Birethanti has been described. The Modi Khola trek could be included with the Thak Khola trek.

From **Birethanti** (3400 ft, 1037 m), the trail begins near the suspension bridge and heads north along the west (R) bank of the Modi Khola through fields and forests. A wooden bridge over a tributary is crossed after an **hour** and the climbing begins on a rock staircase, quite typical of the *Gurung* country you are now entering. Pass through the scattered houses of **Kimche** (5400 ft, 1646 m) and continue up the rock stairs for some 2½ **hours** to **Ghandrung** (6400 ft, 1951 m), one of the largest *Gurung* villages in the country. The views into the sanctuary from this oak-forested area are superb, and it is worthwhile to spend a night in order to get the best views in the morning.

To continue up the valley, pass through the sprawling village of Ghandrung and head north to a notch (7317 ft, 2230 m) an **hour** beyond. Descend to the Kyumnu Khola, a tributary of the Modi Khola. Cross this tributary (5800 ft, 1768 m) and pass through the scattered houses of **Kyumnu** (6000 ft, 1829 m). Then climb up through the forest on the north side of the tributary valley and head north, contouring below a ridge (6700 ft, 2043 m) to the next tributary valley. The trail then descends to the village of **Chomro** (6400 ft, 1951 m) on the south side of the valley. It takes an hour from the notch to Kyumnu and then 2½ **hours** to Chomro. This

Gurung village is the last permanent settlement up the valley. There may be some shepherds beyond in the warmer months, but food must be carried. The most impressive views from Chomro are of Annapurna South, Hiunchuli, and Machhapuchhre. Machhapuchhre means "fishtail" and the reason is quite evident from here.

To continue north toward the sanctuary, descend from Chomro, cross the tributary, ascend the other side of the valley to a shoulder, and reenter the main valley (7000 ft, 2134 m). In case of doubts about the route, take the upper fork at junctions. **Three hours** from Chomro you come to a recently constructed stone hut called **Kuldi Ghar** (7800 ft, 2377 m). Beyond that, the trail descends through jungles to near the river (7300 ft, 2225 m) and continues north through dense growths of bamboo. Periodically, you enter clearings with frame shelters that shepherds use after covering them with bamboo mats. The forest is rhododendron, oak, and hemlock.

Three hours from Kuldi Ghar, pass a wall, which seems to weep because of water dripping from it, on the opposite side of the valley. In another **two hours** reach a large overhanging rock called **Hinko** (9900 ft, 3014 m). It offers excellent shelter. Just beyond it, the trail has been obliterated by a recent landslide, but once found on the far side, it soon leads to the valley floor which has now widened considerably. You leave the trees and in **three hours** from Hinko, pass the gates of the sanctuary (11,700 ft, 3566 m). The trail keeps to the west (R) bank of the river. Before reaching a large lateral moraine laying roughly east-west, head west along its base (12,500 ft, 3810 m). Suitable campsites can be found in this region, but bring a stove and fuel. Roughly **three or four hours** beyond Hinko, you should be well inside the sanctuary. The times given here are for good, snow-free conditions, which are unlikely in late winter and early spring.

You can proceed along the crest of the lateral moraine to near its junction with the moraine of a glacier flowing down from the Annapurna South-Hiunchuli Col, where there is a cairn (13,270 ft, 4045 m) marked CNRSB. From here the view of the south face of Annapurna is magnificent. This face was climbed by a British party in the spring of 1970. There are excellent views from the eastern end of the moraine as well. You can cross the river beyond the moraine and further explore the sanctuary, or climb Rukse Peak or Tent Peak.

There are many ways in which the treks from Pokhara to Tatopani, or to the Modi Khola can be varied. The ones described here cross the Modi Khola between Ghandrung and Landrung. These variations offer alternatives in treks to the sanctuary as well.

From **Suikhet** (3600 ft, 1097 m) some **4½ hours** from the airstrip at Pokhara, a trail goes up the hill to the north of the Yamdi Khola. An **hour** on this trail brings you to **Astam** at the crest of a ridge 1000 ft (300 m) higher.

Follow the ridge westward, passing Henjakat, Dhital, and **Dhampus** (5900 ft, 1799 m). From Dhampus, reached in **two hours** from Astam, continue climbing on or near the ridge to cross a small pass (7100 ft, 2165 m) after **2½ hours**. From here, descend to the *Gurung* village of **Landrung** (5400 ft, 1646 m) in another **2½ hours**. Continue descending and cross the Modi Khola (4500 ft, 1371 m) after **half an hour**. Then climb directly to **Ghandrung** (6400 ft, 1951 m) in **two hours**.

From Ghandrung it is possible to head south in the Modi Khola Valley, remaining at high elevations through Mohariya, Dansing, and Sabit, to reach **Tirkhedunga** (4900 ft, 1493 m) in the valley of the Bhurungdi Khola upstream from

Birethanti. This route takes **less than a day** from Ghandrung, and is better when the higher route going west from Ghandrung or Kyumnu is snowed in. A local person could be engaged to show the way.

The high route west mentioned above can be taken from either Ghandrung or Kyumnu, since both trails join east of Thante. From Ghandrung, climb above the village for about **three hours** through a thick oak and rhododendron jungle to 9000 ft (2743 m) before descending to the upper reaches of the Bhurungdi Khola, where there is a hut in a clearing called **Thante** (8600 ft, 2621 m). From Thante, climb west to an open area, then cross a pass (10,100 ft, 3079 m) **two hours** from Thante.

From this pass you can either keep to the ridge and head west to meet the other trail at the **GhoRapani Pass** in about 1½ **hours**, or you can descend directly to **Chitre** (7700 ft, 2347 m) in a little over **two hours**. Since there are no villages between Ghandrung or Kyumnu and Chitre, food must be carried. It is easy to get lost in the forest, so it is best to take an experienced guide.

TO MANANG AND OVER THE THORUNG LA

The Manang area was only recently opened to trekkers. It offers many of the same attractions of a trek to Jomosom via Thak Khola, except that the Marsyangdi Khola valley lacks the strong winds and associated dry vegetation near the river. Furthermore, the area does not abound with *Thakali bhaTTi,* and the clang-clong of horse bells of long caravans won't be heard. On the other hand, the Manangba, the people of Manang, are a most worldly ethnic group and some of the men may have traveled farther on the globe than you. The mountain scenery is perhaps more breathtaking than on the other side, if only because the peaks in the open Manang Valley are closer.

Enjoy it all. Cross the Thorung La Pass and circle the Annapurna massif. It is a walk of over 150 mi (330 km), but the rewards certainly compensate for the effort. The circuit takes at least three weeks, perhaps a week more than just walking to Manang and then retracing your steps, but this includes time for some diversions. To do the circuit, your entire party, including porters, must be totally self-sufficient for three or four days in order to cross the pass. Otherwise, cooked food and shelter can be obtained over most of the route. Staples for the crossing can usually be purchased in Manang village. Crossings can be difficult or impossible if there is deep, soft snow on the pass. Such conditions can be expected from January to March, and often longer. Storms can threaten the party at any time, and it is prudent to wait them out or turn back rather than risk lives. Needless deaths have occurred here.

The route is described from Dumre on the Kathmandu-Pokhara Road. You could begin by walking directly from Pokhara to intersect the trail described here at either Khudi or near Tarkughat. The Khudi to Pokhara route is described briefly here, while the Tarkughat to Pokhara route is part of the Pokhara-Kathmandu trek described in Chapter 11. **Dumre** (1500 ft, 457 m) is reached in some five hours by bus from Kathmandu, or in 2½ hours from Pokhara. Board the bus in Pokhara at Mahendra Pul. In Kathmandu the staging area is near the post office early in the morning, or on the east side of the Tundikhel later in the day. Dumre is one of many towns that have sprung up along the road to serve the needs of travelers, and to be staging areas for people arriving at the road or heading out from it. This is the last place to get a wide range of provisions at reasonable prices. Beyond, items are either not available or more expensive.

From Dumre head north and just beyond the town, cross a small river by a series of rocks to the north (L) bank. Go upstream a short distance to a road that may be passable by four-wheel-drive vehicle. This road is one of several being constructed to serve as feeders from the few surfaced main roads in Nepal. It has been under construction for several years, and when completed, will go at least as far as Besisahar. The trail follows the road except for shortcuts which provide pleasant relief. In **fifteen minutes**, turn off the road to the right and enter a subtropical deciduous forest, then climb to the first few houses of **Bhansar** (1800 ft, 549 m) in **ten minutes**. Continue past dwellings until you reach a *chautaara* in the center of town and go on **for some fifteen minutes** to reach an oil press (a fuel-driven one that whistles when in operation). Turn right toward the Marsyangdi Khola, the major river that you follow for many days. The trail stays a few hundred feet above the west (R) bank and reaches the small town of Barabise (1650 ft, 503 m) in **twenty minutes**. Reach Chambas (1750 ft, 533 m) in **forty-five minutes**, then **Turturi** (1725 ft, 526 m) in another **forty-five minutes**. A suburb of Turturi called **Paundi Dovan** (1675 ft, 511 m) sits above a suspension bridge over the Marsyangdi Khola **ten minutes** farther. The Palungtar airstrip (called Gorkha on RNAC schedules) directly across the river could be used by trekkers who want to avoid the road trip to Dumre.

From Paundi Dovan, cross a tributary to the north and continue along the west (R) bank of the Marsyangdi Khola. The trail passes through many small towns, including Tharpani (1825 ft, 556 m) in **fifty-five minutes**. Beyond, there are fewer settlements and more farmland until an **hour** later you come to a point across from Tarkughat, a major town on the old trail between Pokhara and Kathmandu. Descend to the large suspension bridge (1725 ft, 526 m) a **few minutes** beyond. If you are returning from Manang and wish to head directly to Pokhara, you could do so from here by following the Pokhara-Kathmandu route description in Chapter 11 in reverse.

To go to Manang, continue north and cross a tributary, the Paundi Khola, on a suspension bridge in **half an hour** and reach **Paundi** (1900 ft, 579 m) a **few minutes** later. There is a good swimming place under the bridge. Continue north along the trail, which sometimes follows the road, sometimes avoids it. The large tributary, the Dardi Khola, that reaches the Marsyangdi Khola on the east (L) bank, is **fifty minutes** beyond. An **hour** farther, cross another tributary to **Udipur** (2450 ft, 747 m) **five minutes** beyond. The forests that remain are tropical sal, but have been cut extensively. In **half an hour** the trail passes above a town called Dalal (or Phalenksangu) (2350 ft, 716 m). Below, there is a suspension bridge across the Marsyangdi Khola. The name Phalenksangu comes from the English word "plank" and the Nepali word for a rather primitive bridge, *sangu*. There was once a plank bridge here and the name stuck. Such combinations of Nepali and English words can often cause difficulty when they are pronounced with a Nepali accent or spelled in the local script. I can well remember a patient asking me for a "satipicket." It took some time to figure out that he wanted a certificate!

An alternative trail here is to cross the bridge and ascend the east (L) bank of the river to rejoin the other trail above Bhulbhule. This east (L) bank route is shorter than the west (R) bank route, and has more spectacular views. The trail can be hard to find since it meanders through rice fields. In the winter, many Manangbas may be found camping and trading on this side of the river. Trekkers who want to use the well-supplied shops at Besisahar might consider a combination route, following the west (R) bank to Besisahar, crossing the river there, and taking the left hand trail to join the east (L) bank route. The west (R) bank trail may be preferable, however, because the road, when completed, will stay on this side where there are more eating and lodging places. The east (L) bank trail is described as an alternative after the west (R) bank description. Another variation, or even a side trip, is to cross the Marsyangdi Khola here, and climb to the lakes on the Bara Pokhari Lekh for fine views of Manaslu, Peak 29, and Himalchuli. You could even head north from the lakes to rejoin the main river-bottom route a day beyond.

If you don't cross the suspension bridge at Phalenksangu, continue on up the west (R) bank through stands of wet subtropical forest. It may be necessary to climb up to the old trail if there is road construction going on. Reach a small town, Nadiwal (2650 ft, 808 m) in **forty-five minutes**, and Bakunde (2675 ft, 815 m) in another **half hour**. Descend to cross a tributary (2675 ft, 815 m) in **forty-five minutes**, then ascend to **Besisahar** (2700 ft, 823 m)—called Bensisahar and Lamjung on some trekking maps—**fifteen minutes** beyond. This major town, situated on a shelf of land above the main river, is the district center of Lamjung District and the site of the first police check post along the way. There is no road construction beyond here at present.

North of town, descend from the shelf, and cross a tributary (2350 ft, 716 m) on stones some **twenty minutes** later. Climb up and continue contouring in wet subtropical forest to Tanaute (2650 ft, 808 m) in **fifteen minutes**. **Over half an hour** later, the trail crosses a slide, and in another **half hour**, a tributary on a suspension bridge (2500 ft, 762 m). Continue above the Marsyangdi Khola, then descend to cross the Khudi Khola (2600 ft, 792 m) in **forty minutes**. Directly across the suspension bridge is the village of **Khudi**, a pleasant town with the last shops for some time. The valley narrows and changes character considerably from the wide valley to here. Himalchuli is the major summit to the east.

If returning from Manang, you might consider walking directly to Pokhara from Khudi and avoiding Dumre. It takes two days or less. The trail goes from Khudi to Baglung Pani, through Lamagaon, across the Badam Khola to Nalma, and across the Midam Khola, passing Kala Pattar to Begnas Tal, the lake in the eastern part of the Pokhara Valley.

To continue to Manang from Khudi, climb over toward the main valley of the Marsyangdi, pass the Khudi school, and reach a tributary (2700 ft, 823 m) in **fifteen minutes**. Continue along the river and pass an old suspension bridge across from the town of Bhulbhule on the opposite bank in **fifteen minutes**. Don't cross it, but continue another **five minutes** farther upstream to a new suspension bridge (2775 ft, 846 m). Cross it to the east (L) bank.

To take the alternative route from Phalenksangu to Bhulbhule, cross the bridge at Phalenksangu and climb the hill for **ten minutes** to the fields above. The trail winds its way through fields, sometimes becoming several trails. The villages are pleasant and the sights are lovely. After 1½ **hours**, the trail drops down into a steep ravine with a stone staircase leading in and out on both sides. Then it traverses along a steeper slope with fine views across the valley and to the high mountains beyond. **Twenty minutes** from the ravine is the bridge crossing to Besisahar. Several trails drop down to the river, but take the one that traverses and continue to another lookout (Deskadanda) **twenty minutes** beyond. It is another 1¼ **hours** to the big pipul tree and small village of Simbachaur, and an additional 1¼ **hours** to Bhulbhule. **Five minutes** beyond, the trail from the west (R) bank crosses to join the east (L) bank trail.

All described routes now continue on the east (L) bank north of Bhulbhule. Continue upstream and in **ten minutes**, pass a beautiful thin waterfall on your right.

This is the first of many handsome waterfalls along the way to Manang. A **half hour** later, cross another tributary (3050 ft, 930 m) and reach Nadi, a winter settlement of Manangbas. Beyond, enter a major tributary valley to the east, that of the Musi Khola. Descend to a suspension bridge (3125 ft, 953 m) in **half an hour**. Cross it to the north (R) bank of the Musi Khola. Continue upstream, pass the suspension bridge, and climb out of the tributary valley to reenter the valley of the Marsyangdi Khola. The trail contours and climbs in a pleasant little valley of terraces and forests to a settlement called **Bahundanda** (literally "hill of Brahmans") on the right of a prominent prow at a saddle (4300 ft, 1311 m). It is 1½ **hours** from the crossing of the Musi Khola. There are good views to the north if the weather is clear.

Descend into an equally pleasant tributary valley and cross its river in **forty-five minutes** on a cantilever bridge (3700 ft, 1128 m). Ascend to the main river valley and follow the trail beautifully carved out of the rock wall of the valley. Pass the houses of Khanegaon (3900 ft, 1189 m) in **forty-five minutes**, and contour to Ghermu in **half an hour**. Do not ascend toward the cliff to the northeast, but from Ghermu on the edge of a shelf above the river, descend to a suspension bridge over the Marsyangdi (3650 ft, 1113 m) and cross it to the west (R) bank in **ten minutes**. Just upstream are the few houses of **Syange** (3725 ft, 1136 m) by the river. The tall waterfall that you may have admired from the other side of the river provides the water for the next tributary that you cross just beyond Syange. The gorge becomes narrower and the trail rises and falls. There are overhanging rocks such as the one you pass in **half an hour** (3800 ft, 1158 m). These rocks can provide campsites. A lone house is passed in **ten minutes**, then the trail continues **fifty minutes** to the village of **Jagat** (4400 ft, 1341 m)—also called Gadi Jagat or Chote—situated in a saddle in the forest. This used to be an old customs post for the salt trade with Tibet.

Continue through broad-leaved forest and pass by another overhang suitable for a campsite. Cross a small tributary (4400 ft, 1341 m) and admire the spectacular waterfalls on the other side of the river. An **hour** beyond Jagat, reach the small settlement of **Chamje** (4700 ft, 1433 m). There are many changes in the people, architecture, and vegetation as you head upstream. Houses are now built of rocks, the vegetation is less tropical, and the culture is more Tibetan-like.

Just beyond the town, the gorge is very impressive. Descend for **less than ten minutes** and cross to the east (L) bank of the Marsyangdi Khola on a suspension bridge (4625 ft, 1410 m). The forests around you are of oak. Continue upstream, usually high above the river for almost 1½ **hours** until you emerge from the gorge with its torrent below. An ancient landslide from the mountain to the east filled the gorge here, creating a lake that has become silted in above. The river itself flows buried beneath the rubble and is heard but not seen. Enter a broad, pleasant, flat valley with a somewhat quieter river. In route, there are impressive falls on both sides. The first house you come to in the flat valley is Tale. There is a suspension bridge across the river, but don't take it. A sign indicates that you have entered Manang District. Continue ahead to the houses of **Tal** in the center of the flat valley (5600 ft, 1707 m) in **ten minutes**. *Tal,* meaning lake in Nepali, refers to the prehistoric one. East of Tal, there is another spectacular waterfall coming into the valley. Try to spend a night here, for there is nowhere else along the trek quite like it. The area of Manang north of here is called Gyasumdo, meaning "meeting place of the three highways." It is inhabited partly by *BhoTiya* who are primarily agro-pastoralists. These people were the real trans-Himalayan traders of the region until 1959 or 1960 when the trade closed with the Chinese takeover of Tibet. Nareshwar Jang Gurung wrote an interesting survey on Manang (see Recommended Reading).

The trail to Manang proper crosses the small tributary beyond Tal on a log bridge and ascends upstream in the valley that again narrows. In **fifty minutes** pass by an older suspension bridge made of steel and bamboo, but with only cables to walk on. Don't cross it, but continue upstream on the east (L) bank to reach another overhang in **twenty minutes**. Then cross a new suspension bridge over the Marsyangdi Khola (6250 ft, 1905 m) to the west (R) bank and reach **Dharapani** (6375 ft, 1943 m) in **five minutes**. There is a police check post here. Continue on upstream and note the valley coming in from the northeast some **ten minutes** beyond. It comes down from the Larkya Pass and leads north of Manaslu to the Buri Gandaki. The village of Thonje lies at the confluence of the Dudh Khola and the Marsyangdi Khola. Don't cross the wooden cantilever bridge over the Marsyangdi Khola upstream of the river junction. Some **ten minutes** beyond the confluence, take the lower fork—the upper leads to some higher villages. Take the upper trail at the two forks a **few minutes** beyond.

A pleasant **half-hour's** walk brings you around a corner to the town of **Bagarchap** (7100 ft, 2164 m)—meaning "butcher's place." This town has flat-roofed houses, indicating that rainfall is less here. The monsoon clouds have less water in them here because they have unloaded it to the south. The waterworks flowing through the town are quite interesting—you will see nothing remotely similar until you reach Marpha in the Thak Khola across the Annapurna range to the west. The Nyingmapa sect has built a small new *gomba* here with handsome frescoes on its walls. There are views of the Annapurnas and part of Lamjung Himal. Just beyond the town, take the left fork. Do not go down to the cantilever bridge crossing the Marsyangdi Khola. Admire the views of Manaslu behind you. Continue in pine forest and in **forty minutes**, cross a tributary (7550 ft, 2301 m) coming down from the Namun Bhanjyang, a high pass crossing the Himalayan barrier east of Lamjung Himal. Once heavily traveled, this pass is now only occasionally used by *Gurung* shepherds who pasture their sheep and goats on the high slopes. The newly constructed trail along the Marsyangdi Khola has replaced the dangerous old route that people avoided by taking the strenuous high route. Beyond the bridge, take the right fork. The left fork heads up to high pastures and the Namun Pass. It provides an alternative route, used formerly, that has a fine campsite at Timung Meadows. The main trail, described here, is rejoined at Koto. On the main trail, continue a short way to the rushing Syalkyu waterfall (7625 ft, 2324 m) with a wooden cantilever bridge in front of it. Beyond, the path, which is carved out of the cliffs, rises on steps and continues in lush oak forests to cross another tributary (7775 ft, 2370 m) in **fifteen minutes**. Unlike similar valleys in eastern Nepal, there are not many rhododendron trees along the trail. Continue to a clearing and the new settlement of Lattemarang (8050 ft, 2454 m)—also called Tanzah Bishe—in **half an hour**.

The trail in this pleasant part of the valley continues along the south side and crosses another tributary on a wooden bridge (8225 ft, 2507 m) **twenty minutes** later. Just beyond is another house. **Fifteen minutes** after the bridge takes the lower fork (8375 ft, 2553 m), the trail continues in blue pine and spruce forests. Don't cross any of the three wooden bridges over the Marsyangdi Khola that you pass in the next few minutes, but continue and cross a tributary on a wooden bridge (8625 ft, 2629 m) **forty minutes later**. Cross another small stream and reach the few houses of **Koto** (or Kotoje) in a pretty clearing (8625 ft, 2629 m) in less than **ten minutes**. Police may check your trekking permit here. The prominent tributary valley heading north is the Nar Khola, which drains the region called Nar Phu. The inhabitants are traditionally pastoralists.

To continue to Manang, cross a tributary, then another, and enter **Chame** (8900 ft, 2713 m) in less than **half an hour.** This government town is the Jilla Panchayat, or district center, for Manang. It has a bank and a police check post. The non-governmental people live at the west end of town where there is a *gomba.* At the far end of town, first cross a tributary from the south, then the main Marsyangdi Khola on a wooden cantilever bridge (8890 ft, 2710 m) to the north (L) bank. There are more houses here and some hot springs right at the river's edge about 200 yards south of the bridge over the Marsyangdi Khola on the north (L) bank. As you go up the valley into pine forest, the trail is not as well built or maintained as it has been up to now. Continue along the pleasant trail to reach the new houses of Taleku (9200 ft, 2804 m) in **half an hour.** Like the other towns since Dharapani, this one has an entrance *chorten* and an exit *chorten.* The trail continues close to the river, even cut out of the clay hillside in places. Above you is an impressive canyon. The Marsyangdi Valley is almost unrelentingly narrow.

Continue along for **half an hour** to the first of four successive tall waterfalls, opposite you on the south (R) side of the valley. Another **half hour** brings you to a wide wooden cantilever bridge (9575 ft, 2919 m) that crosses to the south (R) bank of the Marsyangdi Khola. Previously this bridge was covered, and you can still see the remnants of a gate. The former *Khampa* settlement of **Bhratang** is just beyond. The gate on the bridge was the *Khampa* way of maintaining control of traffic in the valley. Climb up for **five minutes** to the village of Bhratang. The *Khampa,* Tibetan refugee warriors, were all resettled in 1975 and the town is abandoned save for a police check post. One building in this town is remarkable—it is a large open room that must have been used for meetings. Just west of the town is another wooden cantilever bridge (9650 ft, 2941 m) to the north (L) bank. Annapurna II can be seen to the south—you may have wondered along the way what peak it was, for it looks distinctly different from the north than what you may have been accustomed to seeing from Pokhara. Enter a fir and spruce forest. Cross again to the south (R) bank in **thirty-five minutes** on another wooden bridge (10,050 ft, 3063 m), then climb into a serene pine forest. After the days in the gorge, you can appreciate the beauty and silence of the next **forty-five minutes.** A clearing with some *chorten* (10,450 ft, 3185 m) is next, and beyond some meadows and a small lake. Soon you leave the forest and in **fifty minutes,** reach a bridge over the Marsyangdi Khola to the north (L) bank (10,375 ft, 3162 m). It is also possible to stay on the south (R) bank as far as lower Pisang. Look back and admire the incredible slabs above the river valley on the east side. If you seem to see a building on the ridge, you are right—it is a Buddhist shrine.

You are now in the dry, arid region of Manang called Nyesyang. Since it is in the rain shadow of the Himalaya, which act as a barrier to the wet monsoon clouds from the south, the area gets little rain in the summer. Snow falls here in the winter and remains on the ground much of the time. The men are traders and part-time agriculturalists, while the women are full-time agriculturalists. There is comparatively little animal husbandry. You may meet many young men with considerable facility in English who have traveled far and wide in Asia. They may try to sell or trade almost anything. The people of Nyesyang were granted special trading privileges by the King about 180 years ago. This included passports and import and export facilities. These privileges have been extended to all the people of Manang District. Initially they traded local items for manufactured goods, usually in India and Burma, but more recently they have begun using hard currency from export of expensive items to import machines and other manufactured goods from most South Asian countries. The resultant seasonal migration means less development of agriculture and animal husbandry. So you won't see many herds of yak, sheep, or goats at the higher elevations. These people are thus quite dependent on food imports.

From the bridge there are basically two routes, both of which join up the valley below the village of Braga. The direct route keeps to the valley floor, staying mostly on the south (R) side. If you keep close to the river, you come to lower **Pisang** (10,450 ft, 3185 m) in less than **half an hour.** The other trail ascends on the north side of the valley to reach the rather spectacular town of upper Pisang (10,800 ft, 3292 m) in **half an hour.** The view of Annapurna II from here is unforgettable. From upper Pisang, you can descend to lower Pisang and continue along the lower valley route, or you can take a higher route that climbs to several villages on the north (L) side of the valley. The views of the mountains from this route are more impressive than from the other, and the villages are quite interesting, but it takes perhaps two hours more to reach Braga.

To take the low level route, cross the Marsyangdi Khola to its south (R) bank at lower Pisang. Cross a tributary from the south and ascend into pleasant pine and juniper forests. Climb to the upper valley floor beyond a narrowing. Ongre (10,900 ft, 3322 m), a flat area with a few houses, is reached in 1½ **hours.** There is an airstrip here to link this remote area with Kathmandu. Foreign aid from Yugoslavia is being used for a mountaineering school here. A hydroelectric station is also planned to provide electricity for upper Manang Valley. Continue along, crossing another major tributary from the south, and head over toward the Marsyangdi Khola to cross it (11,250 ft, 3429 m) in another **hour.** Ascend along the north (L) bank to a small town, Munchi (11,425 ft, 3482 m), where the high north side route joins the main valley route. Don't cross the wooden bridge some **fifteen minutes** beyond, but round a ridge a **few minutes** later and reach the entrance *chorten* below **Braga** (11,500 ft, 3505 m).

The high north side route begins in upper Pisang. Like many villages here, the town is constructed using flat roofs. The roof of one house serves as the yard or open area of the house above it. There is a long handsome wall of prayer wheels in an open space below a little-used *gomba.* To head up the valley on the north side, take the trail leaving town to the west. Pass through the entrance *chorten,* descend slightly, cross a tributary (10,800 ft, 3292 m), and contour in a pleasant pine and juniper forest. Pass above a small green lake, and contour to a long *mani* wall. Then descend to cross a tributary (10,775 ft, 3284 m) a little over **half an hour** from Pisang. Take the upper fork and begin a steep climb for an hour to **Ghyaru** (12,050 ft, 3673 m). Spectacular views of Annapurnas II and III and Gangapurna are the main attractions, along with the dark, tunnel-like streets of the town. Contour out of the town to the west, cross a tributary (12,075 ft, 3680 m), and reach a ridge crest (12,375 ft, 3772 m) some 100 ft (30 m) above some ruins, perhaps of an old fort, in 1⅔ **hours.** Rest here and enjoy the views of Gangapurna, Glacier Dome, and Tilicho Peak to the west. North of Tilicho Peak lies the "great frozen lake," named by Herzog, although it is out of view from here. If you cross the Thorung La Pass, you will eventually return to Pokhara by heading well north and then west of this peak.

Continue contouring, cross a tributary, and pass three trails joining yours on the left. Cross another tributary to **Ngawal** (11,975 ft. 3650 m) **forty-five minutes** from Ghyaru. Descend to cross a tributary in a **few minutes,** then continue descending, avoiding a left fork (11,625 ft, 3543 m) **ten minutes** beyond town. Descend to to the valley floor (11,325 ft, 3452 m) and in about an **hour,** reach the few houses of Munchi (11,425 ft, 3482 m). Here the trail meets the main lower trail from Pisang. **Braga** (11,500 ft, 3505 m) is less than **half an hour** away.

Braga, a large and interesting village, is the seat of the oldest monastery in the area. The *gomba* is perhaps 500 years old, and belongs to the Kargyupa sect of Tibetan Buddhism. Like most of the *gomba* in this region, it is not very active. Nevertheless, it is well worth a visit, for it contains some unique works of art. The main temple contains 108 terra-cotta statues, each about two ft (60 cm) high, arranged in rows along three of the four walls. They represent much of the Buddhist Pantheon. There is another three-story temple above this main building. The temple is described in detail in David Snellgrove's *Himalayan Pilgrimage* (see Recommended Reading).

The village of **Manang** (11,650 ft, 3351 m) is **half an hour** beyond Braga. In between two tributaries along the way, on a ridge to the north, lies the Bod-zo *gomba*. It is perhaps the most active institution around. The beautiful paintings on its walls that Snellgrove admired in his book have been poorly repainted recently. Reach this *gomba* by climbing upstream before crossing the second of the series of tributaries. Head up the valley for **half an hour** to the ridge crest (11,750 ft, 3581 m). You can most likely restock your provisions in Manang, although prices are quite high. Perhaps you may see an archery contest! Manang itself is spectacularly perched across from a glacial lake formed by water from Gangapurna and Annapurna III. To the west is the village of Khangsar, the last habitation before Tilicho Tal (lake). And beyond is the impressive north face of Tilicho Peak. An approach to the lake has been described from the Kali Gandaki side. It can also be reached from Khangsar in **two days**. Someone familiar with the route could be hired here. In bad weather it can be difficult to find the lake from the east. It is frozen in winter, and periods of thaw vary from year to year.

If you are planning to cross the Thorung La and reach the Kali Gandaki (river) to the west, it is important to spend a day or two acclimatizing here before proceeding. If you have flown to Manang, you should spend at least three or four days in this region before attempting to cross the pass. Those who have walked up should spend one or two days at 12,000 ft (3658 m) or so. Acclimatization days are best spent being active and climbing to high elevations for views, but returning to lower altitudes to sleep.

To proceed from Manang over the Thorung La, the high pass leading to Muktinath and the Kali Gandaki Valley, cross a tributary below a falls beyond Manang and reach **Tengi** (11,950 ft, 3642 m) in **half an hour**. This is the last permanent settlement below the pass. Climb for **half an hour** beyond Tengi to a fork. Take the right fork—the left descends to cross the river to Khangsar—and reach some *goTh* called Khosang (12,725 ft, 3879 m) shortly beyond. **Ten minutes** farther is a higher settlement of *goTh* called Khöra. The trail has now turned northwest up the tributary valley of the Jargeng Khola. To the southwest you can see the summit of Roc Noir, part of the Great Barrier. The countryside around you is quite dry and alpine, with occasional birch groves. Pass some *goTh,* cross small tributaries, and contour along pleasant meadows. If you are here early in the morning or late in the afternoon, look for herds of blue sheep, which may descend for water. Reach Leder, a lone two-storied *goTh* (13,700 ft, 4176 m) 2½ **hours** from Tengi. This is the last shelter before the pass, though there are plenty of suitable canpsites. Do not attempt to cross the pass unless all of the party, including the porters, are equipped for cold and bad weather. If the weather is threatening, and everyone cannot be housed in tents in case of a snowstorm, do not proceed. Lives have been needlessly lost on this pass because parties proceeded in bad weather without accepting responsibility for the welfare of the porters.

From Leder, climb, contour, and then descend to the river by a covered wooden cantilever bridge (14,000 ft, 4267 m) in **forty minutes**. Cross to the west (R) bank of the Jargeng Khola where suitable campsites can be found. This narrow valley is being eroded severely, and some of the landslides cover the river with natural bridges. Climb and contour upstream, crossing some scree (14,325 ft, 4366 m) to reach the riverbed and a campsite (14,450 ft, 4404 m) just beyond called Phedi—meaning foot of hill— an **hour** from the bridge. The trail now leaves the river valley, which continues northwest, and ascends west. In dry weather, water can be scarce the next day, so fill up. There are two high campsites (14,675 ft, 4473 m and 14,875 ft, 4534 m) **ten to fifteen minutes** apart along the trail, which soon disappears. The campsites may not have any water. There are no good campsites with water beyond the pass unless you camp on snow in the appropriate season.

From Phedi, ascend to a notch (15,725 ft, 4793 m) in **1¼ hours** and head left (west), traversing to the base of a prominent lateral moraine (15,900 ft, 4846 m) in **half an hour**. Reach its crest (16,050 ft, 4892 m) a **few minutes** later and continue west along less steep terrain. After many false crests, reach the Thorung La Pass (17,650 ft, 5380 m) in **two hours** if you are adequately acclimatized. A large cairn marks the pass, but it may be almost entirely covered with snow. There is an impressive glaciated peak to the south. It is not very difficult to ascend if you have the requisite skills, experience, and equipment, and if you are well acclimatized. Thorungse, the peak to the north, requires some technical rock climbing. The pass is exhilarating in that it is an abrupt transition from one major Himalayan valley to another, but views from it are probably less impressive than those on either side. Far below you to the west is the Kali Gandaki. Those with sharp eyes and binoculars can pick out the green oasis of Kagbeni.

The descent from the pass is gradual at first and follows the middle of the valley for the first **hour**. It becomes considerably steeper and keeps to the south side of the valley on scree. The first campsites (14,150 ft, 4313 m) are some **two hours** down from the pass just after crossing a tributary to the right. In the dry season, after and just before the monsoon when all the snow has melted, there is no water available, necessitating a descent to near Muktinath. Reach a *goTh* without a roof in **ten minutes**. Cross a tributary (which may be dry) to the left (it flows from the south) and descend to a major tributary in the valley floor (12,650 ft, 3856 m) **2½ hours** from the pass. Cross it to the south (L) bank and ascend a bit to continue down the main valley. Reach **Muktinath** (12,475 ft, 3802 m) after rounding a corner some **fifteen minutes** later.

To continue, reverse the trail descriptions given earlier for the trek from Pokhara to Muktinath.

9 SOLU-KHUMBU (The Everest Region)

Because it is there.
George Mallory, one of the first climbers to attempt Everest. He disappeared into a cloud near the summit in 1924.

There are several possible ways of reaching the Solu-Khumbu District of Nepal. The classical way to Khumbu, the northernmost part of the district, is to walk from Kathmandu, although most parties start walking from Lamosangu or Dolalghat on the Kathmandu-Kodari Road. This shortens the walking time by two days.

There are STOL airstrips in several places along the way, and aircraft charters can be arranged. The airstrips are at Jiri, some three days' walk from Kathmandu; at Phaphlu in Solu, a week's walk; and finally at Lukla, a day's walk from Namche Bazaar. There are now regularly scheduled flights by Royal Nepal Airlines to Lukla. In addition, a strip has been constructed above Namche Bazaar. It is called Shyangboche and is used by visitors to the luxury Everest View Hotel in Khumjung, and to a certain extent by trekkers.

As mentioned earlier, rapid ascent to high altitudes can be dangerous, even fatal. For some people, rapid ascent to even 10,000 ft (3100 m) has been disastrous. Lukla is at 9275 ft (2827 m) while the airstrip at Shyangboche is at 12,435 ft (3790 m). Hence it is best to try to arrange to walk to Khumbu and to fly out, if you want to fly part way. If you must, fly to Phaphlu or Lukla and ascend gradually. In winter, few landings are made at Lukla or Shyangboche because of snow.

If you are walking both ways, the journey from Kathmandu to Khumbu can be combined with the trek from Khumbu to Ilam District in eastern Nepal, followed by air transportation to Kathmandu. Or you can go by jeep and train to Darjeeling. This is described in Chapter 11. You can also reach and leave the Khumbu region via Rolwaling to the east. This involves the crossing of a high glaciated pass, the Trashi Labsta, which requires some mountaineering skills and equipment, and considerable stamina. This long crossing is somewhat hazardous. It is described in Chapter 11.

TO SOLU-KHUMBU *(Map No. 3, Page 158)*

While there are few close views of the mountains until you get to Khumbu, the walk from Lamosangu to Khumbu is recommended as an introduction to the hills of Nepal and their inhabitants. A few pleasant diversions are described along the way. Average walking time to Namche Bazaar is ten to twelve days. Local people have been known to take much less time, but they traveled all day and sometimes at night. After all, a curvilinear distance of eighty miles is involved and with switchbacks and diversions in the trail, it is about 150 miles of walking from Lamosangu to Namche Bazaar. Furthermore, the trip involves a series of ascents that total

Ama Dablang from Khumjung. (Stephen Bezruchka)

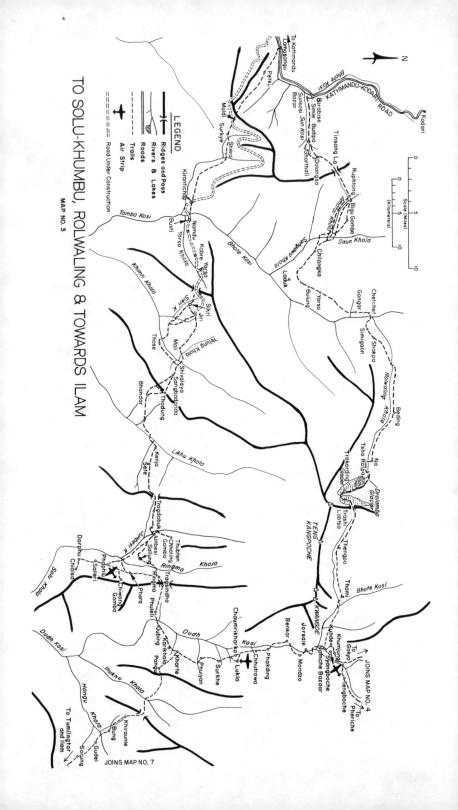

35,200 ft (10,724 m) and a series of descents that total 26,100 ft (7954 m). You more than climb Everest along the way, but it is well worth it.

Generally speaking, the main rivers run south and are separated by high ridges. So the route is a succession of ups and downs, often following tributaries flowing east and west. Compared to the trek between Pokhara and Kathmandu, also going against the grain of the land, the ridges and valleys are much higher and the climbs and descents are more strenuous.

In the past, *bhaTTi* and tea shops were rare along the route except near Khumbu, but this is no longer the case since the trail has become quite popular with Westerners. There is usually no difficulty in obtaining cooked food along the way, but it is wise to carry some food with you. Shelter should also pose no problem.

To save two days of walking from Kathmandu, take the bus heading to Barabise on the Kathmandu-Kodari Road. It leaves every few hours from the staging area north of the Kathmandu City Hall, east of Tundikhel. The bus to Lamosangu—which means "long bridge"—takes some **three to five hours.** You could go by bus only as far as Dolalghat (2080 ft, 634 m) and walk from there. This adds a day to the journey, but avoids a long climb at the beginning. Better to have the extra day to spend in Khumbu.

A new road is being built from Lamosangu to Jiri as part of the Swiss Multipurpose Development Project. Parts of the road can be used as trails for the early part of the trek. Also, minibus transportation is sporadically available along it from Lamosangu to Busti, just over the river from Kirantichap. When completed to Jiri, it will shorten the trekking time considerably. A question often asked is how much vehicular transportation should be used to shorten treks. The Everest trek originally started from the Kathmandu Valley; now the starting point is moving ever closer to Solu-Khumbu. Trekkers who want to experience the hills as well as the mountains may choose not to use all the available roads, or they may choose a trek in which those options aren't available.

The Jiri road begins across the Sun Kosi (river), about 1½ mi (3.3 km) west of Lamosangu. It is not worthwhile to walk up it; the usual foot trail is more direct. From the road at Lamosangu (2430 ft, 741 m), cross the Sun Kosi on a sturdy suspension bridge, and, after passing through the village, climb steeply to the southeast through chilaune forest to gain a ridge. Follow it to the village of **Kaping** (4300 ft, 1219 m) in 1¾ **hours**. Another 1¼ **hours** brings you to **Petku** (5450 ft, 1661 m). Continue climbing through terraced farms, interspersed with thatch-roofed houses and eventually reach a ridge (6850 ft, 2088 m) and the village of Pakhar. The road and trail soon intersect, and the route follows the road to **Muldi** (8350 ft, 2540 m) some **five hours** from Petku.

From Muldi the trail continues along the ridge, passes the settlement of Ningale, and begins to descend. Just before the descent, there are distant views extending from Annapurna in the west to the Khumbu Himal in the east. The path leaves the road and descends east for 1½ **hours** before crossing to the south (R) side of a tributary (5875 ft, 1791 m). Shortly beyond, it reaches the village of **Surkye** (5750 ft, 1735 m). In another **fifteen minutes**, cross to the north (L) bank of the Chandrawati Khola (5175 ft, 1577 m), and reach Shera (4750 ft, 1448 m) some 2½ **hours** after Muldi.

Directly beyond Shera, take a suspension bridge over another tributary from the north and continue on the north (L) side of the valley, at times walking in pleasant chir pine forests, but soon returning to the ubiquitous terracing to reach **Kirantichap** (4325 ft, 1320 m) some **four hours** after Shera. You are now in the area covered by the *Tamba Kosi Likhu Khola* map of the Research Scheme Nepal Himalaya. The map is quite useful for the next five days' walk. Intersect the road at Kirantichap, but keep to the more direct foot path.

From Kirantichap descend for an **hour** through chir pine and sal forests to a sturdy suspension bridge over the beautiful blue waters of the Bhote Kosi (2800 ft, 853 m). The village of Busti lies on the opposite side of the river and is now known for its bakery! Climb up the east (L) bank to the ridge and follow its south side to the village of **Namdu** (4900 ft, 1493 m), reaching its lower part **two hours** after crossing the river. You intersect the road along the way and local conditions dictate whether to follow it. **Kabre** (6025 ft, 1836 m) is reached in 1¾ **hours** from Namdu, the trail mostly following the road. The trail descends slightly to cross the Yarsa Khola before reaching **Yarsa** (6475 ft, 1974 m) in another **hour**. You are now in Jirel country, an area surrounding Jiri populated by a hill ethnic group whose language is related to that of the Sherpas.

From Yarsa the trail rises through oak and chir pine forests, past a small town, **Chisapani**, to a notch in the ridge you are contouring. The road is again intersected here. This pass (8280 ft, 2523 m) is reached in less than **two hours** from Yarsa and provides distant views of Rolwaling Himal. Almost due north is the high ridge crested with a black tower called Chobo Bamare (19,550 ft, 5959 m), which you may have been seeing for several days now. The road heads north, while you descend east through pleasant forests and terraces to the Sikri Khola (6250 ft, 1905 m) and the town of **Sikri**, which is reached in **little more than an hour**.

There are two choices from here, depending on whether you want to visit Jiri, where there is a hospital, a STOL airstrip, a guesthouse, and a dairy and agricultural project financed with Swiss aid. The route which avoids Jiri passes through the Those bazaar.

To go to Jiri, cross the two tributaries of the Sikri Khola before they join and climb through oak and chir pine forests to round a ridge (7000 ft, 2134 m) where there is a market every Saturday. Beyond that, descend to **Jiri** (6250 ft, 1905 m) about 1¾ **hours** beyond the Sikri Khola.

From Jiri there are again two choices. One passes through Those, a *Newar* bazaar and a town with many shops where you can replenish your supplies. The other route ascends higher and offers distant views of mountains.

The route from Jiri through Those follows the west (R) bank of the Jiri Khola south to about 6125 ft (1867 m), crosses to the east (L) bank, and ascends, passing near the village of Kune (6775 ft, 2064 m) to join the trail from Sikri Khola that avoids Jiri. The trail continues to a notch marked with *chorten* (6800 ft, 2070 m) in a chir pine and oak forest and then descends, passing the settlement of Kattike to the south, to the Khimti Khola (5750 ft, 1753 m), which is followed on its west (R) bank to a suspension bridge. Cross it and follow the river north to **Those** (5900 ft, 1799 m). From Jiri to Those takes 2½ **to three hours**.

To take the high route from Jiri, climb the east side of the Jiri Valley to reach a pass (7875 ft, 2400 m) after 1½ **hours**. Then descend through **Mali** to a covered bridge over the Yelung Khola. Cross it to the northeast (L) bank and go on to a suspension bridge over the Khimti Khola. **Shivalaya** (5800 ft, 1767 m), the village on the other side, is 1¼ **hours** from the pass.

To avoid Jiri and go through Those, follow the east (L) bank of the Sikri Khola to near its junction with the Jiri Khola to the south. Cross the Jiri Khola to its east (L) bank and climb up the side of the valley to join the trail from Jiri at 6775 ft (2064 m). Follow this trail to Those as already described. From the first turnoff to Jiri, it takes 2½ **to three hours** to Those. From Those, follow the river on its east (L) bank, walking upstream for 1½ **hours** to **Shivalaya** (5800 ft, 1767 m). There is even an English signpost here.

All the route choices end up at Shivalaya. From here the trail goes up the ridge to the village of **Sangbadanda** with its schoolhouse (7350 ft, 2240 m) in 1¾ **hours**. Just up from the schoolhouse, the trail branches. The left branch heads up past the village of **Buldanda** (8200 ft, 2500 m) to the cheese factory at **Thodung** (10,140 ft, 3091 m) about 2¾ **hours** from Sangbadanda. Besides buying cheese here, you can get a good view of Gaurishankar to the north. This peak (23,459 ft, 7150 m) was once thought to be the highest in the world since it was visible from afar. There is a monastery **half an hour** south of the cheese factory. To rejoin the regular route, head south along the ridge to the pass (8900 ft, 2713 m), reaching it in an **hour**. This is definitely a worthwhile detour. If you take the right branch at Sangbadanda, you come to several tea shops (seasonal) run by Sherpas in about **forty-five minutes**.

The trail continues along the north side of the valley of the Mohabir Khola, crossing numerous tributaries and entering a hemlock forest until the pass (8900 ft, 2713 m) is reached. One of the largest collection of *mani* walls in Nepal is here. It takes 2½ **hours** to reach the pass from Sangbadanda.

From the pass, the trail descends into the beautiful, lush valley to the east and heads toward the two large stupas by a small *gomba* at the town of **Bhandar** (7200 ft, 2194 m), which is called Changma by Sherpas. This takes an **hour** and brings you into the area populated by Sherpas.

From the scattered village of Bhandar, descend the fertile plateau to cross a river (6600 ft, 2012 m). Then go on through forests and terraces to cross the Surma Khola (5100 ft, 1555 m) to its north (L) bank. Continue to the Likhu Khola and cross it on a suspension bridge (5060 ft, 1543 m) to its east (L) bank. It takes 2¼ **hours** to reach the river from Bhandar, then **less than an hour** walking upstream along its east (L) bank through chir pine forest to reach the Kenja Khola, which is crossed to **Kenja** (5360 ft, 1634 m).

The biggest climb of the journey so far, up to the Lamjura Pass (11,580 ft, 3530 m), begins behind the schoolhouse and follows a ridge more or less on its south side through oak forest to the small settlement of **Sete** (8450 ft, 2575 m), which has a small *gomba* above it. Be sure to obtain water from the streams crossing the trail below Sete, as there is little chance of finding more until you have descended the other side of the pass. It takes 2¼ **to three hours** to reach Sete from Kenja. Beyond, the trail continues along the ridge in a fir forest, passing the two bamboo mat houses called Goyun (10,550 ft, 3216 m), which are sometimes occupied. When the trail branches (11,150 ft, 3399 m), take the left fork heading northeast through a rhododendron forest to the pass about two miles away. The pass is **three to four hours** from Sete. In spite of the height of the pass, there is no view of the mountains, but those with time and energy can climb the peak north of the pass (13,159 ft, 4010 m) for views in good weather.

From the Lamjura Pass, the trail descends through a fir forest and emerges at **Tragdobuk** (9380 ft, 2860 m) in 1½ **hours**. Continue on the north side of the valley, round a notch, and drop down to the town of **Junbesi** (8775 ft, 2675 m) in an **hour**. There is an active *gomba* here.

About 1½ hours off the main trail to the north of Junbesi lies Thubten Chholing Gomba, an active monastery. The abbot there, Tulshig Rimpoche, was formerly at the Rongbuk Monastery on the northern slopes of Mount Everest in Tibet. It is a small *gomba*, but exquisitely painted, and definitely worth seeing. To reach it, head north from Junbesi past some *chorten* and *mani* walls to a bridge (9000 ft, 2743 m) over the Junbesi Khola. Continue up the east (L) bank until you spot the monastery on a shelf above you to the east. Follow the main trail past fine Sherpa homes until you are just about under the *gomba* and head directly up to it. The town of Mobung is nearby. The *gomba* is one to 1½ hours from Junbesi.

From Junbesi you can also head south to the major Solu towns of Salleri and Phaphlu and to a Tibetan resettlement center at Chialsa. This area is described later in this chapter. The *Shorong/Hinku* map of the Research Scheme Nepal Himalaya covers the trek from here to Namche Bazaar.

To continue to Namche Bazaar from Junbesi, cross the Junbesi Khola on a log bridge below the stupas (8700 ft, 2552 m) and take the extreme left or upper trail up the valley to the south. The trail passes through pine forests to reach open country. Round the crest (10,000 ft, 3048 m) of the Sallung ridge from which you can see Mount Everest on a clear day! Head north up the valley of the Ringmo Khola to the town of **Sallung** (9700 ft, 2953 m) about **two hours** from Junbesi.

From here the trail descends through oak forests to cross a tributary (8675 ft, 2644 m), then the main river of the Ringmo Khola (8525 ft, 2599 m). The trail then ascends to the few houses of Ringmo (9200 ft, 2805 m) 1½ **hours** from Sallung. In route after crossing the river, the trail branches. The right branch heads south to Phaphlu. This region is described later. From Ringmo the trail ascends east through juniper woods past some rectangular *mani* walls to a pass, Tragsindho La (10,125 ft, 3086 m), with *chorten, mani* walls, and prayer flags. To the east is the valley of the Dudh Kosi which you follow north to Khumbu. Meanwhile, 500 ft (152 m) below you is Tragsindho Monastery. To reach it, take the left branch of the trail at the junction 100 ft (30 m) below the pass on the east side. The other trail passes above the monastery and rejoins the monastery trail 100 ft (30 m) below the *gomba*. It takes **forty-five minutes** to reach the pass from Ringmo and another **fifteen minutes** to reach the monastery, which has a guesthouse.

From Tragsindho the trail descends to the southeast, passes through forests, and emerges at the small Sherpa village of **Manidingma** (7200 ft, 2194 m) in 1¾ **hours**. The trail continues to descend, passing terraces and the scattered villages of **Chorco** (7000 ft, 2134 m) and **Phuleli** (6500 ft, 1980 m). Beyond, descend into oak forests to emerge at a bridge over the Dudh Kosi (4900 ft, 1493 m) 1½ **hours** from Manidingma. Above the bridge on the west (R) bank is an abandoned stone house used by the Swiss who built the bridge. It is a **five-minute** bushwhack from the trail.

The trail crosses the river to the east (L) bank and heads north to reach Namche Bazaar in two to three days. Sometimes it is over a mile above the river, which falls through a steep gorge. This part of Solu-Khumbu is called Pharak. There have been many improvements in agriculture in Pharak over the years. You may notice fruit trees and many varieties of vegetables.

Follow the river for awhile through chir pine forests, then climb through the terraces of the *Rai* village of **Jubing** (5500 ft, 1676 m). Here it is better to take the upper fork at junctions until above the village. Then scamper up a small cliff and emerge on to more terraces. Aim for the prominent notch on the ridge ahead of you. From the notch (6900 ft, 2103 m), contour to the village of **Karikhola** (6800 ft, 2072 m) inhabited by Sherpas, *Rai,* and *Magar.* Karikhola is **two hours** from the Dudh Kosi.

Cross the bridge over the Kari Khola (6600 ft, 2012 m) and ascend its north (R) bank some 1800 ft (549 m) to the scattered settlement of **Kharte** in 1½ **to two hours**. The trail continues to climb out of this tributary valley, passing an oak forest where langur monkeys may be seen occasionally, to a ridge crest, Khari La (10,200 ft, 3109 m), in **two hours**. At this point, you are almost a mile above the Dudh Kosi. Unlike the gorge of the Kali Gandaki in central Nepal, you pass well above the steep slopes.

The next tributary valley to the north has to be passed. Descend 1000 ft (305 m) and cross the tributary after an **hour**. Continue on the north side of the valley to reach **Phuiyan** (9300 ft, 2835 m) in **half an hour**. Again, continue to the crest of a ridge (9800 ft, 2983 m) leading down to the Dudh Kosi and again, enter the valley of another tributary. Shortly after beginning a steep descent, you can see the STOL landing strip at Lukla, almost due north. The village of **Surkhe** (7675 ft, 2339 m) at the bridge crossing the tributary is **two hours** from Phuiyan.

The trail now leaves this tributary valley and heads more directly north toward the town of **Chaumrikharka**, another scattered village. Along the way, pass the inscription "Lukla Road" (8300 ft, 2530 m) painted faintly on a rock to the right of the trail. It indicates the way to the STOL field (9275 ft, 2827 m) reached in an **hour** from here. Before ascending to Chaumrikharka (8500 ft, 2591 m to 8900 ft, 2713 m), the trail crosses a spectacular, deep gorge with a high waterfall (7900 ft, 2408 m). Upper Chaumrikharka (8900 ft, 2713 m), with three large stupas and a *gomba,* is 1¾ **hours** from Surkhe. From here on, the going is easier; the major climbs are over. The trail from Chaumrikharka passes pleasant fields and ascends to a small ridge (8775 ft, 2675 m) where the trail to the north from Lukla joins the main trail up the Dudh Kosi valley. There is a recently built village called Chablung here.

Lukla (9275 ft, 2827 m) has become a major trekking center over the years. In addition to the airstrip nestled among spectacular mountains, there are now many hotels featuring food and accommodations varying from slightly more expensive than the cheapest in nearby places, to quite luxurious and, of course, expensive. Many trekkers try to fly into Lukla, tour Khumbu, and fly out. There never seems to be enough flights out of Lukla to prevent bottlenecks, and bad weather can result in delays of several days or even a week or more. Sometimes several hundred trekkers of many nationalities may find themselves stranded at Lukla. Many of them have come to Nepal to escape the pressures of their jobs and homes. Yet when they find themselves missing flights to Kathmandu to return them to their jobs and homes, they can become very difficult to contend with. Patience wears thin and tempers flare. Although it may be comical to those who remain calm, such displays project an unfortunate image of the visitors on the rather relaxed natives. These problems can be prevented by avoiding Lukla as a point of pickup by air. Shyangboche farther north is certainly no better, as Hotel Everest View guests vie for seats. However, Phaphlu, an airstrip perhaps two days farther from Khumbu, has fewer logistical problems, and the prosperous area of Solu that is visited in route is quite pleasant. Walking out to Lamosangu on the Kathmandu-Kodari Highway is time consuming, but especially worthwhile if you have never traveled this route before. Walking out to the south is another possibility. Flights back to Kathmandu can be arranged from the STOL strips at Lamidanda and Rumjatar, two towns near the route. You can also continue south to the Tarai and either link up with the East-West Highway and go to Kathmandu, or fly from major towns such as Janakpur. Or you could go southeast to Dharan or Ilam. This route is described in Chapter 11. Finally you could walk out of Khumbu by crossing the high and potentially dangerous Trashi Labsta, a pass to the west of Thami, and return to Kathmandu via Rolwaling. Only well-equipped parties of experienced mountaineers should attempt this route.

To proceed from Lukla to Khumbu, head north and join the main trail at Chablung. From here, continue north, crossing another tributary (8850 ft, 2698 m) with a beautiful peak at its head. Soon a bridge over the Dudh Kosi is reached and the village of Ghat (8350 ft, 2545 m) lies on its west (R) bank. There are some hotels on the east (L) bank, too. Proceed on the east (L) bank through **Chhutrawa** (8500 ft, 2591 m) to **Phakding** (8700 ft, 2652 m), now expanded to both sides of the river.

There has been a recent change in the trail due to a flash flood caused by an avalanche from a disrupted glacial lake high on the slopes of Ama Dablang. The water washed out several bridges over the next section, so the river crossings may change in the future as new bridges replace the temporary ones built after the flood. The section in question is between Phakding and the climb up to Namche Bazaar.

About **two hours** beyond Chaumrikharka or 2½ **hours** from Lukla, cross to the west (R) bank (8600 ft, 2621 m) of the Dudh Kosi and continue through blue pine and rhododendron forests to the village of **Benkar** (8875 ft, 2905 m). Watch for large, hanging, tongue-like beehives on the east (L) bank cliffs opposite you above Phakding. The new trail may traverse too high to allow you to see these. In a short while, cross to the east (L) bank and climb up through Chumowa. Here you may notice extensive vegetable farms, which supply the Japanese-built Everest View Hotel in Khumjung. Cross another tributary, the Kyangshar Khola (9100 ft, 2773 m), before climbing to **Mondzo** (9300 ft, 2835 m) about 1½ **hours** from Phakding. The trail then descends to the left of a huge rock and crosses to the west (R) bank of the Dudh Kosi to **Jorsale** (9200 ft, 2805 m) in **forty-five minutes**. This is the last village before Namche Bazaar. Enter Everest (Sagarmatha) National Park here. You can see the route on the *Khumbu Himal* map of the Research Scheme Nepal Himalaya. Jorsale is called Thumbug on this map.

The next stretch is named "bridges" by the Sherpas, after its several crossings. From Jorsale, cross the river shortly, then recross it. The west fork, the Bhote Kosi, joins the main Dudh Kosi just beyond. This west fork is crossed (9325 ft, 2843 m) to its east (L) bank and the climb to Namche Bazaar begins. Some 500 ft (152 m) up at the crest of the prow, Everest can be seen behind the Lhotse-Nuptse ridge. **Namche Bazaar** (11,300 ft, 3446 m) is **two or 2½ hours** from Jorsale. You are now in Khumbu. Stores, hotels, and restaurants are run by Sherpas. Prices are high, but most staples are available. In addition, there is a market on Saturdays. There is much old expedition food and equipment available in shops in Khumbu. The headquarters of Everest National Park is here, and there is a museum on the nearby hill. General regulations of national parks are discussed in Chapter 3. Essentially you and your entire party must be self-sufficient in non-wood fuel.

Namche Bazaar is a remarkable town. As the administrative center for Khumbu, it has many officials and offices, including a police check post. Many of the officials are lowlanders who would rather be elsewhere, though they do enjoy the good things about Namche Bazaar—the clean air, good water, and impressive views. Namche Bazaar used to be the trading center, where grain from the south was exchanged for salt from Tibet, and it remains a trading center, although the salt trade has ended. The weekly market held on Saturday is colorful and well worth seeing, and there are lots of interesting shops. Enterprising Sherpas have set up hotels with hot showers and a variety of foods. It is a good place to be rejuvenated after the rigors of the heights.

KHUMBU *(Map No. 4, Page 166)*

> *To arrive by foot in Sherpa country is to gain some insight into what it was like for the Israelites to reach the promised land.*
> Mike Thompson, anthropologist and climber

You should not regard Namche Bazaar or Tengboche as the turnaround point on the trek. There are enough things to do in Khumbu to occupy two or three weeks. There are four main river valleys which you can explore. Each has spectacular mountain scenery. There are two active monasteries and at least three village *gomba* to visit. And perhaps most appealing are the Sherpa people and their culture. If you have employed a Sherpa whose home is in Khumbu, you will most likely be given the hospitality of his home. Those fortunate enough to be in Khumbu during the full moon in May or November-December may see Mani-rimdu, the Sherpa drama festival depicting the victory of Buddhism over Bon. The May production is usually at the Thami Monastery and the November-December one at the Tengboche Monastery. Several of the trips available in Khumbu are described here.

To Everest Base Camp

From Namche Bazaar the trail rises to the saddle to the east and contours high above the Dudh Kosi until it joins the trail from Khumjung by some large boulders (11,800 ft, 3597 m). It continues through forests of blue pine and rhododendron, passing below the village of Trashinga to the Dudh Kosi (10,650 ft, 3247 m), where there is a small settlement called **Pungo Tenga** with several mills, a series of water-driven prayer wheels, and some hotels. It is **two hours** from Namche Bazaar. The trail climbs past the prayer wheels through very pleasant forest, with occasional impressive views of Kangtega, to **Tengboche** (12,687 ft, 3867 m), about **two hours** from the river. The forest of pine, fir, black juniper, and rhododendron in route is remarkable. Look for blood pheasants feeding near Tengboche in the morning. As from so many places in Khumbu, the views from Tengboche are spectacular. What a place for a monastery! The Tengboche *gomba* can be visited and sometimes respects can be paid to the venerable abbot. When visiting the abbot, be sure to offer him a ceremonial scarf or *kata* obtained from another monk. A donation from each visitor is appreciated. There are several choices for food and lodging. The park maintains some guest houses for trekkers and there are latrines, or *chaarpi*.

From Tengboche the trail heads east and descends slightly past the nunnery at Deboche (12,325 ft, 3757 m) and the few houses of Milingo, all the while in a fine

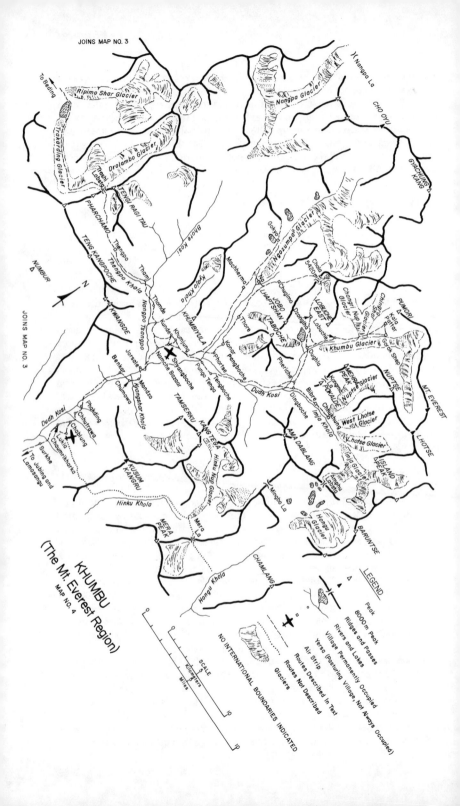

JOINS MAP NO. 3

To Beding

Ripimo Shar Glacier

Trakarding Glacier

Drolambo Glacier

Trashi Labtsa

TENGI RAGI TAU

PHARCHAMO

Thengpo

Thengpo Khola

TENG KANGPOCHE

Nangpo Tsangpo

Thami

Thonde

Bhote Kosi

NUMBUR

N

KWANGDE

Kunde

KHUMBILA

Khumjung

Jorsale
Benkar
Monjo
Namche Bazaar
Shyangboche
Nyongshar Khola
Chumoa

Dudh Kosi
Phakding
Chutrawa
Ghabung
Lukla
Choumikhana

Surkhe

To Jiubing and
Lamosangu

KUSUM
KANGRU

TAMSERKU

KANG TEGA

Hinku Nup Glacier

Hinku Khola

MERA
PEAK

Mera

Hongu Khola

Kyajo Khola

Machhermo

Thore

Konar

Nangpo Tsangpo

Phortse

Pangboche

Pungo Tenga

Dudh Kosi

Nangpa Glacier

Nangpa La

CHO OYU

GYACHUNG
KANG

Ngozumpa Glacier

Gokyo

Choia
5420

NGOJUMBA
KANG

JOBO
LHAPTSHAN

THOBUCHE

Dzonglha

Chugima
Dzonglha

Pheriche

Dughla

LABUCHE
EAST

Changri Nup Glacier

Chang Tsa

Changri Shar Glacier

LABUCHE

Khumbu Glacier

Lobuche

PUMORI

Kala
Pathar

Gorak Shep

MT. EVEREST

Korong
POKALDE

MEHRA
PEAK

Nuptse Glacier

NUPTSE

Bibre
Chhukhung

Imja Khola

West Lhotse
Glacier

LHOTSE

AMA DABLANG

Dingboche

Lhotse Glacier

Imja Glacier

ISLAND
PEAK

Amphu
Labtsa

Mingbo La

Hongu
Glacier

BARUNTSE

CHAMLANG

Hongu Khola

KHUMBU
(The Mt. Everest Region)
MAP NO. 4

SCALE

Kilometers

Miles

LEGEND

Peak

8000 m Peak

Ridges and Passes

Rivers and Lakes

Village Permanently Occupied

Yersa (Pasturing Village, Not Always Occupied)

Air Strip

Routes Not Described

Routes Described In Text

Glaciers

forest of rhododendrons that are spectacular in bloom. Continue to the river, the Imja Khola, and cross it at a narrowing on a wooden bridge (12,400 ft, 3780 m) from which you get a spectacular view of Ama Dablang. Cross to the north (R) bank. Some **five or ten minutes** beyond, near some *mani* stones, the trail forks. The left (higher) fork ascends to the Pangboche Gomba (13,075 ft, 3985 m), while the right goes directly to the village of **Pangboche** (12,800 ft, 3901 m) some **1½ hours** from Tengboche. The *gomba*, the oldest in Khumbu, was built some 300 years ago at the time that Buddhism is said to have been introduced into Khumbu. According to legend, a venerable old lama tore out his hair and cast it around the *gomba*. The large black juniper trees surrounding it sprouted from those hairs. They are so large because it is forbidden to cut them. The *gomba* contains some yeti relics—a scalp and some bones—which you can see for a few rupees.

Continue northeast from either the village itself or from the *gomba*, and reach a trail fork (13,725 ft, 4183 m) **1½ hours** beyond Pangboche. The right fork goes toward Dingboche, while the left, slightly less prominent fork climbs past one hut to the crest of a small ridge (14,050 ft, 4282 m) from which Pheriche can be seen. Descend a short distance to the bridge over the Khumbu Khola (13,875 ft, 4229 m) and cross it to the west (L) bank to reach **Pheriche** (13,950 ft, 4252 m) in some **two or three hours** from Pangboche, depending on acclimatization.

Pheriche, once a *yersa* or temporary yak herding area, is now settled throughout the winter—entirely because of the trekking traffic. It is a very different place from the one I encountered on my first visit in 1969. There are hotels built from blocks of sod, a garbage dump, and some latrines. The place is usually crowded with people, although solitude can be found nearby. There is a Trekkers' Aid Post, which was set up by the Himalayan Rescue Association in 1973. The post does research on altitude illness as well as providing medical care to trekkers and porters. A pressure chamber is currently being tested here to treat altitude illness. Of course, it is even better to prevent it by slow acclimatization. Every party should spend two nights, or at least a complete day and night, at Pheriche. During the day spent here, an ascent or hike is an especially good idea. You could spend this day going to Dingboche and farther east up the Imja Khola as described later. Or you could climb the ridge to the northeast to as high as 17,000 ft (5030 m) for views of Makalu to the east and of nearby summits. There is a hermitage on the way. You could also recross the Khumbu Khola and climb up on the shoulders of Taboche to the west. Or simply do the next day's walk, but return to Pheriche for the night. If you are already bothered by the altitude, it may be best to just walk along the valley floor. Check the section on altitude illness in Chapter 5.

To go on to the foot of Everest, continue north from Pheriche along the flats past the *yersa* of Phuling Karpo, then turn northeast up a grassy lateral moraine of the Khumbu Glacier. The route crosses its crest, descends to cross a glacial stream emerging from the snout of the glacier, which is covered by the moraine (15,025 ft, 4579 m), and ascends to the two stone huts of **Dughla** (15,075 ft, 4593 m). It takes **1½ hours** to reach Dughla from Pheriche. The trail then winds around the moraine to emerge on the other side of the glacier after crossing another stream of melted water from it. The trail continues northeast to the tea shops of **Lobuche** (16,175 ft, 4930 m), situated below the terminal moraine of a tributary glacier. Lobuche is about **1½ hours** from Dughla. A climb to the ridge crest to the west provides fine views, especially at sunset.

There is little shelter beyond Lobuche. Two stone huts at Gorak Shep are not maintained. It is possible to use Lobuche as a base to climb to Kala Pattar for views and to return the same day. This is advisable to avoid altitude problems. If you plan to sleep at Gorak Shep, it is best to have your own tents since space in the drafty huts can't be counted on.

To the southeast of Lobuche lies a pass, the Kongma La (18,135 ft, 5527 m). A good side trip is to cross the Khumbu Glacier, ascend the pass, and head south to Bibre as described later. This would take a very long, strenuous day, and it requires confidence on rock. Pokalde Peak, south of the pass, could also be climbed.

Beyond Lobuche the trail follows a trough beside the Khumbu Glacier, then climbs through the terminal moraine of another tributary glacier. From a high point here, the rubble-covered hill of **Kala Pattar** in front of Pumori can be seen, and at its base, a lake which is often frozen. Those planning to go to Gorak Shep at the northeast end of the lake should descend to the sands and contour the lake on its northeast shore to the rock monuments to persons who have died nearby. Gorak Shep (17,000 ft, 5184 m) is reached in 2¼ **to three hours** from Lobuche. You can no doubt see Tibetan snow cocks here and approach them quite closely.

The cairn of upper Kala Pattar (18,450 ft, 5623 m) to the north of the rounded hill that is the surveyed point of Kala Pattar can be reached in 1½ **hours** from Gorak Shep by ascending directly and keeping slightly to the northeast. You can see the South Col of Everest from here. Alternatively, you can head directly up to Kala Pattar without going to Gorak Shep by proceeding from the terminal moraine. It may be difficult to find the "trail" through the moraine, especially if there has been a recent snowfall. Trail sense is an asset, though small cairns mark the way.

The world's highest mountain was named after Sir George Everest, the head of the Survey of India from 1823 to 1843. Its Tibetan name, that used by the Sherpas, is Chomolongma which means Goddess Mother of the World. Sagarmatha, its Nepali name, means Head of the Seas. It was first climbed in 1953 by Sir Edmund Hillary and Tenzing Norgay.

The sites of the various base camps used for climbing Everest can be reached from Gorak Shep in a few hours by venturing over the rubble-covered surface of the Khumbu Glacier. They are close to the foot of the Khumbu icefall (17,400 ft, 5304 m). As you approach the first evidence of base camp garbage, note that recent base camps are an hour or so beyond, right at the foot of the Khumbu icefall. If you are here during a time that no expedition is climbing Everest, it may be tedious and time consuming to find the exact location. It is possible to visit the base camps from Lobuche and return the same long day. There are no good views from the base camps. If time is limited, it is better to ascend to Kala Pattar.

Better views of the Khumbu icefall and the other side of the Lhotse-Nuptse Wall can be obtained by climbing up the southeast ridge of Pumori. This ridge is reached by going part way to the base camps and turning northwest. Do not go out on the Khumbu Glacier to reach the ridge; stay on the lateral moraine. It is possible to get to where you can see the North Col of Everest before encountering technical difficulties. Lhotse can also be seen. It is best to use Gorak Shep as a base for this.

The times given for the journey beyond Namche Bazaar are quite variable. They depend upon the weather conditions as well as the fitness and acclimatization of the party. Allow at least five days to reach Kala Pattar from Tengboche. Hire local porters to carry your loads since they can handle the altitude much better than you. If you are going to high altitudes, be prepared for cold winds and snow. It is most important to heed the warning signs of altitude sickness described in Chapter 5. Many trekkers have died in this region because they did not do so. And they continue to die!

Yaks grazing near the Tengboche Monastery, with Everest barely visible over the Lhotse-Nuptse ridge to the left and Ama Dablang on the right. (Ane Haaland)

Up the Imja Khola

Reach **Dingboche** as already described or climb up the ridge (14,250 ft, 4343 m) behind Pheriche and descend to it in **half an hour.** You can take a shortcut from Lobuche by crossing the stream emanating from the snout of the Khumbu Glacier and climbing up the lateral moraine. Then follow a trail that contours to the south, passing the small temporary village of Dusa before dropping down to Dingboche. This third possibility is the quickest route from Lobuche.

From a little west of Dingboche you can climb up to Nangkartshang Gomba (15,430 ft, 4703 m) in **1½ hours** for fine views of Makalu to the east. This is a detour if you are going to Chhukhung, but you could then head east to join the trail coming from Dingboche at **Bibre** (15,000 ft, 4571 m). Bibre is reached in **1½ hours** from Dingboche by the direct route. The trail continues east, crossing numerous streams that flow from the Nuptse and Lhotse Glaciers, to a number of yak huts or *yersa* at **Chhukhung** (15,535 ft, 4734 m) perhaps **1½ hours** after Bibre.

You can now see Ama Dablang's east face. It is worthwhile to spend a day or two traveling around to the east and to the northeast for close views of the incredible Lhotse-Nuptse Wall. Either the *Khumbu Himal* or the *Mahalungar Himal* map is very useful here and suggests many hikes. Island Peak, a trekking summit, is northeast of Chhukhung.

Khumjung and Kunde

The STOL strip called Shyangboche (12,435 ft, 3790 m) is carved out of a shelf of land. Climb to it in less than an hour from Namche Bazaar. There are hotels and restaurants here. The government yak breeding farm five to ten minutes to the northwest is recognized by an impressive fence enclosing it. Often the yaks and naks (females) may be pastured much higher. The farm is attempting to preserve and maintain good genetic stocks of yak. This is necessary for the cross-breeding programs in which hearty *chAUmri* (cross between cow and yak) are developed. You can proceed past the preserve to the northwest, climbing to a crest (12,700 ft, 3871 m) in pleasant forests and descending to **Kunde** (12,600 ft, 3841 m). The north end of this town is the site of Kunde Hospital, built by the Himalayan Trust established by Sir Edmund Hillary.

To reach Khumjung, the "sister city" of Kunde, you can either traverse east from Kunde, or go directly from Shyangboche by climbing northeast from the airstrip past a large *chorten* in a blue pine forest. Descend past the Himalayan Trust school to the potato fields below **Khumjung** (12,400 ft, 3780 m). There is a village *gomba* to the north containing yeti relics that can be seen for a donation. The yeti scalp has been around the world during a test of its authenticity. Read *High in the Thin Cold Air* by Sir Edmund Hillary and Desmond Doig (Garden City, New York: Doubleday, 1962) for details. The famed Sherpa artist Kappa Kalden lives in Khumjung.

Finally of interest is the Everest View Hotel, beautifully situated on a shelf (12,700 ft, 3870 m). It can be reached in half an hour or less from the airstrip by following the well-graded path beginning at the lower end of the airstrip. Or you can reach it from the stupa at the eastern end of the potato fields of Khumjung. There is usually a Japanese doctor to look after the guests. You can trace your route on the relief map of Khumbu, which is on display here.

There have been many changes in this area since I first visited it. Immediately noticeable are the new houses with Western-style windows, corrugated tin roofs, and chimneys. Water systems have been constructed, making it somewhat easier to get water. People are much more cautious with their use of firewood since it is so time consuming to search for it. Communal fires are much smaller than at, say, Phortse, where wood is more plentiful. Families have a greater variety of Western goods. Mountaineering equipment and clothes are often used rather than the traditional apparel. Wealth is more often measured in terms of equipment and money rather than traditionally in the size of yak and sheep herds. Indeed, with children going off to school, it is difficult to find laborers to tend the animals. Of course the general level of education is quite good, and there are many Sherpas who are fluent in English. And it is not uncommon to find widows caring for children and looking after homes. Mountaineering expeditions take their toll and the Sherpas as an ethnic group were never large in number. The monasteries are perhaps less well supported now. It was traditional for a family to send the youngest child to the monastery, but now such practices are less common. Some of the changes of development are for the good, and some are questionable. No matter how we perceive it, the Sherpas feel their lot is better now.

To Gokyo

The trip up the Dudh Kosi from Khumjung takes you to summer yak-grazing country, to beautiful small lakes, and to the foot of Cho Oyu and Gyachung Kang peaks. The trail goes northeast of the stupa at the east end of Khumjung and climbs along the side of Khumbiyula to a crest of a ridge (13,100 ft, 3992 m) where there is a stupa. This takes **two hours** from Khumjung. Above you on the slopes of Khumbiyula, watch for a herd of Himalayan tahr (called *goral* by locals). Phortse is across the river. The trail descends steeply to near the river (11,950 ft, 3643 m). Take the left fork at junctions, as those to the right descend and cross the river to Phortse. The trail heads north and, after an **hour** or so, Cho Oyu is visible. You cross many spectacular waterfalls which are frozen in winter. Many landslides have occurred on both sides of this steep valley. After emerging from the woods, the trail passes several summer yak herding huts, or *yersa*, including Tongba (13,175 ft, 4015 m), **Gyele,** and Dole (13,400 ft, 4084 m). It takes 2¾ **hours** from the stupa on the ridge crest to **Gyele.** The next *yersa* at Lhabarma is far from water, but it is available at the one after that, Luza.

From Gyele, **Lhabarma** (14,200 ft, 4328 m) is reached in **less than an hour** and **Luza** (14,400 ft, 4390 m) in another **hour.** In the next tributary valley is **Machherma** (14,650 ft, 4465 m), a farther **forty-five minutes** away. Go on for an **hour** to **Pangka** (14,925 ft, 4548 m), but here again, there is no water near. From Pangka, descend slightly, following one of the melted glacial rivers that flow down the west side of the Ngozumpa Glacier, which is to the east now. The trail crosses this river at a narrowing and soon emerges at the first of several small lakes (15,450 ft, 4709 m) 1½ **hours** beyond Pangka. Another **forty-five minutes** brings you to the next lake, or *tsho*, with the *yersa* Longpanga at its northern end. There is no good shelter here, so continue for another **half hour** to the third lake (sometimes called Dudh Pokhari) and the *yersa* of **Gokyo** (15,720 ft, 4791 m) on its east shore.

From Gokyo, Cho Oyu looms to the north. There are several places to go for views. Currently the most popular is to ascend the ridge to the northwest to a small summit (17,990 ft, 5483 m). This takes **two to three hours** for those well acclimatized and provides an excellent panorama from Cho Oyu, to Everest, to Lhotse, and all the way to Makalu. Some trekkers consider the view from this Kala Pattar, as it is called, better than from the one above Gorak Shep. Alternatively, you can follow the trail north between the lateral moraine of the glacier and the hills to the west until you reach the next lake (16,150 ft, 4923 m) where, near its east shore, there are some roofless huts. This takes about 1½ **hours** from Gokyo. A climb of a few hundred feet up the hill to the north of the lake provides fine views. You could also continue another 1½ **hours** to the last lake. The *Khumbu Himal* map may suggest many other hikes. You could return from Gokyo by following the east side of the valley, reaching it from below the snout of the glacier at Pangka. Or you could cross the glacier directly east of Gokyo. Alternatively, you could follow the route described below in reverse to reach the Khumbu Glacier and the foot of Everest.

Most of the *yersa* settlements in Khumbu belong to the people in the permanent villages to the south. They are usually locked up when no one is there. If you employ a local Sherpa, he can very likely get permission for you to use those owned by his family or acquaintances. You should pay a few rupees a night to use them.

Pass 5420 Meters

For people who want to combine visits to the Everest Base Camp region with one to the upper reaches of the Dudh Kosi beneath Cho Oyu without extensive backtracking, this pass is a scenic and enjoyable route. It does involve a short glacier crossing for which a rope and ice axe are advisable; however, there are no serious dangers or technical difficulties. In the process, you circumnavigate Jobo Lhaptshan (21,128 ft, 6440 m) and Taboche (20,889 ft, 6367 m) and get excellent views of Cho Oyu to the north.

To descend from the Everest Base Camp area, follow the trail down below Lobuche some **fifteen to thirty minutes** as far as the stream crossing on the lateral moraine (16,000 ft, 4877 m) but instead of crossing it, contour on the side of the valley, eventually turning northwest into the valley of the pass. You can thus stay at a high elevation and instead of descending to the shores of the lake below you (Tshola Tsho), cross the main stream that feeds into the lake higher up. Pick the trail up again near the stream crossing if it has been lost. The trail ascends to the *yersa* of Dzonglha (15,889 ft, 4843 m), beautifully situated on a shelf of land with fine views in every direction. It is about **2½ hours or more** from Lobuche. This is a very good spot to camp, either in tents or in the huts. The feeling of sitting under the north face of Jobo Lhaptshan is unforgettable.

Alternatively, if approaching this area from the south, go to Dughla and follow the trail slightly below it before bearing west to the small trail skirting the end of the Tshola Glacier moraine which has almost blocked the valley and formed the Tshola Tsho (lake) above it. Reach the end of the lake (14,804 ft, 4512 m)—it is ice-covered in November—in **half an hour**. The best camping spot for spectacular views is near here, but the only huts are some distance farther on. The trail follows the north shore of the lake and rises gradually until it reaches Tsholo Og (15,306 ft, 4665 m), a *yersa* of three huts, in **forty-five minutes**. All are unoccupied and locked in winter. Water must be carried from a stream **ten minutes** farther on. Dzonglha is another **hour** up the faint trail. Above this *yersa*, the trail is less distinct, and although there is no further shelter, there are signs of people using the pass.

Cross a small crest just above Dzonglha and descend slightly into the gentle valley coming down from the glacier in the pass to the northwest. The pass, sometimes called Chola by locals, is the 5420 m (17,783 ft) crossing marked on the Schneider *Khumbu Himal* map. There is a small trail aiming for the glacier-smoothed rock to the east of the glacier itself. The moraine at the head of the valley is reached in an **hour** from Dzonglha. Ascend to the right of the glacier, sometimes on loose rock, sometimes on large slabs with handsome graining, until you reach a small valley or moat between the rock and the glacier. In route you may find the remnants of a meteorological survey station and a bench mark (E9/GEN). Eventually, gain the glacier around 17,350 ft (5285 m). Keep to its south side and ascend steeply at first (30°) on the snow-covered surface. Watch for crevasses. During the monsoon this may be bare ice and require crampons. The glacier levels out and the pass (17,783 ft, 5420 m) is reached in perhaps **2½ hours** from Dzonglha. A new valley and new vistas open up before you. From the pass there are no views of the giants, but this gives you an opportunity to appreciate the lesser, often more beautiful, mountains. Those with experience and equipment may want to scramble up the snow to the minor summit to the south.

The descent on the west side of the pass is initially down steep, hard snow, then onto variegated talus heading south. Beware of ice avalanches from the hanging glacier on the peak marked 5666 m on the Schneider map. Reach the valley

The spectacular pasture of Dzonglha in Khumbu, with Ama Dablang seen from the north. (Donald Messerschmidt)

floor with its boulders and hummocks. If heading to Gokyo, you can bear west without losing much altitude, then descend to cross the Ngozumpa Glacier. If heading south, continue along the trail through the boulders and hummocks near the main stream in the rather flat valley. Near the end of the shelf, there is a cave by some stone fences called Chugimo (16,175 ft, 4930 m). It is suitable for shelter or camping. Reach it in **two to three hours** from the pass. As you leave the flats, follow the trail on the north (L) side of the stream and reach Dragnag, a beautiful *yersa* (15,100 ft, 4602 m) within sight of the terminal moraine of the Ngozumpa Glacier, in **forty-five minutes**. Cross the river you have been following on a rock bridge to the south (L) bank. The river may be concealed beneath it. Don't descend, but contour **fifteen minutes** to a *yersa* called Tsom (15,000 ft, 4572 m), labeled Gonglha on the *Khumbu Himal* map. Alternatively, you could descend from Dragnag to Na (14,435 ft, 4400 m), labeled Tsoshung on the map, which is below the tongue of the glacier. From here, you can join the route described earlier on the west (R) bank of the Dudh Kosi by crossing the stream west of Na and contouring gently up to the south to reach the shelf above the river in **half an hour**. Before you proceed, note the view of the impressive south face of Cho Oyu to the north.

To head south to Phortse on the east side of the valley, continue contouring below Tsom, crossing a tributary to reach Thare (14,250 ft, 4343 m) in **forty-five minutes**. Another **half hour** of climbing brings you to Thore (14,435 ft, 4400 m), which is probably the spot marked Thare on the Schneider *Khumbul Himal* map. Names do get confusing in Khumbu, especially since names on the Schneider map are Tibetan for the most part, while the inhabitants are Sherpa, and the initial surveyors were Indian! Fortunately the route is completely straightforward. After a couple of tributaries, the *yersa* of Konar (13,425 ft, 4092 m) near another tributary is reached in 1½ **hours**. There is no permanent habitation before Phortse along this valley. All of the huts along the route are in excellent condition, and the area is very beautiful—perhaps there is a relation between this and the paucity of trekkers.

Continue into a handsome juniper and birch forest to a tributary that is the source of the Phortse water supply. Continue through rhododendrons to upper **Phortse** (12,140 ft, 3700 m), some **forty-five minutes** from Konar. Phortse is the impressively perched village you have probably seen from the south. It dominates the entrance to the valley you have descended. To leave Phortse, descend through the fine forest to the west to the Dudh Kosi (11,200 ft, 3414m) in **half an hour** and ascend to meet the trail from Khumjung to Gokyo that has already been described, in another **half hour**.

To Thami

The trail to Thami begins at Namche Bazaar and heads west without going behind the *gomba* as the other trail does. You can also take the trail heading west from Shyangboche before the descent to Namche Bazaar. The trail contours the Nangpo Tsangpo Valley, passing Phurte (11,400 ft, 3475 m), then crossing the main tributary from the north, the Kyajo Khola (11,200 ft, 3414 m) at the small town of Kyajo. Continue on to **Thamo** (11,300 ft, 3444 m) 1½ **hours** from Namche Bazaar, or less from Shyangboche. To the north above the trail is the town of Mende where there is a new monastery with an English-speaking *Rinpoche* (reincarnate abbot). Westerners sometimes study there. Proceed to **Thomde** (11,500 ft, 3505 m) where a miniature hydroelectric project is being planned to provide electricity to Khumbu! The trail continues to follow the river and crosses it (11,550 ft, 3520 m) some **forty-five minutes** beyond Thamo to ascend on its south (R) bank. Pass through pleasant forests and reach the Thengpo Khola flowing east from the Trashi Labsta Pass. Cross it to the north (L) bank (12,075 ft, 3680 m) and ascend a small hill to the north to the valley flats and the town of **Thami**, (12,400 ft, 3780 m) an **hour** from Thomde. There is a small hill just to the north of Thami beyond which you are not permitted to go. To the north up the main riverbed lies the Nangpa La (18,753 ft, 5716 m), an important pass into Tibet that was once the popular trading route. To the west of Thami, where the hill behind the town terminates at the base of a cliff, is a monastery (12,925 ft, 3940 m) which is worth visiting. Farther to the east at the head of the valley is the Trashi Labtsa, a high pass (18,885 ft, 5755 m) leading west to the Rolwaling Valley. It is described in Chapter 11.

SOLU *(Map No. 3, Page 158)*

Those with sufficient time should consider visiting the towns of southern Solu. This region is inhabited by Sherpas who have migrated south from Khumbu and settled where it is much easier to farm and live. They are generally wealthier than their northern counterparts, and signs of this wealth are readily apparent. Another attraction of this area is a successful Tibetan camp at Chialsa.

People who are heading to Khumbu, but who wish to detour to this region, must leave the regular route at Junbesi, while those returning to Kathmandu should turn off from Ringmo, or possibly from Phuleli. There is a high route from Ghat west over the ridge and south to Ringmo, but it is not practical except in the dry season if there has not been any snow at higher elevations.

From **Junbesi**, cross the bridge below the stupa and take the right fork of the level trail that follows above the northeast (L) bank of the Junbesi Khola. In **less than half an hour** you come to **Khamje** (8525 ft, 2599 m). Continue along the river until it flows into the Dudhkunda Khola, also called the Solu Khola, and cross this river (7725 ft, 2355 m) to its east (L) bank. Head south, following close to the river for the most part, but rising to clear bends until a shack (7480 ft, 2250 m) is reached. The trail rises beyond the shack and soon joins the main north-south trail higher on the east bank at a magnificent house with a private *gomba* (8100 ft, 2469 m) in **Phaphlu**. This takes about **two hours** from Khamje. The impressive forests are mostly prickly-leaved oak. A hospital has been built here by Sir Edmund Hillary. Head south for about **forty-five minutes** to **Salleri** (7700 ft, 2347 m), the district center of Solu-Khumbu. Along the way, pass the Phaphlu airstrip (7775 ft, 2370 m). From a distance Salleri is reminiscent of a Wild West town. Another **fifteen minutes** to the south is **Dorphu** (7500 ft, 2256 m), where a colorful market is held every Saturday. To visit the Tibetan camp at **Chialsa**, follow the trail to the southeast from Dorphu for a **little over an hour**. It continues climbing above most of the houses to the camp (9000 ft, 2743 m). Be sure to visit the carpet manufacturing center.

Another attraction of the area is **Chiwong Gomba** (9700 ft, 2953 m), a monastery spectacularly situated high on a cliff overlooking Phaphlu and Salleri. It can be reached by heading north from Chialsa for some **three to four hours**. Trekkers heading south from Ringmo can get to it more directly. It could also be reached from the bridge over the Dudhkunda from which a trail heads directly up to join the main north-south trail on the east side of the valley at 8200 ft (2500 m). From here, head south and shortly, take the fork to the left heading to Chiwong. The *gomba* is well described in *Buddhist Himalaya* (see Recommended Reading).

To reach this area on your return from Khumbu, head south from **Ringmo**. The trail branches left from the one to Sallung at 9050 ft (2758 m) just below the town, and goes south on a wide path. After contouring through a forest, it passes through the attractive town of **Phera** (8300 ft, 2530 m) 1¾ **hours** from Ringmo. Beyond, take the left branch, since the right descends to the river and then to Junbesi. Continue on the main trail, passing the turnoff to the left to Chiwong Gomba and reaching **Phaphlu** in **two hours**. The rest of the route has been described. There is also a route heading directly over the ridge from Phuleli to Chialsa.

Trail scene west of Pokhara. (Stephen Bezruchka)

10 WESTERN NEPAL

The Promised Land always lies on the other side of a wilderness.
Havelock Ellis, English psychologist

Western Nepal, the region west of the Kali Gandaki river, offers interesting country and people to the trekker who has done the popular treks. But it is more difficult to travel here than in the more frequented east. Except for the trek to Dhorpatan, food and accommodations generally cannot be obtained. Very few people in the area speak English, trails tend to be more difficult, and the country seems more rugged. Furthermore, the Himalayan scenery in this part of Nepal is less impressive than in the east. It is very difficult to get the feeling of being in the mountains that Khumbu, Rolwaling, and Langtang provide. However, there are many other attractions. For the person wishing to see impressive forests, rugged and generally high terrain, and interesting peoples, the west has much to offer.

Two areas are described. The first is visited on a circuit from Pokhara to Dhorpatan with the return via Tansen. There are few logistic problems here compared to those encountered in the second area, which is seen on a circuit from Jumla to RaRa Lake.

DHORPATAN-TANSEN CIRCUIT
(Maps No. 2, Page 133 and No. 5, Page 178)

A circuit from Pokhara to Dhorpatan with the return through Tansen offers a pleasant trek through mixed country and includes views of impressive mountains. The Dhorpatan Valley is most unusual for its spaciousness in this tangled country. There are many interesting side trips. In the winter, when snow can make the crossing of the Jaljala Pass into Dhorpatan difficult if not impossible, there is another lower pass providing access. Unfortunately, it is necessary to make the decision to go via this lower pass a day or two out of Pokhara. You could also start from Tansen and return via the more spectacular higher pass. Lodging is available along most of the trek and would only be a concern if the last day into Dhorpatan dragged on.

There are several options for starting this trek. You could fly to Balewa south of Baglung on regular RNAC flights and walk from there. There is also a STOL strip in Dhorpatan, but as yet no regular flights, though a charter could be arranged. Starting from Pokhara, there are two choices. You could walk to Naudanda to the northwest and then to Bhaudari Deorali, Tilhar, Dobila, and Kusma as has been described in reverse in Chapter 8. Alternatively, you could board a bus toward Butwal on the Siddhartha Rajmarg at Mahendra Pul in Pokhara and get off at the other village called Naudanda about **one to 1½ hours'** ride to the south. Finally, you could take the same bus all the way to Tansen, and walk in reverse.

Pokhara to Dhorpatan via Jaljala

Take the bus to Naudanda as already described. From **Naudanda** (3600 ft, 1097 m), head west and contour, then descend to the south to a tributary from the

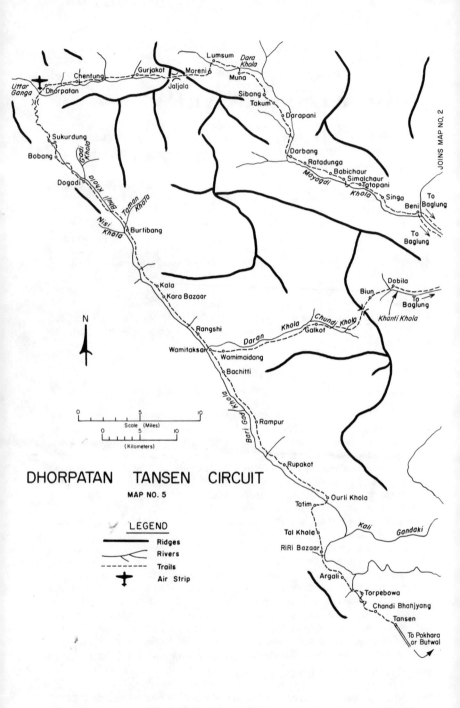

DHORPATAN TANSEN CIRCUIT

MAP NO. 5

LEGEND

━━━ Ridges
〜 Rivers
--- Trails
✈ Air Strip

north. It can be crossed directly, or in high water, **ten minutes** upstream at a suspension bridge. On the east (R) bank, reach **Seti Dovan** (2950 ft, 900 m), a large bazaar town **forty-five minutes** from Naudanda. The uncleared areas are wet sub-tropical forest. Continue west above the north (L) bank of the Andhi Khola to **Rangatani** (3100 ft, 945 m) in **half an hour**. Cross the suspension bridge here and follow the south (R) bank during high water. Either bank can be followed in low water. Continue upstream to **Chilaunabati** (3600 ft, 1097 m) in 1½ **hours**, then to **Phedi** (3850 ft, 1173 m) in another 1½ **hours**. There are usually three fords of the river at places that depend on the river level. This is a main route and the trail is easy to find. Beyond Phedi, begin a steep ascent over a good trail with steps part of the way. The pass and the town of **Karkineta** (5350 ft, 1631 m) are reached in 1½ **to two hours**.

The descent to the Modi Khola now begins. Head southwest from the pass and descend through Potebar (4400 ft, 1341 m) in **half an hour**, Phedi (3225 ft, 983 m) in **half an hour**, and **Yamdi** (3000 ft, 914 m) in another **half an hour**. Stay on the east (L) bank of the river for **half an hour** to reach a tea shop. Ford the river to its west (R) bank. Contour the rice paddies and ascend a small bamboo-forested gulley. Continue past a large, well-built, three-story white cement and stucco modern-style house. All this takes only **fifteen minutes**. Beyond, keep to the right and descend a few stairs to emerge by three houses. Continue to the town of Ghandichaur (2875 ft, 876 m) in another **ten minutes**. The trail then passes through pleasant mixed forests and terraces, and ascends to a large suspension bridge over the Modi Khola (2400 ft, 732 m) in **half an hour**. Cross to the west (R) bank and ascend for **half an hour** to **Kusma** (3000 ft, 914 m), a large town which is the administrative center for Parbat District. The alternative trail starting at Naudanda north of Pokhara joins here. The forests are of sal.

Continue north along a cobbled trail to the small town of **Chamalgai** (3050 ft, 930 m) in **half an hour**. Descend for **half an hour** to Armadi (2575 ft, 785 m), with a few houses. The trail now follows the east (L) bank of the Kali Gandaki, passing through **Shastradara** (2500 ft, 777 m) in **forty-five minutes** and reaching **Khani-yaghat** (2725 ft, 831 m) at a suspension bridge in an **hour**.

There are now two basic routes. One generally heads north to Beni, then west and northwest to cross a pass (11,200 ft, 3414 m) into the Dhorpatan Valley. The other heads west of Baglung, crosses over to the Bari Gad Khola at Wamitaksar, and follows it northwest over a pass (9600 ft, 2926 m) into Dhorpatan. The former is quicker and much more scenic, but in the winter, when snows block the pass, it may be impassable for many days. The other route is almost always feasible. The Baglung to Wamitaksar variation is described later.

In traveling to Beni, there are two variations, depending on whether you want to pass through Baglung, a district center. To avoid Baglung, continue upstream from Khaniyaghat on the east (L) bank, passing through Parse and Parbeni just across the river from Beni. Cross the Kali Gandaki on a suspension bridge just north of *Beni* (2700 ft, 823 m) and enter the town, which is on the west (R) bank of the Kali Gandaki at the junction with the Mayagdi Khola which flows in from the west. Beni is reached in **three hours** from Khaniyaghat. It is the administrative center of Mayagdi District.

To take the other variation through Baglung, cross the river at Khaniyaghat and climb up to **Baglung** (3200 ft, 975 m) in **half an hour**. This town, pleasantly situated on a shelf above the river, is the administrative center for Baglung District. Dhorpatan lies in the northwest corner of this district. From Baglung, one trail heads west to Wamitaksar. It is described later. To continue to Beni, head north and descend from the plateau to the Kali Gandaki. There is another direct route from the bridge crossing, at Khaniyaghat that stays close to the river and does not climb to Baglung. Either way, continue north up the west (R) bank of the Kali Gandaki, passing a tributary and a few tea shops to reach Beni in **three hours**.

Those flying to the Baglung airstrip land at **Balewa** (3425 ft, 1044 m), which is situated on a shelf above the west (R) bank of the Kali Gandaki **three hours'** walk south of Baglung. A little over **two hours** north of Balewa, descend to cross the Khanti Khola (2800 ft, 853 m) to its north (L) bank and ascend to Baglung in another **half hour**.

To proceed from Beni, head west above the north (L) bank of the Mayagdi Khola. Reach **Bagua** (2875 ft, 876 m) in an **hour**, Singhi (3000 ft, 1044 m) in another **forty-five minutes**, Raksho in another **half hour**, and the large town of **Tatopani** (3075 ft, 937 m) in another **fifteen minutes**. Just before you reach Tatopani, closer to the river than the town, are some hot springs. The forests along here are mimosa and alder. About **twenty minutes** farther upstream, cross the river on a suspension bridge, then shortly recross it to the north (L) bank (3100 ft, 945 m). The town of **Simalchaur** (3175 ft, 968 m) is just beyond. An **hour** brings you to **Babichaur** (3350 ft, 1021 m), another large town. Continue through Shastradura (3475 ft, 1059 m), Baloti, and past an impressive landslide on the south (R) bank to reach **Ratadunga** (3475 ft, 1059 m) in 1¼ **hours**. Do not cross the suspension bridge here, but continue west through Dhakarka to **Darbang** (3650 ft, 1113 m) in a **little over an hour**. This large town has a police check post.

Cross the river on a suspension bridge and proceed up its south (R) bank past a landslide to a tributary from the west, the Danga Khola in **less than an hour**. Cross the tributary to its north (L) bank (3750 ft, 1143 m) and begin a steep ascent up the crest of the ridge. To your left is a chir pine forest, while to your right where there is more moisture, the usual wet subtropical forest. In 1½ **hours** reach **Darapani** (5125 ft, 1562 m) high above the west (R) bank of the Mayagdi Khola. Contour to the west to **Takum** (5500 ft, 1676 m) in another **hour**. Another **half hour** of level walking brings you to **Sibang** (5750 ft, 1753 m). After a short climb of **forty-five minutes**, you reach a fine viewpoint north into the Dhaulagiri range. Below is the junction of the Dara Khola, flowing from the west, and the Mayagdi Khola, draining the Dhaulagiris to the north. Continue contouring, pass above the town of Phalaigaon, and reach **Muna** (6350 ft, 1935 m) in 1½ **hours**. Across the valley lies the spectacularly-perched village of Dara.

From Muna, descend to the river, the Dara Khola, and cross it on a suspension bridge (6100 ft, 1859 m) after **fifteen minutes**. Enter a dry oak forest. Climb, then contour for **two hours**, crossing a tributary from the north, and descend to **Lumsum** (7150 ft, 2179 m). There are only a few houses here, but one offers food and lodging. Except during the late spring, summer, and early fall, there is no food or lodging available beyond until Dhorpatan, a full day's walk ahead in good weather.

To continue from Lumsum, head upstream a short distance on the north (L) bank, then cross the Dara Khola on a suspension bridge (7250 ft, 2210 m). A steep **one-hour** climb follows to the few houses of **Moreni** (8500 ft, 2591 m), and another **fifteen minutes** brings you to a *goTh* (8750 ft, 2667 m) where food is obtainable in season. Leave the typical, terraced hill and ascend into an oak, hemlock, and rhododendron forest for 2½ **hours**. Near the top, where oak and hemlock are replaced by fir and birch, pass a small *chorten* on the left and emerge into a broad open plateau (11,200 ft, 3414 m) near a *chautaara*. This area is called Jaljala and is the highest point, but not the watershed. The actual watershed between the Gandaki and the Bheri-Karnali river systems is some distance ahead and is easily missed.

The views from here are excellent. From west to east, you can see Putha Hiunchuli, Churen Himal, Gurja Himal, which is very near you; then Dhaulagiri, the Nilgiris, Annapurna, Annapurna South, Machhapuchhre, Baudha Himal, and Himalchuli. It is worthwhile to camp here for views in the morning. Water can be obtained at a spring a short distance back on the trail to the east.

To continue to Dhorpatan, keep to the south side of the plateau and after **forty-five minutes** pass a large stone *goTh* on the left and descend to cross a tributary. Ascend briefly to a plateau (10,900 ft, 3322 m) and at its western end, drop 300 ft (110 m) to cross a small river on a log bridge. This river, the Uttar Ganga, is reached some **one to 1½ hours** after Jaljala. The trail now follows the north (R) bank of the river for 3½ **to four hours** to Dhorpatan. The forests are of blue pine and black juniper. In an **hour**, reach some stone *goTh* at **Gurjakot** (9900 ft, 3018 m), where food can be obtained except in the cold season. The river here, the Simudar Khola, is crossed at three points, and in another **half hour**, the Gur Gad River is reached. It can be crossed on rocks, or, in high water, on the bridge **ten minutes** upstream. Continue west, reaching a broad flat area which can be wet and boggy. In this case, bypass it to the north below a *gomba*. This monastery is of the Bon-Po sect, a forerunner of Tibetan Buddhism. Pass some *goTh* and cross a river to **Chentung** (9600 ft, 2926 m), the first permanent habitation since Moreni, an **hour** from the Gur Gad. This village, and the one at the west end of the valley an **hour** beyond, are inhabited by Tibetan refugees who settled here in 1960. **Half an hour** beyond Chentung, cross a tributary from the north and continue another **half hour** past more Tibetan houses to **Giraund** (9325 ft, 2842 m), the site of an airstrip.

Near Dhorpatan

Dhorpatan is the name of the area, an unusually broad, flat valley in this rugged hill country. It was probably once a lake that was later filled in. Many Nepalis from villages to the east, south, and west live here during the summer months when they grow potatoes and pasture animals. Their settlements are seen along the perimeter of the valley, especially on its southern aspect.

Although there are few views from the valley floor (Annapurna South can be seen some thirty-five miles to the east), easy climbs of the surrounding hills provide unparalleled views. You can travel a few days to the north into blue sheep country, or up into the snows and glaciers of the western Dhaulagiri range. The base camps of the various expeditions at the head of the Ghustung Khola are worth visiting. You could continue on across Chalike Pahar to the Dogadi Khola, and across to the Seng Khola and the Jangla Bhanjyang trail, which could then be followed back to Dhorpatan. Food and shelter must be carried for all these trips to the north.

To the west and northwest live the *Kham Magar*, an interesting ethnic group with many animistic and shamanistic traditions. Food and shelter are difficult to obtain in this area and are best carried. A four- to five-day circuit through this region can be most interesting. After a long day down the Uttar Ganga, you can reach the villages of Taka and Shera where the flat-roofed houses are reminiscent of Thak Khola, or of areas farther west. Cross the ridge up the tributary valley to the north, and descend to Hukum (Hugaon), or go beyond to Maikot on the north side of the Pelma Khola, in a day. The third day takes you through Puchhargaon and Yamakar to Pelma. Or you could continue across the Ghustung Khola and camp in the meadows of Thankur. A long day across the Phagune Danda Pass (13,100 ft, 3993 m) brings you back to Dhorpatan.

Those with less time should at least walk up one of the hills surrounding the valley for a view. The ridge crest directly south of the airstrip is the easiest viewpoint, and takes less than two hours via one of its north facing spurs. The view from here in clear weather extends to beyond Langtang in the east! The hill to the north of the valley (13,600 ft, 4145 m) can be reached in three to four hours from the airstrip. Suribang, "the writing desk hill" to the southwest, is an excellent viewpoint. Reach it by heading west as the valley narrows for half an hour to a bridge over the Uttar Ganga. Cross and ascend to the top (13,300 ft, 4054 m) in four hours from the airstrip. Hiunchuli Patan is visible to the west. Finally, the highest of the peaks surrounding the valley, Phagune Dhuri (15,500 ft, 4724 m), lying to the northwest, can be reached from the pass to the east. The round trip probably takes longer than a day.

From Dhorpatan, you could retrace your steps. This could be worthwhile if bad weather has prevented good views. Otherwise, heading southeast to Tansen provides an interesting contrast. Although there are essentially no mountain views until Tansen, the trail passes through pleasant typical hill country. The time required is similar for both routes.

Dhorpatan to Tansen

To head south to Tansen from the airstrip, Giraund, go south across the valley toward the obvious pass. Depending on the year, there may be small bridges over the Uttar Ganga, but it is often necessary to wade. Pick up the trail from the east and reach the pass (9625 ft, 2934 m) in **half an hour**. Descend to a stream, and at 9300 ft (2835 m), begin crossing a series of six small bridges over the stream for the next 600 ft (185 m) through a rhododendron, oak, and hemlock forest. Continue descending on the northeast (L) bank of the Bhuji Khola to reach Dowal (7600 ft, 2316 m) in **one to 1½ hours** from the pass. This is the first permanent settlement. Typical terraced Nepali country lies ahead. The forest is of prickly-leaved oak. In an **hour**, cross and recross the river and ascend slightly to **Sukurdung** (6700 ft, 2042 m), where there is a post box. Beyond the large schoolhouse, the trail crosses to the southwest (R) bank of the Bhuji Khola and descends slightly to **Bobang** (5800 ft, 1768 m) in **forty-five minutes**. Continue descending after a level stretch, and cross to the east (L) bank (5200 ft, 1585 m) of the Bhuji Khola in **half an hour**. In **fifteen minutes**, reach another suspension bridge (5052 ft, 1532 m) and cross to the west (R) bank. You are in wet subtropical forest. In another **fifteen minutes**, reach a covered bridge at **Dogadi** (4775 ft, 1455 m). Bypass another covered bridge and a suspension bridge, then cross to the east (L) bank on a suspension bridge (4250 ft, 1295 m) in **forty-five minutes**. Reach another suspension bridge (3600 ft, 1158 m) over the Taman Khola, a tributary to the east, and cross it to **Burtibang**, a large town with a police check post. From here the trail keeps to the east (L) bank for almost **two days**.

Continue along the Bhuji Khola, climbing somewhat through Renam to the small town of **Bingetti** (3400 ft, 1036 m) **two hours** beyond Burtibang. Cross a tributary from the east, the Bing Khola, on a suspension bridge (3100 ft, 945 m) and reach **Kala** (2950 ft, 900 m), a large town, in another **half hour**. Keep on the east (L) side of the river and enter **Kara Bazaar** (2850 ft, 869 m) in an **hour**. Pass through Balua (2700 ft, 823 m) in another **forty-five minutes** and **twenty minutes** later, cross the Labdi Khola, another tributary. Climb through a sal forest before descending to

Transplanting rice. (Ane Haaland)

Rangshi (2575 ft, 785 m) in an **hour**. The main river is now called the Bari Gad Khola. Another **half hour** brings you to the log bridge (2500 ft, 762 m) crossing the Daran Khola from the east. Just beyond, a left fork ascends to Wamitaksar. Baglung can be reached in a **very long day**. The route from Baglung to here is described later.

To continue to Tansen, pass through the few houses of Sutti and reach **Bachitti** (2325 ft, 709 m) in 1½ **hours**. The trail continues along rice paddies through Laureshimal, Jorkale, and Abachor, crosses a tributary from the east, and reaches **Rampur** (2150 ft, 655 m), a large bazaar, in 2¼ **hours**. Continue through **Mojua**, cross a tributary, pass through Rupakot, Churkati, and Dhab, and cross a large slide on a tributary from the east to reach **Ourli Khola** (2075 ft, 632 m) in 3¼ **hours**. Cross the main river to its southwest (R) bank on a large suspension bridge, then climb up steeply for 1¼ **hours** to **Tatim** (3700 ft, 1128 m).

Keep climbing, take the left fork after passing through the town, and round a ridge jutting to the east (4475 ft, 1364 m). Dhaulagiri and Churen Himal can be seen from here. Enter chir pine forests, then drop slightly to a saddle and the town of **Ghiubesi** (4300 ft, 1311 m) an hour from Tatim. Enter a small, beautiful valley and go left through Chautaara (4500 ft, 1372 m) in **twenty minutes**. There is an impressive three-story house at the pass. Descend to the west, pass through **Pataunje Pani** (4400 ft, 1341 m), and drop steeply into a widening valley to reach the town and

183

Building a house in the hills. (Donald Messerschmidt)

river of **Tal Khola** (2500 ft, 762 m) in **forty-five minutes**. Continue dropping down on the west (R) side of the valley to 2275 ft (693 m) before climbing out of the valley and heading downstream above the west (R) bank. Drop into the valley of the Kali Gandaki and descend to the large town of **RiRi Bazaar** (1550 ft, 472 m) 1¾ hours from Tal Khola.

Go through the town, cross the RiRi Khola to its south (R) bank, and climb above the west (R) bank of the Kali Gandaki river through Oruan Pokhari and Sattari Pokhari to reach **Argana** (2350 ft, 716 m) in **forty-five minutes**. Descend into another valley to reach **Argali** (2175 ft, 663 m) in **half an hour**. There is a side trail heading off to the left of the fountain and *chautaara* in this village. It leads to a palace built in 1947 as a retirement home for then Prime Minister Juddha Shumshere J.B. Rana. It is worth a detour.

Continue shortly beyond Argali to the Gurung Khola (2025 ft, 617 m). Cross to the south (R) bank and follow the river upstream. Pass through Torpebowa (2400 ft, 732 m) in **half an hour**, then cross to the east (L) bank and climb for **fifteen minutes** to Tirap (2625 ft, 815 m). Cross the river three times and reach Rossuas (3625 ft, 1105 m) in **an hour**. The town of **Gurung Khola** (4325 ft, 1318 m) is **half an hour** beyond. Soon you see a pipe and a tunnel through the hill, but keep climbing for **fifteen minutes** to **Chandi Bhanjyang** (4625 ft, 1410 m). Enter a new valley and turn right (west) to contour the Shrinagar ridge on a wide trail. The trail passes through a few small settlements before it crosses the ridge to the south and drops into Tansen (4650 ft, 1417 m), the district center for Palpa, in an **hour**. The head of the road is at the lower end of town. Buses leave for Pokhara in the morning. It is also possible to take a bus south to Butwal and Bhairawa. Be sure to catch the view of the mountains from the ridge behind Tansen. There are also many interesting temples in Tansen.

Baglung to Dhorpatan, Avoiding Jaljala

An alternate, less scenic route from Baglung to Dhorpatan is suitable when snow blocks the route over Jaljala. From Baglung, walk west on the main street. Leave the town and contour close to the Khanti Khola. Reach Khare (3450 ft, 1052 m) in an **hour**. Pass, but do not cross, a suspension bridge to reach **Dobila** (3525 ft, 1074 m), a bazaar, in **half an hour**. Cross to the west (R) bank of a tributary to the northwest. The trail climbs a bit as if toward the main river, then forks after a **few minutes**. Take the right (upper) fork to leave the valley floor. The trail ascends a ridge, passing through scattered settlements, most of which are part of **Biun**. Reach Tarakasi (4600 ft, 1402 m) in **forty-five minutes**. From here there are views of Machhapuchhre, Annapurnas II and IV, Dhaulagiri, Himalchuli, and Annapurna South. Reach the part of Biun containing a red post box (5800 ft, 1768 m) in **forty-five minutes**. In another **forty-five minutes** pass through Dokapani on the south side of the ridge and climb for **half an hour** to a notch (7100 ft, 2164 m) in the oak forest. Take the left fork, which drops a bit, then contour to **Ragini** (7000 ft, 2134 m) in a notch in **fifteen minutes**. To reach the valley to the west, take the left fork and drop along the crest of a ridge to the west. Reach Gasgas (5575 ft, 1700 m), a few houses, in **forty-five minutes**. Shortly beyond is a school. Reach a suspension bridge (4650 ft, 1417 m) over the Chundi Khola in **half an hour**. Cross it to the north (R) bank and head downstream for **fifteen minutes** to **Narethanti** (4425 ft, 1364 m), a small town by a suspension bridge which is not crossed. Cross the next suspension bridge to the south (L) bank. The trail follows close to the river to reach the large bazaar of **Galkot HaTiya** (4075 ft, 1242 m) in an **hour**.

Shortly beyond the bazaar, cross a suspension bridge to the north (R) bank (3950 ft, 1204 m) and reach the small bazaar of Banyan (4050 ft, 1234 m) in **half an hour**. Cross a small tributary from the north to reach Bas Khola (3850 ft, 1173 m) in another **half hour**. In **fifteen minutes** cross again to the south (L) bank on a suspension bridge (3675 ft, 1120 m). Cross another tributary to Potsua (3675 ft, 1120 m). Do not cross either of the next two suspension bridges over the river, now called the Daran Khola. Reach Kanebas (3400 ft, 1036 m) in **half an hour**. The trail ascends a bit to **Wamiukaalo** (3775 ft, 1151 m) in 1½ **hours**. There is a trail which keeps closer to the river, but it is more difficult. Continue climbing for **half an hour** to a notch in the ridge at **Wamimaidang** (4550 ft, 1387 m). The trail then descends the south side of the ridge into the valley of the Bari Gad Khola. In **forty-five minutes**, just beyond a few houses, the trail forks and the right branch descends north to the large town of **Wamitaksar** (2900 ft, 884 m) in **fifteen minutes**. Pass through the town and descend for **half an hour** to the crossing of the Daran Khola on the Dhorpatan to Tansen trail. The rest of the route has already been described. Dhorpatan can be reached from here in **two days**.

JUMLA-RARA LAKE CIRCUIT *(Map No. 6, Page 187)*

At the southern edge of Mugu District at an altitude of almost 10,000 ft (3050 m) lies RaRa, the largest lake in Nepal. It has a circumference of almost eight miles (13 km) and is nestled between heavily-forested steep-sided ridges which thrust up from the fault lines that riddle this section of the foot of the Himalaya.

RaRa can sometimes be reached directly by chartered STOL aircraft. Enquiries should be directed to RNAC or to the National Parks and Wildlife Office in Bijuswari, Kathmandu. Otherwise RNAC operates scheduled flights to Jumla (7700 ft, 2347 m), the Zonal Headquarters of Karnali Zone, which is situated in a broad valley **three days'** walk south of RaRa. It is possible to trek to Jumla from Pokhara, more than a **two-week** trip, but most people fly there.

First the usual route from Jumla to RaRa is described. There are two variations. Most people would do well to take the longer route—at least if traveling without a guide familiar with the shorter *lekh* route. The return route described follows a little-used trail to Sinja, an interesting historical town. From here, a former trade and communication route leads to Jumla. Some food must be carried no matter which route you take.

Rice, wheat, potatoes, or beans may sometimes be available in the bazaar in Jumla, but food shortages are a recurring problem in this whole area. As far as possible, all supplies required for trekking should be brought from Kathmandu. Porters can be hired locally, but English-speaking ones are very rare. It is almost essential to carry a tent when trekking in this area. Most of the people on this trek are *Thakuri*, the King's caste. They are loathe to allow anyone below their caste to enter or stay in their homes.

As mentioned, there are regular flights to Jumla by RNAC, but it is difficult to arrange return flights, either in Kathmandu or in Jumla. Once you arrive in Jumla, see the RNAC representative immediately to confirm your return flight. If you are stuck in Jumla, and unable to make direct connections to Kathmandu, consider taking one of the frequent flights to Nepalganj and connecting from there to Kathmandu. It is also possible to walk **seven days** south to Surkhet and fly from there.

Jumla to RaRa Lake

Looking north from the Jumla Bazaar, you can see most of the trail to the top of Danphe Lekh. The trail goes just to the left of the highest point of this *lekh*.

Heading out of the main bazaar from Jumla, the trail forks almost immediately. Take the left fork and pass close to the hospital as you follow the trail along the bank of the stream heading north out of the valley. In **less than an hour**, cross to the east (R) bank on a small wooden bridge. Begin the ascent from the valley floor, climbing toward the right. The trail rises through a series of cultivated fields, passes close to a few scattered houses, and ascends steadily for **over an hour**. While still well below the main tree line, the trail rises steeply for about **fifteen minutes**, crosses a small stream, and enters one of the few clusters of blue pine trees on the open stretch of hillside. Near this spot—above the trail and slightly off to the right—a campsite with a fresh-water spring (9000 ft, 2743 m) can be seen. This is the last water before the pass. It is a good place to rest and cook your morning meal.

Ascending out of the trees, the trail opens out onto wide meadows rising gently to the north. **Fifteen minutes** beyond the trees, it forks near some stone huts. Take the less obvious right fork and reenter the forest shortly. The left fork is

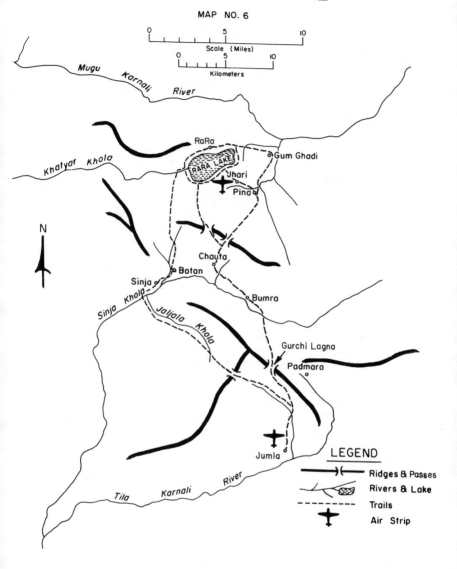

JUMLA & RARA LAKE

MAP NO. 6

Scale (Miles)

Kilometers

Mugu Karnali River

Khatyar Khola

RaRa

RARA LAKE

Gum Ghadi

Jhari

Pina

N

Chauta

Botan

Sinja

Sinja Khola

Jaljala Khola

Bumra

Gurchi Lagna

Padmara

Jumla

Tila Karnali River

LEGEND

Ridges & Passes
Rivers & Lake
Trails
Air Strip

a more level main route to Sinja. The trail emerges into high meadows, visible earlier from below, in 1½ **hours** from the fork. Another **hour** on increasingly difficult rocky terrain brings you to the pass, the Danphe Lekh (12,100 ft, 3688 m). The summit is marked with a small *chorten*. There is a small peak to your left (13,715 ft, 4180 m), and another to your right (13,857 ft, 4224 m). From this point you should have a fine view back down over the Jumla Valley to the 15,000 ft (4500 m) ridges to the south. There is no northern view until you cross the top of the pass.

From the *chorten*, follow the trail across the top of the ridge, winding through patchy forest to the north, before dropping again into open meadows. Note carefully the spot where you emerge from the trees. If you come back this way, it is very easy to miss the opening. If you climb straight on over these meadows, you reach a different pass which leads to the village of Padmara to the southeast, and results in a much longer walk back to Jumla.

Leaving the meadows and crossing a small stream, follow the trail into the trees and descend rapidly through dense mixed forest for **two hours**. Notice the magnificent birch trees, the bark of which is collected for use as paper. And keep your eyes open for a *danphe*—the multi-colored national bird of Nepal.

Near the end of the descent, the trail drops very steeply to the Sinja Khola, which is immediately crossed by a substantial log bridge (8900 ft, 2713 m). Turning west, proceed along the north (R) bank of the river. Within the next hour, choose any suitable campsite along the valley floor by the river.

Approximately an **hour** from the bridge, the trail rises from the riverbed to pass near the village of **Bumra** (9350 ft, 2850 m). An alternative campsite could be in the vicinity of the village. Supplies such as eggs or firewood can sometimes be procured.

From Bumra continue along the side of the hill, proceeding about 500 ft (150 m) above the river. Pass just above another small village within **fifteen minutes**. After another **fifteen minutes**, descend steeply to cross a small stream entering the main river from the north. On the valley floor, pass an unused schoolhouse, cross the main stream (9250 ft, 2819 m), and immediately climb steeply again for **half an hour** to regain your former altitude. Within another **hour**, descend again to cross another stream entering from the north. At the foot of this descent, huddled beneath the steep rock walls on the far side of the stream, stand the two houses comprising the village of **Chauta** (9000 ft, 2743 m). Each of these houses is a "hotel," though sometimes neither food nor accommodation are available. Splendid clay *chilim* (pipes) are made in this area, and are sometimes sold at one of the hotels.

From Chauta, head north, following the trail gently uphill and crisscrossing the stream, the Chauta Khola, in a steep narrow valley. A pleasant walk through groves of large walnut trees takes you to a small *dharmsala* or resting place with a good clear-flowing spring. Reach some isolated cultivated fields in an **hour**. In another **fifteen minutes** the trail passes out of the trees and, leaving the course of the stream, swings left onto the high open pastures. You are now climbing again to the pass of Ghurchi Lagna.

The wide trail proceeds almost directly westward, rising across a broad grassy valley which runs almost at right angles to the final ridge. After you pass groups of large boulders for **half an hour**, the valley you are following splits into two distinct valleys. One heads northwest, and the other, containing the main trail, goes slightly northeast. The main trail heads up the right valley, climbing more or less north to the pass of Ghurchi Lagna (11,300 ft, 3444 m), which is marked by a small stone *chorten*. The pass is some **three hours** from Chauta.

From the junction of the two valleys below the final approach to the pass, a lesser trail into the valley that heads northwest leads directly to RaRa in **five or six hours** along a high ridge trail. Though it offers spectacular views and a much shorter route to the lake, this trail should not be attempted by inexperienced trekkers, or when snow or monsoon clouds threaten to impair vision. In places, the trail is less than 18 in (45 cm) wide, often passing near the edge of high rock cliffs. Attempt it only with a guide.

If taking this alternative less-used trail, follow the bed of a small stream in the valley and rise gradually through a birch forest for **half an hour**. The trail breaks to the right (north) to follow a valley of scrub vegetation. When it wears thin in coarse grassland, there is no alternative but an **hour** of rough scrambling to the top of the ridge. Follow the ridge to the northwest, trying to stay as close as possible to the crest. Within 1½ **hours** you should reach a small *chorten* (13,300 ft, 4054 m) and see the lake far below. From the *chorten*, follow the ridge as it descends about 200 ft (60 m) across the rocky terrain. Then traverse, climb, and descend again for **ten minutes** or so before reaching a trail breaking off to the right. It drops quickly through rhododendron scrub into the dense forest slopes and leads down to the lake. Continue descending steeply through the trees, emerging in 1½ **to two hours** on the southern shores of the lake.

On the regular trail from the Ghurchi Lagna Pass, descend north again into forest. Some **five minutes** below the top is a *dharmsala* near a small stream. From here the trail is difficult, dropping very steeply away from the stream over a series of rocky outcrops. It descends in and out of belts of trees and emerges almost **two hours** later. Traverse for another **half hour** to the village of **Pina** (8000 ft, 2438 m). Pass a water source and suitable camping sites on the way to the village. About **five minutes** before the village, you pass Pina's only hotel, an isolated house directly on the main trail. If you are lucky, it may be open for business. The hotel is open only about half the year, generally during the spring and monsoon.

The village of Pina is grouped into upper and lower clusters connected by an intricate maze of paths through the fields. The main trail from lower Pina proceeds in the direction of the river below, reaching Gum Ghadi (6500 ft, 1981 m) in about **three hours**. This is the government headquarters and police check post for Mugu District. One trail from Gum Ghadi cuts back, ascending steeply to the northern ridge of RaRa. The other trail from the village continues dropping steeply to the Mugu Karnali river, the gateway to the trails into Humla and Mugu.

To proceed most directly to RaRa from Pina, take the new trail that splits from the main trail about **ten minutes** above the hotel. It passes through upper Pina after beginning on the side of a valley at the edge of the village. To find the trail when descending from the Gurchi Lagna Pass, take the left fork at the first stream you come to after leaving the pass a **few minutes** outside of Pina. Bearing to the left, the trail traverses the side of this westward heading valley, passes through cultivated fields for **half an hour** and gradually meets the valley floor and a stream at the end of the traverse. Cross this small stream by a mill (7500 ft, 2286 m) and climb again for **fifteen minutes** before dropping almost immediately to the main valley stream. Follow the stream for another **half hour** through more fields in an ever narrowing valley. Cross the stream on a substantial wooden bridge and climb steeply to the north for **half an hour** to the village of **Jhari** (8350 ft, 2530 m). Continue up through the village to the north, pass some huge cedars, climb again through the forest, and emerge after about **two hours** onto high open pasture. Cross the easily-gained summit (10,050 ft, 3063 m) and emerge at the "airstrip" on the south side of **RaRa Lake** (9800 ft, 2987 m). The airstrip is the only flat area around the shores of the lake. Directly across toward the northwestern side of the lake is the village of Chhabru, then the newer building of the national park headquarters, and farthest to the northeast, the village of RaRa. In late 1978, the residents of Chhabru and RaRa were resettled in the Tarai.

RaRa

The area surrounding the lake, which was designated as a national park in 1975, offers spectacular scenery, although views of snow-capped peaks are limited. Magnificent examples of fir, pine, spruce, juniper, cedar, birch, and rhododendron are found in the forest. Wildlife, including bears, cats, wolves, and deer, have been observed in the area. Around the shores of the lake are some fine "Malla Stones"—pillars of rock bearing Devanagari inscriptions and figures of the sun and moon. The inscriptions probably date from the Malla kings who reigned over much of the western Himalayan region in the twelfth century.

The best camping areas are on the lake's south side, which has much more diverse topography and vegetation than the north side. Meadow lands, virgin spruce forest, and some streams on the southwest corner of the lake make for ideal camping.

Legend and folklore provide the bulk of knowledge about RaRa Lake. The villagers believe it is at least 1800 ft (550 m) deep. They feel it is fed from underground springs flowing from the Mugu Karnali river, which is located about 1800 ft (550 m) downhill from the lake on the other side of the north *lekh*. Given its size and location near one of the main trade routes to Tibet, it is surprising that the lake does not have greater historical or religious significance. Unlike many Himalayan lakes, it is not a pilgrimage site. An annual festival in July and August commemorates the intervention of the great God, Thakur, who changed the direction of the outlet of the lake. Firing an arrow to the west, he opened the western hill to form the present outlet, and taking huge quantities of earth, he filled in the eastern outlet and stamped it firmly with his great feet. His footprints, imbedded in a rock, are visible to this day at the eastern end of the lake. They are the festival's main objects of interest—other than the attractive dancers and the local brew.

The lake's inaccessible location has kept many of its secrets undiscovered. The potential for discovery may be one of the most exciting aspects of this trek.

RaRa to Jumla via Sinja

You can return by taking a less-traveled, longer route through Sinja, the historical summer capital of the Malla Kingdom (twelfth to fourteenth centuries). Food, shelter, and a good map or a local guide familiar with the route are necessary.

From the village of RaRa (9900 ft, 3018 m), take the shore trail southwest to the lake outlet, the Khatyar Khola (9780 ft, 2981 m)—also called the Nisha Khola—in **forty-five minutes**. Do not cross the bridge here, but continue down the north (R) bank for **half an hour**, then cross the stream on a log bridge. One trail continues west on the south (L) bank of the *khola* after ascending a 100 ft (30 m) knoll. Instead, take the left fork (heading south) up a small valley. Climb through the woods on a sometimes indefinite trail which keeps to the western side of the valley. Reach a meadow with a *goTh* (10,740 ft, 3274 m) on a crest in an **hour**.

Continue south, climbing steeply though oak, then birch, then rhododendron forests to reach an alpine ridge (12,500 ft, 3810 m) in **2½ hours**. Above to the left is Chuchuemara Danda. Traverse on its west shoulder for **fifteen minutes** and come out on a saddle above the Ghatta Khola. Descend 500 ft (150 m) to the headwaters of the river and continue down through the valley for an **hour** to Ghorasain, site of the national park's guard quarters (10,500 ft, 3200 m), in **1½ hours**. Here the stream turns southwest. This is an appropriate and beautiful place to camp.

From here it is possible to reach Sinja by climbing to the southwest to 11,500 ft (3505 m) and descending to Lum (9500 ft, 2896 m) before following the Mindrabali Khola to Sinja. This would take a **short day**. The other route proceeds to the southeast, down the left side of the glacial valley of the Ghatta Khola for 1½

hours. Reach the terminal moraine and descend it for 300 ft (90 m). Continue down the valley another 1½ **hours** to a bridge (8700 ft, 2652 m) underneath the town of **Botan** lying to your left. Cross the log bridge and head downstream, meeting the Sinja Khola. Continue on its north (R) bank past some scattered houses to reach **Sinja** (8000 ft, 2438 m) in **two hours**.

Sinja lies in a highly cultivated valley. To the south on a prominent knoll are the remains of the former capital of this area. It is presently the site of a temple, Kankasundri. This area is well worth visiting by climbing the 400 ft (120 m) to the top of the knoll.

To return to Jumla, follow the historical route between Sinja and Kalanga, the old name for Jumla. The two-day route through beautiful forests ascends a river valley to a *lekh* and descends to Jumla. A camp roughly half way on the crest of the *lekh* (11,500 ft, 3505 m) is ideal.

From Sinja ascend the Jaljala Khola to the southeast, keeping to the south (L) bank on a very good, clear trail for **six hours**. On the far watershed, the trail descends through forests and pastures south to **Jumla** (7700 ft, 2347 m). The 25 mi (40 km) of this stretch takes about **ten hours**.

Camp below the Trashi Labsta. (Stephen Bezruchka)

11 OTHER TREKS

Two roads diverged in a wood, and I—
I took the one less travelled by,
And that has made all the difference.

Robert Frost

Four other treks are described in this chapter. The first is an exit from Khumbu to Rolwaling and on to Kathmandu. The second is another exit from the Khumbu region, going southwest to Ilam from where you can proceed by road and train to Darjeeling. The third is the route from Pokhara to Kathmandu, a pleasant introduction to hill Nepal. Finally there is a trip through the Tarai to Chitwan National Park, home of much interesting wildlife.

THAMI TO ROLWALING AND BARABISE VIA THE TRASHI LABSTA *(Maps No. 3, Page 158 and No. 4, Page 166)*

This is a spectacular high route which leaves Khumbu via a glaciated pass and reaches the Rolwaling Valley to the east and its major settlement, Beding, in a minimum of four days. There are no villages or shelters along the way and the route is dangerous even in the best of conditions. Only experienced mountaineers should attempt it and then, only with a party that includes some Sherpas who have been over it before. The entire party, including all the porters, should be equipped for severe conditions of cold and high altitude. Since it is necessary to camp on ice, parties should carry tents and fuel for everyone as well as ice climbing equipment (ice axe, rope, crampons, and ice screws). Under ideal conditions the crossing need not require technical climbing, but such conditions cannot be counted on. Storms are to be expected and food for at least five days should be carried in order to be able to wait out bad weather. Temperatures below freezing are always encountered. Crossings have been made at all times of the year, but the best time is probably April to early December. Falling rock is the danger most often encountered. Ice avalanches are also possible. Many people have died attempting this crossing, but competent, well-equipped parties should have little trouble. Sherpas even take yaks over it! You must be very aware of the hazards of rapid ascent to altitude and of hypothermia. There are no quick escape routes, especially on the Rolwaling side of the pass, should altitude illness become serious.

The route is described from Thami to Rolwaling, thus offering a route out of Khumbu that avoids the traffic jams at Lukla. This direction is also preferable because parties attempting the crossing have usually acclimatized first in Khumbu. Furthermore, if altitude problems strike on the ascent, it is easier to retreat to lower altitudes from this side than from the other side where technically difficult terrain and long glaciers must be negotiated.

From **Thami** (12,500 ft, 3810 m), described in Chapter 9, head west, passing below the monastery to reach a *yersa*, Kure (13,875 ft, 4229 m), in **seventy minutes**. The next *yersa* (14,050 ft, 4282 m) is **ten minutes** beyond. Proceed as the valley of the Thami or Thengpo Khola opens up and admire the peaks on its south side, especially the north face of Teng Kangpoche. The extensive *yersa* of Thengpo (14,175 ft, 4321 m) is reached in **twenty-five minutes**. Climb through the various fenced-in fields of this *yersa* and continue up the north side of the valley. Traverse a rock slide from the north to the end of the slide (15,465 ft, 4714 m) 1⅓ **hours** from lower Thengpo. The best views east, including the west face of Makalu behind Ama Dablang, are along here. Continue on a grassy slope, then begin climbing a loose moraine to reach a flat area suitable for camping (15,910 ft, 4849 m) in **half an hour**. Climb the moraine for an **hour** to Ngole (16,745 ft, 5104 m) below an icefall to the north. Ngole, which has tent sites and overhanging rocks for shelter, is protected from the icefall and is a good place to camp below the pass. In order to avoid rockfall off the southern slopes of Tengi Ragi Tau, the peak to the north, it is wisest to ascend beyond here in the early morning. There is another possible campsite (17,150 ft, 5227 m) **half an hour** beyond. Below and to the south a lake lies in the moraine.

Continue climbing beyond this last site on snow or rock as the season dictates to another level area (17,700 ft, 5395 m) in **half an hour**. Some **fifteen minutes** more climbing, closer to the face of Tengi Ragi Tau, brings you to yet another small campsite (17,850 ft, 5441 m). These last two campsites are not entirely protected from rockfall, a hazard that varies with the time of year. Be on the lookout for serious symptoms of altitude illness, and descend if they occur.

The icefall before you, which has been visible for some time, is from the Trashi Labsta Pass. Ascend a scree slope to the northeast of the icefall and traverse to a sheltered spot (18,250 ft, 5563 m) under the rock face of Tengi Ragi Tau in another **half hour**. The times taken, of course, depend on the acclimatization of the party. If coming from Rolwaling, this sheltered spot could be an appropriate place to pitch a tent and camp. It is safer to camp lower, but you should not descend late in the day if much rock is falling. To proceed over the pass, climb on snow east of the icefall to a long, more gradual slope. There are sheltered spots under overhanging rocks under the face of Tengi Ragi Tau, but it is not a good idea to camp this high, because the risk of altitude illness is greater. Better to sleep low and climb high. Proceed west to the height of land and the Trashi Labsta Pass (18,882 ft, 5755 m)—the name means "luck bringing prayer flags"—in another **forty-five minutes**. There is a cairn with prayer flags at the pass. The times listed here are actual traveling times, and most parties take at least **half a day** from Ngole to here when rests are included. New vistas open up to the west, but the views to the east are limited to Teng Kangpoche. Directly south is the peak Pharchamo (20,582 ft, 6273 m), a trekking summit.

The descent is over a snow-covered moderately steep glacier with crevasses, and requires roped travel and the ability to do crevasse rescues. Reach the Drolambo Glacier (17,850 ft, 5440 m) in perhaps **forty-five minutes**. Parties wishing to explore further can get plenty of ideas from the Schneider map. Note that the route marked on Schneider's *Rolwaling Himal* map is not the one described here, as the marked route is no longer in use. The route described here is less hazardous. Head south along the Drolambo, proceeding near a medial moraine. It is safest to camp above the icefall that lies at the snout of the Drolambo which in turn lies above the Trakarding Glacier. This will minimize the danger that rocks from the medial moraines might melt out of the ice on the stretch above the Trakarding Glacier and tumble down. A campsite (17,750 ft, 5410 m) can be found in about **half an hour**. Unlike the narrow upper part of the eastern side of the Trashi Labsta, the country here is open.

Continue descending the Drolambo, staying east of the first medial moraine and of an icefall that you pass in **half an hour**. Most likely you can travel in a trough that is easy and quite safe, providing you have made an early start and the sun hasn't hit you. Late in the day everything here is usually quite loose and you may feel like a target in a shooting gallery, in a waterfall! In the usual trough, there is one steep ice step, perhaps 40 to 50 ft (15 m) high, where it is best to belay the party down. Crampons, ice axes, rope, and ice screws are a big help here. Descend carefully on snow and ice-covered rock, keeping close to the rock face to the right to avoid falling rocks and ice. In 2½ **to three hours** from the camp above, reach a spectacular rocky spur (16,950 ft, 5166 m) below the icefall on the Drolambo, but still considerably above the Trakarding Glacier below. There are plenty of campsites here which are safe from falling rock and ice. If ascending to the pass from Rolwaling, it would be prudent to camp here if you arrive late in the day, unless it is very cold and the rocks are frozen in place. If there is no sound of falling rock when you stop here on the way to the pass, it is probably fairly safe to continue.

The Trakarding Glacier is the long rubble-covered ice river flowing northwest below you. It is reached in **half an hour** from the spur (16,125 ft, 4915 m). Rock overhangs that provide shelter should be apparent. Traverse northwest under the icefall of the Drolambo Glacier to a campsite called Thakar (16,075 ft, 4900 m) in **fifteen minutes**. There are few if any good camping sites on the extensive moraine of the glacier until the lake is passed. Finding water is also a problem. Keep close to the northwest side of the glacier, following an indistinct trail marked with cairns. There is sometimes falling rock from the northwest, so be cautious. The going is slow along this moraine. Occasional rock overhangs are passed which would make possible campsites if water could be found.

As you near the big lake, Tsho Rolpa or Chu Pokhari, keep to the south of the extensive lateral moraine on the northeast side of the glacier. Along this moraine there is a hazard from falling rock and fine dust is constantly being blown along. After traversing about one-third of the way along the lake, make a steep ascent northeast to meet the rock, then traverse an avalanche chute off Tsoboje—be quick here—and descend a scree slope on the other side of it. Continue in the trench between the wall to the southwest surrounding the lake and the steep walls to the northeast. Contour a snow cone from an avalanche chute to a large sandy area (15,050 ft, 4587 m). It takes some 3½ **to four hours** to get here from Thakar. There is a good campsite here some two-thirds to three-fourths of the way along the lake, but water may be hard to find. There may be a small stream here (often frozen), or you might have to climb over the moraine to the lake, which may be frozen. An ice axe is helpful in getting water.

Continue along the trail, contouring around the terminal moraine at the end of the lake in **half an hour** and continuing around the terminal moraine of the Ripimo Shar Glacier which comes down from the northeast. In **fifteen minutes,** pass through a small *yersa* of unroofed frames, Sangma (14,175 ft, 4321 m), and descend to cross the outflow (13,900 ft, 4237 m) of the lake to the left a **few minutes** later. Descend the broad valley, enjoying the fragrant shrubs. In **half an hour** cross to the north (R) bank of the Rolwaling Khola (13,725 ft, 4163 m). There is a route to the south over the ridge via the Yalung La, a pass to the Khare Khola. But continuing on the usual route, reach the west end of the settlement of Na and the limit of the glaciated valley. Downstream, the Rolwaling Valley is a sharp river-worn *V*. Na is a large *yersa* at the base of an impressive peak to the north. It is occupied by

Beding people part of the year, depending on the potato harvest. The Sherpas of Rolwaling believe that their valley was formed by the sweep of a giant horse and plow—*rolwa* means one furrow, while *ling* is a country—guided by Padmasamblava, who brought Buddhism to Tibet from India. They also feel it is one of the eight *beyul*, or hidden valleys in the Himalaya. Because of this, they do not allow anyone to kill animals in the valley.

Descend 125 ft (38 m) to the lower part of Na and in an **hour**, reach rhododendron and juniper forests, a pleasant contrast to the barren landscape above the lake. Pass through another *yersa*, Dokare (12,575 ft, 3833 m) **fifteen minutes** later and continue to **Beding** (12,120 ft, 3694 m) 1½ **hours** from Na. This is the main settlement for the Sherpa inhabitants of the Rolwaling Valley. It is located in a narrow gorge and gets little direct sunlight. There is no farmland or mountain view, save that of Gaurishankar before you reach the village. The *gomba* here is impressively located and worth visiting to see the fine paintings. There is a school built by Sir Edmund Hillary and some interesting flour mills. People wishing to take a side trip with a view of spectacular Menlungtse (Jobo Garu on the Schneider map) can ascend to the Manlung La in 1½ **days** from Beding, if they are already acclimatized. There is some trade to Palbugthang and Thumphug over this pass during the summer, mostly rice for Tibetan salt.

Leave Beding and pass through a *yersa* (11,975 ft, 3650 m) in **ten minutes**. Then cross a tributary (11,875 ft, 3584 m) in another **ten minutes**. This river, the Gauri Shankar Khola, has eroded a gap in the wall, allowing a pretty waterfall to cascade through. Just beyond is a *yersa*, Chumigalgya, and there are two more in **five and ten minutes** respectively (the last at 11,700 ft, 3566 m). The trail continues into a pleasant fir, rhododendron, and birch forest and descends in **twenty minutes** to a small sanctuary (11,275 ft, 3437 m) to the Nepali deities Sita Mahadev and Kanchi Mahadev. A cantilever bridge here to the south (L) bank of the Rolwaling Khola is the beginning of a trail that leads to the Daldung La. It offers a higher route out of the Rolwaling Valley to use in the monsoon when the main route may be too wet. Don't take it unless so advised by the locals. Continue in forest for **thirty-five minutes** until you cross a tributary from the north. Here there is a good, but very foreshortened view, of Gauri Shankar to the north. Some **ten minutes** beyond, come to a covered bridge crossing the Rolwaling Khola (10,200 ft, 3108 m). Cross to the south (L) bank and keep to the south side of the narrow valley. Notice how everything is much greener and lusher here, perhaps because this north facing slope receives less direct sun. In addition to the deciduous vegetation, there are impressive fir trees.

Continue on the south side above the valley floor and enter a burned area (9350 ft, 2850 m) in **thirty-five minutes**. Some **twenty minutes** beyond reach some steep slabs (9150 ft, 2789 m). Leave the riverbed and ascend the slabs along an impressive locally-made ramp. Reach a clearing in **half an hour**—you are still in the burn which has more growth the farther west you go. **Ten minutes** beyond is a campsite under an overhanging rock, and nearby is a fault cave. Continue high on the side of the valley to stands of oak. Pass under a swirling waterfall (9175 ft, 2797 m) an **hour** beyond the slabs. Continue contouring for **almost an hour** before descending to reach the few *goTh* of Shakpa (8700 ft, 2652 m). Descend in **less than an hour** to the village of **Simigaon** (6550 ft, 1996 m). Sherpas and hill Nepalis inhabit this lush oasis, which has interesting fruits and vegetables in addition to the predominant millet fields.

Descend steeply to the river, the Bhote Kosi, passing under some impressive rock overhangs. Cross to the east (R) bank on a suspension bridge (5000 ft, 1524 m)

forty-five minutes from Simigaon. To the south is an impressive gorge, and the trail rises over difficult stretches of it. Traverse the few fields of Chetchet **fifteen minutes** beyond and admire the falls which tumble at least 300 ft (100 m) down the east (R) bank. Some **thirty-five minutes** beyond Chetchet, the trail forks. The lower fork keeps close to the river and is suitable during low water. The upper fork is for the monsoon. In **half an hour** the valley widens and in its floor ahead is the village of **Gongar** (4525 ft, 1410 m). Cross the Gongar Khola, a tributary from the west, to the trail fork beyond. The left fork keeps close to the river and goes to Charikot. You can take it to join the usual Everest Base Camp route from Lamosangu. The right fork ascends and heads to Barabise. This route is described here. Climb on a spur through terraces to a *chautaara* (5150 ft, 1570 m) **half an hour** from Gongar. Contour and cross two tributaries in **half an hour**. Climb another **twenty-five minutes** to a Shiva sanctuary (5825 ft, 1775 m) to the left of the trail. Surrounded by a rock wall, this sanctuary contains a few bells and innumerable tridents of iron in various shapes and sizes. Climb another **half hour** to **Thare** (6475 ft, 1974 m), a scattered *Tamang* village. It is not marked on Schneider's *Lapchi Kang* map.

Continue contouring to **Dulang** (6225 ft, 1897 m), the next scattered village. Another **fifty minutes** brings you to the ridge where the Warang school (6600 ft, 2012 m) is located. Enjoy the views of Gauri Shankar to the northeast. Pass through the settlement of **Yarsa** (6225 ft, 1897 m) **twenty-five minutes** beyond, then contour and descend for **twenty minutes** to cross the Warang Khola (5775 ft, 1760 m). Contour another **twenty-five minutes** to the scattered village of **Bulung** (5850 ft, 1783 m). Continue to a high clearing, the site of the local middle school (6335 ft, 1931 m), some **twenty-five minutes** beyond. You are now leaving the valley of the Bhote Kosi for the tributary valley of the Sangawa Khola. Contour for **forty-five minutes** to a stupa, then a *chautaara* with Tibetan-style religious paintings. Pass above the scattered village of Laduk and reach the school situated above it (6810 ft, 2075 m) in **twenty minutes**. Don't climb beyond, but take the lower fork and descend slightly. Cross a recent slide, then the Thuran Khola (6260 ft, 1908 m) in another 1¼ **hours**. Above you is the town of Charsaba, but the main trail ascends and contours below it. Beyond a main ridge, the town of Chilangka (6310 ft, 1923 m) is reached in **sixty-five minutes**. Descend past another small slide and cross the Jorang Khola (5585 ft, 1702 m) in **twenty-five minutes**. Contour through chir pine forest to reach **Lading** (5835 ft, 1778 m) in **fifty minutes**.

Beyond there is a choice of routes. The left fork descends to the river, the Saun Khola, crosses it to the east (R) bank on a log bridge, ascends near a tributary, the Amatal Khola, and passes the village of Amatal to the few houses of Ruphthang (7670 ft, 2335 m) in approximately **four hours**. This route is more direct than the other, but it avoids the climb up to Bigu Gomba, one of the most fascinating Buddhist nunneries in Nepal.

To head to Bigu Gomba, also known locally as Tashi Gomba, don't descend the Saun or Sangawa Khola, but contour around a ridge and descend to the Samling Khola, a tributary from the north. Cross it on a cantilever bridge (5710 ft, 1710 m) to the west (R) bank in **forty-five minutes**. Begin climbing up to **Bigu Gomba**. The entire terraced hillside has numerous houses and is called Bigu. It takes **two hours** or more to reach the actual monastery (8235 ft, 2310 m) with its long white building, the home of the nuns, in front of the temple itself, which is set among juniper trees. This nunnery was built around 1933 and houses thirty-six nuns, most of them Sherpas. It is unusual because its east and west walls are lined with interlacing statues of Avalokiteswara, each with eleven heads and 1000 arms, hands, and eyes. You are not allowed to photograph the inside of the *gomba*.

A typical hill Nepal scene with houses interspersed among the terraces. (Brot Coburn)

This convent of the Kargyupa sect is described by Christoph von Fürer-Haimendorf in "A Nunnery in Nepal" (see Recommended Reading).

To leave Bigu, traverse north on a high trail, then contour and drop to join a main trail west of the *gomba* near three stupas (7895 ft, 2406 m) in less than **half an hour**. Continue until you spot **Ruphtang**, one house on top of a small hill, and take a left fork to descend and cross a tributary from the north on a covered bridge by some mills (7460 ft, 2275 m). Climb the hill to Ruphtang (7660 ft, 2335 m) **half an hour** from the stupas. This may be the last habitation below the pass, the Tinsang La. Climb beyond, steeply at first, then more gradually in a forest of prickly-leaved oak. There is a tea shop (8740 ft, 2664 m) some **fifty-five minutes** above Ruphtang. Continue climbing in impressive fir forest with numerous camping sites. There is a *goTh* (10,240 ft, 3121 m) **two hours** from Ruphtang, and a pleasant stream some 500 ft (150 m) higher. The pass itself (10,890 ft, 3319 m), with several *goTh* nearby, is **half an hour** beyond. The view of the Himalaya, although somewhat distant, is breathtaking. The tower of Chobo Bamare is quite close.

From the pass, descend into rhododendron and fir forest which becomes almost pure rhododendron forest lower down, then blends again into prickly-leaved oak forest. A small *gomba* above **Dolangsa** (8165 ft, 2489 m) is reached in **sixty-five minutes** from the pass. There are many variations in the route down the

Sun Kosi river to its junction with the Bhote Kosi below Barabise. You can head south through Nangarpa and cross the main river west of Gorthali before proceeding along its north (R) bank. Or you can keep to the north side of the valley, crossing tributaries and going below a pretty waterfall (7390 ft, 2252 m) **sixty-five minutes** beyond the *gomba*. Beyond, you can continue contouring, or you can descend closer to the river. If descending, reach **Kabre** (5265 ft, 1605 m) in **seventy minutes** from the waterfall. Continue west, crossing a tributary from the north on an old suspension bridge (3890 ft, 1185 m) in **thirty-five minutes**. Contour another **ten minutes** to the first stores of **Budipa** (3790 ft, 1155 m). The main trail continues contouring about 500 ft (150 m) above the main river and passes through the scattered houses of **Simle** (3550 ft, 1080 m) in **fifty-five minutes**. The solace and freedom from the noises of the twentieth century are almost over. Horns can soon be heard. The trail rounds a ridge to descend to **Barabise** (2690 ft, 820 m) on the west (L) bank of the Bhote Kosi in **forty-five minutes**. Buses leave this staging center for Kathmandu periodically during the day.

There is another high pass leading out of the upper Rolwaling Valley, the Yalung La (17,422 ft, 5310 m). The descent is made to the southwest to Suri Dhoban. Inquire at Beding for a guide.

An alternative route from Rolwaling branches from Simigaon, and, instead of crossing to the west (R) bank of the Bhote Kosi, heads south on its east (L) bank, passing through Tashinam to Manthali (3450 ft, 1080 m) approximately **one day** from Simigaon. The Sieri Khola, a tributary from the east, is crossed in route. Continue on the east (L) bank of the main valley and cross the Suri, or Khare, Khola at Suri Dhoban (3215 ft, 980 m). Continue to Tyanku in **a day**. Cross the main river, the Tamba, or Bhote Khosi, at Biguti (3150 ft, 960 m) and climb up to Dolakha (5580 ft, 1700 m) which has several interesting temples. Shortly beyond, reach Charikot (6560 ft, 2000 m) **less than a day** from Tyanku. The main trail to Solu-Khumbu is soon intersected and Lamosangu is 1½ **days** farther. This trail is somewhat shorter than the higher Tinsang La trail, but less scenic.

NAMCHE BAZAAR TO ILAM AND DARJEELING
(Maps No. 3, Page 158 and No. 7, Page 201)

Of the various routes of return from the scenic splendor of Khumbu to areas where conventional motorized travel is possible, this is one of the best because it involves a minimum of backtracking and provides a fine terminal point after traversing the entire eastern section of Nepal. However, the route is somewhat longer (about two weeks is required) than retracing your steps to Barabise or Lamosangu, or going south via Salleri and Okhaldhunga to Janakpur. Also the trails are much less traveled by Westerners, making food and sleeping arrangements more difficult for those who don't speak Nepali. In addition, Westerners are unfortunately not permitted at this time to cross the Indian-Nepali border directly from Ilam to Darjeeling. Instead, they must take a jeep south from Ilam to the East-West Highway and follow it east to cross the border into India.

It is wise to stock up on provisions in Namche Bazaar. There is always *daal bhaat tarkaari* available along the trail, but the shop in Chaumrikharka is the only one until you reach Dingla in almost a week. But if you leave Namche Bazaar a few days before the Saturday market, you meet hundreds of porters carrying goods to sell at the market, and you may be able to buy provisions from them. It is a good idea to hire a local guide for the stretch up to Dingla, as it is easy to get lost in some of the forests near the ridges. Beyond Dingla, there are weekly markets in several places, including Chainpur, Terhathum, Yasak, and Ilam.

Start the route by retracing steps for **1½ days** down the valley of the Dudh Kosi to **Kharte** (8400 ft, 2560 m), which is characterized by a single large white house near the top of the hill above Karikhola. From here, do not descend to Karikhola; instead, head southeast toward Pangu which is visible from Kharte. It is about **three hours** away at a slightly higher elevation. The trail has several forks, but the ones that go more steeply downhill are correct. The trail makes a moderately successful attempt at contouring as it goes up and down to cross numerous streams. **Pangu** (9338 ft, 2864 m) is a Sherpa village characterized by *mani* walls and a *gomba*. From the village, proceed east for **half an hour** on a gentle trail up to the pass, the Pangkongma La (10,410 ft, 3173 m). From here you can see across the Inukhu Khola to the next ridge and to Nachi Dingma in a clearing two-thirds of the way up to the next pass. Follow the trail that goes left (north) out of the pass. It goes down gently for an **hour** to a ridge crest with some houses and fields. The trail now goes down the end of the ridge, becoming steeper until it drops by many nearly vertical switchbacks down to the Inukhu Khola (6090 ft, 1856 m) **two hours** from the pass.

Cross the river on a makeshift bridge and go slightly upstream across boulders and sand to where the trail begins again in dense growth. Climb up steeply to the terraces in **half an hour**, and continue up through terraces and poor houses for the next **hour**. Another **hour** through the forest finally brings you across a stream to **Nachi Dingma** (8531 ft, 2600 m), which has an abandoned open house. From the house, go left diagonally across the flat clearing to a stream in about **five minutes**, then up again through forests to a sharp, notched pass, the Surkie La (10,122 ft, 3085 m), in a **little more than an hour**. All the passes are exhilarating for the views, the sense of accomplishment, and the chance to rest.

Descend to reach a shelter with water in **ten minutes**. Then bear right and go down, sometimes steeply, sometimes less so, to **Khiraunle** (7875 ft, 2400 m) in an **hour**. This is a spread-out Sherpa village with an interesting stupa surrounded by trees. Continue down diagonally to the right (south) across numerous streams to reach a ridge crest in **half an hour**. Descend straight down through the large, spread-out *Rai* village of **Bung** (5250 ft, 1600 m) for an **hour**, then cross a small river to the north via a curvy bamboo bridge. Finally, go down the north (L) bank of the river to reach the Hongu Khola (4320 ft, 1316 m) in another **half hour**. There is a spectacular waterfall where the tributary joins the main stream, and also a good pool for bathing. After crossing the Hongu Khola on another temporary bridge, ascend steeply through rice fields for **1½ hours** to **Gudel** (6560 ft, 2000 m), a *Rai* village somewhat higher than Bung across the valley. Now the trail leaves the ridge crest and proceeds gently up along the right side to reach the Sherpa village of **Sorung** (8530 ft, 2600 m) in **two hours** and **Sanam** (8530 ft, 2600 m) in another **hour**. The prayer flags and solid houses have a more prosperous appearance here than in the *Rai* villages below.

The trail descends slightly for **half an hour** to meet a stream that earlier was far below the trail. There is a shelter here. Follow the stream for **half an hour** until the trail turns right along a small tributary, which is followed for **half an hour** to another shelter near the last water source before the pass, **Saalpa Bhanjyang** (10,990 ft, 3350 m), another **half hour** up.

The trail goes down rather gently to the east-southeast for **two hours**, but some luck is needed to keep on it. Finally, the trail goes diagonally left onto a ridge crest, then down steeply for an **hour** to the *Rai* village of **Phedi** just above a river. From here, Dingla can be reached in **one day** with the aid of moonlight.

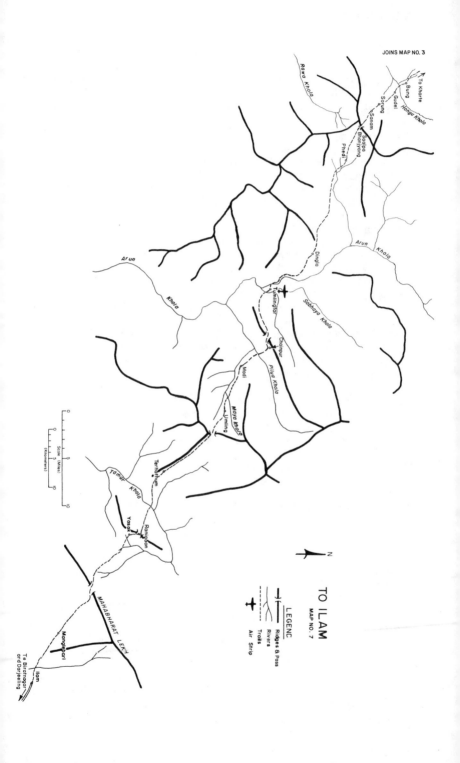

TO ILAM

MAP NO. 7

LEGEND

Ridges & Pass

Rivers

Trails

Air Strip

N

Scale
(Kilometers)
(Miles)

Rawa Khola

To Kharte

Bung

Gudel

Hongu Khola

Sorung

Sanam

Salpa Bhanjyang

Phedi

Arun Khola

Dingla

Arun

Khola

Tumlingtar

Sabhaya Khola

Chainpur

Piluo Khola

Modi

Maya Khola

Umling

Tembathum

Tamur Khola

Yasok

Ranigaon

MAHABHARAT LEKH

Mangalbari

Ilam

To Biratnagar
and Darjeeling

The trail follows close to the river, predominantly on the south (R) bank, until a small shop by a bridge is reached in **three hours**. Now contour gently up (east) to reach a ridge crest in 1½ **hours**. Then go west to cross a small stream before reaching the true ridge crest in another **hour**. When I was here, a strong aroma led us to a tree groaning with tangerines. Its owner gladly sold us eighty-seven for one rupee and probably laughed to think how we nearly broke our backs trying to carry them off. Dingla sits on the next ridge to the south. Reach it by going diagonally down and west, sometimes on a good trail, sometimes on paddy walls, to reach the stream in an **hour**. Beyond the bridge, the correct trail goes fairly directly up to **Dingla**. The town has a few shops, some eating places, a college, and a temple.

Two side trips start from Dingla: one goes up the Arun Khola and the other goes down it. The trek up takes you to the base of Makalu and a Himalayan region that is much less visited than the Everest area. The trek down the river goes to Dhankuta and Dharan. It is a fast exit to a road. But to continue east, proceed southeast down the end of the ridge to reach the Arun Khola in 1½ **hours**. As it is impossible to cross the river at this point, follow the west (R) bank south via a jungle trail to reach a bridge in **half an hour**. Once across the river, the trail ascends steeply up the bank for **ten minutes** to the **Tumlingtar** airstrip on an immense flat area. Follow the trail on the far east side of the airstrip for **half an hour** to a shop where excellent food and lodging can be obtained. Now descend from the flat area to a smaller river which must be waded before beginning the ascent to Chainpur. Go up to the left to reach the crest of the ridge at **Kerang** in **two hours**. Follow the broad level trail on the right side of the ridge for another **hour** to **Chainpur**, a large, pleasant bazaar town where the police check trekking permits. The town boasts a hotel which can provide separate rooms and good food.

Here again there is a choice of routes. You can go east to Taplejung in **two days**, then head south via Phidem to Ilam in **three days**. The second, more expedient choice is to go south to Terhathum in 1½ **days**, then on to Ilam in another 2½ **days**. A description of the latter route is given here.

Leaving Chainpur, the trail descends for **forty-five minutes** and crosses a stream, the Pilua Khola. Then it ascends for 1¼ **hours** to **Madi** at about the same elevation as Chainpur. Now proceed on a level trail to the right to reach **Palomadi** in another **hour**. Another **hour** on level ground brings you to **Alimela** from which it is only a short descent and climb to reach a crossing of the Maya Khola in **half an hour**. Then climb through the widely scattered village of **Umling** and eventually to the pass over Mungabori Lekh in 2½ **hours**. The last part is through an extremely beautiful meadow and forest with a few tea shops **fifteen minutes** before the pass. Now the trail descends rather gradually and follows the long ridge stretching out to Terhathum. Pass through the pleasant village of **Jirikimpti** in **two hours** and keep fairly level on one side of the ridge or the other to reach **Terhathum** in another **hour**. This is a dense little bazaar town with three parallel streets, a Chinese bookstore, and district offices.

The trail to Ilam now continues down the left side of the ridge to **Keorimi** in 1½ **hours**. Beyond, it goes down more steeply on the end of the ridge into the furnace-hot valley of the Tamur Khola. The river is reached in 1½ **hours**. Go upstream for **ten minutes** to where a man in a dugout boat can take you across the river for a small charge, or go **half an hour** farther upstream and walk across the bridge for free. From either place, there is a stiff climb of some **three hours** to **Ranigaon**. If you cross by the dugout, go to the small, extremely steep direct trail just opposite the landing place of the boat. It becomes somewhat cooler after a **one-hour** climb. From the saddle at Ranigaon, it is **half an hour** up the left side of the ridge to **Yasak**, a small Brahman bazaar town.

Another **hour** of reasonably level going brings you to **Milkrode**. Its high school is visible from afar. **Two more hours** of traversing the left side of the hill eventually bring you to a stream. Once across the stream, the trail finally goes steeply up through a village to the barren crest of the Mahabharat Lekh in **two hours**. Follow this crest to the left for an **hour**, taking the right fork at the base of a small hill shortly after a tea shop. The bazaar town of **Manglebari** is visible across a valley. Descend to the stream and follow it until the trail gradually goes diagonally up and crosses various streams and ridges to reach the town in **four hours**. It is now only **four hours** to **Ilam**. Along the way, descend to a small stream, then climb slightly before descending a long way to the stream at the base of the Ilam hill an **hour** from the town.

In Ilam, there are jeeps for the first time in many weeks. Take a jeep south to Sanishari, a **day's** journey. Then continue by jeep for another **hour** to the junction with the East-West Highway. To return to Kathmandu by bus or plane, go either to Biratnagar, where there are daily flights, or to Bhadrapur, where there are fewer air connections. It is possible to motor directly to Kathmandu in **two days**. But to proceed to Darjeeling, take a bus east to Kakarbhitta on the border. Pass through customs and take a **one-hour** jeep ride to Siliguri. From Siliguri, you can take a train, a jeep, or a bus to Darjeeling, or you can go by a jeep or bus to Kalimpong, or to Gantok, Sikkim. Most vehicles leave early in the morning or around noon.

POKHARA TO KATHMANDU
(Maps No. 2, Page 133 and No. 8, Page 205)

The swiftest traveller is he that goes afoot.

Thoreau

Despite the availability of regular flights and the new road between Pokhara and Kathmandu, it is still worthwhile to walk this stretch in order to see typical hill villages and learn much about local life and customs. Besides, there are good views of Himalchuli, Peak 29, Manaslu, Ganesh Himal, and the Annapurnas along the way. As with trails heading east from Kathmandu, the route goes against the grain of the land, but in contrast with those trails, the difference in altitude between the hills and the valleys is less, which makes this trek much easier. There are numerous *Newar* villages in route where you can get cooked meals. Because this is a low, level trek through typical hill areas with good food and reasonable lodging available, it is an excellent introduction to trekking. Travel here is most comfortable during the winter months—December through February. The trek is described from Pokhara to Kathmandu.

Begin at the Pokhara airstrip (2686 ft, 819 m) by crossing the runway. Pass through a gate and head across the narrow gorge of the almost invisible Seti Khola. The valley suburb of **Pinchin Camp** or **Ram Bazaar** is soon reached, and in an **hour**, you meet the main road from the Pokhara Bazaar. Another **half hour** brings you to the Bijayapur Khola, which is forded or crossed on a temporary bridge. Another **forty-five minutes** brings you to **Arghaumpauwa** (2550 ft, 777 m), a large village in the valley floor. Continue for **half an hour** around a hill and descend into the valley to **Sisuwa**. In **forty-five minutes** you come to the far end of Kuti and then to **Sat Muni** in **half an hour**. The Tal Khola, reached in **half an hour** from Sat Muni, is at the end of the valley, and a trail leads from it to a village at the foot of the Deorali ridge in **half an hour**. A **one-hour** climb brings you to the pass and the big village of **Deorali** (3000 ft, 913 m). There are sal forests along the valleys and wet subtropical forests on the ridges.

From Deorali, head northeast and drop to the base of the ridge after **forty-five minutes** to a stream which you follow to near the Madi Khola. Follow either the streambed or a trail up on its north (L) bank to reach several seasonal houses by the stream in an **hour**. The trail then keeps to the south (R) bank for another **hour** before turning right (southeast) to reach the village of **Sisaghat** (1300 ft, 396 m) on the Madi Khola in **half an hour**. The river is crossed by a ferry which is best hailed from high on the west (R) bank. This process is time consuming and you must bargain with the ferryman. Expect to be held up for **at least an hour**.

Once on the east (L) bank, follow it downstream for **fifteen minutes** until you reach the entrance of a tributary valley to the east. Head up this valley, staying above the north (R) bank of the river, for **1½ hours** to **Suti Pasal**. Then head up to the pass at the head of the valley, following the stream closely most of the way. It becomes very steep just below the pass. **Kunchha** (2800 ft, 853 m) is reached some **two hours** after Suti Pasal.

From Kunchha, go west, cross a stream, and head down the valley for an **hour** to a village called **Turi Pasal** or **Naya Bazaar**. Another **hour** brings you to a large town called **Mani Chauk**. Cross the stream at the lower end of the town and follow the north (L) bank of the Poundi Khola, passing the village of **Sundar Bazaar** (2100 ft, 640 m) in **forty-five minutes**. Cross the Poundi Khola to its south (R) bank on a suspension bridge (1700 ft, 518 m) about **forty-five minutes** beyond Sundar. The trail then heads south along the west (R) bank of the Marsyangdi Khola, keeping close to the telephone line until it crosses a massive suspension bridge to reach the large town of **Tarkughat** (1650 ft, 503 m) on the east (L) bank in **half an hour**.

From Tarkughat the trail heads south on a shoulder (1950 ft, 594 m) above the east bank of the Marsyangdi. It is shaded by many banyan and pipul tree *chautaara* and is very pleasant. The Chepe Khola appears to the east, and after **1½ hours** you descend to cross it on a good suspension bridge by a few houses (1550 ft, 573 m). The trail continues up the south (L) bank to reach a plateau and town called **Tadi Pokhari** (2025 ft, 617 m) in **half an hour**. There is an RNAC office here for the Palungtar Airfield (called Gorkha on RNAC schedules) which lies **half an hour** to the south. Continue southeast for **half an hour** to **Barapiiki Bazaar** (2050 ft, 625 m), then another **forty-five minutes** to **Luitel Bhanjyang** (2350 ft, 713 m) in a small pass.

There is a United Mission hospital and a primary school at **Ampipal** (4000 ft, 1219 m) on the ridge north of **Luitel Bhanjyang**. You can reach it by heading north from Tadi Pokhari and asking the way. This will take some **two to three hours**. Another route starts east of Luitel at the Darondi Khola near Chor Kuta, goes part of the way up the Basundi Khola, and continues on its southwest (R) bank past Simpani to Ampipal Bhanjyang. Again, it is necessary to ask the way. From the Darondi Khola, it takes **two to three hours**. A third route proceeds north from Luitel Bhanjyang, while a fourth begins from the east (L) bank of the Chepe Khola and takes the uphill (L) route.

From Luitel Bhanjyang, the trail descends and heads east to a ridge separating the Basundi Khola Valley to the north from that of the river flowing east from the pass at Luitel. The town of **Khoplang** (2100 ft, 640 m) is situated on this ridge **1½ hours** from Luitel. From Khoplang, the trail descends into the tributary valley of the Basundi Khola, passes a small town called **Basundi** (1600 ft, 488 m), and reaches the Darondi Khola (1450 ft, 442 m), another large river, in **1½ hours** from Khoplang. The river usually has to be forded.

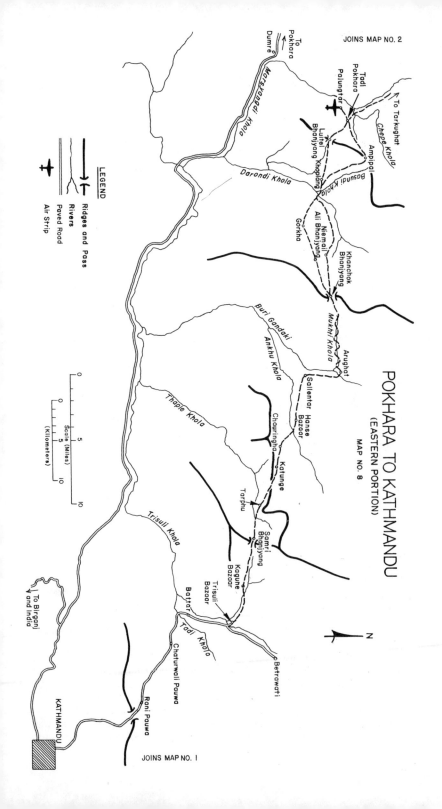

Other Treks

There are two routes from here, depending on whether you wish to detour to Gorkha, home of the founder King of Nepal, Prithvinarayan Shah. To go to Gorkha, go south from the east (L) bank of the Darondi Khola for **fifteen minutes** past a tributary valley on your left to a *chautaara* at the base of a hill. The main trail to Gorkha begins here and goes up through forests and fields to reach **Gorkha** (4000 ft, 1219 m) from the west in 2½ **hours**. This large town with many shops and temples is reminiscent of Kathmandu, but is smaller and has very few tourists.

The Shah family of Gorkha was simply one of many important family alliances in Nepal until Prithvinarayan Shah became master of the House of Gorkha at the age of twenty in 1743. Following a dream of which he never lost sight, Prithvinarayan Shah took twenty-six years, from 1744 to 1769, to conquer the Kathmandu Valley. He managed the near impossible task of building a powerful army out of the small population of Gorkha and maintaining its morale through two generations of fighting. He even retained the vital support of the small peasant and subsistence population of Gorkha. These people bore the brunt of feeding a large standing army over an extended period. Finally, the Gorkha army under Prithvinarayan Shah succeeded in uniting Nepal in the face of numerous and more powerful adversaries by engaging in surprise attacks rather than in large battles, and by keeping its enemies so divided that they were never able to unite in successful opposition to the conquerors.

The home of the founders of Nepal is still very much characterized by its fascinating history. By far the most spectacular site is the old palace of Prithvinarayan Shah, now a very holy shrine. The palace is situated amid terracing and gardens looking out on a panoramic view of the Himalaya. Reach it by climbing 1000 ft (304 m) up a beautiful stone staircase from Gorkha Bazaar. The palace is well-guarded, and only a special caste of Brahmans, who serve the gods within the palace shrine, are allowed to go beyond the courtyard. It is believed that if any ordinary person looks at the gods, he or she will die. All the stone work in Gorkha is unique and beautifully crafted, but the palace and surrounding area are outstanding in Nepal.

About 30 ft (10 m) below the palace is the cave where the hermit Gorkhanath once lived. Gorkha received its name from this famous saint, and the cave, which is presently filled with statues, is an extremely holy place.

To head on toward Kathmandu, descend to the north side of the main ridge from the notch near the shrine and go east to reach a town called **Koke** or **Ali Bhanjyang** (3800 ft, 1158 m) in 1¾ **hours**. There are some shops here. Continue to the east, climbing along beautiful open ridges, and pass through a Brahman village called **Tapli** (4800 ft. 1463 m) an **hour** beyond. There are good views of Himalchuli Baudha, Peak 29, Manaslu, and Ganesh Himal from this ridge. Descend from the ridge to **Khanchok Bhanjyang** (3600 ft, 1098 m) in 1¼ **hours**. The forests are of chir pine and chilaune.

To bypass Gorkha, ford the Darondi Khola and head upstream to the valley of the Khanchok Khola—also called the Masel Khola—1½ **hours** to the east. There is a town called **Niemail** or **Sikhar** to the southeast near the junction of the two rivers. Follow the Khanchok Khola for **three hours** to **Khanchok Bhanjyang** to join the route passing through Gorkha.

From Khanchok Bhanjyang, climb northeast for 300 ft (91 m) to Sano Khanchok **half an hour** beyond. Shortly, begin the descent of the Mukhti Khola which flows east to join the Buri Gandaki at Arughat. Spend some **three hours** in this valley, crossing and recrossing the river on an ill-defined trail. You are back in wet subtropical forest. After the first 2¼ **hours**, the trail keeps to the south (R) bank until it crosses the river on a twisting cantilever bridge. Cross the suspension bridge over the Buri Gandaki just beyond at **Arughat** (1600 ft, 488 m).

Once on the east (L) bank of this river, head south, keeping quite close to the river for almost **two hours** until you climb slightly to reach the Sallentar Plateau and the town of **Sallentar** (2000 ft, 609 m). From Sallentar the trail heads east, descending to the Ankhu Khola (1550 ft, 473 m). Follow the river on its north (R) bank to the town of **Hanse Bazaar** (1550 ft, 473 m) an **hour** beyond Sallentar. Continue along the north (R) bank, avoiding the log and mud bridge east of town. Continue past some Brahman villages until you come to a steel suspension bridge in an **hour**. Cross to the south (L) bank and enter the small village of **Ankhugursanger** (1700 ft, 518 m).

The trail continues east over a small saddle and ascends to **Thasoranpheri** (2000 ft, 609 m) in **forty-five minutes**. Beyond, the trail ascends on an ill-defined ridge past the town of **Chauringha** (3000 ft, 913 m) to a notch in the ridge with a tree on a *chautaara* (4200 ft, 1281 m) in 1¾ **hours**. It then contours the south side of the ridge, passing **Katunge** (4450 ft, 1356 m), several intervening hamlets, and **Bundi** (4450 ft, 1356 m) **half an hour** past the notch. The trail winds along up a ridge with commanding views of the mountains in good weather. The forest is again chir pine and chilaune. Descend past several clusters of houses, Bhotini, and reach a prominent notch in the ridge called **Tarphu** (4200 ft, 1281 m) **two hours** beyond Bundi. The telephone line makes its appearance along this section again.

From Tarphu, descend 1000 ft (304 m) and cross the Barang Khola in **half an hour**. As along many parts of the trail from Pokhara, there are dry and wet weather sections. Except during the monsoon, the river is crossed by a temporary log bridge near a few mills. In the monsoon, however, use a steel suspension bridge a little upstream. Follow the valley upstream, passing the towns of **Tarksank** (3250 ft, 990 m) and **Kirichowa** (3650 ft, 1112 m), to **Samri Bhanjyang** (4250 ft, 1296 m) 1½ **hours** beyond Tarphu.

The trail now descends the valley of the Samri Khola to Trisuli. The forest again becomes wet and subtropical. For **over an hour** the trail keeps to the south (R) bank, passing **Kapri Bas** (3600 ft, 1097 m), Ulangaro (2660 ft, 808 m), and **Kagune Bazaar** (2375 ft, 724 m) before crossing to the north (L) bank of the river to **Morwah Bazaar**. A little over **two hours** after Samri you should reach the outskirts of Trisuli. Go through the upper part of the town past the Indian Aid Compound responsible for an electrical generation project which produces large amounts of power. From the project's penstocks, you can see down to the Trisuli Khola and **Trisuli Bazaar** by a bridge (1766 ft, 538 m). Regular bus service to Kathmandu is available from here. The trip takes **four to five hours**. Buses leave between 7 A.M. and 8 A.M. and between noon and 1 P.M.

The **two-hour** climb from Trisuli Bazaar to Nuwakot, a famous historical fort, is a worthwhile side trip. From the bus stop in Trisuli Bazaar, go back to the east (L) bank of the river. Take the first stony path going up to the left immediately after the bridge, and climb to where it joins the main road. Follow the main road north for a **few minutes** until you reach a three-story red brick house on the left. Take the stone path going upward across the road from this house, and climb for approximately 1½ **hours** to the old city of Nuwakot.

This strategic town was captured by Prithvinarayan Shah, the first king of a united Nepal, in 1744. Its capture was a major victory in his twenty-six-year campaign to conquer the Kathmandu Valley. He later built a seven-story palace in the fortified town. It is still in excellent condition and can be visited simply by requesting the police who guard the area to open it for you. The seventh story commands a view in every direction. Looking out from the highest point, you can easily imagine the following historic battle.

In 1792 the Chinese army, which, until that time, had been making a largely successful incursion into Nepal, made the colossal blunder at Nuwakot of attacking uphill against the skilled Nepali mountain troops. The Chinese were thrown into confusion by a hail of boulders, logs, and every kind of missile. As they retreated in panic, they were halted at the bridge by their own generals, who refused to accept the possibility of retreat. Cut down by the famous Gurkha kakris (curved knives), or drowned in the monsoon-swollen river, the Chinese army was routed in this decisive battle.

To go on to Kathmandu on foot from Trisuli, cross the bridge to the east (L) bank of the river and follow the automobile road south to the village of **Battar** in **forty-five minutes**. Then turn east around the foot of the mountain on which the fort of Nuwakot stands. Go through a low pass and down to the Tadi Khola which joins the Trisuli Khola to the south. Cross a steel suspension bridge **half an hour** upstream from Battar. After the crossing, follow a smaller stream up to the town of **Chaturwali Pauwa** (3400 ft, 1037 m) about **three hours** beyond the Tadi Khola. You have now begun the climb to the rim of the Kathmandu Valley. Continue for another **half hour** to **Barmandi** (4000 ft, 1219 m), a village consisting of a group of large farm houses on a level stretch. Another **1½ to two hours** of climbing brings you to **Tungi Pauwa**. Along the way, pass through the village of **Tarpu Gaon**, distinguished by a huge tree growing on a level stretch. Reach the village of **Ranipauwa** and the automobile road in **half an hour**. The road has taken quite a detour compared to this direct trail, but, of course, it rises much less steeply.

The hill you have been climbing is popularly known as the five *maanaa* climb, since it is said that a loaded porter needs to eat five *maanaa* of rice to climb it. Alas most cargo now goes by truck! From Ranipauwa it is easier to continue along the road to the pass, Kaulatana Bhanjyang (6000 ft, 1829 m).

The remaining forests are oak. The pass is reached in about **forty-five minutes**. The auto road then descends gradually for about three miles until the main walking trail cuts off to the side of the ridge and descends to the rim of the Kathmandu Valley. On the right side of the rim, the remains of a monument of five mounds to represent the five *maanaa* of rice can still be seen. A short descent brings you to **Jitpui Phedi** (4600 ft, 1402 m) and a police check post. Shortly beyond is Balaju with a swimming pool and twenty-two fountains. Expect to spend **1½ to two days** covering the journey from Trisuli to Kathmandu.

CHITWAN NATIONAL PARK
(Map No. 9, Page 209)

Chitwan National Park, covering 210 square miles some sixty miles southwest of Kathmandu, is perhaps the best place in Nepal to see jungle wildlife. Tours to the park can be arranged by several commerical agencies (see Addresses in Appendix). The usual format includes round trip by air, elephant rides, stays at either a jungle lodge or a tent camp, hikes, boat rides, and animal observation. Rhinos are usually seen, and occasionally a leopard or tiger. These tours are quite expensive, but for those who can afford them, well worth it.

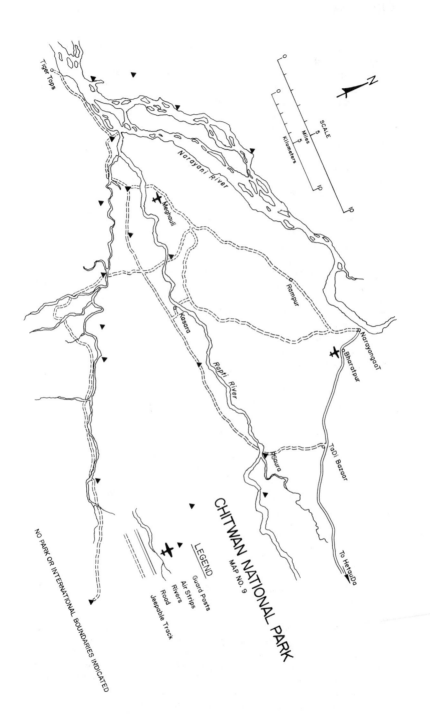

CHITWAN NATIONAL PARK
MAP NO. 9

LEGEND

▼ Guard Posts
✈ Air Strips
Rivers
Road
Jeepable Track

Tiger Tops

Narayani River

Meghauli

Rampur

Kasara

Rapti River

Narayangaat

Bharatpur

TaDi Bazaar

Kasaura

To HetouDa

NO PARK OR INTERNATIONAL BOUNDARIES INDICATED

SCALE

Miles

Kilometers

N

Other Treks

But for the cost-conscious and adventuresome trekker-tourist, there is another way to see the park. Although there are as yet no real facilities for tourists choosing the trekking alternative, the rewards, like those of trekking in a similar style in the hills, are great. The time necessary for such a visit is at least two days in the park and two days getting to and from it from Kathmandu. The travel time could be shortened by traveling by road between Birgunj and Kathmandu. The best season is from October to April. Late October, November, and early December are ideal.

To reach the park by air, you can fly by Royal Nepal Airlines from Kathmandu to **Bharatpur** on regularly scheduled flights. Then take a local bus or truck east along the East-West Highway to **TaDi Bazaar** (ten miles) and walk south along the motorable track to **Saura** (four miles). Porters can be hired in TaDi Bazaar. This is easily done in a day.

To proceed by road, take either a bus or a truck from Kathmandu toward Birgunj. The buses leave from diagonally across from the post office. Get off at **HetauDa** after a six-hour ride. You may want to spend the night here. To continue, take a bus or truck along the East-West Highway to TaDi Bazaar. This takes three hours, and is followed by a four-hour walk south along the motorable road to **Saura**. It is possible to drive this road in a four-wheel-drive vehicle. Several rivers must be crossed, and the road is usually impassable during the monsoon, though there are ferries for people. It is possible to get to Saura in a long, hard day—about fourteen hours—from Kathmandu, but most people break up the journey.

It is also possible to reach the park by flying to **Meghauli** on a charter, but this is rather expensive. There is also a road from Bharatpur to Meghauli. Trucks going along it leave Bharatpur early in the morning. You can arrange rides on them.

Saura, a small village located at the northeast corner of the park, is the starting point for venturing into it. Simple accommodations, camping sites, and Nepali food are available at the tea shop. There are also several simple hotels. A modern campsite has been constructed and there is a small shelter. Water is available nearby in the Rapti river or from local wells. Some wood can be procured locally, but campers are encouraged to bring their own stoves and fuel in order not to contribute to deforestation. There is a guard station in Saura, and a permit must be obtained to enter the park.

Elephants can be rented at the government elephant camp (*haatisaar*) at Saura. Usually two people can ride one elephant. The ride lasts around three hours. The rental is up to the people wo:king at the camp, and is not currently under the park auspices. On such a ride in the park you may see rhinoceroses, spotted deer, sambar, rhesus monkeys, peafowl, and jungle fowl.

Another interesting venture is to ride canoes down the Rapti river. The assistant warden at Saura can help you hire a canoe from one of the villagers. The twelve-mile trip down the river to Kasara, the park headquarters, takes about 3½ hours. There are no facilities at the headquarters, but camping is allowed. A longer trip downstream, lasting five to six hours, brings you to within a one-hour walk of the Tiger Tops Hotel. The best time is late October to February. Along the way you can see many interesting birds and crocodiles.

A popular trip is to go partway down the Rapti by canoe and make a side excursion east up a small stream where crocodiles are normally seen sleeping on the banks. At the Tiger Tops Hotel, you may be able to arrange elephant rides with the management. You might be able to hitch a ride back from the hotel in a jeep, but it is usually necessary to walk back to Saura, a very long day. This could be dangerous since you must walk through long stretches of grassland inhabited by rhinos. In route, pass two guard posts, then a sign pointing to the park head-quarters and a small museum a quarter mile off to the left. Pass two more guard posts before reaching Saura. It could be necessary, or interesting, to spend a night at a guard post.

Finally, you can walk in the jungle. It is not advisable to wander through dense jungle on foot without an experienced guide. Rhinos and sloth bear are the main hazards. Rhinos are quite common in forests, grasslands, and water. Their sight is poor, but their sense of smell is excellent. You can be on top of a rhino before noticing it. They do charge people, and are amazingly fast and agile. If a rhino charges, climb the nearest tree immediately. If there are no trees, run in an arc, as rhinos usually charge in a straight line. Best of all, avoid walking in tall grasslands.

Several blinds (*machaan*) have been constructed in the jungle, usually next to water holes, for observing animals. Ask at the guard station in Saura for directions. They can be reached by elephant, or on foot. Consider spending a night at one to observe the active feeding times and to hear the nocturnal sounds of the jungle. The view is best during a full moon. Animals can be seen undisturbed rather than flushed out as when riding on elephants. Lucky trekkers have seen tigers and leopards, and most people observe rhinos, wild boar, deer, monkeys, and colorful birds.

VEGETATION AND ANIMALS

Most of Chitwan National Park is covered with sal forests. There are small areas on the highest ridges where chir pine occurs, but sal predominates, becoming best developed below the base of the hills. Sal is a hard, heavy, slow-growing species, typically reaching eighty to 100 feet. It is valuable as the principal commercial species of southern Nepal.

Low regions of the park are subject to flooding and are dominated by tall grass species. *Saccharum* and *Phragmites* are common. Stable tracts near the large rivers are covered by a distinct riverain forest characterized by the red silk cotton tree, or *simal (Bombax ceiba)*. The massive red flowers of this tree make a remarkable display in January and February. Some of its common associates are *belar (Trewia nudiflora), sissu (Dalbergia sissoo)*, and more occasionally, the Flame of the Forest, *palos (Butea frondosa)*, which provides beautiful floral displays in spring.

Vegetative cover is at a maximum just following the monsoon. By March and April, grazing, cutting, and burning have reduced the cover to a relative minimum until the rains bring growth again in late June. Thus, from February on is a good time to see wildlife.

Perhaps the greatest attraction of the Chitwan area is its wildlife. The one-horned rhinoceros is the most conspicuous of the large species. It is estimated that there are between 250 and 300 rhinos in the area. Rhinos prefer riverain and grassland habitat, seeking the shelter of the forest during the hot months. In May and June they may often be seen in considerable congregations at wallows or water holes, where they seek relief from the heat.

Another of the more famous species of the park is the royal bengal tiger. While research being carried out in the area indicates that tigers may spend considerable time near areas of human activity, they are seldom observed except by careful effort or fortunate chance.

The large gaur is found in the hilly areas of the park. At least four species of deer, including chital, or spotted deer, hog deer, barking deer and sambar, occur in the lower parts of the forest and grasslands. They are an important prey species of the tiger.

Other mammals that occur in the park include sloth bear, leopard, fishing cat, jungle cat, jackal, wild boar, otter, langur and rhesus macaque monkeys, several kinds of mongooses, and several species of civet cats. During periods of high water the gangetic dolphin is seen in the large rivers.

Reptiles include large crocodiles—the fish-eating gharial, common in the Narayani river, and the mugger, found in the Narayani and in ponds near the river. Numerous species of snake are found in the park including the king cobra, common krait, rat snake, and Indian python.

Birds are the most conspicuous fauna of the park with close to 300 visitor and resident species. Among the larger species are peafowl, red jungle fowl, bengal florican, black partridge, giant hornbill, white-backed vulture, grey-headed fishing eagle, crested serpent eagle, and several species of stork and egret. Waterfowl, such as the brahminy duck and barheaded goose, come to winter along the rivers.

Many smaller birds occur as well. The most colorful and conspicuous are parakeets, kingfishers, woodpeckers, pigeons, and bee-eaters. Songbirds are common with the black-headed oriole among the best known.

SECTION III
THE COUNTRY AND
THE PEOPLE

A small girl in front of a garuda, the carrier of the Hindu God, Vishnu. (Ane Haaland)

Top: Common mongoose, occasionally spotted in the hills. (D. L. Golobitsh) Left: The elusive red panda, photographed in Langtang by a lucky trekker. (D. L. Golobitsh) Right: The spiny pink Morina longifolia, *one of the multitudes of plants that will delight you in the Himalaya. (Mary Lynn Hanley)*

12 NATURAL HISTORY

To a person uninstructed in natural history, his country or sea-side stroll is a walk through a gallery filled with wonderful works of art, nine-tenths of which have their faces turned to the wall.

Thomas Huxley

The flora and fauna of Nepal, its magnificent terrain, its people and their culture, are the great attractions of this remarkable country. In an effort to help the trekker interpret what he sees, a brief guide to the geology, climate, and ecological divisions is presented here with descriptions of the animals that might be encountered along a trek. The scientific study of Nepal's flora and fauna is still going on, so this chapter should not be taken as the final word. Instead, it should be considered a stepping stone to the more comprehensive references cited in Recommended Reading. The Tribhuvan Natural History Museum in Swayambhunath, Kathmandu, can provide some information, as can the Nepal Nature Conservation Society. The society can be contacted through the Kathmandu Guest House, Thamel, Kathmandu.

GEOLOGY

There appears to be some agreement that the origins of the Himalaya can be explained by the theories of plate tectonics and continental drift. Geologists believe that convection currents in the upper mantle of the earth are fueled by heat generated from radioactivity in the core. These currents move continents milimeters per year. Where there are ascending currents, the land mass on the earth's surface above the current thins out, stretches, and breaks apart. Where descending currents meet, initially the crust is pulled in to form a depression (geosyncline); then the land masses overlying very slowly crash together and strong compressive forces crumple the land, producing the folds we call mountains. Erosion and glaciation sculpt them to their present form.

Current theories on the formation of the Himalaya suggest that before the beginning of orogeny (mountain building) some seventy million years ago in the Mesozoic geologic era, there was a large ocean, caused by a geosyncline, separating the Asian from the Indian continent. The Mediterranean Sea is a remnant of this ancient ocean, called the Tethys Sea. The Tethys Sea was fed by rivers from the two continents, which deposited their sediments into it. The Asian continent from the north slowly moved into the Tethys Sea, whose sediments were folded into the Tibetan Marginal Range, the mountains south of the present Tibetan Plateau. This area lies on the Nepal-Tibet border today. After compression, the sediments rose up and the sea disappeared. The rivers originating in these mountains flowed north and south. The next phase occurred ten to fifteen million years ago in the Miocene period. The Indian continent began to overthrust itself against the Asian, resulting in the uplifting of the main Himalayan chain, called the Main Central Thrust. The Tibetan Marginal Range was also lifted higher, and the

Tibetan Plateau was formed by the stretching of the land mass to the north. The rivers flowing south were given a steeper gradient by the overthrusting of the Indian continent. Because of the increased precipitation on the southern parts, the rivers had enough force and water to cut through the mountains faster than they were being lifted up.

The third phase took place 600,000 years ago in the Pleistocene period, when further thrusting from the continental collision gave more uplift to the main Himalaya. Some of the rivers could not erode fast enough and were dammed into lakes such as Tilicho and RaRa.

The final phase during the later Pleistocene period was the rise of the Mahabharat Lekh, the outer foothills. This dammed some of the rivers flowing south, resulting in the formation of lakes such as the one in the prehistoric Kathmandu Valley. It dried up only some 200,000 years ago. Forced to run in longitudinal valleys, the rivers broke through the Mahabharat Lekh in three weak places—the Karnali at Chisapani in the west, the Gandaki at Deoghat in the middle, and the Kosi at Barahchhetra in the east.

The mountains of the Himalaya, the highest in the world, are unique among the great mountain ranges in that they themselves do not form the watershed. It lies almost one hundred miles to the north on the edge of the Tibetan Plateau. The result is the world's greatest gorges, through which the trans-Himalayan rivers penetrate the mountain barriers on their way to the Indian Ocean. The Himalayan mountains are the youngest in the world and may still be rising from the pressures of the collision of continents.

Today three main geological zones can be recognized in Nepal. The Tropical Plains and Foothills lie over Tertiary (twenty-five to seventy million years old) sediments consisting of conglomerate sandstone, shale, and marine limestone. Many fossils are found in the Siwaliks or outer foothills. Minerals found here include placer gold and coal. The Middle Region, intensely folded, is made up primarily of Paleozoic (270 to 500 million years old) sediments consisting of phyllite (derived from shale) and micaceous quartzite. Also found are limestone, dolomite, carbonaceous shale, slate, granite, and iron formations. Copper, lead, zinc, iron, cobalt, and nickel are some of the minerals found there. Few of these deposits are economically retrievable. The Himalaya is made of Mesozoic and more recent sediments consisting of metamorphic elements containing few minerals. In western and northeastern Nepal, there are granitic intrusions and hydrothermal activity. The hot springs, which trekkers enjoy, correspond to rupture lines in the terrestrial crust. They appear at low points of geological relief and are close to the Main Central Thrust. Indeed hot springs do not occur outside of this area. The Nepalis use the springs for certain rituals and pilgrimages as well as for bathing. The *BhoTiya* tend to ascribe therapeutic benefits to them.

CLIMATE

Nepal has a monsoon climate. The heavy rains of the monsoon occur from June to September, and begin in the eastern parts. Two to three weeks can separate the onset of the monsoon in the east from in the west. Similarly, more rain falls in the east, although local conditions are very important in determining the amount of precipitation. At high altitudes, above about 20,000 ft (6000 m), there is snow rather than rain. In addition, there is a less well-defined winter monsoon from December to the end of March. This precipitation takes the form of snow at higher altitudes, above about 8000 ft (2440 m).

The monsoon is caused by the movement of moist air north and west from the Bay of Bengal. As the moist air rises, it cools and condenses as rain. This precipitation falls on the southern side of the main Himalayan range. Generally there is less at higher altitudes since the clouds have already given up much moisture at the lower altitudes. When the resulting dry air mass gets across the Himalaya, it has very little moisture left to deposit on the northern sides. A rainscreen thus exists on the north sides of the Himalaya. The result is visible in Dolpo and Mustang.

The winter rains enable Nepalis to grow a second crop at lower altitudes. Generally, crops are grown up to the altitude at which clouds hang during the monsoon, as the clouds limit the amount of sun available. Local factors are immensely important in determining the rainfall and climate. Rain falling on north and west faces evaporates less, and more rain falls on steeper slopes, so there tends to be greater variety in the flora in these areas. Shady areas also have a more varied vegetation. While trekking, observe the changes in vegetation on different terrain, and try to predict local climatic factors that produce them.

VEGETATION

Nepal's vegetation can be classified in several ways. Amateur botanist J.D.A. Stainton, author of *Forests of Nepal* (see Recommended Reading), characterized thirty-five different forest types or plant communities. They can be divided into four biomes determined by altitude: Tropical and Subtropical; Temperate and Alpine Broad-leaved; Temperate and Alpine Conifer; and Minor Temperate and Alpine Associations. There is usually a transition zone in which one biome gradually drops out and is replaced by the next. Thus perhaps 3500 ft (1070 m) is the limit of Tropical and Subtropical vegetation. Temperate and Alpine Broad-leaved forests are found above this up to 9000 ft (2800 m). Generally, the vegetation becomes more familiar to trekkers from temperate climates as they ascend. Temperate and Alpine Conifer forests begin above 7000 ft (2130 m) and are found to perhaps 12,000 ft (3600 m). Above the tree line, Minor Temperate and Alpine Associations, the familiar alpine plants, grow to about 16,000 ft (5000 m). These altitudes are only approximate and vary immensely with local conditions.

The country can also be divided into topographical divisions. Some forest types are denoted here by their indexing species. Botanical names are given with common names where possible. No descriptions of species are given, but the terminology should be general enough to identify some forest groups while trekking. Consult *Forests of Nepal* for a complete treatment. There is no comprehensive guide to the floral species of Nepal, but *Himalayan Flowers and Trees* (see Recommended Reading) is a significant, popular, pictorial treatise.

The best way to learn about the plants of Nepal is to trek with someone who knows. Treks organized by a few agencies include a naturalist who can interpret the vegetation for trekkers. The Department of Medicinal Plants has published floral lists for several regions of the Kathmandu Valley including Godavri and Phulchowki. The amateur botanist can become familiar with many of Nepal's forest types by visiting these areas and comparing plants with the lists. The lists are available from the department's offices in Thapathali.

TARAI AND BHABAR

The Tarai, the flat region of Nepal that is the continuation of the Gangetic Plains of India has been substantially cleared for cultivation. The mosquitoes that carry malaria are found only in and around the large, impressive stands of sal forest in this area. The steady rise from the Tarai to the foothills is called the Bhabar. Again, sal forest predominates in these flat regions.

DUN VALLEYS AND OUTER FOOTHILLS

The first outer foothills are termed the Siwalik or Churia hills. They rise to 4000 ft (1220 m) and parallel the Indian border. Then come the heavily forested Dun Valleys. And farther north is the Mahabharat Lekh, rising to 9000 ft (2740 m). In western Nepal, sal and subtropical deciduous forests are found at the lowest altitudes, and forests of chir pine (*Pinus roxburghii*), with needles in bunches of three, occur from above 2000 ft (610 m) up to 6000 ft (1830 m). The upper regions are mostly oak forests (*Quercus incana* and *Q. lanuginosa*) containing some rhododendrons. In eastern Nepal, sal and tropical evergreen forests predominate at the lower altitudes, followed by subtropical evergreen forests at midrange, and topped by temperate mixed broad-leaved forests in the upper altitudes.

MIDLANDS

Nepal's midlands, the large region between the outer foothills and the Himalaya, vary considerably in different areas of the country. The West Midlands is the region between the Kali Gandaki river and the western border. Chir pine forests occur in this area to about 6500 ft (1980 m), while the oaks (*Quercus incana* and *Q. lanuginosa*) occur to 8000 ft (2440 m). At higher altitudes, forests of prickly-leaved oak (*Q. semecarpifolia*) and fir (*Abies spectabilis*) as well as birch (*Betula utilis*) are found, especially above 11,500 ft (3500 m). Rhododendron forests, so spectacular in eastern Nepal, are not found here to as great an extent. Coniferous forests up to the tree line include hemlock (*Tsuga dumosa*) and blue pine (*Pinus excelsa*) with needles in bunches of five. In selected locations such as around Dhorpatan, black juniper (*Juniperus wallichiana*) grows. Forests generally resemble those found in Kumaon, India, to the west.

The East Midlands is the region between the Arun Kosi river system and the eastern border. The flora is eastern Himalayan in character. In the lower altitudes, the Bengal subtropical hill forest (also known as the wet subtropical forest) includes a kind of chestnut (*Castanopsis indica*) and chilaune (*Schima wallichi*), but has been much affected by habitation. There are areas with subtropical semi-evergreen hill forests containing tree ferns and screw pine (*Pandanus furcatus*). Lower temperate mixed broad-leaved forests occupy middle elevations, followed by evergreen forests. Rhododendron forests are common from middle elevations to tree line. On one species (*Rhododendron arboreum*), the blooms become lighter as altitude increases.

The Central Midlands is the area between the Kali Gandaki and the Arun Kosi rivers, excepting the region south of Annapurna and Himal Chuli. It is a complex mixture of East and West Himalayan forest types. This is especially evident in that western forests occur on south slopes, while eastern forests are found on north slopes. In wet areas, alder (*Alnus nepalensis*) is common in erosion pockets and broken areas.

The area south of Annapurna and Himal Chuli differs from the midlands nearby in that it receives much more rainfall, mostly because the moisture-laden clouds from India have relatively low hills to cross before reaching it. At lower elevations, chilaune and *castanopsis* forests and subtropical semi-evergreen hill forests occur. At middle altitudes, lower temperate mixed broad-leaved forests are found on north and west faces. Slightly higher, oak (*Q. lamellosa*) occurs on north and south faces. Due to the excess rainfall, coniferous forests are not predominant, even at higher elevations. Upper temperate mixed broad-leaved or rhododendron forests predominate in the higher areas.

DRY RIVER VALLEYS

Impressive rivers cut through the Himalaya and produce remarkable gorges in their upper elevations before settling down in their lower courses. Strong prevailing winds usually blow upstream and create a rain shadow that extends several thousand feet up the valley. In the gorges, however, eastern slopes get little sun and tend to be quite damp. Above the damp regions close to the river itself, the next few thousand feet of the gorge may be quite dry. These are followed by wet slopes higher still. Instead of the usual vegetation succession due to altitude, the dry middle section may have pine forests topped by broad-leaved forests.

INNER VALLEYS

Valleys lying within the Himalayan ranges receive less rainfall than those lying south of the range. Valleys in the west receive even less rainfall at lower altitudes than those in the east. In the upper reaches of eastern valleys such as Khumbu, Rolwaling, and Langtang, the valley shape changes from a water-worn, heavy rainfall V to a glacier-worn U. Travel is easier in the broad, open, upper reaches of these valleys. Terminal moraines of glaciers become evident and the glaciers can be seen at work. There is extensive grazing in the upper valleys, and temporary shelters, inhabited during the monsoon, are found. The forests to tree line are not much different from forests at similar altitudes south of the main Himalaya. Above tree line, however, the predominant species of juniper changes from *Juniperus recurva* to *Juniperus wallichiana*, which grows as a small tree at times. In addition, the alpine shrubs are those found in more xerophilous (desert-type) areas of flora. Similarly, the herbs are those of the Trans-Himalaya rather than of monsoon country.

The upper Kali Gandaki or Thak Khola exhibits a tremendous change of climate and vegetation over a short distance. The valley begins below Ghasa in the monsoon vegetation of the midlands. Here there are subtropical rain forests with alder (*Cedrella toona*) and mimosa (*Albizzia mollis*). This gives way to blue pine, cypress (*Cupressus torulosa*), hemlock, some horse chestnut (*Aesculus indica*), rhododendron, and yew (*Taxus spp.*). Beyond Kalopani are stands of fir, birch, and some cypress with steppe forests beyond. Above the valley floor are black juniper and cypress. The valley floor is quite dry, but the wetter slopes above have forests of fir, birch, and blue pine. Some spruce (*Picea smithiana*) occur in side valleys. Between Marpha and Jomosom the floor contains only xerophilous shrubs which continue for several thousand feet above the valley floor. Higher up are, first, steppe forests, then dry alpine scrub, and finally wetter slopes. The prevailing upstream winds produce a rain shadow in the valley floor and for several thousand feet above it. Treeless steppe country continues into Mustang and there are no forests beyond until the Tibetan Plateau and the Takla Makan desert, a distance of over 1000 miles.

HUMLA-JUMLA AREA

The Humla-Jumla area is somewhat drier than might be expected due to a chain of *lekh* (hills) to the south which intercept much of the rain. Here the Himalaya are not so impressive and, correspondingly, the countryside is more open and less deeply eroded. Cultivation generally extends to higher altitudes than in the midlands. Much of the area is covered with blue pine, especially on south facing slopes, while spruce is found on north and west facing slopes. Himalayan cedar (*Cedrus deodara*) and cypress also occur. Apricots and walnuts sometimes grow wild. Generally the flora are west Himalayan in character.

ARID ZONE

North of the Dhaulagiri and Annapurna Himals, the country is generally treeless and the climate and vegetation is much like that of Tibet. Rainfall is minimal since the area lies in the rain shadow of the Himalaya. Few trees are found. The vegetation is that of a treeless steppe. Shrubs, grasses, and alpine flowers predominate.

ALPINE ZONE

The zone above tree line in Nepal is much the same as in most mountainous parts of the world. Plants grow to very high altitudes, even to 20,000 ft (6100 m), and bloom from April to October. First to bloom are the primulas and polygonums, followed by dwarf rhododendrons. Primulas, potentillas, and other moisture-loving alpine species bloom during the monsoon. Also found are sandworts (*Arenaria*), edelweiss (*Leontopodium*), rock jasmines (*Androsace*), sage brush (*Artemisia*), and joint pines (*Ephedra*). Toward the end of the season, there are gentians, larkspurs (*Delphinium brunonianum*), *Allardia glabra,* and *Selimum cortioides*.

AROUND HABITATION

Deforestation for terracing and grazing is common in areas of habitation. Trees such as kafal, walnut, fig, tamarind, *Bassia butyracea, Eugenia jambos, Ficus cunea,* and *Moringa pterygospermum* are grown for their food value. Trees and shrubs producing fodder such as camel's foot (*Bauhinia variegata* and *B. purpurascens*), hackberry (*Celtis australis*), and mimosa (*Albizzia chinehsis*) are planted. *Sarauja nepalensis, Brassaiopsis hainla, B. aculeata, Grewia oppositifolia,* and oak are trimmed for fodder. The pipul (*Ficus religiosa*), with pointed leaves, and banyan (*Ficus bengalensis*), with rounded leaves and branch roots, are usually planted together at *chautaara* to represent the male and female principles. Bamboo clumps are often planted near villages and are harvested to make baskets, trays, bridges, irrigation pipe, mats, swings, and in the construction of buildings. Bamboo occurs naturally on large rocky slabs with poor soil.

Most villages and terraces are built on south facing slopes in order to get sufficient sun for agriculture. By contrast, north facing slopes are usually forest and grazing lands.

Rice is grown in the hills up to 6500 ft (2000 m). It is planted before the monsoon, transplanted after the monsoon begins, and harvested in the autumn. Below 2100 ft (650 m), two crops can be grown. Rice straw is used for making mats, thatched roofs, and other items. Wheat is planted in late autumn in the rice fields, then harvested in the spring. In the dry northern areas, however, it is grown in the summer. Corn is planted in the spring and harvested during the monsoon. Millet is planted in the spring, then transplanted into corn fields before the corn is harvested. The millet is then harvested in the fall. Barley, a common high altitude crop, is planted in the spring and harvested in the fall. At lower elevations it is planted in the fall and harvested in the late spring. Buckwheat, another crop of the heights, is planted in late spring, and harvested in the autumn. At lower elevations, it is planted in the autumn and harvested in the early spring. Potatoes, often a staple at high altitudes, are planted in the spring and harvested in the fall.

Vegetables such as chillies, other spices, lentils, soybeans, mustard, turnips, radishes, pumpkins, and spinach are grown in small gardens surrounding houses. Fruit trees found in low lying areas include bananas, tangerines, papayas, and mangoes. Also many semi-cultivated plants such as nettles are eaten or used for making thread. Nearby forest trees have many uses. Sal is carved into many useful items and is used for house and bridge construction. Pine is used for shingles and timber. Oak makes good agricultural tools such as plough parts and hammers. Rhododendron wood is used for making wooden containers to hold yogurt because the wood enhances the flavor. Birch bark is used as wrapping paper.

MAMMALS

Zoogeographically, the world is divided into four realms, and each of these is then divided into regions and subregions. Characteristic species of animals are found in each. Nepal is strategically placed in the overlap zone of the Oriental Region (which includes most of India and much of South East Asia), and the Holarctic (or Palearctic) Region (which includes Europe, North Africa, and Northern Asia). The Oriental Region is found in the Tarai, while the Holarctic Region is represented in areas north of the Himalaya, especially Mustang, Dolpo, Manang, and Humla. Generally, where two zoogeographical regions meet, there is a broad intermediate zone in which both regions contribute species. The result is usually a diversity of animals.

But Graeme Caughley, who studied the animals of Nepal in the 1960s, has observed, "Nowhere else is the boundary between two faunas so abrupt. Over a distance of forty miles, one fauna gives way to another." Moreover, in this forty miles, the number of species of animals is surprisingly low. As in vegetation types, there is a characteristic eastern and western Himalayan pattern. Furthermore, species found to the east and west of Nepal do not seem to occur in the intervening area. Thus the red deer is found in Bhutan, and in Garhwal, but not in Nepal. Also, animals found in the western Himalaya, such as the ibex, markhor, wild goat, and urial, do not occur in Nepal. Similarly, animals found in the eastern Himalaya, such as the takin, are absent in Nepal. One might expect to find species unique to the Himalaya, but this is not the case, perhaps because the area is geologically so young.

Not only are few species encountered in the areas where most trekking takes place, but the population of these animals is low. This is most likely due to human habitations which modify the vegetation. Superstition may also contribute to increased destructive pressure on certain species. The faunal zones in Nepal have been characterized by Caughley as follows:

In the **Tarai Zone**, Oriental Region fauna is typically found, with representations from both the Indian and Indo-Chinese subregions. Several areas have been set aside as wildlife sanctuaries and national parks. Wildlife reserves are planned at Sukhla Phanta, Karnali, and Koshi Tappu. There is a national park at Chitwan. The one-horned rhinoceros, tiger, swamp deer, wild buffalo, gaur, leopard, clouded leopard, sloth bear, wild boar, monkeys, and many small animals are found in the Tarai region.

The **Foothill Zone**, the area from the Tarai to the monsoon-affected tree line, was originally all forested, but is now often cleared for agriculture. Leopard, goral, serow, barking deer, sambar, musk deer, Himalayan black bear, wild boar, red panda, red fox, jackal, and the monkeys—common langur, common rhesus, and Assam rhesus—are found in the forested areas. Smaller animals include porcupine, yellow-throated marten, orange-bellied squirrel, civet, river otter, weasel, shrew, and Indian hare.

The **Himalayan Zone** is the area above the tree line within the monsoon region. Surprisingly few species are found there. The Himalayan mouse hare (pika) and the Himalayan tahr may be seen.

The **Northern Slope Zone** is the area in the rain shadow north of the Himalaya. The fauna are of the Holarctic Region. Lynx, wolf, brown bear, snow leopard, musk deer, fox, and blue sheep are found. There are areas, such as in Khumbu, where the Holoarctic fauna penetrate south of the main Himalaya. Similarly, to the north of Dhorpatan, but south of the Himalaya, blue sheep are found. This is probably because the area receives less precipitation than other areas of the Himalayan Zone, and because the grass vegetation needed to support them grows above tree line.

Nepali names are given for some of the animals in the following list of mammals of the Foothill and Himalayan zones:

Barking deer (*mriga, ratuaa, rate*) are small reddish animals that make a barking sound when alarmed. These solitary deer live in forest and scrub to 8000 ft (2438 m).

Musk deer (*kasturi, mriga*) are hornless nocturnal animals with pronounced canine teeth. They live in rhododendron and birch forests near tree line, although they sometimes venture above it. They are poached for the musk pod found only in the male.

Serow (*thar*) are solitary goat-antelopes with mule-like ears. They live in thickly-wooded, inaccessible bamboo river valleys and may venture into open slopes at dawn or dusk.

Himalayan tahr (*jhaaral*) are hairy, goat-like mammals found throughout the mountains at around 12,000 ft (3650 m). They graze along the open patches of steep cliffs.

Goral (*ghoral*) are small goat-like animals that inhabit steep ravines and gullies at, or shortly above, tree line. They prefer grass and shrub-covered slopes near the shelter of rocks or forest, and are found in small groups in the morning and evening.

Blue sheep (*naaur*) are not really blue, but tan. These beautiful animals inhabit the grassland above tree line, usually near rocky areas. Herds sometimes venture close to forests in late winter and early spring. Look for them north of Dhorpatan and on the Manang side of the Thorung La.

Wild boar (*bAdel*) are large omnivorous pigs that live in forests at various altitudes and are known for rooting the ground and destroying crops.

Common langurs (*lAngur*) are large monkeys which can be seen in groups in dense forests and even open country above 12,000 ft (3650 m).

Rhesus monkeys (*bAAdar*) are smaller macaque monkeys which are found in open country, rocks and cliffs, and pine forests to 8000 ft (2450 m), as well as near villages.

Himalayan black bears (*himaali kaalo bhaalu*) are large, sometimes dangerous animals that live in steep, thick forests near tree line. They descend in winter.

Red pandas (*hobre, raato baa saano pADaa*) are secretive animals that live high in hemlock and fir forests near bamboo and brush. During the day, they sleep in trees.

Jackals (*shyaal*) are wide-ranging animals found near villages. They can steal poultry and attack small domestic animals. Their eerie howls are unforgettable.

Red foxes (*raato phaauro*) live singly or hunt in pairs. They are nocturnal and tend to be found in brush or cultivated areas up to elevations as high as 10,000 ft (3050 m).

Leopards (*chituwAA*) are found at or below timberline. These solitary cats attack many domestic animals.

Snow leopards (*him chituwAA*) are beautiful cats found in the heights. They are difficult to spot.

Common mongooses (*nyaauri muso*) may be seen running along roads or walls as they hunt.

Himalayan weasels are wide-ranging animals that can be seen in dense forests, dry sandy valleys, low swamps, or among rocks. They also lodge in holes in high pasture fences.

Beech or stone martens (*dhunge malsAApro*) are squirrel-cats that live in the high forests in holes or among rocks. They prey on small animals.

Common otters (*ot*) can sometimes be spotted playing near cold mountain streams and lakes.

Himalayan marmots live higher than any other animal in the world—up to 18,000 ft (5500 m).

Himalayan mouse-hares (*muse khraayo*) are also small high altitude dwellers.

BIRDS

Unlike mammals, for which there is a species gap between the Oriental and Holarctic regions, the species of birds found in Nepal is overwhelming. Perhaps some 750 different species occur—half the number found in all of South Asia. In the Tarai, the birds are characteristically of the Indian subregion of the Oriental Region, while at high altitudes, and on the northern slopes, Eurasian (a subregion of the Holarctic Region) birds predominate. Besides the mixture in the midlands, Indo-Chinese (a subregion of the Oriental Region) birds are also common. Also, in the far west, some Mediterranean (a subregion of the Holarctic Region) birds occur. Many birds pass through Nepal on spring and fall migrations. In the winter, visitors from the north arrive, and in the summer, birds, like people, come from the Indian plains to the hills of Nepal.

Birds of Nepal (see Recommended Reading) is invaluable to those interested in the amazing diversity of Nepali birds. Good treks for birdwatching include Khumbu for its high altitude birds, Manang and north of Jomosom for Tibetan species, and Chitwan National Park for jungle birds. Kathmandu Valley itself is excellent. Some 375 species have been observed there. In order to see as many different species of birds as possible, go from low to high elevations.

The following descriptions of many of the bird families of Nepal illustrate some of the sights the birdwatcher may see.

Grebes are aquatic birds and are often seen in winter on the lakes of Pokhara or on RaRa Lake.

Herons are water feeders that can be seen along streams and open flooded fields, or feeding upon insects near pasturing bovines. Egrets are especially common in rice paddies.

Cranes may be seen in flocks during their migration. They often land in open areas.

Ducks and geese are not native to Nepal, but they may occasionally be seen in winter flying overhead along the major rivers or over high altitude lakes.

Hawks, eagles, and vultures are winter visitors from Asia. They can be found at high altitudes near and above the tree line.

Pheasants, partridges, and quail are common throughout much of Nepal. The national bird of Nepal, the *danphe* or impeyan pheasant, is found in scrub and trees near tree line, especially in the spring. The snow cock may be seen running along hillsides in alpine scrub.

Pigeons and doves of many species are common. The trekker may be surprised to find the familiar city pigeon along rocky streams. The spotted dove is often heard around towns, while the rufous turtle dove is found in forests. The snow pigeon flies in flocks in higher regions.

Parakeets range over several elevations, and may often be encountered in noisy flocks.

Cuckoos are usually heard first, then sometimes spotted. These large, colorless birds are found in the higher hills.

Owls are often heard at night.

Barbets are chunky, colorful birds that have loud, monotonous calls and are found at low to middle elevations.

Woodpeckers thrive in the many forests throughout much of the country.

Larks are somewhat drab birds, but they are unforgettable when observed courting. They do this by singing and fluttering in circles at high altitudes.

Swifts, as their name implies, speed through much of Nepal. Indeed, the fastest bird in the world (white-rumped swift) is found in Nepal. Their flight is a fast flutter compared to the swallow's deep graceful wingbeats.

Swallows are found near habitations or nesting on cliffs.

Orioles are found at low and middle elevations.

Drongos are slim, black birds with scissor tails. They are found in various habitats, and often chase crows, kites, and other large birds.

Mynas, members of the starling family, are often found near man or on the outskirts of towns.

Crows, magpies, and jays of various species are found all over Nepal. House crows frequent the low and middle hills; the jungle crow, a larger, all-black bird, ranges into the high mountains. At the high altitudes, the Tibetan raven may be seen.

Bulbuls are crested birds which have a conspicuous call and perch near treetops or flowers.

Babblers are a large family of birds. They live in groups quite close to the ground and produce a variety of songs. Nepal is the only place where the spiny babbler is found.

Flycatchers are small birds which may be seen in clearings, darting about in search of insects.

Warblers are small, nondescript birds which live near the ground, in grassy areas, or in trees.

Thrushes are fine songsters found in various habitats—mountain streams, wooded ravines, low forests, and rooftops.

Titmice are small birds, many with conspicuous crests, found in oak forests at high elevations.

Nuthatches and tree creepers are small birds found moving up and down tree trunks and branches looking for insects in the bark. Nuthatches go down, while tree creepers go up!

Sunbirds and flowerpeckers are tiny birds with long curved bills. They are the Asian counterpart of hummingbirds. Look for them in oak and rhododendron forests in the spring.

Munias, sparrows, and weavers are common. The so-called house sparrow is common near settled areas; other species live in forests. The weaver builds long pendulous nests in ravines, grassy cliffs, and trees.

Finches and buntings of many species are found in the mountains.

BUTTERFLIES

Nepal has over 500 species of butterflies. They can be observed almost anytime. The following notes on their habitat are from Colin Smith, the resident authority on Nepal's butterflies.

Butterflies are attracted to flowers, both in gardens, and in flowering cultivated fields. Damp sand beside rivers, small streams, and water channels attract butterflies. Areas where humans or animals have been are also attractive to them. Ridges, forested on both sides with a slight clearing at the top, or clear with a few trees near the ridge crest, are good places to find them. Butterflies often tend to return to a favorite spot. Some do not range much, while others go on very long migrations. Bamboo attracts a disproportionate number. Although butterflies usually like sun, sometimes forests with sunlight bouncing through the trees are a favored habitat. The best time to see them is probably during the early monsoon, although just after the monsoon in the prime trekking time is also good.

Collections of butterflies may be seen at the Tribhuvan University Natural History Museum in Swayambhunath, or at the Prithvinarayan Campus in Pokhara.

REPTILES

The distribution of reptiles in Nepal is still poorly understood. Among the non-poisonous species encountered in the hills are the common wolf snake (*Lycodon aulicus*), the keelback (*Amphiesma platyceps*), the striped keelback (*Amphiesma stotala*), and the *dhaman*, or rat snake (*Ptyas mucosus*). The only poisonous species at all common in the hills is the mountain pit viper (*Trimeresurus monticola*), although the green pit viper (*Trimeresurus albolabris*) is sometimes found. The harmless common wolf snake is often mistaken for the poisonous common krait (*Bungarus caerulens*). To date, I have not heard of any non-herpetologist trekker seeing poisonous snakes, let alone being bitten by them. Fear too rapid ascent to altitude, not snakes.

The people of Nepal. Left: A Gurung *woman of the hills. (Donald Messerschmidt) Right: An old* Tamang *gentleman. (Donald Messerschmidt) Bottom: Children. (Ane Haaland)*

13 HILL AND MOUNTAIN PEOPLE OF NEPAL

by Donald A. Messerschmidt, Ph.D.*

Nepal has always been a meeting ground for different people and cultures.

Dor Bahadur Bista, Nepali anthropologist

Nepal is a land of great diversity. Its social, cultural, religious, geographical, floral, and faunal varieties fascinate and challenge the imagination. The diversity across the land is quickly seen and felt by trekkers and travelers. In a relatively few miles (although it may be days of arduous walking) a trekker can leave the low, sub-tropical Tarai forests and ascend northward into the high alpine meadows—the *lekh* of the Himalaya. The scenery changes from elephant grass to rhododendron forests; from water buffalo wallows to yak pastures, all set against the clear Tibetan sky. The *Tarai-wala* (a person of the Tarai) is left behind for the *PahAARi* (hillsman), *Lekhali* (alpine herdsman), and *BhoTiya* (Tibetan) of the highlands.

Variations in social and cultural expression seem to parallel the physical, geographic, and biotic changes associated with altitude and latitude. The trekker sees an ever changing variety of farmsteads, villages, and bazaars; passes the shrines of Hindu, Buddhist, and animist; encounters farmer, trader, merchant, innkeeper, and herdsman; and notes houses of many styles, sizes, and shapes. The colorfully diverse expressions of human adaptation to the Himalaya are unexpectedly fascinating for a land to which most visitors come expecting only spectacular mountains, Sherpa guides, herds of yak, and temples.

Nepal has dozens of ethnic and caste groups, each differentiated by unique aspects of language, dress, locale, life-style, religion, and other subtle criteria. At one level of analysis, however, certain elements of uniformity tend to knit all the diversity together. Take language, for example. It can be said to divide Nepalis into only two major camps: those who speak Nepali as their mother tongue—primarily the caste groups; and those who speak languages identified by linguists as part of the Bodic division of Sino-Tibetan (formerly called "Tibeto-Burman")—ethnic groups and those of close Tibetan affinities.

Another of the more visible attributes of uniformity in Nepal is a marked association between the cultural groups and the particular altitudes and latitudes.

* Donald Messerschmidt is a Nepal anthropologist who provided information on trekking to me before I first traveled there. His Nepal experience began in the Peace Corps in 1963 and continued as a teacher in Lincoln School in Kathmandu before he studied the *Gurung* people of west-central Nepal for his Ph.D. from the University of Oregon. He has published extensively on Nepal and edits the *Nepal Studies Association Bulletin*. Currently he teaches in the anthropology department at Washington State University in Pullman, Wash. and continues to study Nepal. He is one of the foremost authorities on the people of Nepal, and he has generously provided this chapter for the book.

In short, each distinct group can be identified in great part by the ecological niche it occupies in the physical-cultural landscape. Each niche is characterized by similarities in dress, house style, patterns of trade and subsistence, and other physical accouterments and modes of expression.

In the brief anthropological description of Nepal that follows, the many ethnic and caste groups are described in terms of both their differences and their similarities to one another. It is inevitable in a discussion this non-specific that much of the uniqueness of the people will be blurred, and generalizations will be made that may not fit all situations. The discussion focuses on those peoples most often met on trails in the hills and mountains. Because few trekkers travel in the Tarai valleys and plains adjacent to India, discussion of the castes and ethnic groups of that region is omitted. The intent here is only to provide the trekker with enough general information to better understand and appreciate the sights he sees and people he meets. An abbreviated list of hill and mountain peoples—the caste and ethnic populations—is provided, and some major festivals of Nepal are described at the end of the chapter.

Nepal's rich cultural traditions have been heavily influenced, and sometimes irrevocably changed, by the recent influx of tourism, education, technology, mass communications, and other aspects of modernization. How should we begin to describe Nepal's culture? We will start by categorizing it according to religious tradition, social type, and known historical origins and development. Following that, we will discuss and describe some of the common aspects of Nepali cultural expression in various areas of Nepal.

RELIGION

Nepali culture is based on two "great" or "high" traditions—Hinduism and Buddhism—each undergirded by many fundamental expressions of local "little" traditions of animism and shamanism. A very small percentage of Nepalis are Muslim, or "Musalman." They will not be considered here.

Hinduism is reflected both in the system of caste, which defines social status and hierarchy, and in an economic system based on rice agriculture and a highly ritualized cattle culture. *Buddhism*, principally the Mahayana ("Great Vehicle") Tibetan form, is found among the *BhoTiya* people of the northern border area. Many of the *Newar* people of Kathmandu Valley are Buddhists, and many are Hindus. The various local expressions of these two religions are historically and conceptually interwoven, but it would take much more than this short account to untangle and explain their interrelationships clearly.

Animism and shamanism are concerned with spirits that exist in the natural environment, and with the condition of the souls and spirits of each individual, alive and dead. Animistic beliefs and shamanic ritual permeate both the "high" cultures of Buddhism and Hinduism. At virtually every wayside shrine, in almost every religious rite, in ceremonies performed by lay people as well as by the Hindu temple priest (*pujaari*), the Buddhist monk (*lama*), or the village shaman (*jhAAkri*), you will see some form of worship (*pujaa*) focusing on both the animate and inanimate objects of nature. Funerals, rites of passage, and curing ceremonies are all richly ornamented with the animist's and shaman's concern for placating local spirits and natural forces. If you happen on a religious ceremony during your trek, your presence may be offensive (your close proximity to food preparation, for example, may be deemed ritually polluting). As you observe ritual events, be aware of the sensitivities of the officiants and participants. And open your senses to the

A village lama conducting a pujaa *(worship) in Jharkot. (Ane Haaland)*

fullness of their expression, especially to the sometimes awesome respect shown for nature—to the moon, earth, fire, water, and air; to cow dung and smoky incense; to cow's urine and curds; and to the blood sacrifice of chickens, pigeons, and goats. Therein you will begin to glimpse a very close and necessary association between mankind and nature that many people, caught up in the frenetic pace of the modern world elsewhere, have forgotten or uncaringly abandoned.

HISTORY

The Himalayan region of South Asia has always been viewed, it seems, as a safe haven for immigrants and refugees. One large movement of people into the Himalaya of Nepal dates from the twelfth to the fifteenth centuries A.D. when many Hindus—particularly of Rajput origins—fled the Moghul invaders plains. Some refugees settled in Kathmandu Valley, but great numbers remained more rural, populating the lower valleys and hills all across the land. The *PahAARi* people of adjacent India are culturally, physically, and linguistically the "cousin-brothers" of these Nepali Hindu hillsmen.

The Rajput arrivals were mostly Brahman (priests) and *Thakuri-Chetri* (warriors, also known as *Kshatriya* in India), with a smattering of craftsmen and menial labor castes. They encountered a local population of *Khas* people and many ethnic peoples, with whom they intermixed to various degrees linguistically, economically, religiously, and socially. The caste Hindu migrants brought certain strong social and cultural traditions—a status hierarchy, language, religion, and a rice- and cattle-based economy that blended with the local life-style and world view to make what is today's unique Nepali national culture.

Nepali history until the Gorkha Conquest of the eighteenth century A.D. is the history of petty principalities. One such principality was the Malla Kingdom. It grew up in the far west of Nepal and encompassed parts of neighboring Tibet and influenced the chiefdoms of the Bheri and upper Kali Gandaki river valleys. The Mallas (not to be confused with unrelated and later Mallas among the *Newar* of Kathmandu) ruled west Nepal from about the twelfth century to the fourteenth century A.D. They were apparently a *Khas* people, an ancient group whose presence as a powerful force in the region has had profound effects on all of Nepal's subsequent social history. They ruled simultaneously with the arrival of the migrant Rajput *Thakuri-Chetri* and Brahmans from the plains.

The Malla Kingdom was followed by several loosely-federated Rajput *Thakuri* Kingdoms in the west—the so-called Twenty-two (*Baisi*) Raja and the Twenty-four (*Chaubisi*) Raja. Several of these kingdoms rose to prominence, but it was the mountain kingdom of Gorkha and its leader, Prithvinarayan Shah, that eventually emerged as the strongest. In the 1760s Prithvinarayan laid siege to the *Newar* stronghold of Kathmandu Valley and ultimately went on to unify all of Nepal in the Gorkha Conquest. The House of Gorkha eventually controlled a vast Himalayan region stretching to Bhutan in the east, to Kashmir in the west, into Tibet in the north, and into the territories of the British East India Company in the south. By the mid-1800s, however, Nepali expansion had been halted, and the Gorkha domain was cut back to approximately the present bounds of Nepal. The Nepalis were pushed back by the British who thereafter chose to hire rather than subdue the men of Gorkha, whom they called "Gurkhas." The present Shah kings of Nepal are the direct descendants of Prithvinarayan Shah.

This brief historical overview is given here only to alert the trekker to part of the story of an earlier life in central and west Nepal in particular. There the local ethnics (especially *Magar* and *Gurung*) were conscripted to fight for the Hindu kingdoms. And, throughout these regions, from the modern town of Gorkha west to Pokhara and Palpa and beyond across the Bheri and Karnali rivers, the ruins of mountaintop forts (*kot*) are still visible. Similarly, and dating roughly to the same period, the ruins of walled towns (*dzong*) are seen in the Tibetan borderlands. All of these ruins speak silently to a rich and as yet little studied feudal past—part of the untapped, colorful, socio-historic archaeological heritage of Nepal.

THE PEOPLE

The inhabitants of Nepal can be classified culturally in several ways. Here they are first classified into three general cultural groups: the Hindu castes, the ethnic groups of the hills, and the northern border people, or *BhoTiya*. Then they are classified geographically into four areas: the Kathmandu Valley, east Nepal, central Nepal, and west and far west Nepal. The Hindu castes are of the physical type sometimes called by the now archaic classification of "Caucasoid" (Aryan or Mediterranean), while the ethnic groups of the hills and the northern border people are "Mongoloid" in physical type.

BY CULTURE

Hindu Castes

The Hindu castes are called by the general term *PahAARi* (hillsmen). Their origins can be traced back many centuries to India. They prefer to live in the middle hills and lower valleys, generally below 6000 ft (1800 m). Many people of the three lower menial castes no longer pursue their ascribed professions, but work as day laborers on the land of others, or often as porters for large trekking parties or for merchants.

HIGH CASTES

Brahman—the traditional priest caste. Today it includes peasant farmers, civil servants, moneylenders, landowners, schoolteachers, and others.
Chetri (including *Thakuri*)—the traditional warrior caste. It includes the same occupations as the Brahmans, as well as soldiers in the Gurkha armies. The King's family is of *Thakuri* Rajput origin.

MENIAL CASTES

Damai or **Darji**—tailors and musicians for Hindu weddings and festivals.
Kaami—ironworkers, makers of tools, and sometimes silversmiths and goldsmiths.
Saarki—cobblers and leatherworkers.

Ethnic Groups of the Hills

The ethnic groups of the hills have been in the Himalaya somewhat longer, it is thought, than the Hindu castes. They are descendants of several waves of migration from the north and northeast. These groups tend to cluster between 6000 ft (1800 m) and 9000 ft (2700 m).

Newar—merchants, civil servants, artisans, craftsmen, and farmers of the Kathmandu Valley and the hill bazaars. Many are hotel keepers. *Newar* are stratified into numerous subcastes modeled on the Hindu caste system. There are both Hindu and Buddhist *Newar.*

Kiranti (Rai and **Limbu)**—peasant hillsmen of east Nepal. Some are Gurkha soldiers.

Tamang—peasant farmers, day laborers, and porters of east and central Nepal. They are particularly abundant around Kathmandu Valley.

Magar—peasant farmers of central and west Nepal. Some are Gurkha soldiers. They are much influenced by Hinduism.

Gurung—peasant farmers and shepherds of central Nepal. They live generally higher than their *Magar* neighbors. Some are Gurkha soldiers. Some *Gurung* have recently become successful businessmen in and around Pokhara.

Sunwar and **Jirel**—small groups of peasant farmers east of Kathmandu Valley.

Thakali and **PaunchgaaUle**—agro-pastoralists, traders, and businessmen of Thak Khola in central Nepal. They are often found trading or keeping inns in and around Pokhara and in surrounding districts as far south as the Tarai and the Indian border. They are aggressive entrepeneurs.

Northern Border People or *BhoTiya*

Like the ethnic groups of the hills, these people came to Nepal from the north and northeast long before the Hindu castes. They inhabit the northern valleys and mountainsides, usually above 9000 ft (2700 m), and are the true "Himalayan Highlanders." Their cultural affinities are clearly with Tibet. They are Buddhist and pursue economies such as long distance trade, yak and sheep herding, and more recently, portering and guiding for trekking and mountaineering parties.

Listed as they occur from east to far west Nepal across the backbone of the great Himalaya, they include: **Lhomi** (upper Arun River); **Sherpa** (Solu-Khumbu and Mount Everest region, Rolwaling, and Helambu); **Langtang** (north of Kathmandu); **Nupri** (northern Gorkha District and upper Buri Gandaki river); **Nyeshang** and **Nar** or **Manangbo** (Manang District and upper Marsyangdi river); **Baragaun** and **Lopa** (north of Thak Khola); **Dolpo, Tarap** *BhoTiya,* and **Tarali** (Dolpo District, northwest of Thak Khola); **Mugu** *BhoTiya* (Mugu Karnali Valley); **Limi** *BhoTiya* (Limi Valley and northwest of Jumla); and **Byansi** (far northwest corner of Nepal and the adjacent Almora District of India). There are many other *BhoTiya* groups scattered throughout the high Himalaya.

BY GEOGRAPHY

People of the Kathmandu Valley

The early inhabitants of the Kathmandu Valley were the *Newar.* Today they make up the bulk of the merchants and shopkeepers (alongside many businessmen of Indian origin) in the three cities of Kathmandu, Patan, and Bhatgaon, and in outlying hill bazaars. They also fill a large number of civil service posts in the government.

Kathmandu Valley is also populated by large numbers of Brahmans, and *Chetri,* in both the cities and the countryside. Other peoples often seen in the streets of the capital are Hindus from the Tarai, *Tamang* hillsmen who work as coolies and day laborers, *BhoTiya* (including many Sherpas) from the north, *Gurung* and *Magar* from central and west Nepal, and *Kiranti* from the east. Since

Nepali women making the pilgrimage to Muktinath, passing a boulder with the mantra, Om Mani Padme Hum, *carved on it. As a sign of respect, they keep it to their right. (Brot Coburn)*

1959, many Tibetan refugees have also settled in the valley. Monks and other Tibetan men and women are found at the Buddhist temples and monasteries of Bodhnath and Swayambhunath on the outskirts of Kathmandu, and at the refugee and handicraft center at Jawalakhel near Patan. Tibetan handicrafts—especially articles of clothing and colorful carpets—are well-known to travelers in Nepal.

In medieval times, *Newar* craftsmen developed the distinct architectural and decorative motifs and religious arts of the valley. They became active traders when, for centuries, a main trade route between India and Tibet passed through Kathmandu. In time, *Newar* extended their craftsmanship and business enterprises to Lhasa and other Tibetan centers of trade. After the defeat of their valley kingdoms by the Shah rulers of Gorkha in 1769, the *Newar* proceeded to take economic advantage of the Gorkha Conquest. As Gorkha military and administrative outposts were established to tie the new Himalayan kingdom together, *Newar* merchants arrived to set up shops. They created many of the hill bazaars that trekkers encounter throughout Nepal.

Not all *Newar* are businessmen or civil servants. Members of one sub-group known as *Jyapu* are seen tilling the vast fields of rice, wheat, and vegetables in the valley. Others are stone and wood carvers, carpenters, potters, goldsmiths, blacksmiths, and Hindu or Buddhist temple priests. *Newar* peasant communities are even occasionally found in the outlying districts. Most *Newar*, no matter how far dispersed, try to keep kinship and ritual ties with Kathmandu Valley because it is their homeland.

People of East Nepal

The east is the home of Brahmans and *Chetri* at the lower elevations, of *Kiranti* (*Rai* and *Limbu*), *Tamang*, *Sunwar*, and *Jirel* peoples at the middle elevations,

233

and of *Lhomi*, Sherpa, and other *BhoTiya* groups in the high valleys and mountains up to 14,000 ft (4000 m).

The *Kiranti* live in the easternmost districts, and are found even around Darjeeling in West Bengal. Like the *Gurung* and *Magar* farther west, the *Kiranti* are renowned for their exploits in the British and Indian Gurkha armies. They speak a number of interrelated dialects that are often unintelligible from one watershed village to the next.

Kiranti economy is fairly self-sufficient. (The description that follows fits most of the Nepali hill people in general.) Rice is raised in the lower, well-watered fields. Upland crops, such as corn, millet, barley, wheat, and potatoes, are raised on the higher, drier, and steeply sloped or terraced hillsides. No mechanized farm equipment is found in the hills (except an occasional threshing machine or rice mill). Tilling is done either by hand with a short-handled hoe (seen most often in Kathmandu Valley), or with bullocks pulling iron-tipped wooden plows. All hillsmen eat what they raise and market what little surplus they may have. Some supplement their incomes by marketing oranges or selling fish caught in the rivers and streams. The wealthier may also engage in money-lending. Others engage in seasonal employment as migrants to neighboring India or as mercenary Gurkha soldiers. In the far eastern hills bordering the Darjeeling district of West Bengal, there are tea plantations—Nepal's own brand of Ilam tea is exceptionally good. Some hillsmen make and sell bamboo baskets and mats, and where sheep are raised on the higher slopes, the people weave and sell the woolen blankets, rugs, and felt-like capes and jackets that are often seen in Kathmandu's street bazaar.

The *Tamang* are a very large and widespread hill group. They and the Sherpas are among the most recent groups to settle along the northern border regions and higher hills, having come, it appears, from farther north and east. *Tamang* have retained much of their Tibetan heritage and are Buddhist. There are *Tamang* villages all around the Kathmandu Valley, especially north toward Helambu and east on the Mount Everest trek. *Tamang* are known to Himalayan climbers who hire them for the long haul into base camps, although at the higher elevations the Sherpas tend to dominate the portering.

Eastward toward Everest are the territories of such groups as the *Sunwar* and *Jirel*. *Sunwar* people inhabit the valleys of the Likhu Khola and Khimti Khola rivers. Some of them have been recruited into Gurkha British and Indian regiments. The *Jirel* are found in the Jiri and Sikri valleys.

Next to the Gurkha soldiers of Nepal, it is perhaps the Sherpas, famous as mountain guides and porters, who have attracted the most worldwide attention. Some Sherpas dwell in the remote Rolwaling Valley, and as far west as Helambu Valley. But the most renowned come from the villages of Shar-Khumbu (Solu-Khumbu) along the upper valley of the Dudh Kosi and its tributaries in the Mount Everest region. Sherpas are relatively recent newcomers to Nepal. Pangboche, their oldest village, and one of the highest, is thought to have been built a little over 300 years ago. The Sherpas speak a Tibetan dialect, dress like their Tibetan neighbors—or often like Western trekkers—and live as traders and agro-pastoralists, farming their high fields (mostly potatoes, wheat, barley, and buckwheat) and herding yak and sheep in alpine pastures up to 17,000 ft (5000 m). Their region is divided into three subregions: Solu, Pharak, and Khumbu. Solu to the south includes such villages as Junbesi and Phaphlu, and the monastery at Chiwong in picturesque valleys at approximately 9000 ft (2700 m). Pharak is situated between Solu and Khumbu along the steep banks of the Dudh Kosi. Most Sherpa mountaineers hail from Khumbu, the highest of the three regions, ranging

Top: Plowing the fields with a metal-tipped wooden plow drawn by bullocks. (Brot Coburn) Bottom: Harvesting millet. (Brot Coburn)

from 11,000 ft (3300 m) on up. Their villages include Namche Bazaar, Thami, Khumjung, Khunde, and Pangboche as well as the famous and beautiful Buddhist monastery of Tengboche. Among the Sherpas, the practice of Tibetan Lamaism remains strong.

The Sherpas have received considerable attention from anthropologists, mountaineers, and traveling journalists, so we need not go into much detail here (see Recommended Reading). Namche Bazaar's Saturday markets, however, are interesting from a traveler's perspective because of the chance to see several ethnic groups and a wide variety of local handicrafts and trade goods on display. If traveling toward Namche Bazaar immediately before or after a Saturday, trekkers may see many groups of lowlanders, mostly *Rai* and a few Brahmans and *Chetri*, carrying baskets of produce such as rice, corn, and fruits to sell or trade for highland produce such as wheat, wool, potatoes, *ghiu* (clarified butter), and other animal by-products. The lowlanders are easily singled out from the Sherpas and Tibetans by their style of dress—light tie-across Nepali shirts and baggy trousers that fit snugly at the calves. Sherpa and Tibetan men, by comparison, prefer heavy woolen cloaks and trousers with leather or woolen boots. At the market itself, Tibetan boots and handicrafts of silver, wool, and leather are displayed. A market day is a lively occasion, a time when Tibetans, Sherpas, *Rai,* and others (including visitors) join in trade, gossip, eating, drinking, and perhaps some spirited dancing and singing.

People of Central Nepal

Central Nepal is here considered to be the region from Kathmandu Valley west to and just beyond Pokhara. It is the home of Brahmans, *Chetri, Magar, Gurung,* and a number of northern border peoples, including the *Thakali* of Thak Khola. Brahmans and *Chetri* are often seen on the lower trails from Kathmandu to Pokhara, especially around the historic site of the old Gorkha kingdom. *Newar* bazaars line the road between Kathmandu and Pokhara. Many caste and ethnic groups have also been attracted to these new settlements. *Magar* villages are most often encountered in the lower hills of the region. *Gurung* inhabit the higher north slopes of the Annapurna, Lamjung, Chuli, and Ganesh Himalayan massifs. There are many *Tamang* in the region as well. To restrict the *Magar* to the lower hills is not entirely correct since several *Magar* sub-tribes live at higher and more northerly locations, notably on the flanks of the Annapurna and Dhaulagiri Himalaya on tributary streams of the Kali Gandaki river. In these higher regions the *Magar* are variously known as *Pun, Chantel, Kaiki,* and *Tarali.* Part of their culture blends into that of the *BhoTiya*.

Tibetan *BhoTiya* groups include *Gurung BhoTiya* in the region called Nupri between Himalchuli and Ganesh Himal, *Manang BhoTiya (Nyeshangba)* in the upper Marsyangdi river valley north of the Annapurna range, *Lopa* in Mustang north of Thak Khola, and other *BhoTiya* in Dolpo and Tarap to the west around and behind the Dhaulagiri Himalayan massif.

During the winter months, large numbers of these mountain people trek south to the lower hills and are often encountered in and around bazaar towns where they engage in trading and sometimes running inns and small shops. One well-known central Nepal ethnic group is the *Thakali*. Their language is very close to *Gurung,* but their cultural history has been more influenced by Tibet. *Thakali* are noted for their aggressive trading spirit, which they developed as middlemen in the formerly very active Nepal-Tibet rice and salt trade. Since 1959 when the Tibetan border trade dried up, the salt business has come to a virtual standstill in Thak Khola, and many *Thakali* have turned southward for other economic opportunities. Many have recently turned away from their Tibetan cultural heritage and become Hindus—worshipping the Hindu pantheon, dressing as their Nepali business associates dress, and speaking Nepali. Some have moved south permanently to take full advantage of new business opportunities in Pokhara, in the Tarai, and in Kathmandu.

The Thak Khola trek passes through villages of several ethnic and caste groups. Pokhara, the starting point for many central and west Nepal treks, is inhabited by all sorts of peoples—Brahmans, *Chetri,* lower castes, *Magar, Gurung, Newar, Thakali, BhoTiya,* and Tibetans. The surrounding hills are dotted with *Gurung* villages. The wealth of the ex-Gurkha soldiers is obvious from their large, cut-stone houses with slate or corrugated metal roofing. There is a Tibetan refugee settlement at Pardi near the Pokhara airport, and another at Hyangja, a half-hour walk north of the main Pokhara bazaar.

A day's walk north of Pokhara through a number of hill villages and small *Newar* towns is the Kali Gandaki river gorge. There, especially on the lower trail between Baglung and Dana, the trekker may meet *Pun Magar* people who live high on the steep ridges along some of the tributaries of the Kali Gandaki. Their villages are difficult to ascend to and seldom visited by outsiders. The *Pun Magar* are noted for their skill in rock cutting, as can be seen on the cliff-side trails along the river. Some of the more northerly rock cutting was done in the 1960s by Tibetan refugee *Khamba.*

Above the dramatic gorge of the Kali Gandaki between the towns of Ghasa and Jomosom is the Thak Khola itself in what appears to be one general cultural area. *Thakali* villages line the route north along the now slowly meandering Kali Gandaki. The largest town is Tukche, a former salt-trading center and caravanserai (a place for the overnight accommodation of caravans). Today, however, many of the *Thakali* inhabitants of Tukche have moved south into the lower hills permanently.

In the winter when trekkers usually reach Thak Khola, the villages look more empty and lifeless than ever. This is the season of trade and travel in Nepal, and many *Thakali* have gone south temporarily to run tea shops and inns (*bhaTTi*) along the trails. The rainy season will see them back home, planting and tending their wheat and buckwheat fields, filling the streets and alleys of their towns with gaiety and laughter, and enjoying local summer festivals and weddings.

Despite some uniform appearances, Thak Khola is the home of two somewhat distinct ethnic groups—the *Thakali* majority (as far north as Tukche) and the *PaunchgaaUle* (literally, "people of the five villages") who live in Marpha, Syang, Chiwong, Cherok, and Jomosom-Thinigaon. The *PaunchgaaUle* people in turn recognize several sub-groupings among themselves on the basis of marriage customs and other more subtle differences. To the common traveler and many Nepalis, it is, however, difficult to distinguish the *PaunchgaaUle* from the *Thakali.*

North of *PaunchgaaUle,* at Kagbeni and in the valley of the Muktinath shrine, live the *BaaragaauN BhoTiya* people. Muktinath is a central attraction for tourists and trekkers as well as Hindus and Buddhists. Muktinath shrine is dedicated to Lord Vishnu, and is the site of a very large annual Hindu pilgrimage on the full moon day (*janai purnima*) of August. There is another, smaller pilgrimage each spring. At the same time as the August pilgrimage, the local *BhoTiya* Buddhists have a large, colorful fair (*mela*) highlighted by horse racing. The region around the Muktinath temple includes several renowned Buddhist temples (*gomba*). In this region the style of life is close to that of Tibet proper, particularly among the *BaaragaauN BhoTiya* inhabitants of Kagbeni and Dzong.

The *Lopa* people of Mustang north of Kagbeni are politically Nepalis, but culturally much like their Tibetan neighbors, especially in dress, language, material culture, economy, and allegiance to the Tibetan Buddhist religion. Some of them—and some neighboring peoples—practice the ancient pre-Buddhist religion of Bon which is heavily infused with animistic and shamanic belief and ritual. These people are all agro-pastoralists who farm their oasis-like fields wherever enough water is available in the arid countryside, and herd yak, goats, and sheep in the higher alpine meadows along the border. They were formerly a link in the salt and rice trade through Thak Khola.

People of West and Far West Nepal

West and far west Nepal are regions lesser known to anthropologists than the central and eastern hill and northern border regions. There are several reasons for this—the difficulty of travel in the area, the remoteness from centers of trade and government, and the relatively low population, sparse settlement, and dearth of ethnic groups. These hills are drier and the people suffer from more difficult environmental circumstances; their production is lower and it takes much more land to support the average family. The great distances and time involved to travel from either the Tarai towns to the south or the capital at Kathmandu farther east are also important factors.

Part of the west is the home of the *Magar*, but only as far as the Sallyan District. Beyond that to the western border with India, Hindu caste groups predominate. In great measure these Hindu villagers are closely related to the *PahAARi* (hillsmen) of Almora, Kumaon, and Garhwal in the neighboring Indian Himalaya. The Nepali language here blends into the central *PahAARi* dialect of north India, and to some extent there is greater socio-cultural interaction with Indian neighbors and kinsmen than with the peoples of central Nepal or Kathmandu. In recent years the national government has taken a more active interest in the problems and potential of the far west. There has been a concerted effort to further integrate and unite all of the Nepali people as one nation, and to improve the local standard of living.

Living north of the Hindu caste groups of the west and far west are more of *BhoTiya* people, named after particular valleys in which they dwell, such as Limi, Mugu, Tarap, and Dolpo. Some of these have only recently been studied by anthropologists, and as yet most accounts of them are found only in scholarly journals and dissertations.

There are some spectacular treks in this region, particularly to the lakes (RaRa and Phoksumdo) and mountains. And there are some equally attractive social systems, cultural patterns, and historic and archaeological reminders of the past.

This is the land of the ancient Malla Kingdom, and it is literally "littered" with many of the cultural and historical artifacts of that era. For instance, along the former "royal highway" of the Mallas, a walking route stretching north from the inner Tarai through Jumla to Tibet, there are various inscribed stones that scholars have used to determine the nature and extent of the Malla domain. And there are ancient shrines dedicated to the locally prominent deity, Masta. Trails here are festooned with carved wooden spirit effigies, and with bells, flowers, and strips of colored cloth set out to appease the spirits that haunt each locale. The trekkers are

Magar *women in the western region of Nepal. (Ane Haaland)*

admonished—please—to respect local custom here and throughout Nepal and to refrain from handling or taking souvenirs beyond what can be captured on film. Much of what is seen and admired here is holy, and local feeling toward holy objects is not unlike the reverence and respect Westerners feel in the sanctuaries of the great cathedrals of Europe, or in their home town churches and synagogues.

One fascinating cultural feature of some of the more northerly dwelling Hindus of this region is their apparent "Tibetanization." Unlike elsewhere in Nepal, some *Chetri* and *Thakuri* of the west and far west are indistinguishable at first glance from their Buddhist *BhoTiya* neighbors. They wear the same style of clothing, construct the same kind of flat-roofed houses, and pursue some of the same patterns of trade and subsistence economy as the *BhoTiya*. Their way of living is unlike that of their more "pure" Hindu caste neighbors to the south, who look down on them.

Many people whom the trekker encounters on the trails of this region—along the Bheri and Karnali river routes, for example—are *BhoTiya* traders and travelers who prefer to spend their winters in the warmer, lower southlands of Nepal. At times, in the fall and spring, the trekker may encounter a veritable kaleidoscope of people in caravans, including Byansi traders who live mostly in the Indian frontier district of Almora, Uttar Pradesh.

The salt trade was once a flourishing business here. Salt was procured from Tibetan traders from the great salt lakes of west Tibet, then traded through several hands for cereal grain and other commodities in Nepal and India. Today, traders deal more often in wood products, animal by-products (*ghiu*, hides), and cereal grains as well as a plethora of manufactured goods generally of Indian origin.

Despite the recent growth of tourism and travel in this far end of the country, and the government's increasing interest in development (witness the new roads, schools, and other services), Nepal's west and far west remain remote from the national center. It is a region touched by certain exotic feelings, a place as romantic as its curious place names: Dang, Dandeldhura, RaRa, Limi, Humla-Jumla.

MAJOR FESTIVALS

SECULAR FESTIVALS

Several national holidays are celebrated throughout the country. The most colorful from the standpoint of national culture and the prospect of photography is *Prajaatantra Divas,* or Nepali National Day, February 19. It is highlighted by parades on the Tundikhel (parade ground) in Kathmandu. National ethnic groups, dancing troupes, the military, and various peasant, class, and cooperative organizations participate. There is much military pomp and splendor.

HINDU FESTIVALS

Hindu festivals are celebrated in Kathmandu Valley and in many hill bazaars and Tarai towns. Many smaller festivals, especially those of the *Newar*, are not mentioned here; information about them and the exact dates of all festivals, which are reckoned by the lunar cycle, can be obtained in Kathmandu. The following Nepali words are often used in relation to certain festivals and religious occasions:

—*ekadasi,* the eleventh day of every fortnight during the lunar year, is observed by fasting, worship, and ceremonial bathing.

—*jaatraa* means festival.

—*pujaa* means worship.

—a *Tikaa* is a mark of religious and decorative significance on the forehead of Hindus. They are given and received, particularly at festive and religious occasions, to express good wishes, friendship, respect, and honor.

The Hindu holidays include:

Shiva Ratri, literally "Shiva's Night," is at Pashupatinath, a famous large Hindu temple on the banks of the Bagmati river in Kathmandu Valley northeast of the capital city. This festival attracts thousands of pilgrims from the Tarai and from India. They walk, take planes, or ride buses to the valley for the occasion. The Nepali Army parades on the Tundikhel, and bonfires burn for several nights.

Holi is in early March. Its climax is on the full moon day when red powder is thrown and passersby are doused with colored water.

GhoRa Jaatraa is in late March and includes horse racing and athletic events on the Kathmandu Tundikhel.

Janai Purne is the full moon day of August on which high caste Hindus bathe ceremonially and ritually change their sacred threads (*janai*) which are worn over their shoulders. Yellow threads to be worn until the Tihar festival are also tied around the wrists of all Hindus for good luck. Hardy and pious Hindus take pilgrimages to bathe and worship at some of the high Himalayan lakes, such as Gosainkunda, north of Kathmandu, and to other equally auspicious holy sites such as Muktinath north of Thak Khola. In Kathmandu, large numbers gather at the water tank of Kumbeshwar in Lalitpur, a site which has religious affinities with Gosainkunda.

Indra Jaatraa lasts eight days at the end of September and beginning of October. The center of activities is Hanuman Dhoka (the square near the old Royal Palace in Kathmandu), but preparations can be seen at various other places for many days prior to the main celebrations. A tall pole is erected and a golden elephant is placed there, attracting worshippers with offerings of sweets, fruit, and flowers. Dancing troupes perform, and drama productions are given. Special tribute is made to those who have died during the past years; their family members parade through the streets carrying burning lamps and incense, and chanting religious hymns. Various manifestations of the God Indra are shown throughout the city, the most famous being the huge head of Bhairab at Indrachok, and the metal head gilded with gold at Hanuman Dhoka. Each evening the temples of Hanuman Dhoka and the old palaces are lighted with numerous oil lamps.

On the day before the full moon, *Raths Jaatraa,* thousands of Nepalis crowd the streets to glimpse the "Living Goddess," Kumari, and two "Living Gods," Ganesh and Bhairab, as they are paraded in ancient temple carts through the lower part of the city. The young virgin deity and her two boy attendants are specially selected from the Bada subcaste (silversmiths and goldsmiths) of the *Newar* caste. The Kumari is considered the protectoress of Kathmandu Valley.

DasAAl (Dusserah in India) lasts for ten days at the time of the new moon in mid-October. This is Nepal's most important festival. It commemorates the legendary victory of the Goddess Durga over the evil demon-buffalo, Mahisashur. One highlight is the ceremonial decapitating of buffaloes at the *kot* (fort) near Hanuman Dhoka on the ninth day of the festival. Schools and government offices are closed and the holiday is considered a time for family reunions all over the country. Goats and sheep from the north and buffaloes from the Tarai, are herded into Kathmandu for the occasion. There is much feasting and merrymaking.

Tihar or *Diwali* is a five-day festival in mid-November. The last three days are the most interesting. The third day is *Lakshimi Pujaa*, dedicated to Lakshmi, Goddess of wealth and associated with light. Houses are trimmed with hundreds of tiny oil lamps which transform Kathmandu at night into a unique and beautifully-lighted city. Lakshmi's blessings are invoked, and a new business year is officially begun.

BUDDHIST FESTIVALS

Bhuddhist festivals include:

Losar, the Tibetan New Year, is in mid-February. There are activities at Baudhnath and Swayambhunath temples, and at the Tibetan refugee center near Patan. Buddhist pilgrims arrive and reunions are held during this colorful occasion. There is much trading and merrymaking.

Buddha's Birthday in May is a solemn occasion. Foreign dignitaries are usually invited to observances during the day at Swayambhunath. Observances are also held in other Buddhist temples and monasteries. Prayer flags fly overhead, and at night the Swayambhunath hilltop is brightly lighted.

Dalai Lama's Birthday on July 6 is a time for prayers, invocation of blessings, and feasting, especially by Tibetan refugees.

Mani-rimdu is a Sherpa dance-drama. This colorful festival is uniquely Sherpa, but has its origins in ancient Tibetan theatrical genre. It is performed during November or early December at Tengboche monastery and in May at Thami monastery, both of which are in the Solu-Khumbu district near Mount Everest. The performers are traditionally monks, but the occasion is highlighted by much gaiety and feasting by monks and lay spectators alike.

Buddhist monks about to play instruments for a pujaa (worship). (Ane Haaland)

MELA

These rural fairs are country-wide and occur throughout the year at various locations, especially in the spring. The fairs are traditionally associated with local rural Hindu shrines, quite often at the confluence of two rivers. They tend to coincide with religious occasions.

During August, fairs are held in Thak Khola, Dhorpatan, and at the Muktinath shrine, a Buddhist and Hindu pilgrimage quest north of the Annapurna Himalaya. Horse racing is a main event at *BhoTiya* fairs.

WEDDINGS

Hindu weddings can be almost anytime, but most are in mid-winter, especially during January and February. Weddings among the hill ethnic groups are more randomly contracted. Hindu marriages are traditionally arranged by the parents of the couple; horoscopes are compared by a priest, and an auspicious date is set. The weddings, especially those of the upper castes, are loud, musical affairs attended by much drumming and horn blowing as the bride's and groom's parties travel to and from each other's villages, sometimes over a period of several days. Solemn ritual activities can be observed during the evenings.

APPENDIX A

ADDRESSES

The following addresses—**all located in Kathmandu**—should be helpful for those planning a trek in Nepal. Naturally, businesses come and go, and addresses change, but these will at least provide a place for the reader to start. Inclusion in this list does not imply endorsement by the author or publisher.

Trekking (T) and River Rafting (RR) Agencies

(T, RR) Alpine Adventure
G.P.O. Box 105, Durbar Marg
Phone: 11786

(T) Annapurna Mountaineering
and Trekking
G.P.O. Box 795, Durbar Marg
Cable Address: AMTREK
Phone: 12736

(T) Dolkha Trekking
Kanti Path
Phone: 15620

(T) Exploring Nepal
G.P.O. Box 1856,
Ram Shah Path
Phone: 14424

(T) Express Trekking
G.P.O. Box 339, Naxal
Cable Address: GREATREK
Phone: 13017

(T) Gauri Shankar Trekking Service
G.P.O. Box 681, Jamal
Phone: 12112

(T, RR) Great Himalayan Adventure
G.P.O. Box 1033, Kanti Path
Cable Address: HIMTREK
Phone: 14424

(T, RR) Himalayan Journeys
G.P.O. Box 1566, Kanti Path
Phone: 16626

(T) Himalayan Rover Treks
G.P.O. Box 1081, Hathisar
Cable Address: ROVTREK
Phone: 12691

(T,RR) Himalayan Sangrila Treks
G.P.O. Box 1985
Ram Shah Path
Cable Address: WILDLIFE
Phone: 13303

(T) Himalayan Travels and Tours
G.P.O. Box 234, Durbar Marg
Phone: 11682

(T) Himalayan Trekking
G.P.O. Box 391,
Ram Shah Path
Phone: 11808

(T) Himal Trek
G.P.O. Box 1501
Ram Shah Path

(T) International Trekkers
G.P.O. Box 1293, Bansbari
Cable Address: INTREK
Phone: 11786

(T) Kanchenjunga Trekking
G.P.O. Box 1296
Ram Shah Path
Cable Address: HIT
Phone: 14139

Appendices

(T)   Manaslu Trekking
G.P.O. Box 1519, Durbar Marg
Cable Address: MANASTREK
    Phone: 12422

(T)   Mountain Hiking Service
G.P.O. Box 2120
Ram Shah Path
    Phone: 11804

(T, RR)   Mountain Travel (Himalayan
    River Exploration)
G.P.O. Box 170, Durbar Marg
Cable Address: TREKKERS
    Phone: 12808, 11262

(T)   Natraj Trekking
G.P.O. Box 1606
Kanti Path
    Phone: 13533

(T)   Nepal Natural Trek
G.P.O. Box 1852, New Road
Cable Address: NNTREK
    Phone: 16578

(T)   Nepal Trekking
G.P.O. Box 368, Thamel
Cable Address: NETREKKING
    Phone: 14681

(T)   Nepal Treks and Natural
    History Expeditions
G.P.O. Box 459, Ganga Path
Cable Address: NEPTREK
    Phone: 12985, 12511

(T)   Sherpa Cooperative Trekking
G.P.O. Box 1338
Kamal Pokhari
Cable Address: SHERPAHUT
    Phone: 15887

(T)   Sherpa Society
G.P.O. Box 1566
Chabahil, Chuchepati
    Phone: 16361, 16757

(T)   Sherpa Trekking Service
G.P.O. Box 500, Kamaladi
Cable Address: SHERPTREK
    Phone: 12489

(T)   Transhimalayan Trekking
G.P.O. Box 283, Durbar Marg
Cable Address: TRANSVIEW
    Phone: 13854, 15271

(T)   Yeti Mountaineering
    and Trekking
G.P.O. Box 1034
Ram Shah Path
Cable Address: MOUNTAIN
    Phone: 14619, 16341

(T)   Yeti Trekking
Kanti Path
    Phone: 13533
    (Head office in Pokhara
    at Box 40, Naghdunga,
    Phone: 283)

Chitwan National Park Tour Agencies

Gaida Wildlife Camp
G.P.O. Box 1273, Durbar Marg
Cable Address: MANASTREK
    Phone: 11786

Hotel Elephant Camp
G.P.O. Box 1281, Durbar Marg
Cable Address: ELECAMP
    Phone: 13976

Jungle Safari Camp
G.P.O. Box 1530
Kanti Path
Cable Address: JSCAMP
    Phone: 13533

Tiger Tops
G.P.O. Box 242, Durbar Marg
Cable Address: TIGERTOPS
    Phone: 12706

Nepal Book Dealers

Educational Enterprise
G.P.O. Box 425, Mahankal

Himalayan Booksellers
G.P.O. Box 528, Ghantaghar
Durbar Marg

Ratna Pustak Bhaudar
G.P.O. Box 98, Bhotahity

APPENDIX B

GLOSSARY OF NEPALI AND TIBETAN WORDS

bhaat	cooked rice
bhaTmaas	soybeans
bhaTTi	traditional Nepali inn
BhoTiya	Buddhist highlander of Nepal
chaarpi	latrine
chang	locally brewed beer
chAUmri or **zopkio**	a cross between a yak and a cow
chautaara	rectangular resting platform on a trail
chilim	clay pipe for smoking
chorten	Buddhist religious cubical structure
daal	lentil-like sauce poured over rice
daru or **rakshi**	a Thakali distilled spirit
dhaarni	measure of weight (approximately 6 lb, 2.7 kg)
dharmsala	rest house
Doko	conical basket for carrying loads
ghiu	clarified butter (**ghee** in India)
gomba	Tibetan Buddhist temple
goTh	shelter used by shepherds
haatisaar	elephant camp
himal	mountain
jAAR	locally brewed beer
kata	ceremonial scarf of white cheesecloth
khola	river
lekh	hill
loTa	vessel for carrying water to clean oneself after defecating
maanaa	volume measure (20 oz, 2½ cups, 0.7 l)
machaan	blind for observing animals
mani	prayer
memsahib	honorific title used by Nepalis for female foreigners
naamlo	tumpline
namaskaar	traditional greeting (very polite and formal)
namaste	traditional greeting (less formal)
paathi	volume measure equal to eight **maanaa**
paau	weight measure (8 oz, 0.2 kg)
paisaa	smallest denomination of money (0.085 U.S. cents)
rakshi	distilled spirit
rupiyAA	100 **paisaa** (about 8½ cents at 1980 U.S. exchange rate)
sahib	honorific title used by Nepalis for male foreigners
ser	weight measure equal to four **pau** (2 lb, 0.8 kg)
tal	lake
thangka	Buddhist scroll painting
tsampa	roasted barley flour, usually consumed by **BhoTiya**)
yersa	a cluster of **goTh** in Khumbu, but also applies to other northern regions
zopkio or **chAUmri**	a cross between a yak and a cow

APPENDIX C

RECOMMENDED READING

> *Many people come, looking, looking . . .*
> *some people come, see.*
>
> Dawa Tenzing, a Sherpa

The maximum enjoyment of Nepal comes from becoming familiar with its history, its culture, its geography, and other aspects. This book basically concerns itself with the practical matters related to trekking. However, the annotated list below deals mostly with literature on Nepal outside of the Kathmandu Valley, and should help the trekker learn about various aspects of Nepal.

The books listed are either still in print, recently reprinted, or recently out of print. Those published in Nepal can normally be purchased there only. Some sources from which you may be able to order these books by mail are listed in the Addresses section of the Appendix. Many of these books can be read at the Tribhuvan University Library in Kirtipur, Kathmandu.

BIBLIOGRAPHIES

Boulnois, L. and Millot, H. *Bibliographie du Nepal Volume 1.* Paris: Editions du Centre National de la Recherche Scientifique, 1969.

Boulnois, L. *Bibliographie du Nepal Volume 1 Supplement 1967-1973.* Paris: Editions du Centre National de la Recherche Scientifique, 1975.

Malla, Khadga Man. *Bibliography of Nepal.* Kathmandu: The Royal Nepal Academy, 1975.

GENERAL

Foreign Areas Studies Division. *Area Handbook for Nepal (with Sikkim and Bhutan).* Washington: U.S. Army, 1972. A survey of the country in its many aspects.

Hagen, Toni. *Nepal, The Kingdom of the Himalayas.* Berne: Kummerley and Frey, 1971. A large-scale, illustrated book by the first man to travel widely through the country.

Hamilton, Francis Buchanan. *An Account of the Kingdom of Nepal.* New Delhi: Manjusri Publishing House, 1819. A classic reprinted in 1971 in the Bibliotheca Himalayica series. It deals with much of Nepal's history and culture.

Hodgson, Brian. *Essays on the Languages, Literature, and Religion of Nepal and Tibet.* New Delhi: Manjusri, 1874. Another classic reprinted in 1972 in the same series. It was written by an incredibly eclectic scholar.

Kazami, Takehide. *The Himalayas, a Journey to Nepal.* Tokyo: Kodansha International, 1968. A brief description of the author's treks with a series of excellent color photographs.

Kirkpatrick, W. *An Account of the Kingdom of Nepaul.* New Delhi: Manjusri, 1811. The account of the first visit to "Nepaul" by an Englishman. It was reprinted in 1969 in the Bibliotheca Himalayica series.

Landon, Perceval. *Nepal.* Kathmandu: Ratna Pustak Bhandar, 1928. Reprinted in the Bibliotheca Himalayica series in 1976. It is a veritable wealth of information on many topics.

Nicolson, Nigel. *The Himalayas.* Amsterdam: Time-Life, 1974. A useful survey with excellent photographs.

Rieffel, Robert. *Nepal Namaste.* Kathmandu: Sahayogi Prakashan, 1978. The best general guide to Nepal. A new edition is forthcoming.

Shumshere, Pashupati; Rana, J.B.; and Malla, Kamal P. *Nepal in Perspective.* Kathmandu: Centre for Economic Development and Administration, 1973. A superb series of essays by distinguished Nepalis on diverse aspects of Nepal.

Tucci, Giuseppe. *Tibet, Land of Snows.* London: Elek Books, 1967. Of interest here because so much of the culture, art, and ways of life of the northern people are Tibetan in nature.

ANTHROPOLOGY

Anderson, Mary M. *The Festivals of Nepal.* London: George Allen & Unwin, 1971. Mostly concerned with Kathmandu, but also helpful for the hills.

Aziz, Barbara Nimri. *Tibetan Frontier Families.* New Delhi: Vikas, 1978. A good source of information on Tibetan social life.

Berreman, Gerald D. *Hindus of the Himalaya.* Berkeley: University of California Press, 1972. Deals mainly with the Paharis of the Indian Himalaya, but also helpful in understanding the Hindus in the hills of Nepal.

Bista, Dor Bahadur. *People of Nepal.* Kathmandu: Ratna Pustak Bhandar, 1974. Presents an excellent synopsis of most of the ethnic groups found in Nepal. If a trekker were to restrict himself to one book, this should be it.

Caplan, A. Patricia. *Priests and Cobblers.* San Francisco: Chandler Publishing Company, 1972. Helpful for understanding the caste system in Nepal.

Caplan, Lionel. *Administration and Politics in a Nepalese Town.* London: Oxford University Press, 1975. Helpful for understanding a district center.

Ekvall, Robert B. *Fields on the Hoof.* New York: Holt, Rinehart and Winston, 1968. Deals with Tibetan nomads. It pertains to many of the Tibetan refugees found in Nepal.

Hitchcock, John T. *The Magars of Banyan Hill.* New York: Holt, Rinehart and Winston, 1966. The study of a particular hill ethnic group. It contains a great deal of material relevant to many of the other hill people.

Hitchcock, John T., and Jones, Rex L. *Spirit Possession in the Nepal Himalayas.* Warminster, England: Aris & Phillips, 1976. A series of articles on shamans of Nepal. It is useful should you encounter any during your treks.

Macfarane, Alan. *Resources and Population.* Cambridge: Cambridge University Press, 1976. A study of economic and demographic change in a *Gurung* village.

Messerschmidt, Donald A. *The Gurungs of Nepal.* Warminster: Aris & Phillips, 1976. An excellent description of the social and political organization of these people.

Von Fürer-Haimendorf, Christoph. *The Sherpas of Nepal, Buddhist Highlanders.* London: John Murray, 1964. An excellent account. A shortened version is available in the book *Mount Everest* (see Regional books).

_____.*Caste and Kin in Nepal, India, and Ceylon.* New York: Asia Publishing House, 1966. A series of essays by anthropologists. They cover, among others, the *Chetri, Newar,* and *Thakali.*

_____.*Himalayan Traders.* London: John Murray, 1975. An interesting look at changes in the economic patterns of Nepal's high altitude dwellers.

Appendices

ART

Aran, Lydia. *The Art of Nepal*. Kathmandu: Sahayogi Prakashan, 1978. Deals primarily with the Kathmandu Valley, as do most books on Nepali art. It is also a useful guide to the art of this country seen through the religions.

Sharma, Prayag Raj. *Preliminary Study of the Art and Architecture of the Karnali Basin, West Nepal*. Paris: Centre National de la Recherche Scientifique, 1972. One of the few art studies pertaining to Nepal outside the Kathmandu Valley.

Singh, Madanjeet. *Himalayan Art*. London: Macmillan, 1968. A survey of most of the Himalayan region with beautiful reproductions. There is a paperback edition published by UNESCO.

GEOGRAPHY

Thapa, .N.B., and Thapa, D.P. *Geography of Nepal*. New Delhi: Orient Longmans, 1969. A superficial account that nevertheless answers many of the newcomer's questions.

HISTORY

Regmi, Mahesh Chandra. *A Study in Nepali Economic History, 1768-1846*. New Delhi: Manjusri, 1971. Invaluable for understanding how life in the hills evolved.

Stiller, L.F. *The Rise of the House of Gorkha*. New Delhi: Manjusri, 1973. Provides an understanding of the problems involved in unifying Nepal in the 1700s.

_____. *The Silent Cry*. Kathmandu: Sahayogi Prakashan, 1976. A continuation of the author's study of the growth of unity in Nepal. It covers the pre-Rana period, 1816 to 1839.

LANGUAGE

Clark, T.W. *Introduction to Nepali*. London: School of Oriental and African Studies, 1977. The only formal text. It is difficult to use, but valuable to those seeking a good knowledge of the language.

Hari, Anna Mari. *Conversational Nepali*. Kathmandu: Summer Institute of Linguistics, 1971. An excellent course, though not practical for use while trekking.

Karki, Tika B., and Shrestha, Chij K. *Basic Course in Spoken Nepali*. Kathmandu: published by the authors, 1979. Written for Peace Corps volunteers. It may be useful for the serious trekker. Chij Shrestha's language institute in Naxal is also a source for language lessons.

Meerendonk, M. *Basic Gurkhali Dictionary*. Singapore: published by the author, 1960. An excellent pocket dictionary. Some grammar is needed to use it.

Summer Institute of Linguistics. *Trekker's Pocket Pal Word and Phrase Guide*. Kathmandu: Summer Institute of Linguistics. A simple, helpful language aid.

NATURAL HISTORY

Bhatt, Dibya Deo. *Natural History and Economic Botany of Nepal*. Calcutta: Orient Longman, 1977. An excellent survey with a wealth of detail.

Fleming, Robert L., Sr.; Fleming, Robert L., Jr.; and Bangdel, Lain. *Birds of Nepal*. Kathmandu: Avalok, 1979. A comprehensive field guide. It can be ordered from Mrs. Vern Beieler, 1028 Crestwood Street, Wenatchee, Wash. 98801.

Fleming, Robert L., Jr. *The General Ecology, Flora, and Fauna of Midland Nepal*.

Kathmandu: Tribhuvan University Press, 1978. A reprinting of this very useful work at last!

Gee, E. P. *The Wild Life of India.* London: Collins, 1964. Especially interesting for those visiting Chitwan National Park.

Hooker, J. D. *Himalayan Journals.* New Delhi: Today and Tomorrow's Printers and Publishers, 1969. A reprint of an account by the first scientist to travel in Nepal.

Le Fort, Patrick. "Himalayas: The Collided Range; Present Knowledge of the Continental Arc," *American Journal of Science,* (1975) 275-A:1-44. An interesting, technical survey of the formation of the Himalaya.

Malla, S. B. *Flora of Langtang and Cross Section Vegetation Survey.* Kathmandu: Department of Medicinal Plants, 1976. One of several books published by the government. It is technical, but useful to those with botanical knowledge.

Mierow, Dorothy, and Shrestha, Tirtha Bahadur. *Himalayan Flowers and Trees.* Kathmandu: Sahayogi Prakashan, 1978. A wealth of pictorial material to aid in identifying plants.

Mishra, Hemant Raj, and Mierow, Dorothy. *Wild Animals of Nepal.* Kathmandu: Ratna Pustak Bhandar, 1976. A useful species survey with line drawings.

Prater, S. H. *The Book of Indian Animals.* Bombay: Bombay Natural History Society, 1971.

Schaller, George. *Stones of Silence: Journeys in the Himalaya.* New York: Viking Press, 1980. A book on the wild cats, sheep, and goats of the Himalaya. It is a fascinating synthesis of the author's observations and feelings about this ecosystem.

_____.*Mountain Monarchs: Wild Sheep and Goats of the Himalaya.* Chicago: University of Chicago Press, 1977. A volume more technical than the above. Those with a zoological background could appreciate it.

Sharma, Chandra K. *Geology of Nepal.* Kathmandu: Educational Enterprise, 1977. Very detailed. It is useful to those with a geological background.

Shrestha, Tirtha Bahadur. *Gymnosperms of Nepal.* Paris: Centre National de la Recherche Scientifique, 1974. A useful guide to identification of conifers.

Smith, Colin. *Commoner Butterflies of Nepal.* Kathmandu: Natural History Museum, 1976.

Stainton, J. D. A. *Forests of Nepal.* London: John Murray, 1972. A detailed survey requiring knowledge of specific species.

POLITICAL SCIENCE

Mihaly, Eugene Bramer. *Foreign Aid and Politics in Nepal.* London: Oxford University Press, 1965. An early study. Its conclusions remain valid today.

Rose, Leo E. *Nepal Strategy for Survival.* Berkeley: University of California Press, 1971. A fascinating political history.

Shaha, Rishikesh. *Nepali Politics—Retrospect and Prospect.* Delhi: Oxford University Press, 1978. A controversial book. It is invaluable for understanding Nepal today.

REGIONAL

Cronin, Edward W., Jr. *The Arun: A Natural History of the World's Deepest Valley.* Boston: Houghton Mifflin, 1979. An entertaining description with a wealth of material on natural history.

Downs, Hugh R. *Rhythms of a Himalayan Village.* New York: Harper and Row,

Appendices

1980. A photo documentary of a Sherpa village in Solu.

Fleming, Robert L., Jr., and Fleming, Linda F. *Kathmandu Valley*. Tokyo: Kodansha International, 1978. A beautiful book.

Gurung, Nareshwar Jang. "An Introduction to the Socio-Economic Structure of Manang District." *Kailash* (1976) 4:295-308.

Hagen, Toni; Dyhrenfurth, Gunter-Oscar; Von Fürer-Haimendorf, Christoph; and Schneider, Erwin. *Mount Everest: Formation, Population and Exploration of the Everest Region*. London: Oxford University Press, 1963. The best single volume to take with you to Khumbu. It includes chapters on geology, mountaineering and the Sherpas.

Hall, Andrew R. "Preliminary Report on the Langtang Region." *Contributions to Nepalese Studies* (June 1978) 5:51-68.

Hillary, Edmund. *Schoolhouse in the Clouds*. Harmondsworth, England: Penguin Books, 1968. An interesting account of Hillary's attempts to aid the Sherpas of Nepal.

Hornbein, Thomas F. *Everest: The West Ridge*. Seattle: The Mountaineers, 1980. Superb photographs and a sensitive text.

Jest, Corneille. *Tarap*. Paris: Seuil, 1974. A photo documentary of life in a Dolpo Valley.

Matthiessen, Peter. *The Snow Leopard*. New York: Viking & Bantam, 1978. A personal trekking account that deals primarily with the author's inner journey.

Snellgrove, David. *Himalayan Pilgrimage*. Oxford: Bruno Cassirer, 1961. An account of this scholar's treks through north-central and northwestern Nepal. His wide range of interests and acute powers of observation make for fascinating reading.

RELIGION

Bernbaum, Edwin. *The Way to Shambhala*. New York: Anchor Press, 1980. An exploration of the myth of the mystical kingdom hidden behind the Himalaya, believed in by many of Nepal's highlanders.

Detmold, Geogrey, and Rubel, Mary. *The Gods and Goddesses of Nepal*. Kathmandu: Ratna Pustak Bhandar, 1979. Deals primarily with the Kathmandu Valley. But it is nevertheless very useful for Nepal in general.

Humphreys, Christmas. *Buddhism*. Harmondsworth: Penguin Books, 1952. An excellent account of the basic tenets of Buddhism and, as such, prerequisite to an understanding of the various kinds of Buddhism practiced in Nepal.

Jerstad, L.G. *Mani-rimdu, Sherpa Dance Drama*. Seattle: University of Washington Press, 1969. Invaluable for a fuller understanding of the festival. It also contains introductory chapters on religion and the Sherpas.

Sen, K. M. *Hinduism*. Harmondsworth: Penguin Books, 1961.

Snellgrove, David. *Buddhist Himalaya*. Oxford: Bruno Cassirer, 1957. An understanding of Buddhism is a prerequisite for this book. It deals with the Solu-Khumbu region and the Buddhism of Sherpas and of Kathmandu.

Von Fürer-Haimendorf, Christoph. "A Nunnery in Nepal," *Kailash*. (1976) 4:121-154.

Waddel, L. A. *The Buddhism of Tibet or Lamaism*. Cambridge, England: W. Heffer, 1967. A reprint of an 1895 book. It describes the religion and its practices.

TREKKING

Armington, Stan. *Trekking in the Himalayas*. Victoria, Australia: Lonely Planet, 1979. A guide slanted for those on organized treks.

Baume, Louis C. *Sivalaya: Explorations of the 8000-Metre Peaks of the Himalaya.* Seattle: The Mountaineers, 1979. A fascinating detailed chronology for those interested in mountaineering.

Gurung, Harka. *Vignettes of Nepal.* Kathmandu: Sajha Prakashan, 1980. A fascinating account of a Nepali geographer's many treks in his country's remote regions. It is a source of inspiration for the veteran-trekker looking for new horizons.

Iozawa, Tomoyo. *Trekking in the Himalayas.* Tokyo: Tama-to-Keikoku Sha, 1976. Has good color photographs, sketches, detailed drawings, and maps. The text is disappointing. An English edition is due.

Kleinart, Christian. *Nepal Trekking.* Munchen: Bergverlag Rudolf Rother, n.d., c. 1976. An attractive guide. It has sixteen fold-out pages containing brief route descriptions, maps, and excellent panoramic photos.

Thompson, Mike. "Sahibs and Sherpas," *Mountain* (July-Aug. 1979) 68:45-49. An interesting insight into this interaction.

TREKKING MEDICINE

Hackett, Peter. *Mountain Sickness: Prevention, Recognition, and Treatment.* New York: American Alpine Club, 1980. A small but complete and useful booklet. The author is the medical director of the Himalayan Rescue Association.

Houston, Charles S. "High Altitude Illness Updated: How Fast is Slow Enough." *Summit* (Feb.-Mar. 1979) 25:1.

Hultgren, Herbert N. "High Altitude Medical Problems." *Western Journal of Medicine* (July 1979) 131:8-23. An excellent review by a pioneering high altitude researcher. It is suitable for those with a medical background.

Steele, Peter. *Medical Care for Mountain Climbers.* London: Heinemann, 1976. Comparable to *Medicine for Mountaineering* listed below, but somewhat simplified and reflecting the British point of view.

Summer Institute of Linguistics. *Field Workers Medical Manual.* Huntington Beach, California: S. I. L. 1973. Comparable to *Medicine for Mountaineering.* It is directed to those dealing with medical problems in remote areas.

Ward, Michael. *Mountain Medicine.* London: Crosby Lockwood Staples, 1975. An excellent survey of problems associated with cold and high altitudes. It is not practical in clinical situations.

Wilkerson, James A. *Medicine for Mountaineering.* Seattle: The Mountaineers, 1975. A superb practical book designed for the layman, yet dealing with the entire spectrum of medical problems encountered in the mountains. The second edition is up to date.

Wilson, Rodman. "Acute High Altitude Illness in Mountaineers and Problems of Rescue," *Annals of Internal Medicine* (1973) 78:421. An excellent, practical, clinical survey. It is useful to those with a medical background.

Worth, Robert M., and Shah, Narayan K. *Nepal Health Survey.* Honolulu: The University of Hawaii Press, 1969. Interesting to those with a medical background. It is helpful in understanding the type of health conditions that prevail among Nepalis.

INDEX

Page numbers in italics refer to photo captions.

Index

(Nick Langton)

As I write these last words, my thoughts return to you who were my comrades: the stubborn and indomitable peasants of Nepal. Once more I hear the laughter with which you greeted every hardship. Once more I see you in your bivouacs or about your fires, on forced march or in the trenches, now shivering with wet and cold, now scorched by a pitiless and burning sun. Uncomplaining, you endure hunger and thirst and wounds; and at the last, your unwavering lines disappear into the smoke and wrath of battle. Bravest of the brave, most generous of the generous, never had country more faithful friends than you.

> Ralph Lilley Turner, author of *Dictionary of the Nepali Language*,* describing the Gurkhas with whom he served in the British Army. He learned Nepali from these soldiers, and wrote the definitive Nepali dictionary without ever having visited Nepal.

---

* Routledge and Kegan Paul Limited, London, 1931, 1965.

About the Author

Stephen Bezruchka, a Canadian physician, has spent many years in Nepal, both trekking and working on a health project in the remote western region. He was a graduate student in mathematics at Harvard University when his love of mountains and mountaineering brought him to Nepal in 1969. This was when he first went on many of the treks described here. These treks and the year he spent there led him to an enduring fascination with the endless variety of the land and peoples of Nepal. Thus when he returned to North America, it was to study medicine at Stanford University with the intention of returning to Nepal to work in one of its remote hill areas. This he did for several years. It was one of the most meaningful and fulfilling times of his life. Currently he is practicing medicine in Seattle and planning his next trip to Nepal.

Stephen Bezruchka and friends. (Mary Murphy)